THE UNCANNY X-MEN

TARGET: ANGEL

BACKPACK MARVELS

TABLE OF CONTENTS

COVER ART: **GREG HORN**

BOOK DESIGN: **COMICRAFT**

REPRINT EDITOR: **POLLY WATSON**

EDITOR IN CHIEF: **BOB HARRAS**

BACKPACK MARVELS: X-MEN® Vol. 1 No. 1, November, 2000. Contains material originally published in magazine form as UNCANNY X-MEN #'s 167-173. Published by MARVEL COMICS, Bill Jemas, President; Bob Harras, Editor-in-Chief; Stan Lee, Chairman Emeritus. OFFICE OF PUBLICATION: 387 PARK AVENUE SOUTH, NEW YORK, N.Y. 10016. Copyright © 1983, 2000 Marvel Characters, Inc. All rights reserved. Price $6.95 per copy in the U.S. and $9.95 in Canada. BACKPACK MARVELS: X-MEN (including all prominent characters featured in this issue and the distinctive likenesses thereof) is a trademark of MARVEL CHARACTERS, INC. No part of this book may be printed or reproduced in any manner without the written permission of the publisher. Printed in Canada. First Printing, November, 2000. ISBN #0-7851-0763-0. GST. #R127032852. MARVEL COMICS is a division of MARVEL ENTERPRISES, INC. Peter Cuneo, Chief Executive Officer; Avi Arad, Chief Creative Officer.

10 9 8 7 6 5 4 3 2 1

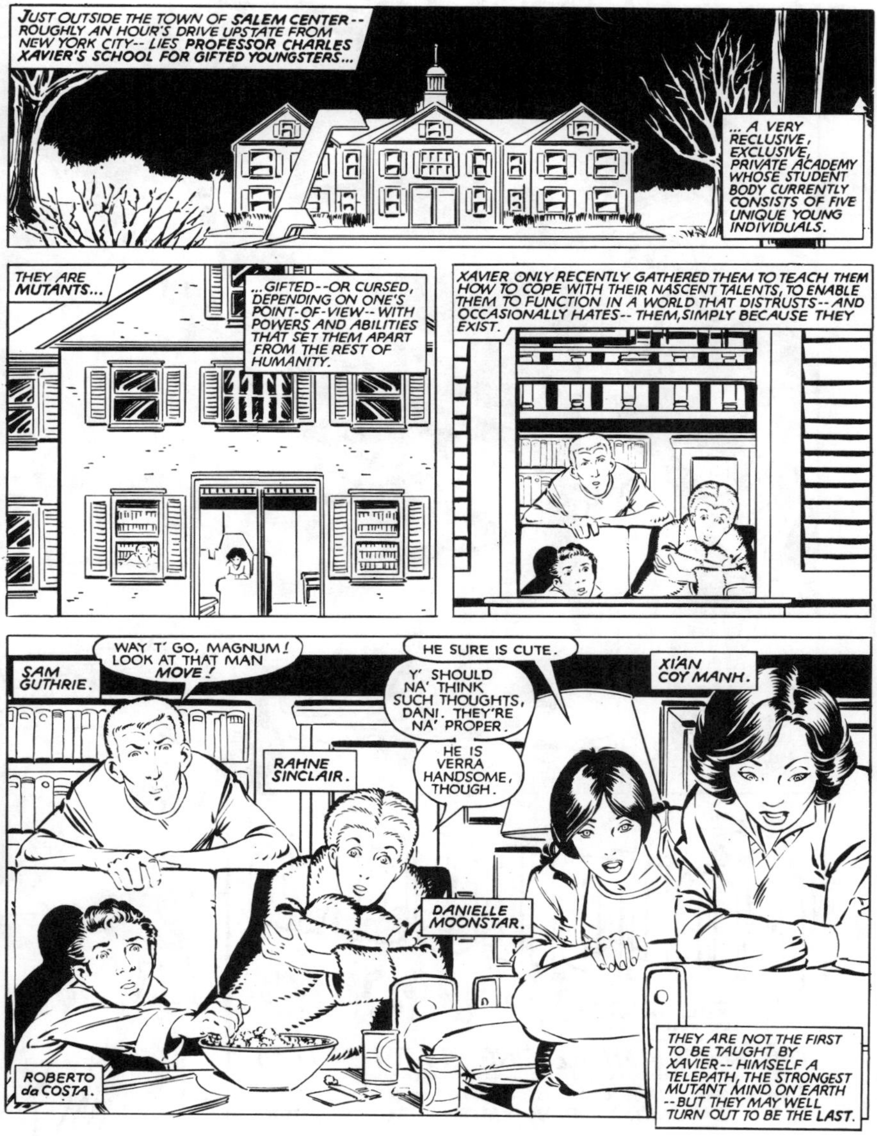

JUST OUTSIDE THE TOWN OF SALEM CENTER-- ROUGHLY AN HOUR'S DRIVE UPSTATE FROM NEW YORK CITY-- LIES PROFESSOR CHARLES XAVIER'S SCHOOL FOR GIFTED YOUNGSTERS...
... A VERY RECLUSIVE, EXCLUSIVE, PRIVATE ACADEMY WHOSE STUDENT BODY CURRENTLY CONSISTS OF FIVE UNIQUE YOUNG INDIVIDUALS.
THEY ARE MUTANTS...
...GIFTED--OR CURSED, DEPENDING ON ONE'S POINT-OF-VIEW--WITH POWERS AND ABILITIES THAT SET THEM APART FROM THE REST OF HUMANITY.
XAVIER ONLY RECENTLY GATHERED THEM TO TEACH THEM HOW TO COPE WITH THEIR NASCENT TALENTS, TO ENABLE THEM TO FUNCTION IN A WORLD THAT DISTRUSTS-- AND OCCASIONALLY HATES-- THEM, SIMPLY BECAUSE THEY EXIST.
SAM GUTHRIE.
WAY T' GO, MAGNUM! LOOK AT THAT MAN MOVE!
HE SURE IS CUTE.
Y' SHOULD NA' THINK SUCH THOUGHTS, DANI. THEY'RE NA' PROPER.
HE IS VERRA HANDSOME, THOUGH.
XI'AN COY MANH.
RAHNE SINCLAIR.
DANIELLE MOONSTAR.
ROBERTO da COSTA.
THEY ARE NOT THE FIRST TO BE TAUGHT BY XAVIER-- HIMSELF A TELEPATH, THE STRONGEST MUTANT MIND ON EARTH --BUT THEY MAY WELL TURN OUT TO BE THE LAST.

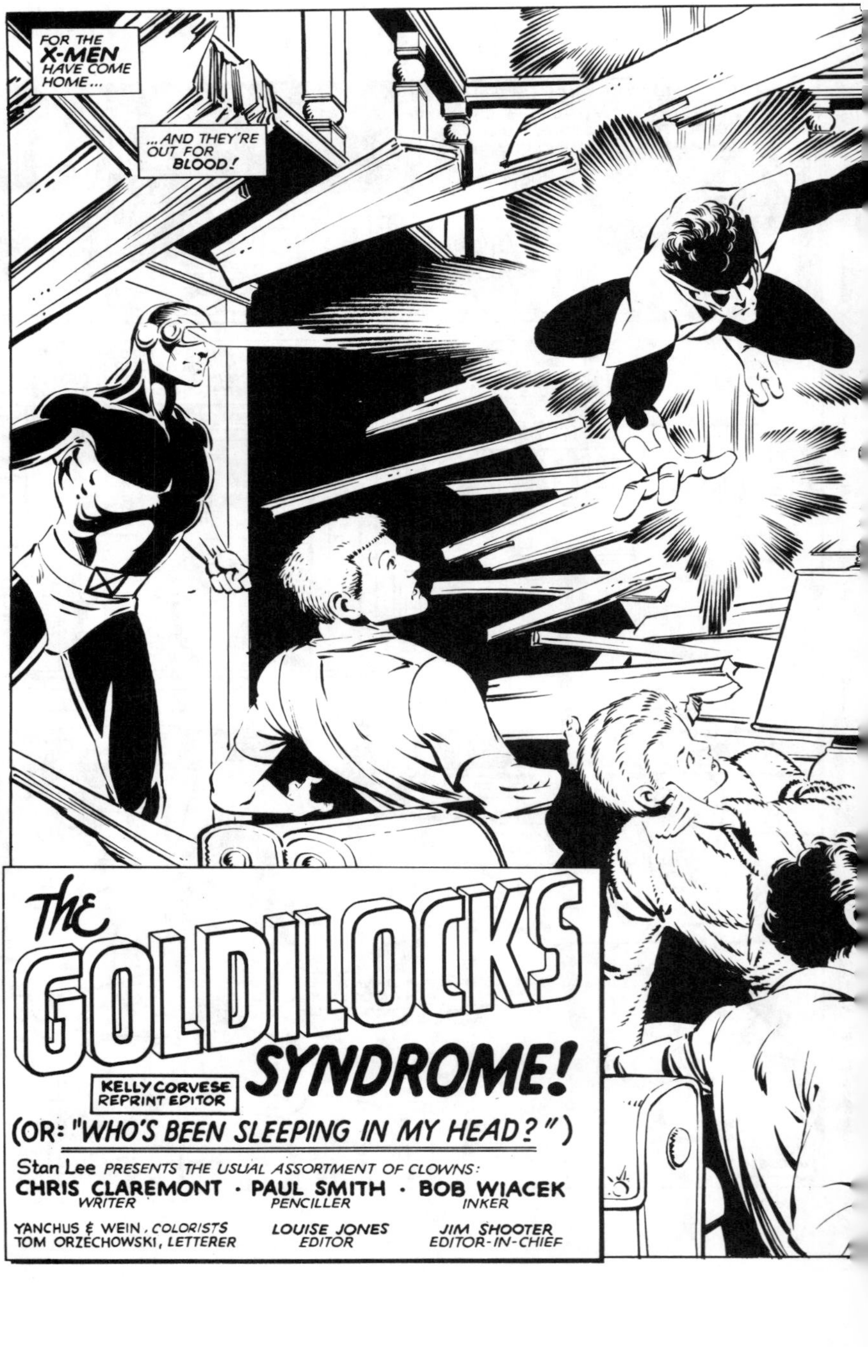

FOR THE X-MEN HAVE COME HOME...
...AND THEY'RE OUT FOR BLOOD!
THE GOLDILOCKS SYNDROME!
KELLY CORVESE REPRINT EDITOR
(OR: "WHO'S BEEN SLEEPING IN MY HEAD?")
Stan Lee PRESENTS THE USUAL ASSORTMENT OF CLOWNS:
CHRIS CLAREMONT WRITER · PAUL SMITH PENCILLER · BOB WIACEK INKER
YANCHUS & WEIN, COLORISTS
TOM ORZECHOWSKI, LETTERER
LOUISE JONES EDITOR
JIM SHOOTER EDITOR-IN-CHIEF

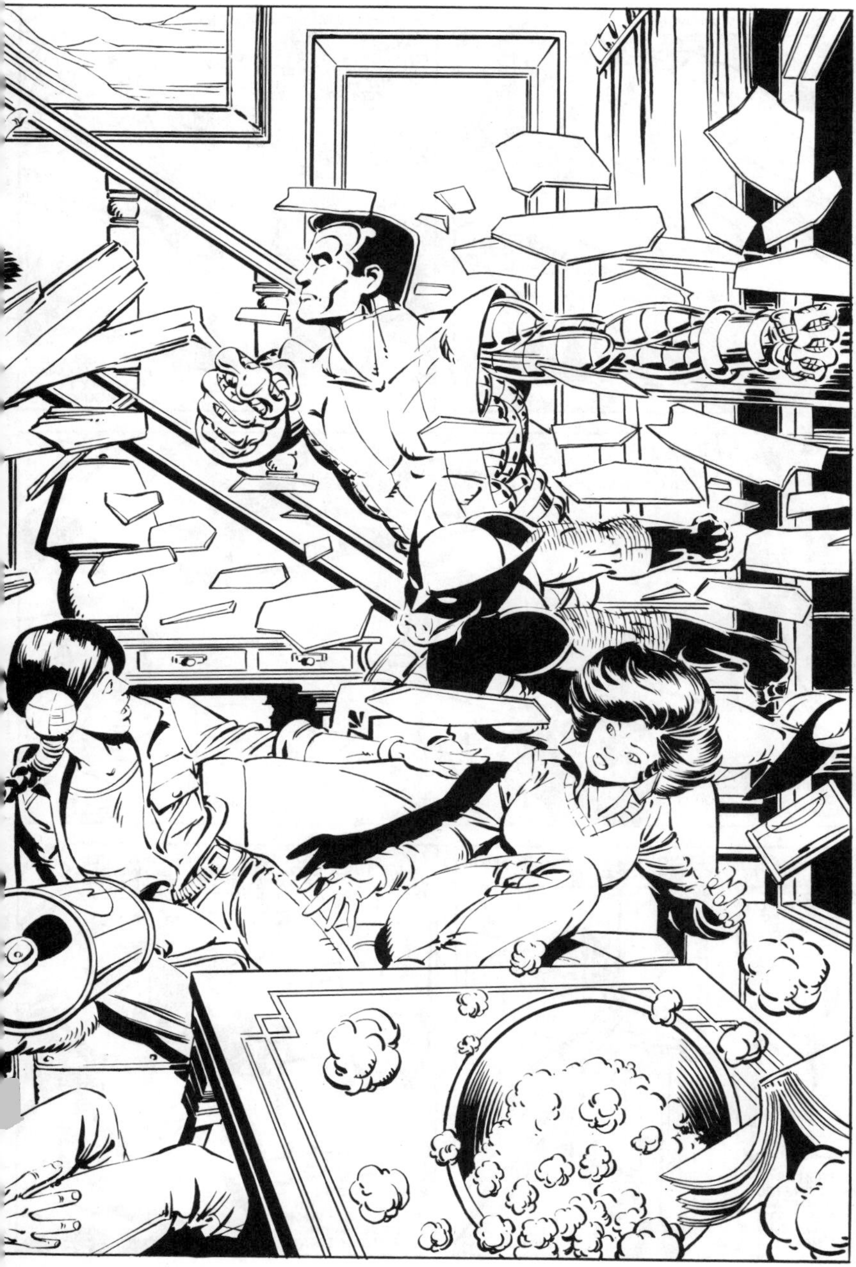

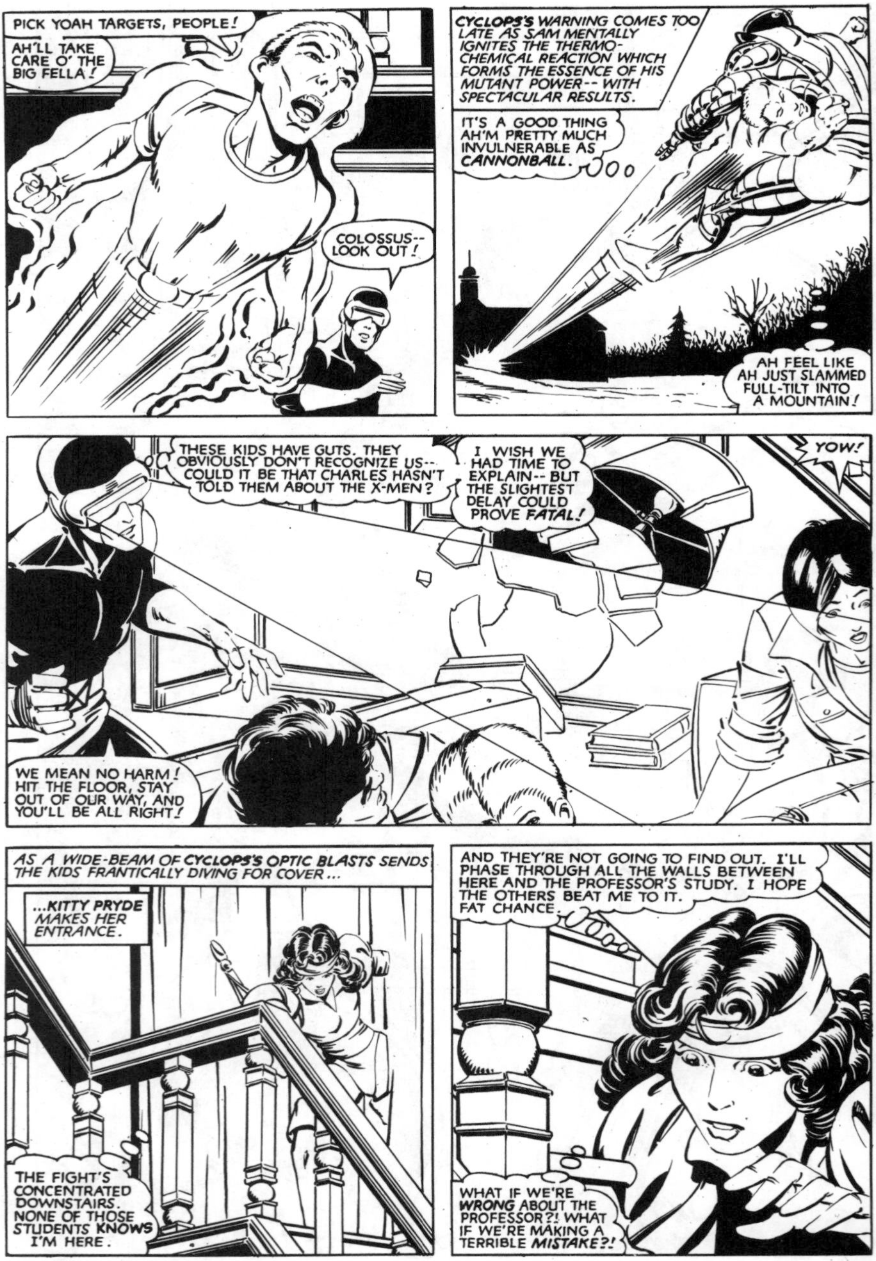
PICK YOAH TARGETS, PEOPLE!
AH'LL TAKE CARE O' THE BIG FELLA!
COLOSSUS-- LOOK OUT!
CYCLOPS'S WARNING COMES TOO LATE AS SAM MENTALLY IGNITES THE THERMO-CHEMICAL REACTION WHICH FORMS THE ESSENCE OF HIS MUTANT POWER-- WITH SPECTACULAR RESULTS.
IT'S A GOOD THING AH'M PRETTY MUCH INVULNERABLE AS CANNONBALL.
AH FEEL LIKE AH JUST SLAMMED FULL-TILT INTO A MOUNTAIN!
THESE KIDS HAVE GUTS. THEY OBVIOUSLY DON'T RECOGNIZE US-- COULD IT BE THAT CHARLES HASN'T TOLD THEM ABOUT THE X-MEN?
I WISH WE HAD TIME TO EXPLAIN-- BUT THE SLIGHTEST DELAY COULD PROVE FATAL!
YOW!
WE MEAN NO HARM! HIT THE FLOOR, STAY OUT OF OUR WAY, AND YOU'LL BE ALL RIGHT!
AS A WIDE-BEAM OF CYCLOPS'S OPTIC BLASTS SENDS THE KIDS FRANTICALLY DIVING FOR COVER...
...KITTY PRYDE MAKES HER ENTRANCE.
THE FIGHT'S CONCENTRATED DOWNSTAIRS. NONE OF THOSE STUDENTS KNOWS I'M HERE.
AND THEY'RE NOT GOING TO FIND OUT. I'LL PHASE THROUGH ALL THE WALLS BETWEEN HERE AND THE PROFESSOR'S STUDY. I HOPE THE OTHERS BEAT ME TO IT. FAT CHANCE.
WHAT IF WE'RE WRONG ABOUT THE PROFESSOR?! WHAT IF WE'RE MAKING A TERRIBLE MISTAKE?!

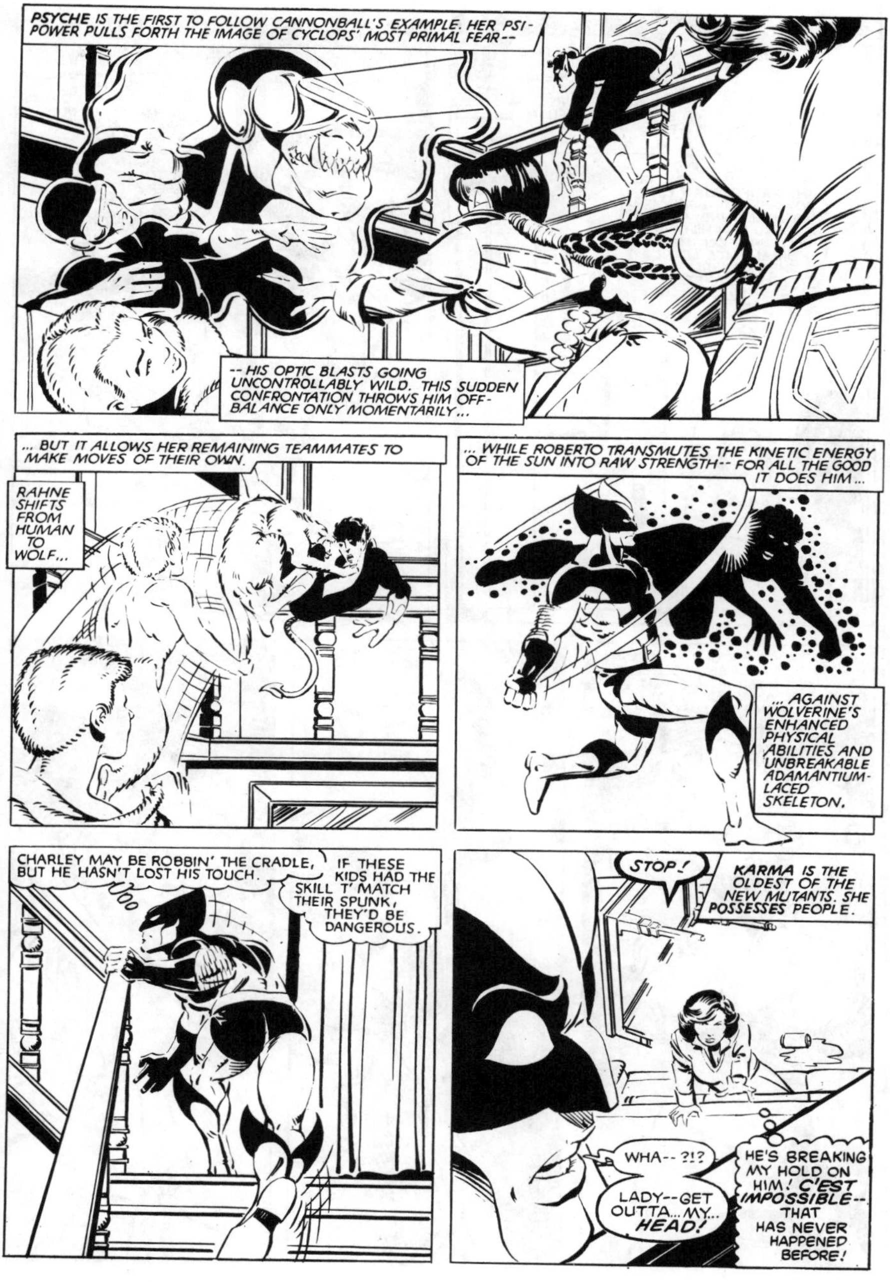
PSYCHE IS THE FIRST TO FOLLOW CANNONBALL'S EXAMPLE. HER PSI-POWER PULLS FORTH THE IMAGE OF CYCLOPS' MOST PRIMAL FEAR--
--HIS OPTIC BLASTS GOING UNCONTROLLABLY WILD. THIS SUDDEN CONFRONTATION THROWS HIM OFF-BALANCE ONLY MOMENTARILY...
... BUT IT ALLOWS HER REMAINING TEAMMATES TO MAKE MOVES OF THEIR OWN.
RAHNE SHIFTS FROM HUMAN TO WOLF...
... WHILE ROBERTO TRANSMUTES THE KINETIC ENERGY OF THE SUN INTO RAW STRENGTH-- FOR ALL THE GOOD IT DOES HIM...
... AGAINST WOLVERINE'S ENHANCED PHYSICAL ABILITIES AND UNBREAKABLE ADAMANTIUM-LACED SKELETON.
CHARLEY MAY BE ROBBIN' THE CRADLE, BUT HE HASN'T LOST HIS TOUCH.
IF THESE KIDS HAD THE SKILL T' MATCH THEIR SPUNK, THEY'D BE DANGEROUS.
STOP!
KARMA IS THE OLDEST OF THE NEW MUTANTS. SHE POSSESSES PEOPLE.
WHA--?!?
LADY--GET OUTTA...MY... HEAD!
HE'S BREAKING MY HOLD ON HIM! C'EST IMPOSSIBLE--THAT HAS NEVER HAPPENED BEFORE!

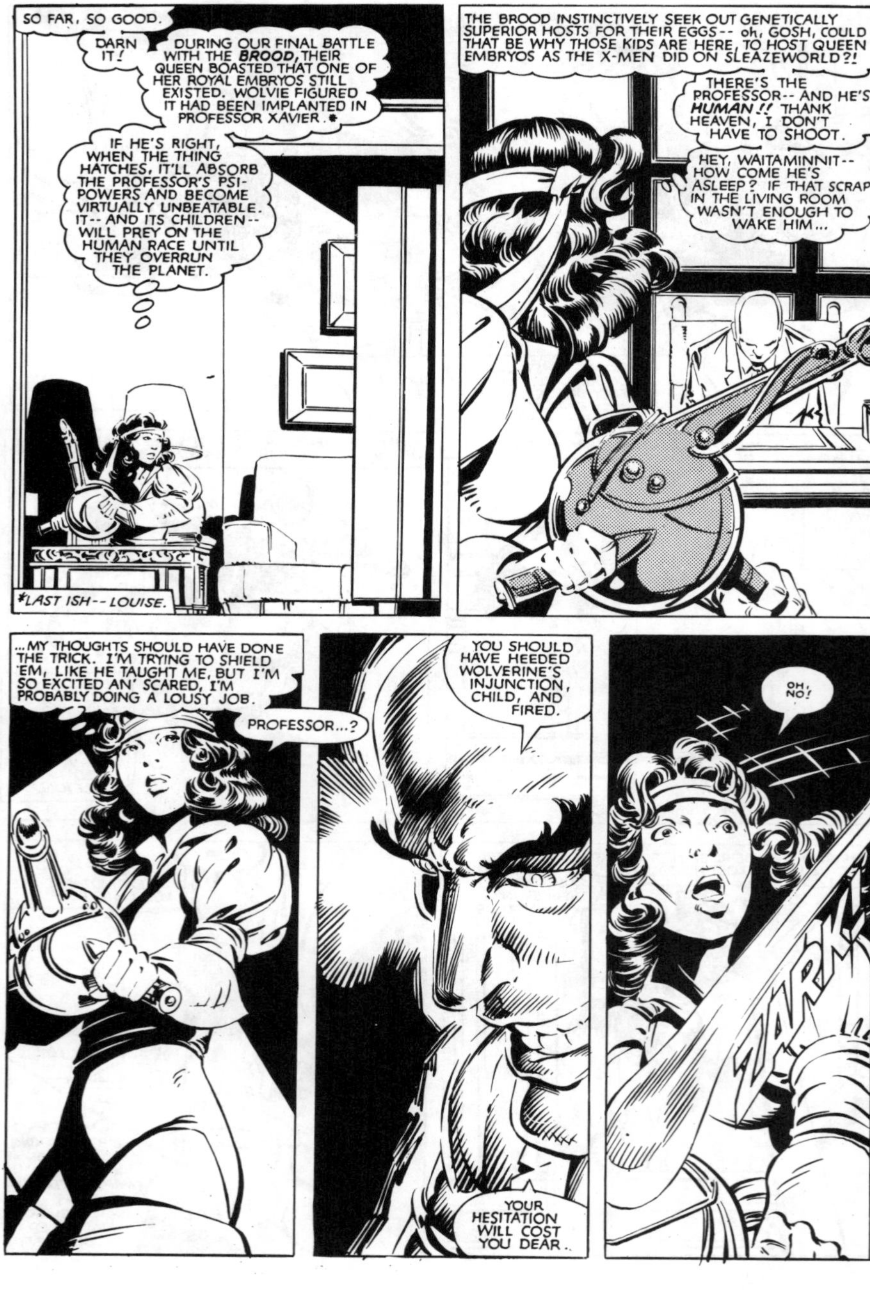
SO FAR, SO GOOD.
DARN IT!
DURING OUR FINAL BATTLE WITH THE BROOD, THEIR QUEEN BOASTED THAT ONE OF HER ROYAL EMBRYOS STILL EXISTED. WOLVIE FIGURED IT HAD BEEN IMPLANTED IN PROFESSOR XAVIER.*
IF HE'S RIGHT, WHEN THE THING HATCHES, IT'LL ABSORB THE PROFESSOR'S PSI-POWERS AND BECOME VIRTUALLY UNBEATABLE. IT-- AND ITS CHILDREN-- WILL PREY ON THE HUMAN RACE UNTIL THEY OVERRUN THE PLANET.
*LAST ISH-- LOUISE.
THE BROOD INSTINCTIVELY SEEK OUT GENETICALLY SUPERIOR HOSTS FOR THEIR EGGS-- oh, GOSH, COULD THAT BE WHY THOSE KIDS ARE HERE, TO HOST QUEEN EMBRYOS AS THE X-MEN DID ON SLEAZEWORLD?!
THERE'S THE PROFESSOR-- AND HE'S HUMAN!! THANK HEAVEN, I DON'T HAVE TO SHOOT.
HEY, WAITAMINNIT-- HOW COME HE'S ASLEEP? IF THAT SCRAP IN THE LIVING ROOM WASN'T ENOUGH TO WAKE HIM...
...MY THOUGHTS SHOULD HAVE DONE THE TRICK. I'M TRYING TO SHIELD 'EM, LIKE HE TAUGHT ME, BUT I'M SO EXCITED AN' SCARED, I'M PROBABLY DOING A LOUSY JOB.
PROFESSOR...?
YOU SHOULD HAVE HEEDED WOLVERINE'S INJUNCTION, CHILD, AND FIRED.
YOUR HESITATION WILL COST YOU DEAR..
OH, NO!
ZARK!

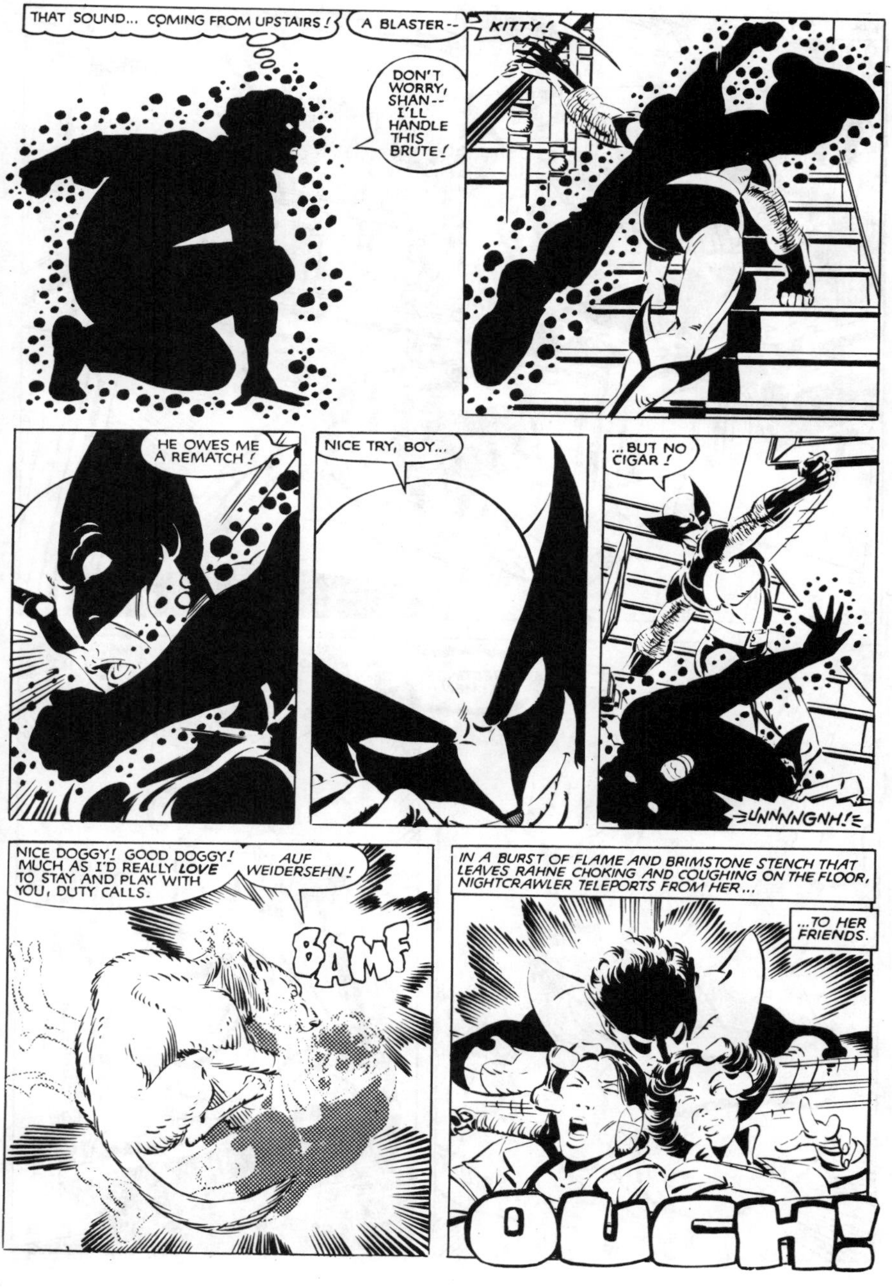
THAT SOUND... COMING FROM UPSTAIRS!
A BLASTER--
DON'T WORRY, SHAN-- I'LL HANDLE THIS BRUTE!
KITTY!
HE OWES ME A REMATCH!
NICE TRY, BOY...
...BUT NO CIGAR!
UNNNNGNH!
NICE DOGGY! GOOD DOGGY! MUCH AS I'D REALLY LOVE TO STAY AND PLAY WITH YOU, DUTY CALLS.
AUF WEIDERSEHN!
BAMF
IN A BURST OF FLAME AND BRIMSTONE STENCH THAT LEAVES RAHNE CHOKING AND COUGHING ON THE FLOOR, NIGHTCRAWLER TELEPORTS FROM HER...
...TO HER FRIENDS.
OUCH!

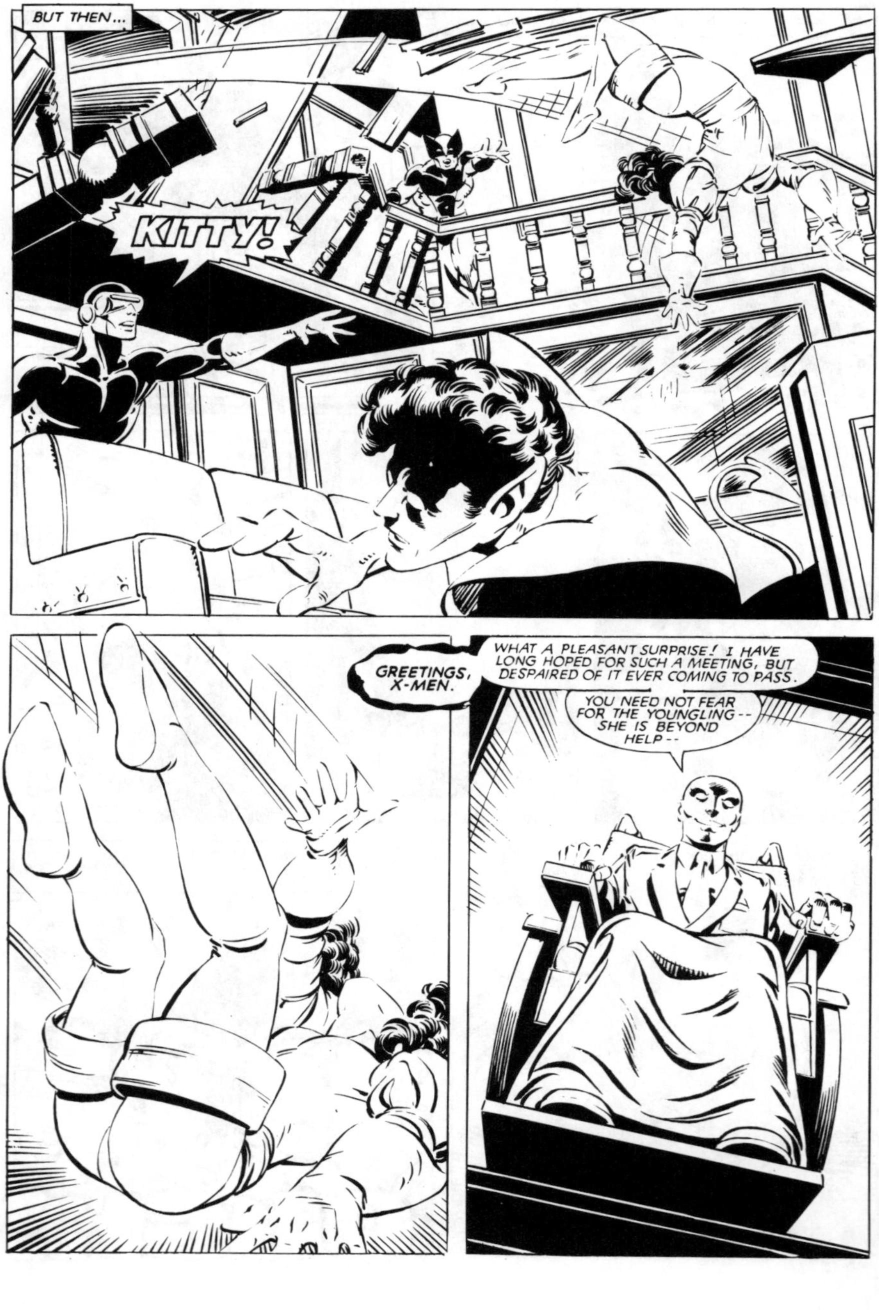
BUT THEN...
KITTY!
GREETINGS, X-MEN.
WHAT A PLEASANT SURPRISE! I HAVE LONG HOPED FOR SUCH A MEETING, BUT DESPAIRED OF IT EVER COMING TO PASS.
YOU NEED NOT FEAR FOR THE YOUNGLING -- SHE IS BEYOND HELP --

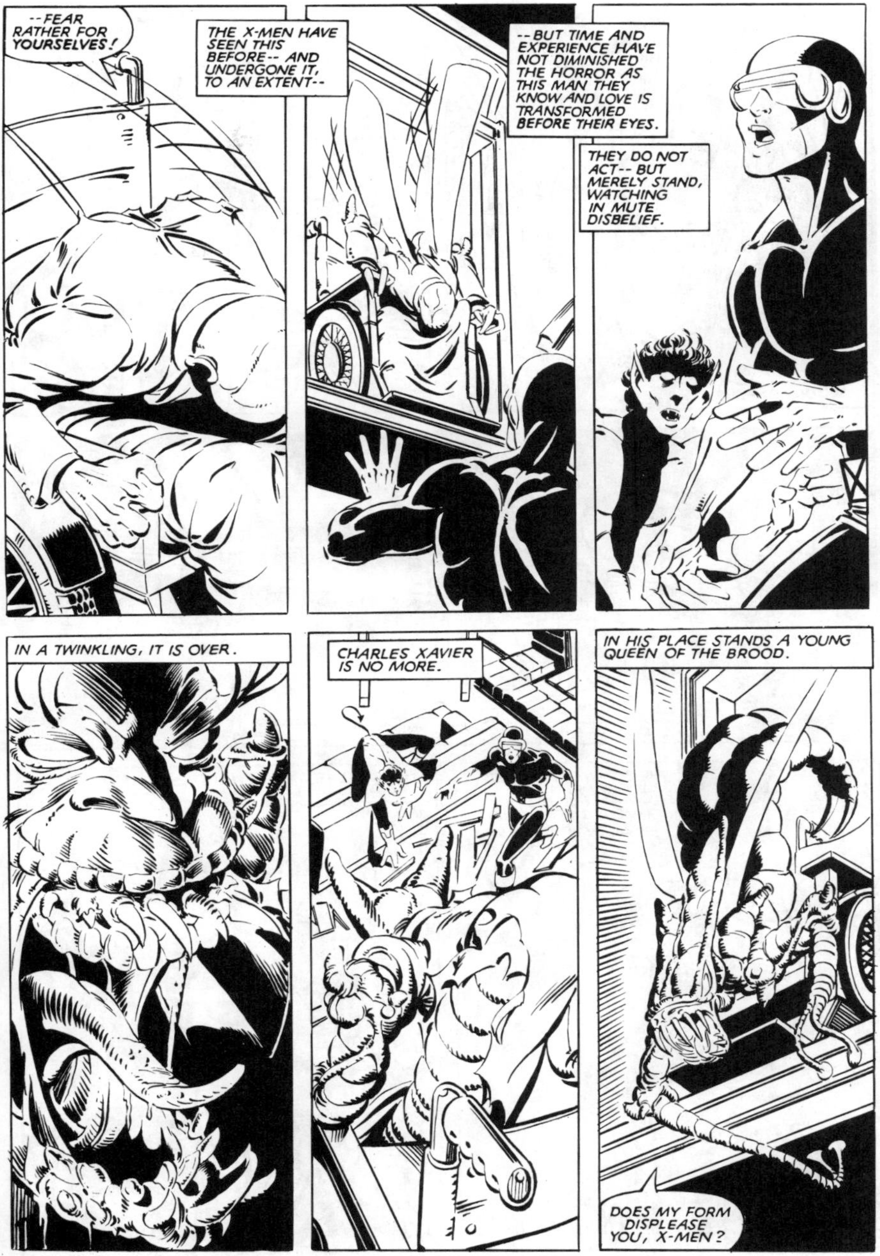
--FEAR RATHER FOR YOURSELVES!
THE X-MEN HAVE SEEN THIS BEFORE-- AND UNDERGONE IT, TO AN EXTENT--
--BUT TIME AND EXPERIENCE HAVE NOT DIMINISHED THE HORROR AS THIS MAN THEY KNOW AND LOVE IS TRANSFORMED BEFORE THEIR EYES.
THEY DO NOT ACT-- BUT MERELY STAND, WATCHING IN MUTE DISBELIEF.
IN A TWINKLING, IT IS OVER.
CHARLES XAVIER IS NO MORE.
IN HIS PLACE STANDS A YOUNG QUEEN OF THE BROOD.
DOES MY FORM DISPLEASE YOU, X-MEN?

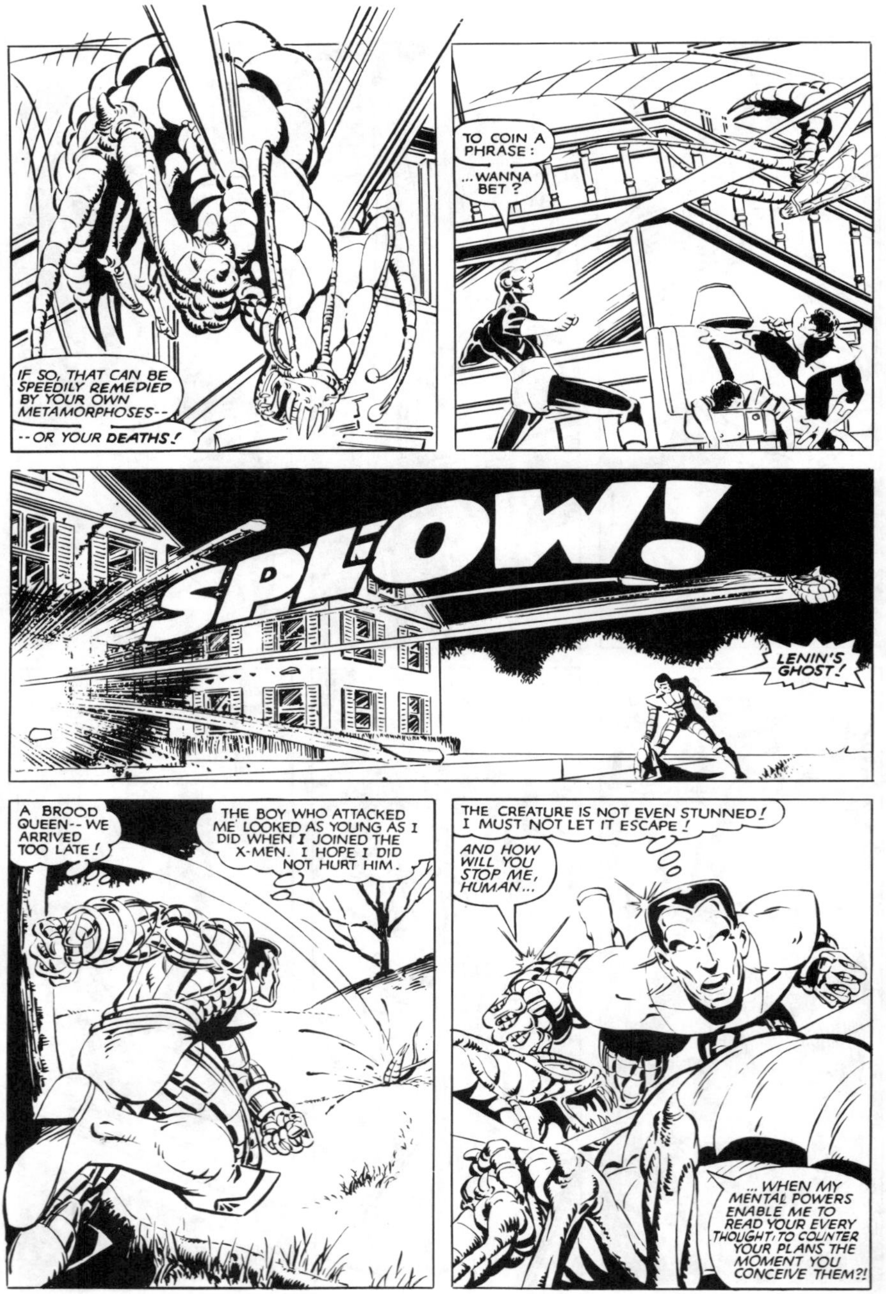
IF SO, THAT CAN BE SPEEDILY REMEDIED BY YOUR OWN METAMORPHOSES--
--OR YOUR DEATHS!
TO COIN A PHRASE:
...WANNA BET?
SPLOW!
LENIN'S GHOST!
A BROOD QUEEN-- WE ARRIVED TOO LATE!
THE BOY WHO ATTACKED ME LOOKED AS YOUNG AS I DID WHEN I JOINED THE X-MEN. I HOPE I DID NOT HURT HIM.
THE CREATURE IS NOT EVEN STUNNED! I MUST NOT LET IT ESCAPE!
AND HOW WILL YOU STOP ME, HUMAN...
...WHEN MY MENTAL POWERS ENABLE ME TO READ YOUR EVERY THOUGHT; TO COUNTER YOUR PLANS THE MOMENT YOU CONCEIVE THEM?!

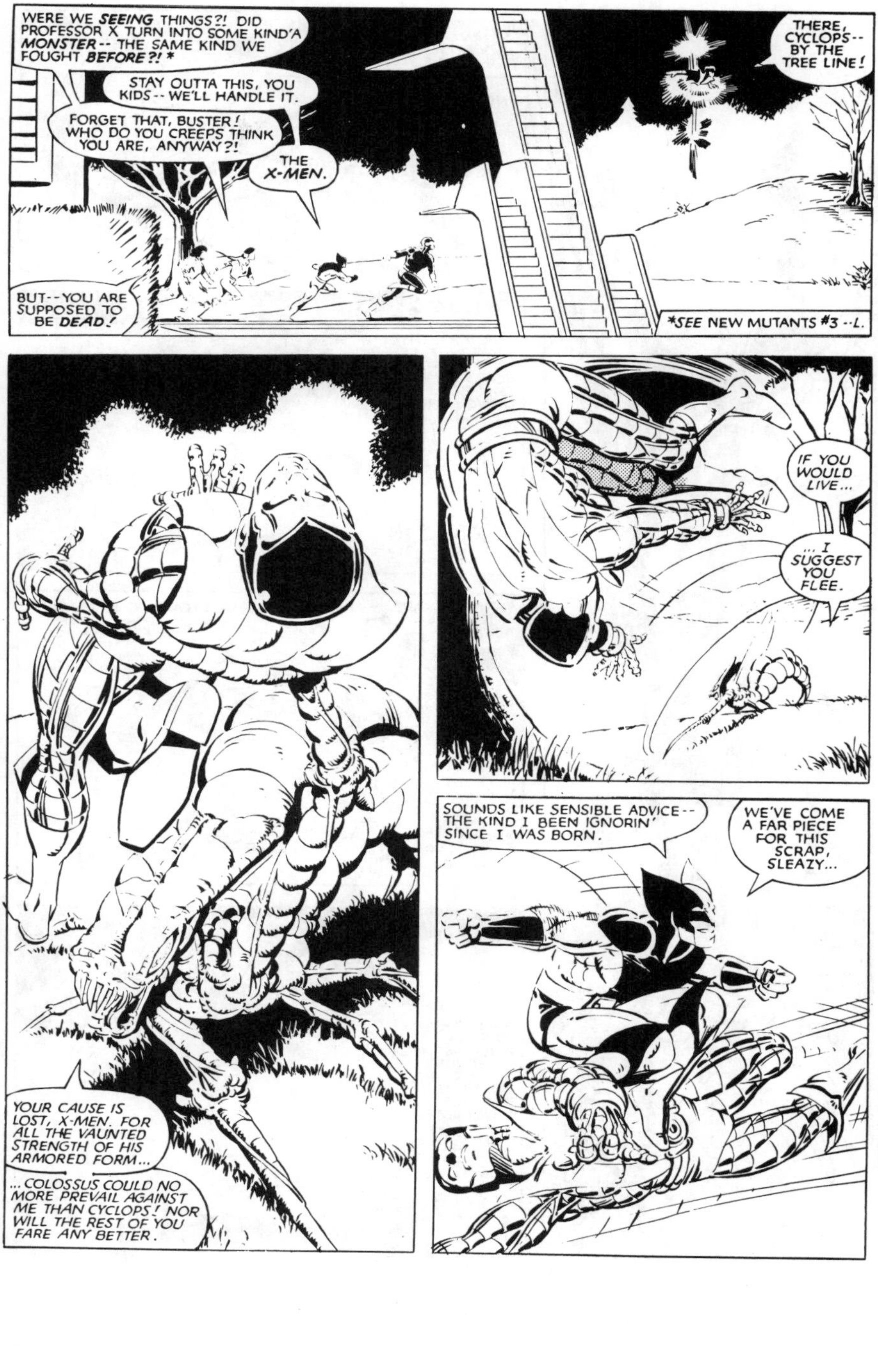
WERE WE SEEING THINGS?! DID PROFESSOR X TURN INTO SOME KIND'A MONSTER -- THE SAME KIND WE FOUGHT BEFORE?! *
THERE, CYCLOPS -- BY THE TREE LINE!
STAY OUTTA THIS, YOU KIDS -- WE'LL HANDLE IT.
FORGET THAT, BUSTER! WHO DO YOU CREEPS THINK YOU ARE, ANYWAY?!
THE X-MEN.
BUT -- YOU ARE SUPPOSED TO BE DEAD!
*SEE NEW MUTANTS #3 --L.
YOUR CAUSE IS LOST, X-MEN. FOR ALL THE VAUNTED STRENGTH OF HIS ARMORED FORM...
... COLOSSUS COULD NO MORE PREVAIL AGAINST ME THAN CYCLOPS! NOR WILL THE REST OF YOU FARE ANY BETTER.
IF YOU WOULD LIVE...
... I SUGGEST YOU FLEE.
SOUNDS LIKE SENSIBLE ADVICE -- THE KIND I BEEN IGNORIN' SINCE I WAS BORN.
WE'VE COME A FAR PIECE FOR THIS SCRAP, SLEAZY...

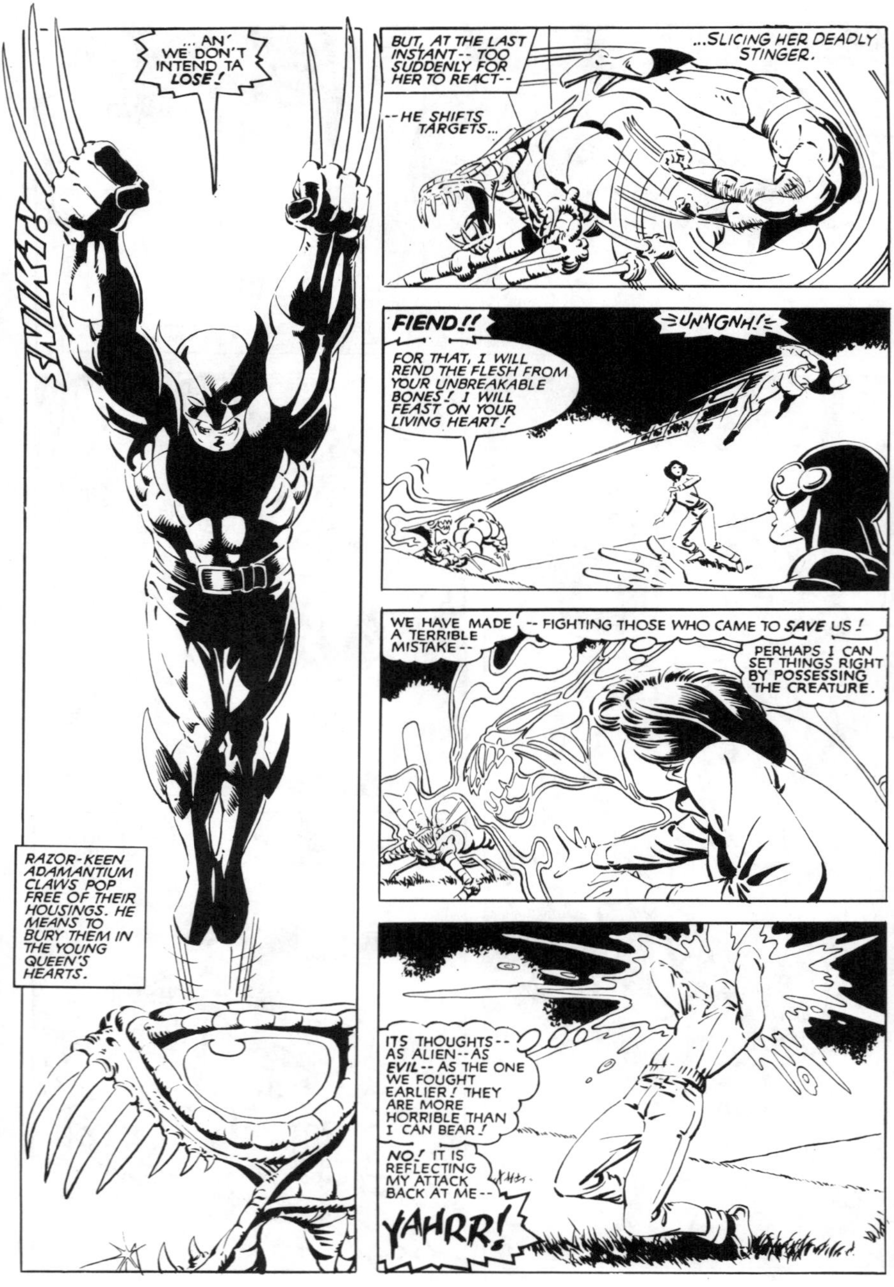
... AN' WE DON'T INTEND TA LOSE!
SNIKT!
RAZOR-KEEN ADAMANTIUM CLAWS POP FREE OF THEIR HOUSINGS. HE MEANS TO BURY THEM IN THE YOUNG QUEEN'S HEARTS.
BUT, AT THE LAST INSTANT-- TOO SUDDENLY FOR HER TO REACT--
--HE SHIFTS TARGETS...
...SLICING HER DEADLY STINGER.
FIEND!!
FOR THAT, I WILL REND THE FLESH FROM YOUR UNBREAKABLE BONES! I WILL FEAST ON YOUR LIVING HEART!
UNNGNH!
WE HAVE MADE A TERRIBLE MISTAKE--
-- FIGHTING THOSE WHO CAME TO SAVE US!
PERHAPS I CAN SET THINGS RIGHT BY POSSESSING THE CREATURE.
ITS THOUGHTS-- AS ALIEN--AS EVIL-- AS THE ONE WE FOUGHT EARLIER! THEY ARE MORE HORRIBLE THAN I CAN BEAR!
NO! IT IS REFLECTING MY ATTACK BACK AT ME--
YAHRR!

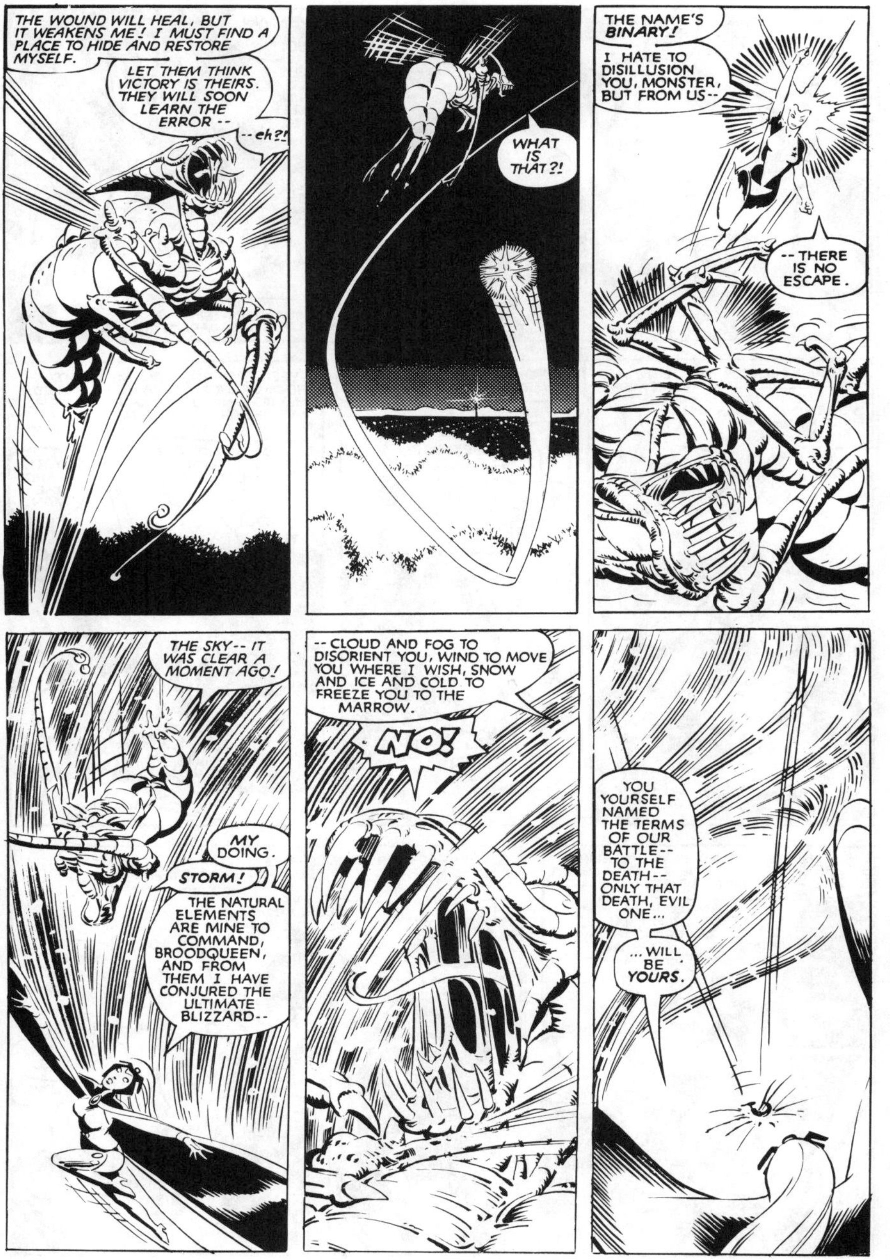
THE WOUND WILL HEAL, BUT IT WEAKENS ME! I MUST FIND A PLACE TO HIDE AND RESTORE MYSELF.
LET THEM THINK VICTORY IS THEIRS. THEY WILL SOON LEARN THE ERROR --
--eh?!
WHAT IS THAT?!
THE NAME'S BINARY!
I HATE TO DISILLUSION YOU, MONSTER, BUT FROM US--
--THERE IS NO ESCAPE.
THE SKY-- IT WAS CLEAR A MOMENT AGO!
MY DOING.
STORM!
THE NATURAL ELEMENTS ARE MINE TO COMMAND, BROODQUEEN, AND FROM THEM I HAVE CONJURED THE ULTIMATE BLIZZARD--
--CLOUD AND FOG TO DISORIENT YOU, WIND TO MOVE YOU WHERE I WISH, SNOW AND ICE AND COLD TO FREEZE YOU TO THE MARROW.
NO!
YOU YOURSELF NAMED THE TERMS OF OUR BATTLE-- TO THE DEATH-- ONLY THAT DEATH, EVIL ONE...
...WILL BE YOURS.

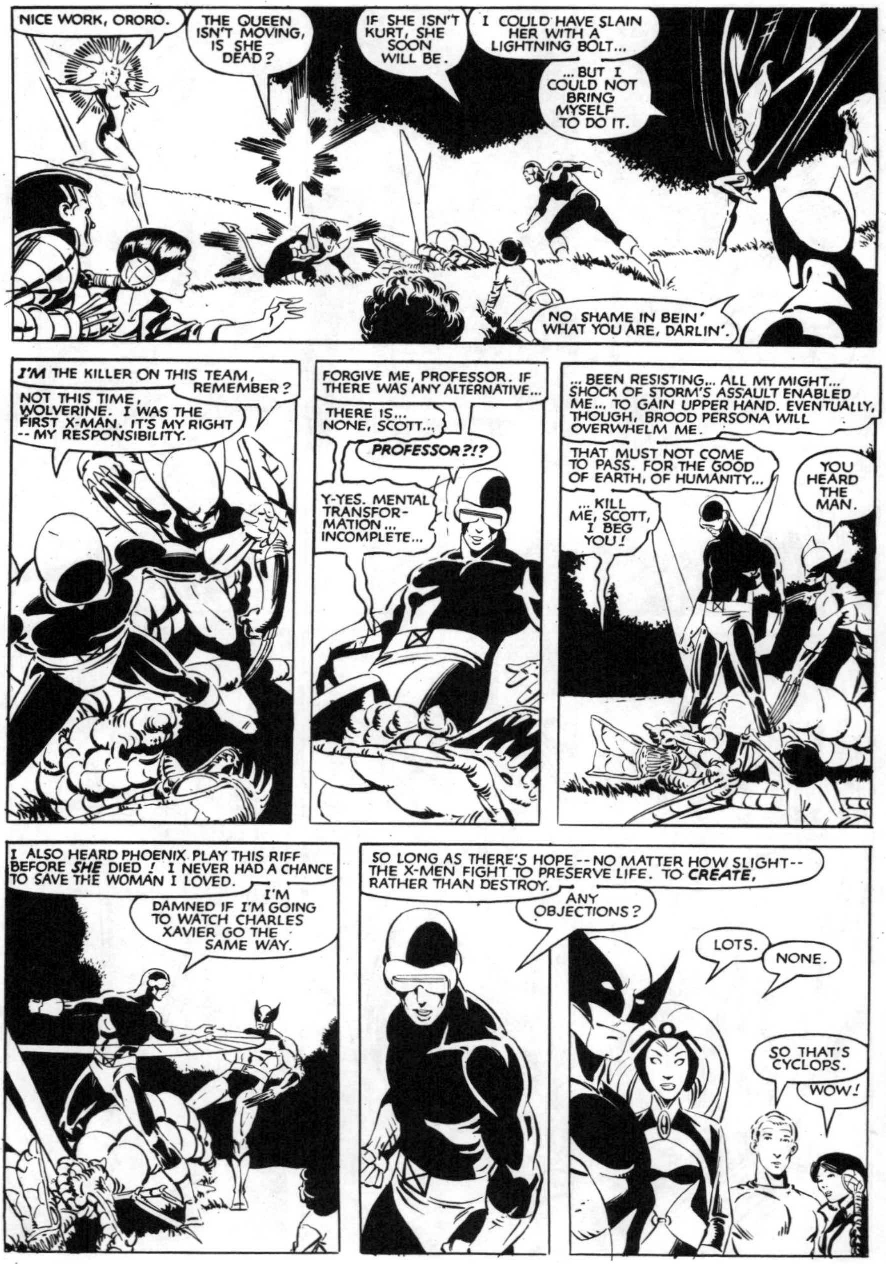
NICE WORK, ORORO.
THE QUEEN ISN'T MOVING, IS SHE DEAD?
IF SHE ISN'T KURT, SHE SOON WILL BE.
I COULD HAVE SLAIN HER WITH A LIGHTNING BOLT...
... BUT I COULD NOT BRING MYSELF TO DO IT.
NO SHAME IN BEIN' WHAT YOU ARE, DARLIN'.
I'M THE KILLER ON THIS TEAM, REMEMBER?
NOT THIS TIME, WOLVERINE. I WAS THE FIRST X-MAN. IT'S MY RIGHT -- MY RESPONSIBILITY.
FORGIVE ME, PROFESSOR. IF THERE WAS ANY ALTERNATIVE...
THERE IS... NONE, SCOTT...
PROFESSOR?!?
Y-YES. MENTAL TRANSFORMATION... INCOMPLETE...
... BEEN RESISTING... ALL MY MIGHT... SHOCK OF STORM'S ASSAULT ENABLED ME... TO GAIN UPPER HAND. EVENTUALLY, THOUGH, BROOD PERSONA WILL OVERWHELM ME.
THAT MUST NOT COME TO PASS. FOR THE GOOD OF EARTH, OF HUMANITY...
... KILL ME, SCOTT, I BEG YOU!
YOU HEARD THE MAN.
I ALSO HEARD PHOENIX PLAY THIS RIFF BEFORE SHE DIED! I NEVER HAD A CHANCE TO SAVE THE WOMAN I LOVED.
I'M DAMNED IF I'M GOING TO WATCH CHARLES XAVIER GO THE SAME WAY.
SO LONG AS THERE'S HOPE -- NO MATTER HOW SLIGHT -- THE X-MEN FIGHT TO PRESERVE LIFE. TO CREATE, RATHER THAN DESTROY.
ANY OBJECTIONS?
LOTS.
NONE.
SO THAT'S CYCLOPS.
WOW!

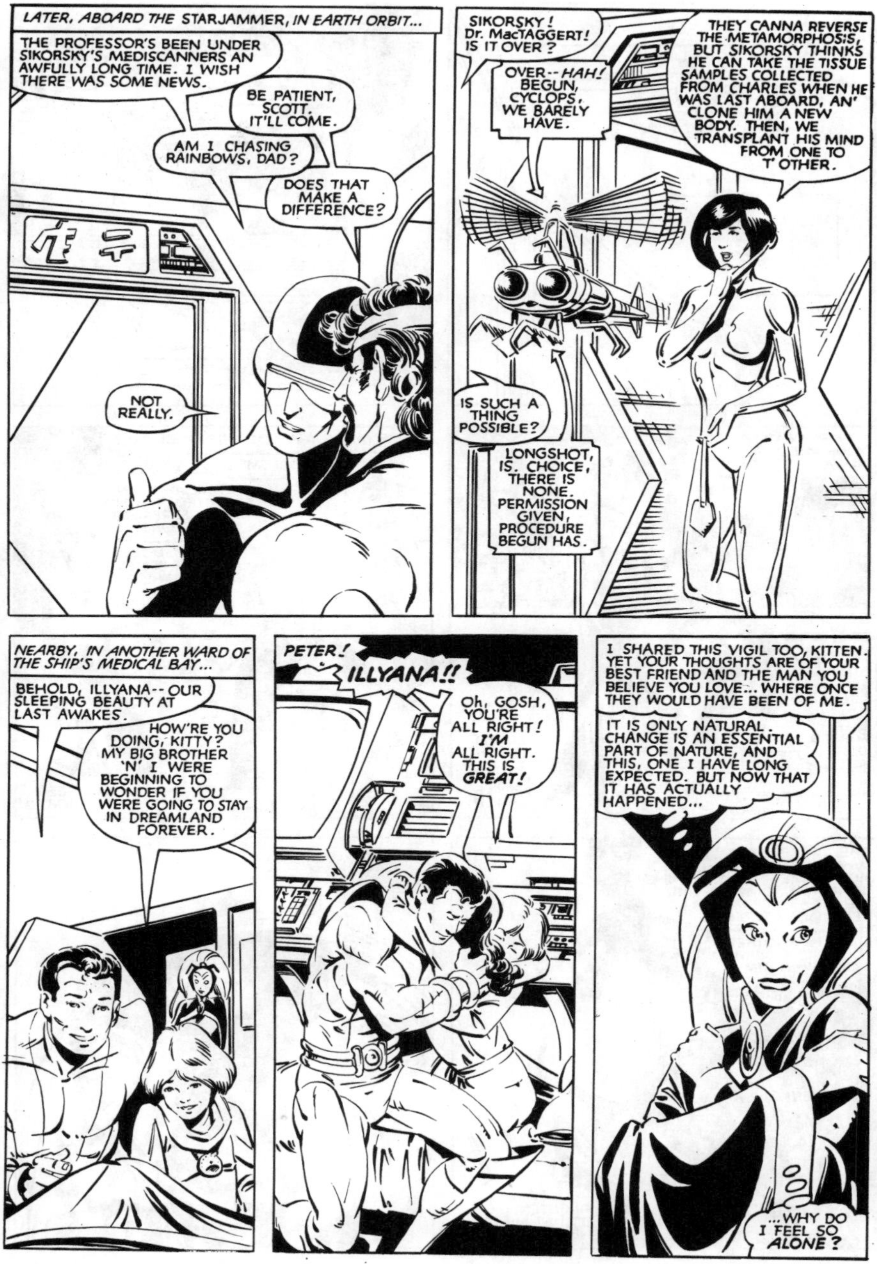
LATER, ABOARD THE STARJAMMER, IN EARTH ORBIT...
THE PROFESSOR'S BEEN UNDER SIKORSKY'S MEDISCANNERS AN AWFULLY LONG TIME. I WISH THERE WAS SOME NEWS.
BE PATIENT, SCOTT. IT'LL COME.
AM I CHASING RAINBOWS, DAD?
DOES THAT MAKE A DIFFERENCE?
NOT REALLY.
SIKORSKY! Dr. MacTAGGERT! IS IT OVER?
OVER--HAH! BEGUN, CYCLOPS, WE BARELY HAVE.
THEY CANNA REVERSE THE METAMORPHOSIS, BUT SIKORSKY THINKS HE CAN TAKE THE TISSUE SAMPLES COLLECTED FROM CHARLES WHEN HE WAS LAST ABOARD, AN' CLONE HIM A NEW BODY. THEN, WE TRANSPLANT HIS MIND FROM ONE TO T'OTHER.
IS SUCH A THING POSSIBLE?
LONGSHOT, IS. CHOICE, THERE IS NONE. PERMISSION GIVEN, PROCEDURE BEGUN HAS.
NEARBY, IN ANOTHER WARD OF THE SHIP'S MEDICAL BAY...
BEHOLD, ILLYANA--OUR SLEEPING BEAUTY AT LAST AWAKES.
HOW'RE YOU DOING, KITTY? MY BIG BROTHER 'N' I WERE BEGINNING TO WONDER IF YOU WERE GOING TO STAY IN DREAMLAND FOREVER.
PETER!
ILLYANA!!
Oh, GOSH, YOU'RE ALL RIGHT! I'M ALL RIGHT. THIS IS GREAT!
I SHARED THIS VIGIL TOO, KITTEN. YET YOUR THOUGHTS ARE OF YOUR BEST FRIEND AND THE MAN YOU BELIEVE YOU LOVE... WHERE ONCE THEY WOULD HAVE BEEN OF ME.
IT IS ONLY NATURAL. CHANGE IS AN ESSENTIAL PART OF NATURE, AND THIS, ONE I HAVE LONG EXPECTED. BUT NOW THAT IT HAS ACTUALLY HAPPENED...
...WHY DO I FEEL SO ALONE?

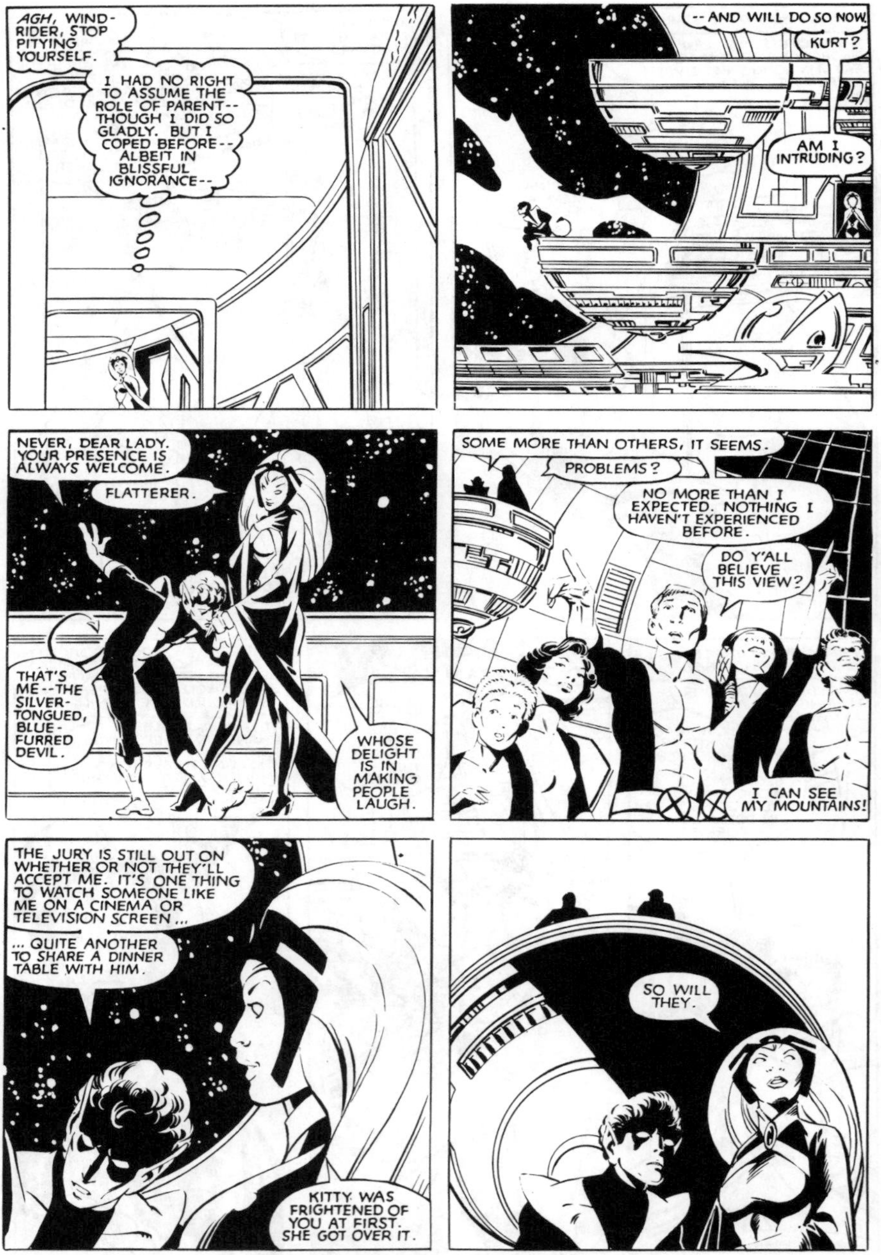
AGH, WIND-RIDER, STOP PITYING YOURSELF.
I HAD NO RIGHT TO ASSUME THE ROLE OF PARENT-- THOUGH I DID SO GLADLY. BUT I COPED BEFORE-- ALBEIT IN BLISSFUL IGNORANCE--
--AND WILL DO SO NOW.
KURT?
AM I INTRUDING?
NEVER, DEAR LADY. YOUR PRESENCE IS ALWAYS WELCOME.
FLATTERER.
THAT'S ME--THE SILVER-TONGUED, BLUE-FURRED DEVIL.
WHOSE DELIGHT IS IN MAKING PEOPLE LAUGH.
SOME MORE THAN OTHERS, IT SEEMS.
PROBLEMS?
NO MORE THAN I EXPECTED. NOTHING I HAVEN'T EXPERIENCED BEFORE.
DO Y'ALL BELIEVE THIS VIEW?
I CAN SEE MY MOUNTAINS!
THE JURY IS STILL OUT ON WHETHER OR NOT THEY'LL ACCEPT ME. IT'S ONE THING TO WATCH SOMEONE LIKE ME ON A CINEMA OR TELEVISION SCREEN...
... QUITE ANOTHER TO SHARE A DINNER TABLE WITH HIM.
KITTY WAS FRIGHTENED OF YOU AT FIRST. SHE GOT OVER IT.
SO WILL THEY.

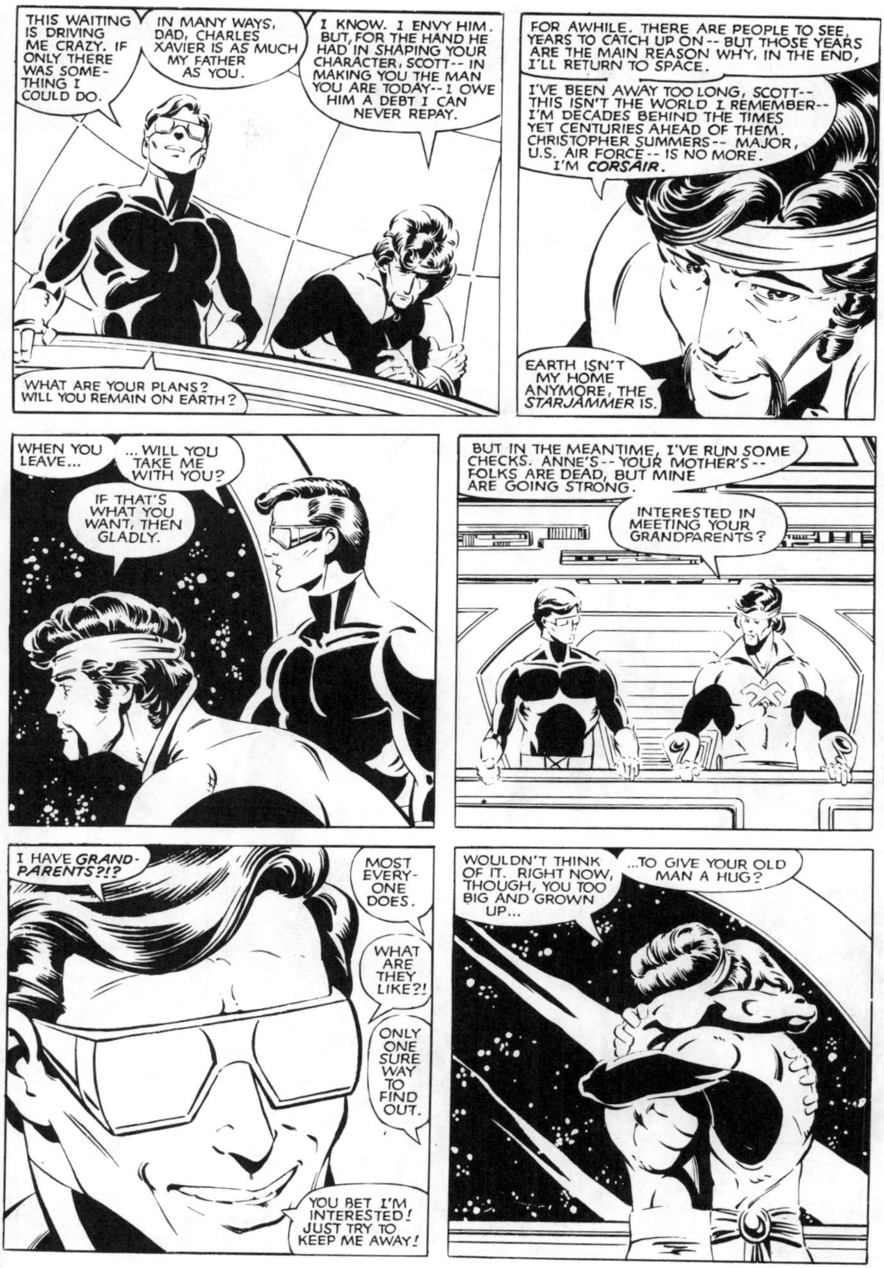
THIS WAITING IS DRIVING ME CRAZY. IF ONLY THERE WAS SOMETHING I COULD DO.
IN MANY WAYS, DAD, CHARLES XAVIER IS AS MUCH MY FATHER AS YOU.
I KNOW. I ENVY HIM. BUT, FOR THE HAND HE HAD IN SHAPING YOUR CHARACTER, SCOTT-- IN MAKING YOU THE MAN YOU ARE TODAY-- I OWE HIM A DEBT I CAN NEVER REPAY.
WHAT ARE YOUR PLANS? WILL YOU REMAIN ON EARTH?
FOR AWHILE. THERE ARE PEOPLE TO SEE, YEARS TO CATCH UP ON -- BUT THOSE YEARS ARE THE MAIN REASON WHY, IN THE END, I'LL RETURN TO SPACE.
I'VE BEEN AWAY TOO LONG, SCOTT-- THIS ISN'T THE WORLD I REMEMBER-- I'M DECADES BEHIND THE TIMES YET CENTURIES AHEAD OF THEM. CHRISTOPHER SUMMERS-- MAJOR, U.S. AIR FORCE -- IS NO MORE. I'M CORSAIR.
EARTH ISN'T MY HOME ANYMORE, THE STARJAMMER IS.
WHEN YOU LEAVE...
...WILL YOU TAKE ME WITH YOU?
IF THAT'S WHAT YOU WANT, THEN GLADLY.
BUT IN THE MEANTIME, I'VE RUN SOME CHECKS. ANNE'S-- YOUR MOTHER'S-- FOLKS ARE DEAD, BUT MINE ARE GOING STRONG.
INTERESTED IN MEETING YOUR GRANDPARENTS?
I HAVE GRAND-PARENTS?!?
MOST EVERYONE DOES.
WHAT ARE THEY LIKE?!
ONLY ONE SURE WAY TO FIND OUT.
YOU BET I'M INTERESTED! JUST TRY TO KEEP ME AWAY!
WOULDN'T THINK OF IT. RIGHT NOW, THOUGH, YOU TOO BIG AND GROWN UP...
...TO GIVE YOUR OLD MAN A HUG?

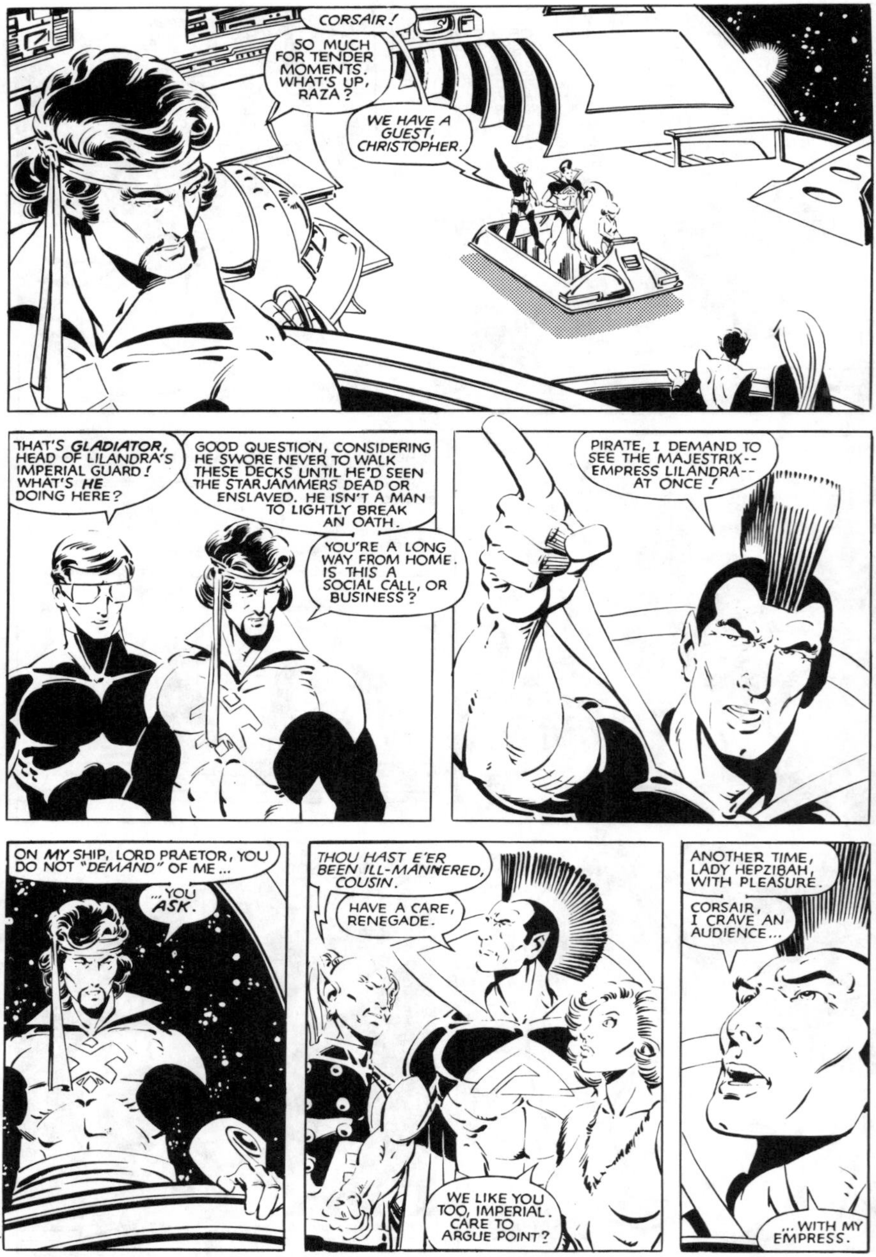
CORSAIR!
SO MUCH FOR TENDER MOMENTS. WHAT'S UP, RAZA?
WE HAVE A GUEST, CHRISTOPHER.
THAT'S GLADIATOR, HEAD OF LILANDRA'S IMPERIAL GUARD! WHAT'S HE DOING HERE?
GOOD QUESTION, CONSIDERING HE SWORE NEVER TO WALK THESE DECKS UNTIL HE'D SEEN THE STARJAMMERS DEAD OR ENSLAVED. HE ISN'T A MAN TO LIGHTLY BREAK AN OATH.
YOU'RE A LONG WAY FROM HOME. IS THIS A SOCIAL CALL, OR BUSINESS?
PIRATE, I DEMAND TO SEE THE MAJESTRIX-- EMPRESS LILANDRA-- AT ONCE!
ON MY SHIP, LORD PRAETOR, YOU DO NOT "DEMAND" OF ME...
...YOU ASK.
THOU HAST E'ER BEEN ILL-MANNERED, COUSIN.
HAVE A CARE, RENEGADE.
WE LIKE YOU TOO, IMPERIAL. CARE TO ARGUE POINT?
ANOTHER TIME, LADY HEPZIBAH, WITH PLEASURE.
CORSAIR, I CRAVE AN AUDIENCE...
...WITH MY EMPRESS.

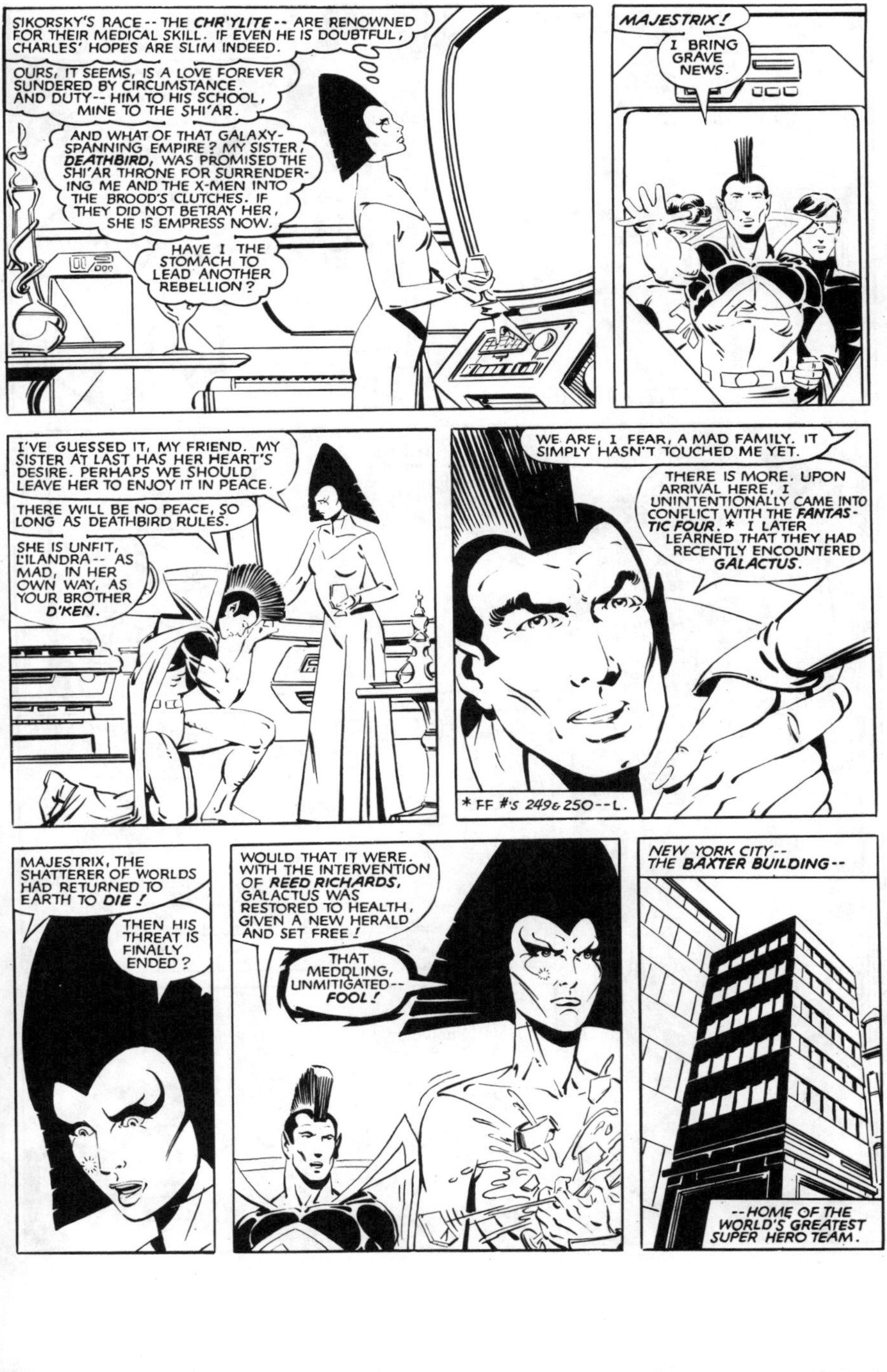
SIKORSKY'S RACE -- THE CHR'YLITE -- ARE RENOWNED FOR THEIR MEDICAL SKILL. IF EVEN HE IS DOUBTFUL, CHARLES' HOPES ARE SLIM INDEED.
OURS, IT SEEMS, IS A LOVE FOREVER SUNDERED BY CIRCUMSTANCE. AND DUTY-- HIM TO HIS SCHOOL, MINE TO THE SHI'AR.
AND WHAT OF THAT GALAXY-SPANNING EMPIRE? MY SISTER, DEATHBIRD, WAS PROMISED THE SHI'AR THRONE FOR SURRENDERING ME AND THE X-MEN INTO THE BROOD'S CLUTCHES. IF THEY DID NOT BETRAY HER, SHE IS EMPRESS NOW.
HAVE I THE STOMACH TO LEAD ANOTHER REBELLION?
MAJESTRIX!
I BRING GRAVE NEWS.
I'VE GUESSED IT, MY FRIEND. MY SISTER AT LAST HAS HER HEART'S DESIRE. PERHAPS WE SHOULD LEAVE HER TO ENJOY IT IN PEACE.
THERE WILL BE NO PEACE, SO LONG AS DEATHBIRD RULES.
SHE IS UNFIT, LILANDRA-- AS MAD, IN HER OWN WAY, AS YOUR BROTHER D'KEN.
WE ARE, I FEAR, A MAD FAMILY. IT SIMPLY HASN'T TOUCHED ME YET.
THERE IS MORE. UPON ARRIVAL HERE, I UNINTENTIONALLY CAME INTO CONFLICT WITH THE FANTASTIC FOUR.* I LATER LEARNED THAT THEY HAD RECENTLY ENCOUNTERED GALACTUS.
* FF #'S 249 & 250 -- L.
MAJESTRIX, THE SHATTERER OF WORLDS HAD RETURNED TO EARTH TO DIE!
THEN HIS THREAT IS FINALLY ENDED?
WOULD THAT IT WERE. WITH THE INTERVENTION OF REED RICHARDS, GALACTUS WAS RESTORED TO HEALTH, GIVEN A NEW HERALD AND SET FREE!
THAT MEDDLING, UNMITIGATED-- FOOL!
NEW YORK CITY-- THE BAXTER BUILDING--
--HOME OF THE WORLD'S GREATEST SUPER HERO TEAM.

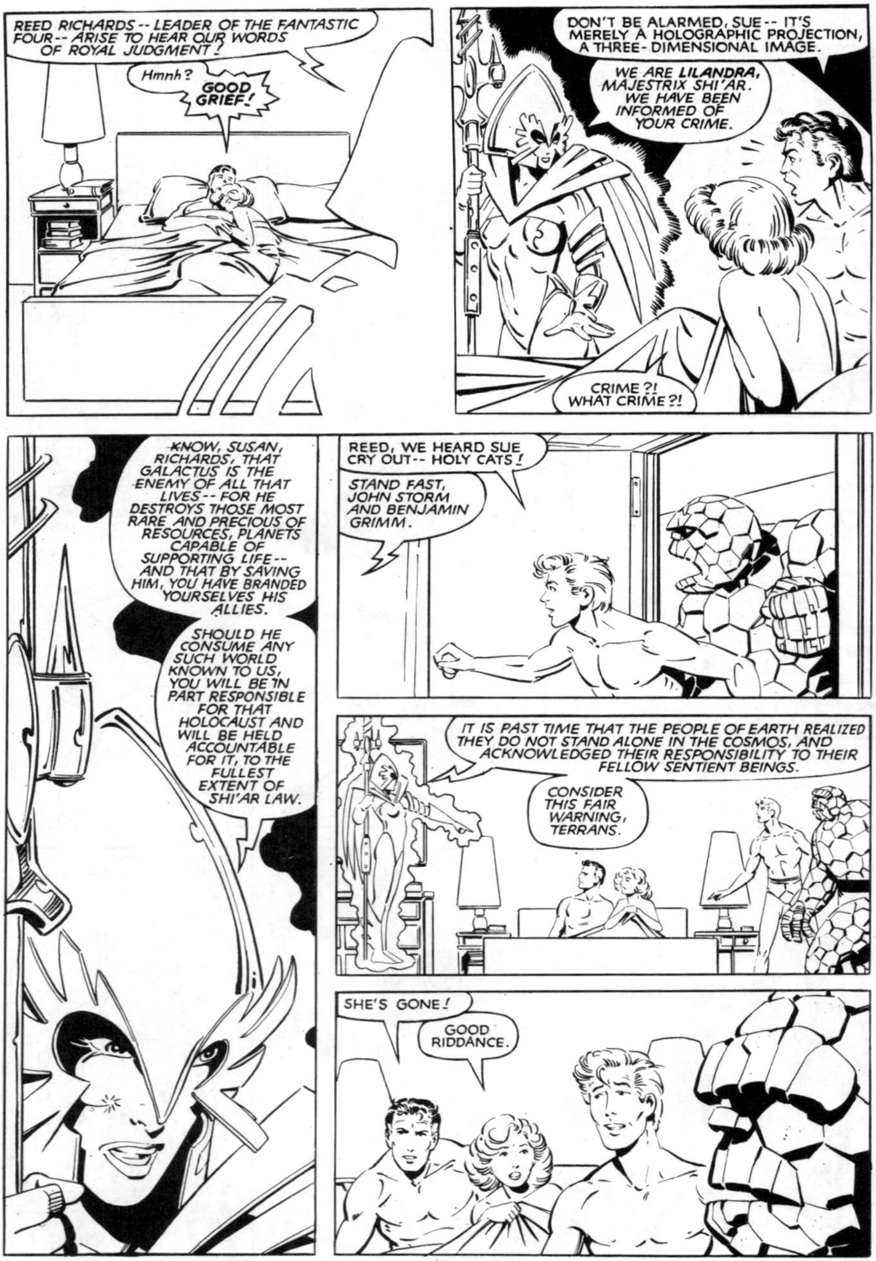
REED RICHARDS -- LEADER OF THE FANTASTIC FOUR -- ARISE TO HEAR OUR WORDS OF ROYAL JUDGMENT!
Hmnh? GOOD GRIEF!
DON'T BE ALARMED, SUE -- IT'S MERELY A HOLOGRAPHIC PROJECTION, A THREE-DIMENSIONAL IMAGE.
WE ARE LILANDRA, MAJESTRIX SHI'AR. WE HAVE BEEN INFORMED OF YOUR CRIME.
CRIME?! WHAT CRIME?!
KNOW, SUSAN RICHARDS, THAT GALACTUS IS THE ENEMY OF ALL THAT LIVES -- FOR HE DESTROYS THOSE MOST RARE AND PRECIOUS OF RESOURCES, PLANETS CAPABLE OF SUPPORTING LIFE -- AND THAT BY SAVING HIM, YOU HAVE BRANDED YOURSELVES HIS ALLIES.
SHOULD HE CONSUME ANY SUCH WORLD KNOWN TO US, YOU WILL BE IN PART RESPONSIBLE FOR THAT HOLOCAUST AND WILL BE HELD ACCOUNTABLE FOR IT, TO THE FULLEST EXTENT OF SHI'AR LAW.
REED, WE HEARD SUE CRY OUT -- HOLY CATS!
STAND FAST, JOHN STORM AND BENJAMIN GRIMM.
IT IS PAST TIME THAT THE PEOPLE OF EARTH REALIZED THEY DO NOT STAND ALONE IN THE COSMOS, AND ACKNOWLEDGED THEIR RESPONSIBILITY TO THEIR FELLOW SENTIENT BEINGS.
CONSIDER THIS FAIR WARNING, TERRANS.
SHE'S GONE!
GOOD RIDDANCE.

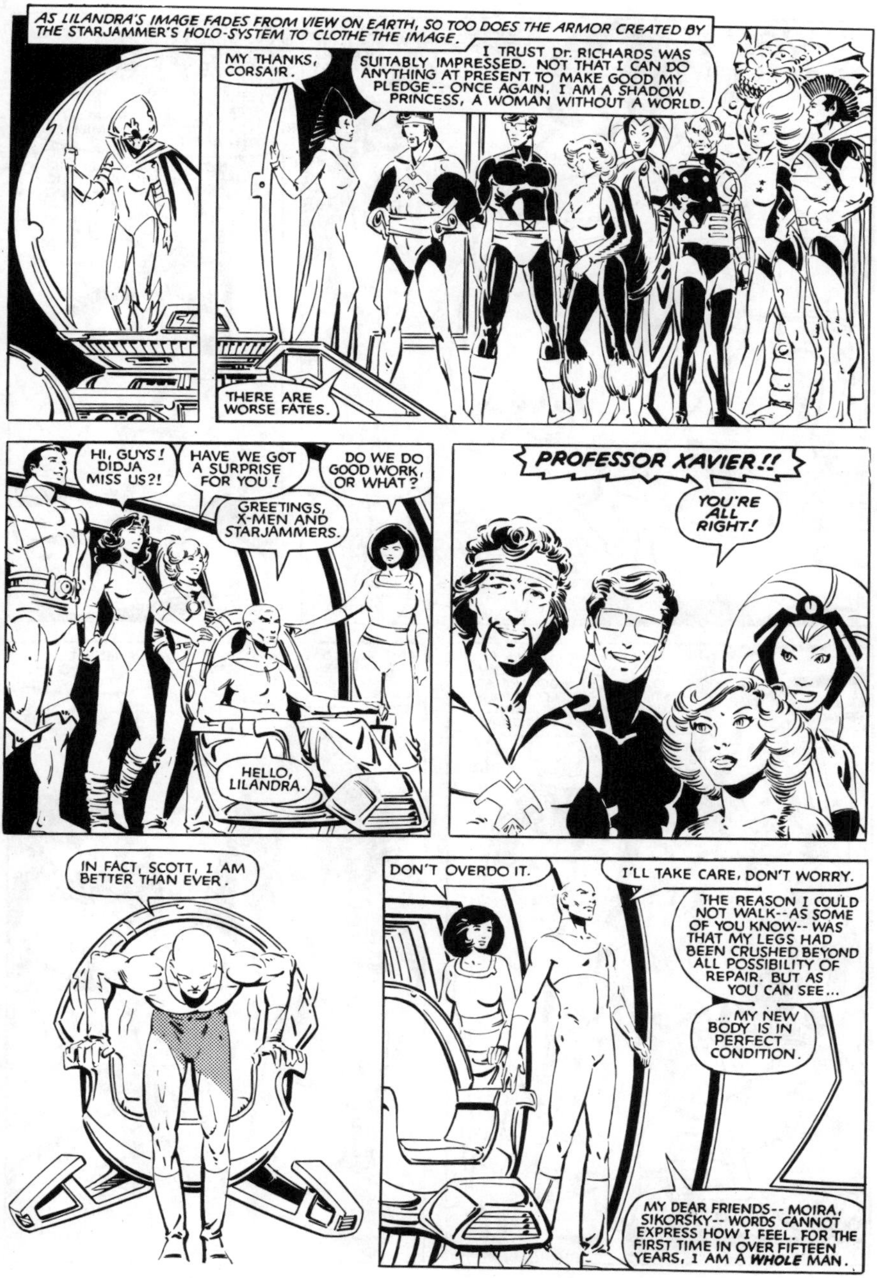
AS LILANDRA'S IMAGE FADES FROM VIEW ON EARTH, SO TOO DOES THE ARMOR CREATED BY THE STARJAMMER'S HOLO-SYSTEM TO CLOTHE THE IMAGE.
MY THANKS, CORSAIR.
I TRUST Dr. RICHARDS WAS SUITABLY IMPRESSED. NOT THAT I CAN DO ANYTHING AT PRESENT TO MAKE GOOD MY PLEDGE-- ONCE AGAIN, I AM A SHADOW PRINCESS, A WOMAN WITHOUT A WORLD.
THERE ARE WORSE FATES.
HI, GUYS! DIDJA MISS US?!
HAVE WE GOT A SURPRISE FOR YOU!
DO WE DO GOOD WORK, OR WHAT?
GREETINGS, X-MEN AND STARJAMMERS.
HELLO, LILANDRA.
PROFESSOR XAVIER!!
YOU'RE ALL RIGHT!
IN FACT, SCOTT, I AM BETTER THAN EVER.
DON'T OVERDO IT.
I'LL TAKE CARE, DON'T WORRY.
THE REASON I COULD NOT WALK--AS SOME OF YOU KNOW-- WAS THAT MY LEGS HAD BEEN CRUSHED BEYOND ALL POSSIBILITY OF REPAIR. BUT AS YOU CAN SEE...
...MY NEW BODY IS IN PERFECT CONDITION.
MY DEAR FRIENDS-- MOIRA, SIKORSKY-- WORDS CANNOT EXPRESS HOW I FEEL. FOR THE FIRST TIME IN OVER FIFTEEN YEARS, I AM A WHOLE MAN.

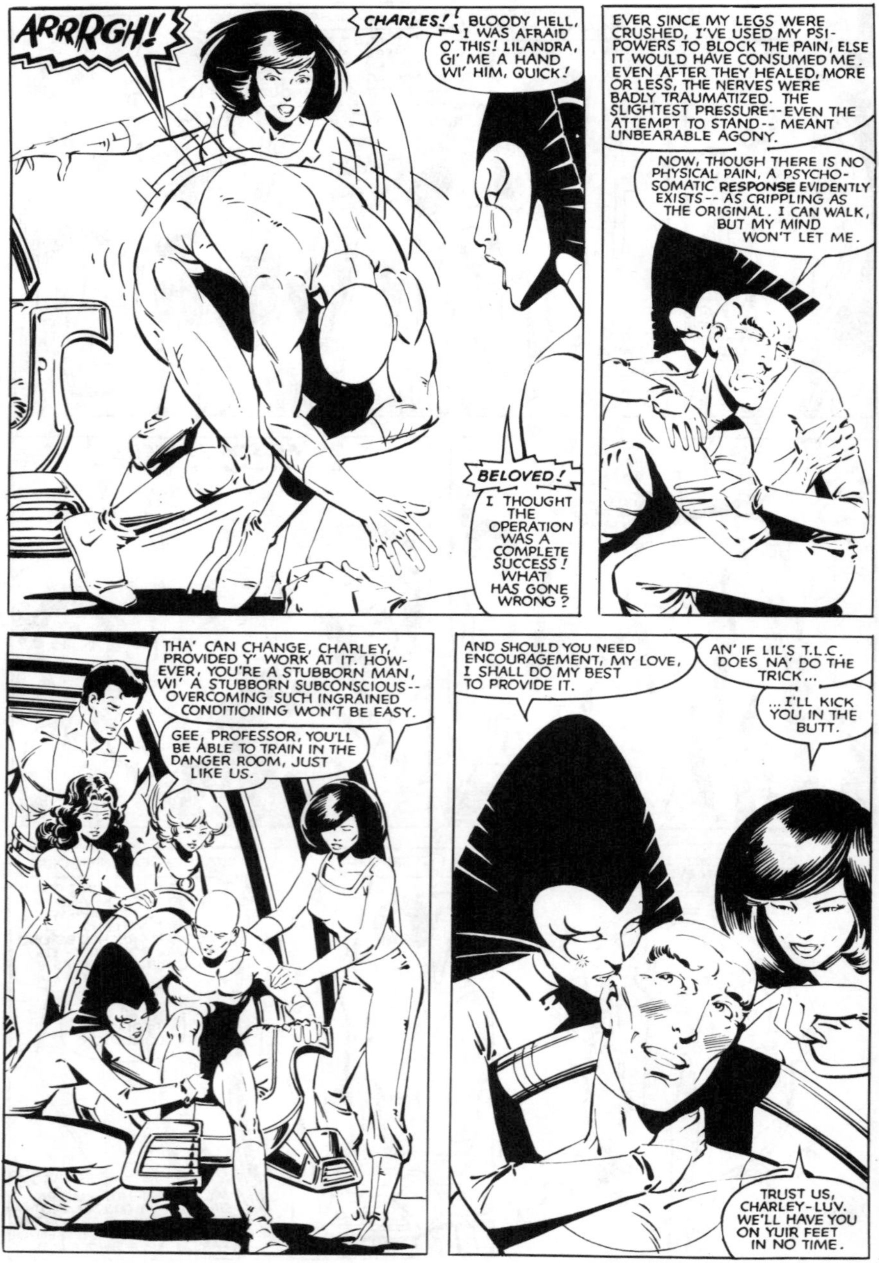

ARRRRGH!
CHARLES!
BLOODY HELL, I WAS AFRAID O' THIS! LILANDRA, GI' ME A HAND WI' HIM, QUICK!
BELOVED!
I THOUGHT THE OPERATION WAS A COMPLETE SUCCESS! WHAT HAS GONE WRONG?
EVER SINCE MY LEGS WERE CRUSHED, I'VE USED MY PSI-POWERS TO BLOCK THE PAIN, ELSE IT WOULD HAVE CONSUMED ME. EVEN AFTER THEY HEALED, MORE OR LESS, THE NERVES WERE BADLY TRAUMATIZED. THE SLIGHTEST PRESSURE--EVEN THE ATTEMPT TO STAND--MEANT UNBEARABLE AGONY.
NOW, THOUGH THERE IS NO PHYSICAL PAIN, A PSYCHO-SOMATIC RESPONSE EVIDENTLY EXISTS--AS CRIPPLING AS THE ORIGINAL. I CAN WALK, BUT MY MIND WON'T LET ME.
THA' CAN CHANGE, CHARLEY, PROVIDED Y' WORK AT IT. HOW-EVER, YOU'RE A STUBBORN MAN, WI' A STUBBORN SUBCONSCIOUS--OVERCOMING SUCH INGRAINED CONDITIONING WON'T BE EASY.
GEE, PROFESSOR, YOU'LL BE ABLE TO TRAIN IN THE DANGER ROOM, JUST LIKE US.
AND SHOULD YOU NEED ENCOURAGEMENT, MY LOVE, I SHALL DO MY BEST TO PROVIDE IT.
AN' IF LIL'S T.L.C. DOES NA' DO THE TRICK...
...I'LL KICK YOU IN THE BUTT.
TRUST US, CHARLEY-LUV. WE'LL HAVE YOU ON YUIR FEET IN NO TIME.

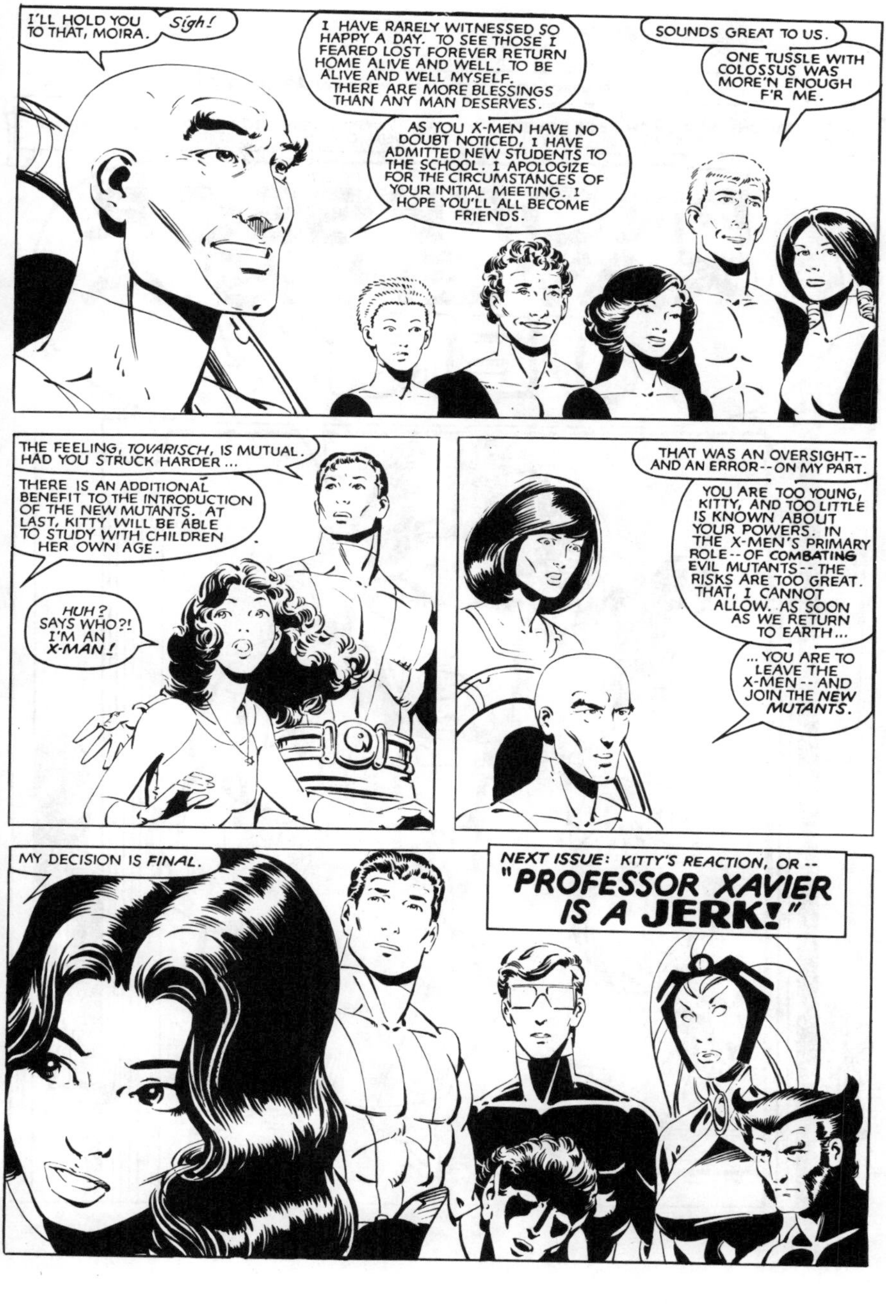
I'LL HOLD YOU TO THAT, MOIRA.
Sigh!
I HAVE RARELY WITNESSED SO HAPPY A DAY. TO SEE THOSE I FEARED LOST FOREVER RETURN HOME ALIVE AND WELL. TO BE ALIVE AND WELL MYSELF. THERE ARE MORE BLESSINGS THAN ANY MAN DESERVES.
AS YOU X-MEN HAVE NO DOUBT NOTICED, I HAVE ADMITTED NEW STUDENTS TO THE SCHOOL. I APOLOGIZE FOR THE CIRCUMSTANCES OF YOUR INITIAL MEETING. I HOPE YOU'LL ALL BECOME FRIENDS.
SOUNDS GREAT TO US.
ONE TUSSLE WITH COLOSSUS WAS MORE'N ENOUGH F'R ME.
THE FEELING, TOVARISCH, IS MUTUAL. HAD YOU STRUCK HARDER ...
THERE IS AN ADDITIONAL BENEFIT TO THE INTRODUCTION OF THE NEW MUTANTS. AT LAST, KITTY WILL BE ABLE TO STUDY WITH CHILDREN HER OWN AGE.
HUH? SAYS WHO?! I'M AN X-MAN!
THAT WAS AN OVERSIGHT-- AND AN ERROR-- ON MY PART.
YOU ARE TOO YOUNG, KITTY, AND TOO LITTLE IS KNOWN ABOUT YOUR POWERS. IN THE X-MEN'S PRIMARY ROLE-- OF COMBATING EVIL MUTANTS-- THE RISKS ARE TOO GREAT. THAT, I CANNOT ALLOW. AS SOON AS WE RETURN TO EARTH...
... YOU ARE TO LEAVE THE X-MEN-- AND JOIN THE NEW MUTANTS.
MY DECISION IS FINAL.
NEXT ISSUE: KITTY'S REACTION, OR --
"PROFESSOR XAVIER IS A JERK!"

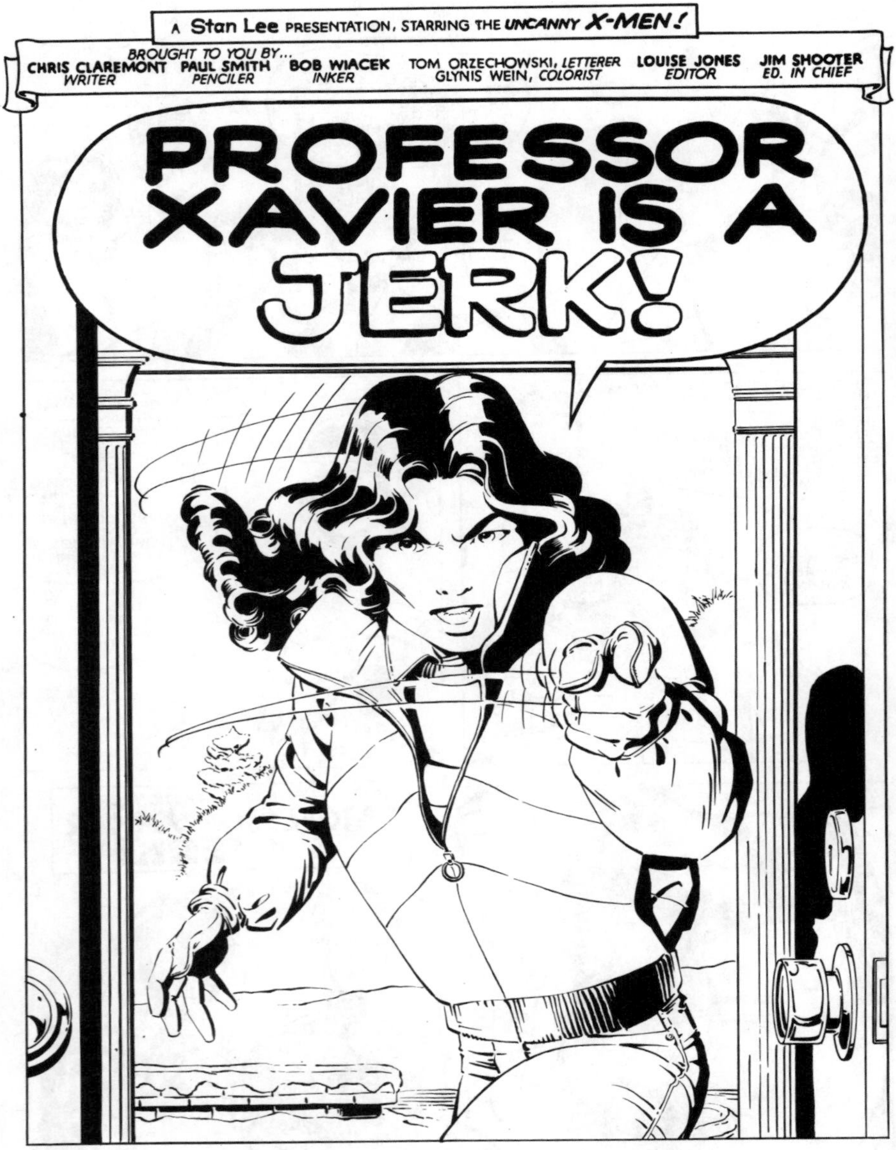
A Stan Lee PRESENTATION, STARRING THE UNCANNY X-MEN!
BROUGHT TO YOU BY...
CHRIS CLAREMONT WRITER
PAUL SMITH PENCILER
BOB WIACEK INKER
TOM ORZECHOWSKI, LETTERER
GLYNIS WEIN, COLORIST
LOUISE JONES EDITOR
JIM SHOOTER ED. IN CHIEF
PROFESSOR XAVIER IS A JERK!

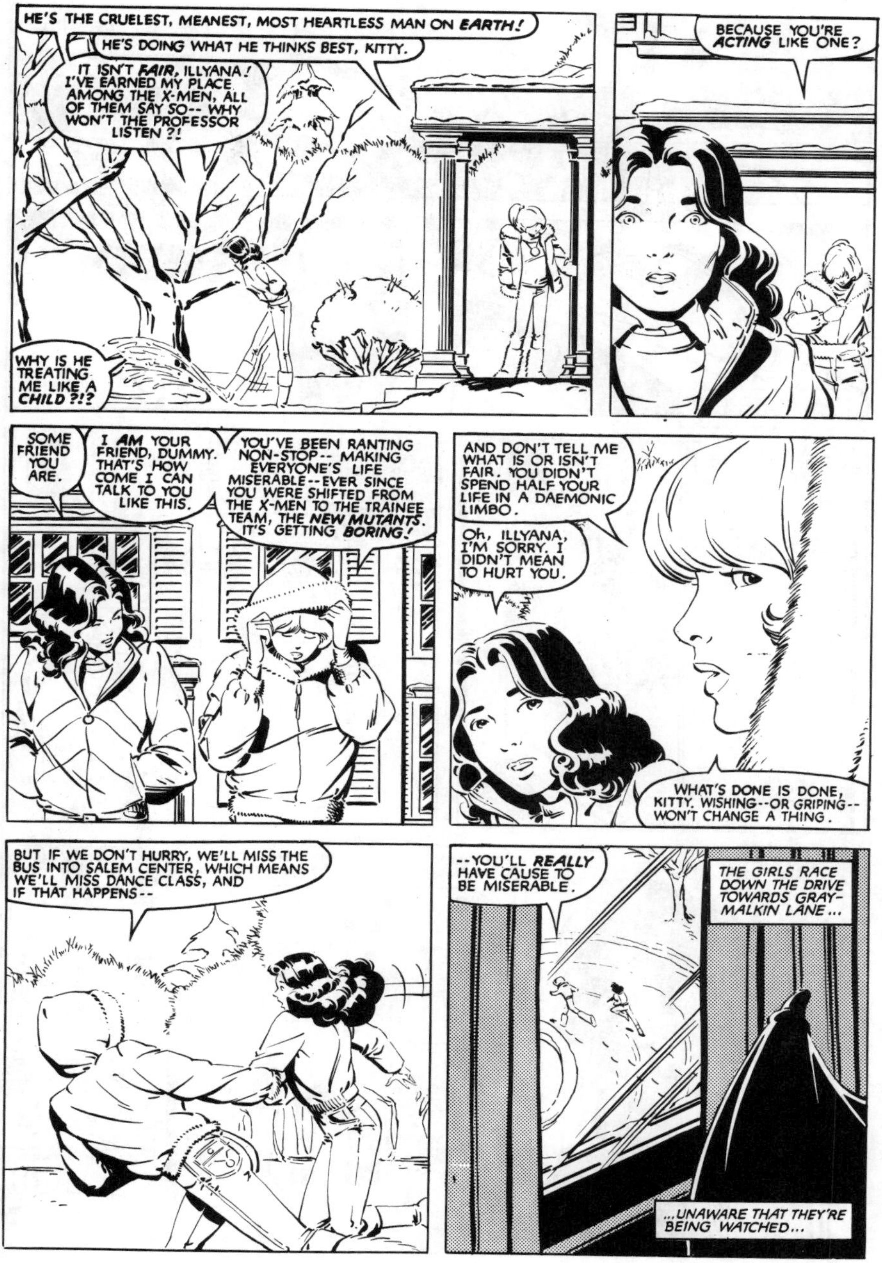
HE'S THE CRUELEST, MEANEST, MOST HEARTLESS MAN ON EARTH!
HE'S DOING WHAT HE THINKS BEST, KITTY.
IT ISN'T FAIR, ILLYANA! I'VE EARNED MY PLACE AMONG THE X-MEN, ALL OF THEM SAY SO-- WHY WON'T THE PROFESSOR LISTEN?!
WHY IS HE TREATING ME LIKE A CHILD?!?
BECAUSE YOU'RE ACTING LIKE ONE?
SOME FRIEND YOU ARE.
I AM YOUR FRIEND, DUMMY. THAT'S HOW COME I CAN TALK TO YOU LIKE THIS.
YOU'VE BEEN RANTING NON-STOP-- MAKING EVERYONE'S LIFE MISERABLE--EVER SINCE YOU WERE SHIFTED FROM THE X-MEN TO THE TRAINEE TEAM, THE NEW MUTANTS. IT'S GETTING BORING!
AND DON'T TELL ME WHAT IS OR ISN'T FAIR. YOU DIDN'T SPEND HALF YOUR LIFE IN A DAEMONIC LIMBO.
Oh, ILLYANA, I'M SORRY. I DIDN'T MEAN TO HURT YOU.
WHAT'S DONE IS DONE, KITTY. WISHING--OR GRIPING--WON'T CHANGE A THING.
BUT IF WE DON'T HURRY, WE'LL MISS THE BUS INTO SALEM CENTER, WHICH MEANS WE'LL MISS DANCE CLASS, AND IF THAT HAPPENS--
--YOU'LL REALLY HAVE CAUSE TO BE MISERABLE.
THE GIRLS RACE DOWN THE DRIVE TOWARDS GRAYMALKIN LANE...
...UNAWARE THAT THEY'RE BEING WATCHED...

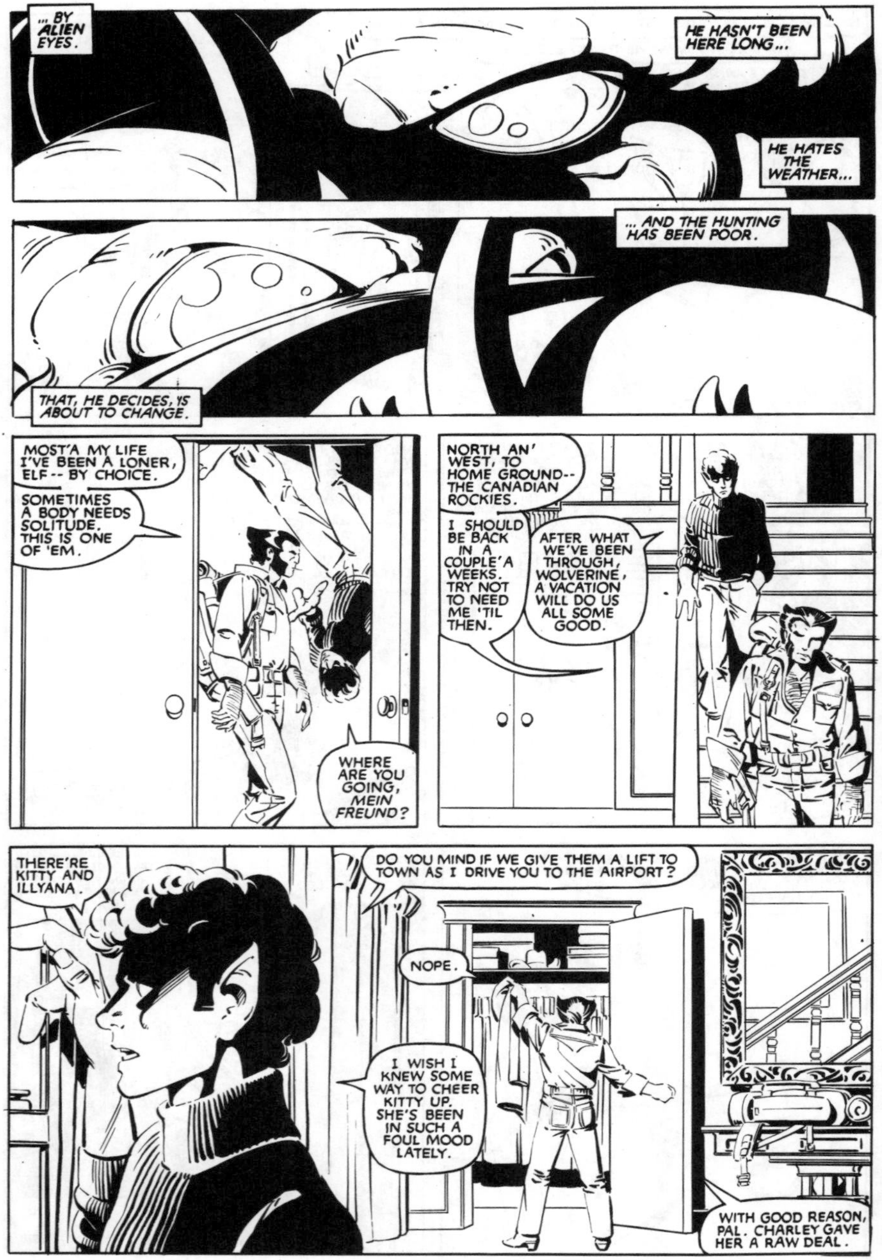
... BY ALIEN EYES.
HE HASN'T BEEN HERE LONG...
HE HATES THE WEATHER...
... AND THE HUNTING HAS BEEN POOR.
THAT, HE DECIDES, YS ABOUT TO CHANGE.
MOST'A MY LIFE I'VE BEEN A LONER, ELF -- BY CHOICE.
SOMETIMES A BODY NEEDS SOLITUDE. THIS IS ONE OF 'EM.
WHERE ARE YOU GOING, MEIN FREUND?
NORTH AN' WEST, TO HOME GROUND-- THE CANADIAN ROCKIES.
I SHOULD BE BACK IN A COUPLE'A WEEKS. TRY NOT TO NEED ME 'TIL THEN.
AFTER WHAT WE'VE BEEN THROUGH, WOLVERINE, A VACATION WILL DO US ALL SOME GOOD.
THERE'RE KITTY AND ILLYANA.
DO YOU MIND IF WE GIVE THEM A LIFT TO TOWN AS I DRIVE YOU TO THE AIRPORT?
NOPE.
I WISH I KNEW SOME WAY TO CHEER KITTY UP. SHE'S BEEN IN SUCH A FOUL MOOD LATELY.
WITH GOOD REASON, PAL. CHARLEY GAVE HER A RAW DEAL.

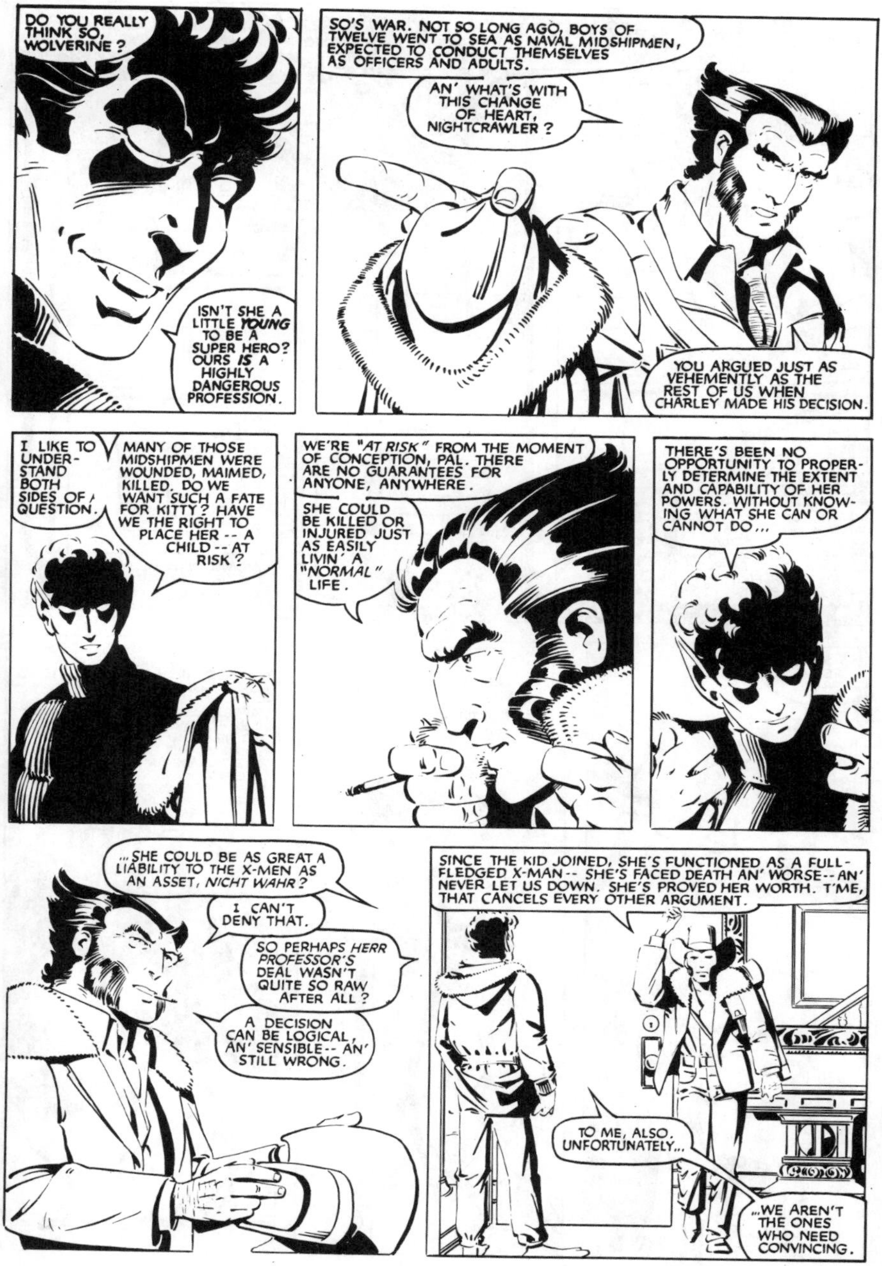

DO YOU REALLY THINK SO, WOLVERINE?
ISN'T SHE A LITTLE *YOUNG* TO BE A SUPER HERO? OURS *IS* A HIGHLY DANGEROUS PROFESSION.
SO'S WAR. NOT SO LONG AGO, BOYS OF TWELVE WENT TO SEA AS NAVAL MIDSHIPMEN, EXPECTED TO CONDUCT THEMSELVES AS OFFICERS AND ADULTS.
AN' WHAT'S WITH THIS CHANGE OF HEART, NIGHTCRAWLER?
YOU ARGUED JUST AS VEHEMENTLY AS THE REST OF US WHEN CHARLEY MADE HIS DECISION.
I LIKE TO UNDER-STAND BOTH SIDES OF A QUESTION.
MANY OF THOSE MIDSHIPMEN WERE WOUNDED, MAIMED, KILLED. DO WE WANT SUCH A FATE FOR KITTY? HAVE WE THE RIGHT TO PLACE HER -- A CHILD -- AT RISK?
WE'RE *"AT RISK"* FROM THE MOMENT OF CONCEPTION, PAL. THERE ARE NO GUARANTEES FOR ANYONE, ANYWHERE.
SHE COULD BE KILLED OR INJURED JUST AS EASILY LIVIN' A *"NORMAL"* LIFE.
THERE'S BEEN NO OPPORTUNITY TO PROPER-LY DETERMINE THE EXTENT AND CAPABILITY OF HER POWERS. WITHOUT KNOW-ING WHAT SHE CAN OR CANNOT DO...
...SHE COULD BE AS GREAT A LIABILITY TO THE X-MEN AS AN ASSET, *NICHT WAHR?*
I CAN'T DENY THAT.
SO PERHAPS *HERR PROFESSOR'S* DEAL WASN'T QUITE SO RAW AFTER ALL?
A DECISION CAN BE LOGICAL, AN' SENSIBLE-- AN' STILL WRONG.
SINCE THE KID JOINED, *SHE'S* FUNCTIONED AS A FULL-FLEDGED X-MAN-- SHE'S FACED DEATH AN' WORSE-- AN' NEVER LET US DOWN. SHE'S PROVED HER WORTH. T'ME, THAT CANCELS EVERY OTHER ARGUMENT.
TO ME, ALSO. UNFORTUNATELY...
...WE AREN'T THE ONES WHO NEED CONVINCING.

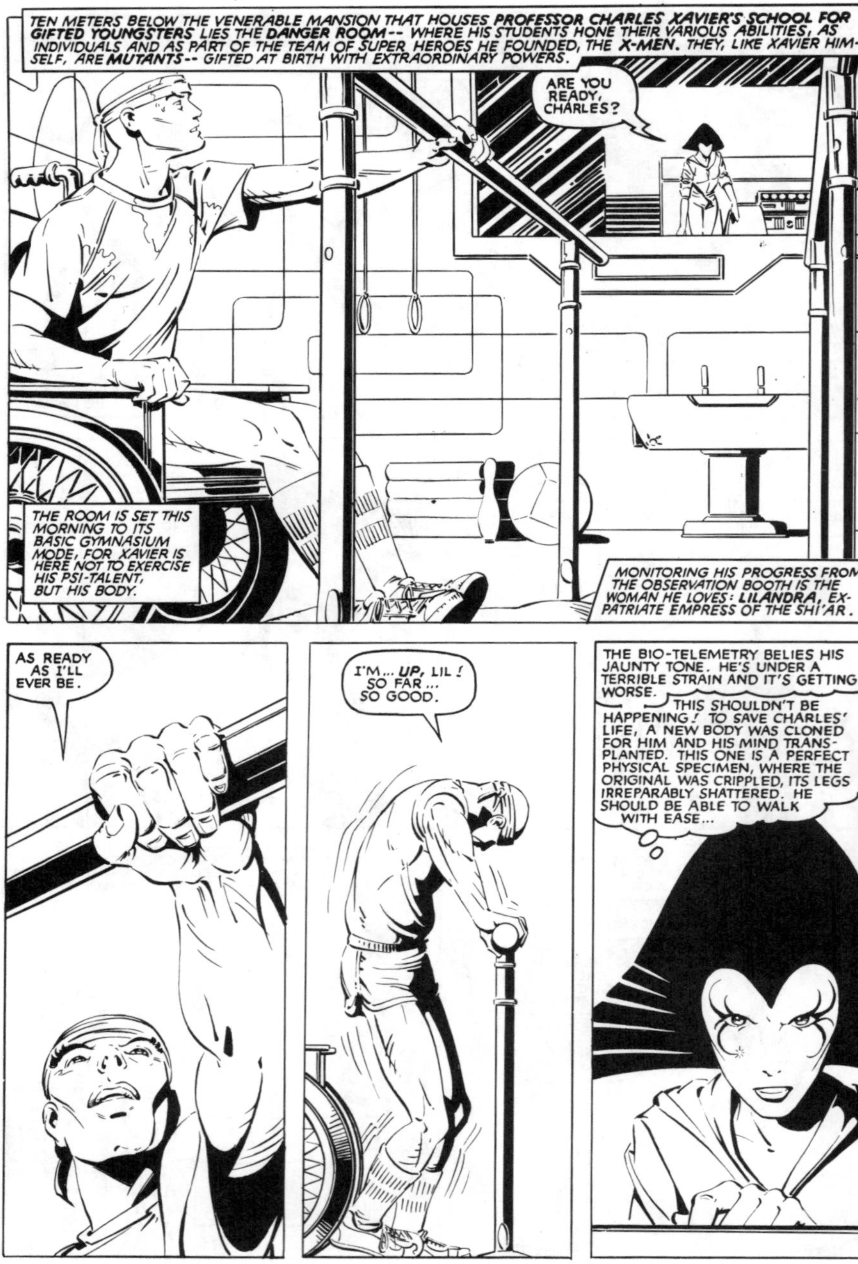
TEN METERS BELOW THE VENERABLE MANSION THAT HOUSES PROFESSOR CHARLES XAVIER'S SCHOOL FOR GIFTED YOUNGSTERS LIES THE DANGER ROOM-- WHERE HIS STUDENTS HONE THEIR VARIOUS ABILITIES, AS INDIVIDUALS AND AS PART OF THE TEAM OF SUPER HEROES HE FOUNDED, THE X-MEN. THEY, LIKE XAVIER HIMSELF, ARE MUTANTS-- GIFTED AT BIRTH WITH EXTRAORDINARY POWERS.
ARE YOU READY, CHARLES?
THE ROOM IS SET THIS MORNING TO ITS BASIC GYMNASIUM MODE, FOR XAVIER IS HERE NOT TO EXERCISE HIS PSI-TALENT, BUT HIS BODY.
MONITORING HIS PROGRESS FROM THE OBSERVATION BOOTH IS THE WOMAN HE LOVES: LILANDRA, EXPATRIATE EMPRESS OF THE SHI'AR.
AS READY AS I'LL EVER BE.
I'M... UP, LIL! SO FAR... SO GOOD.
THE BIO-TELEMETRY BELIES HIS JAUNTY TONE. HE'S UNDER A TERRIBLE STRAIN AND IT'S GETTING WORSE.
THIS SHOULDN'T BE HAPPENING! TO SAVE CHARLES' LIFE, A NEW BODY WAS CLONED FOR HIM AND HIS MIND TRANSPLANTED. THIS ONE IS A PERFECT PHYSICAL SPECIMEN, WHERE THE ORIGINAL WAS CRIPPLED, ITS LEGS IRREPARABLY SHATTERED. HE SHOULD BE ABLE TO WALK WITH EASE...

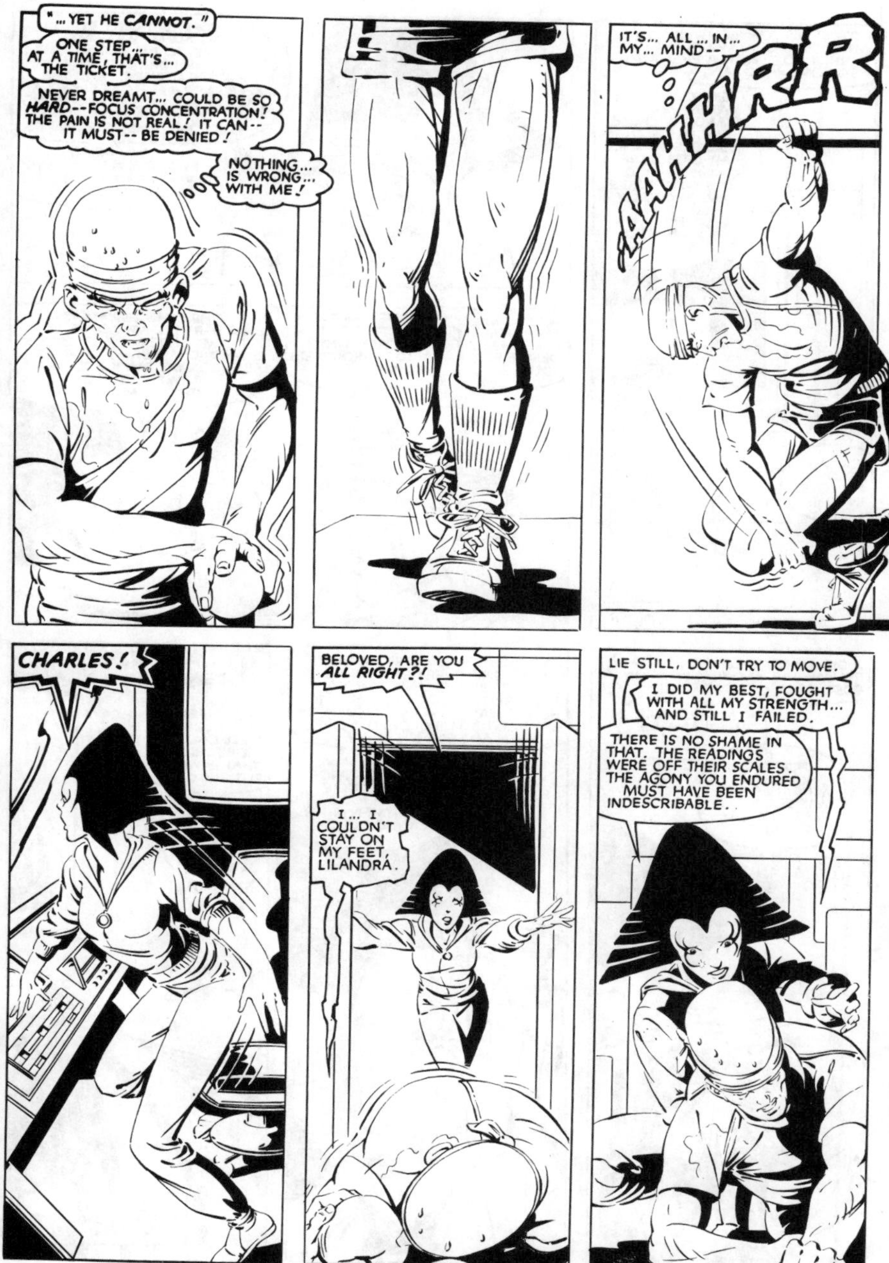
"... YET HE CANNOT."
ONE STEP... AT A TIME, THAT'S... THE TICKET.
NEVER DREAMT... COULD BE SO HARD--FOCUS CONCENTRATION! THE PAIN IS NOT REAL! IT CAN-- IT MUST-- BE DENIED!
NOTHING... IS WRONG... WITH ME!
IT'S... ALL... IN... MY... MIND--
AAHHRR
CHARLES!
BELOVED, ARE YOU ALL RIGHT?!
I... I COULDN'T STAY ON MY FEET, LILANDRA.
LIE STILL, DON'T TRY TO MOVE.
I DID MY BEST, FOUGHT WITH ALL MY STRENGTH... AND STILL I FAILED.
THERE IS NO SHAME IN THAT. THE READINGS WERE OFF THEIR SCALES. THE AGONY YOU ENDURED MUST HAVE BEEN INDESCRIBABLE.

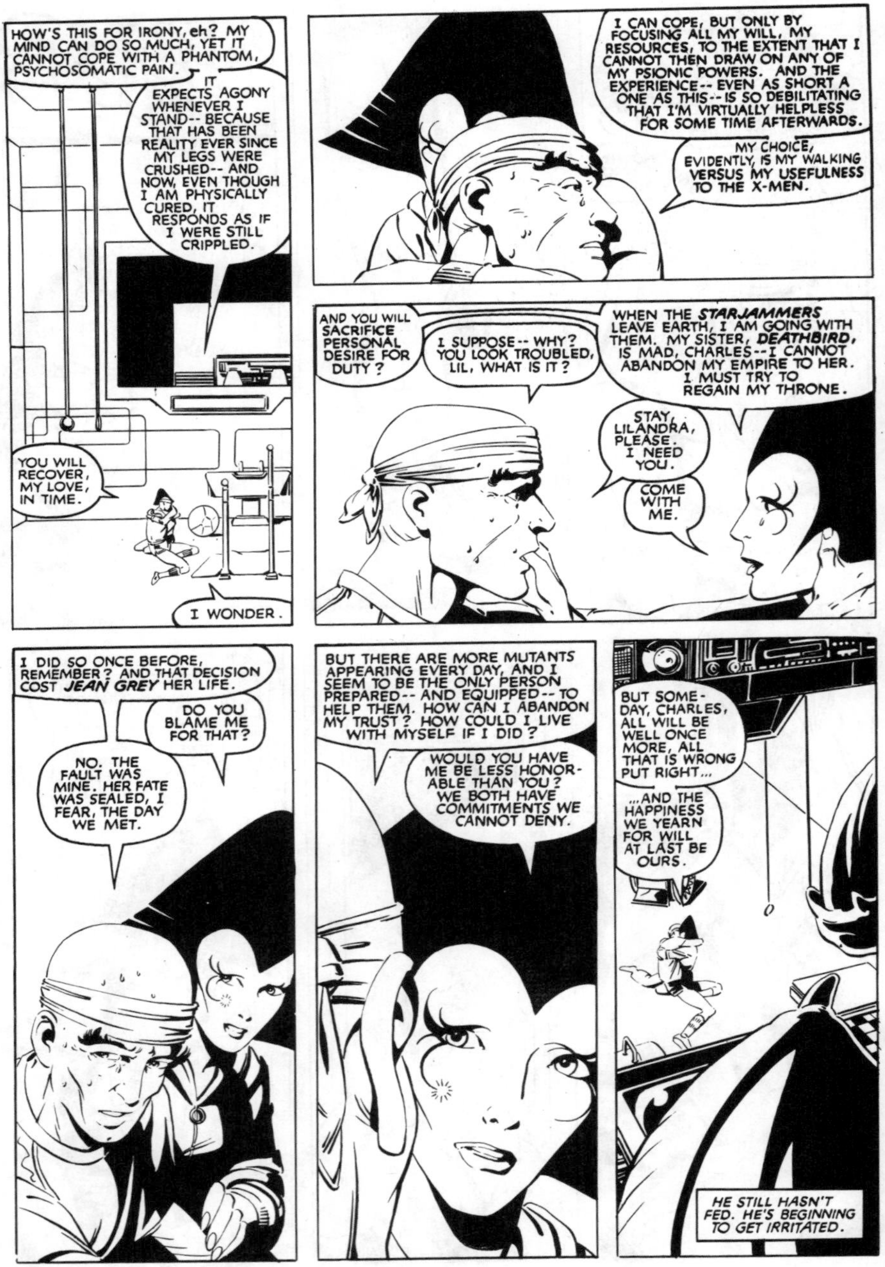
HOW'S THIS FOR IRONY, eh? MY MIND CAN DO SO MUCH, YET IT CANNOT COPE WITH A PHANTOM, PSYCHOSOMATIC PAIN.
IT EXPECTS AGONY WHENEVER I STAND-- BECAUSE THAT HAS BEEN REALITY EVER SINCE MY LEGS WERE CRUSHED-- AND NOW, EVEN THOUGH I AM PHYSICALLY CURED, IT RESPONDS AS IF I WERE STILL CRIPPLED.
YOU WILL RECOVER, MY LOVE, IN TIME.
I WONDER.
I CAN COPE, BUT ONLY BY FOCUSING ALL MY WILL, MY RESOURCES, TO THE EXTENT THAT I CANNOT THEN DRAW ON ANY OF MY PSIONIC POWERS. AND THE EXPERIENCE-- EVEN AS SHORT A ONE AS THIS--IS SO DEBILITATING THAT I'M VIRTUALLY HELPLESS FOR SOME TIME AFTERWARDS.
MY CHOICE, EVIDENTLY, IS MY WALKING VERSUS MY USEFULNESS TO THE X-MEN.
AND YOU WILL SACRIFICE PERSONAL DESIRE FOR DUTY?
I SUPPOSE-- WHY? YOU LOOK TROUBLED, LIL, WHAT IS IT?
WHEN THE STARJAMMERS LEAVE EARTH, I AM GOING WITH THEM. MY SISTER, DEATHBIRD, IS MAD, CHARLES--I CANNOT ABANDON MY EMPIRE TO HER. I MUST TRY TO REGAIN MY THRONE.
STAY, LILANDRA, PLEASE. I NEED YOU.
COME WITH ME.
I DID SO ONCE BEFORE, REMEMBER? AND THAT DECISION COST JEAN GREY HER LIFE.
DO YOU BLAME ME FOR THAT?
NO. THE FAULT WAS MINE. HER FATE WAS SEALED, I FEAR, THE DAY WE MET.
BUT THERE ARE MORE MUTANTS APPEARING EVERY DAY, AND I SEEM TO BE THE ONLY PERSON PREPARED-- AND EQUIPPED-- TO HELP THEM. HOW CAN I ABANDON MY TRUST? HOW COULD I LIVE WITH MYSELF IF I DID?
WOULD YOU HAVE ME BE LESS HONOR-ABLE THAN YOU? WE BOTH HAVE COMMITMENTS WE CANNOT DENY.
BUT SOME-DAY, CHARLES, ALL WILL BE WELL ONCE MORE, ALL THAT IS WRONG PUT RIGHT...
...AND THE HAPPINESS WE YEARN FOR WILL AT LAST BE OURS.
HE STILL HASN'T FED. HE'S BEGINNING TO GET IRRITATED.

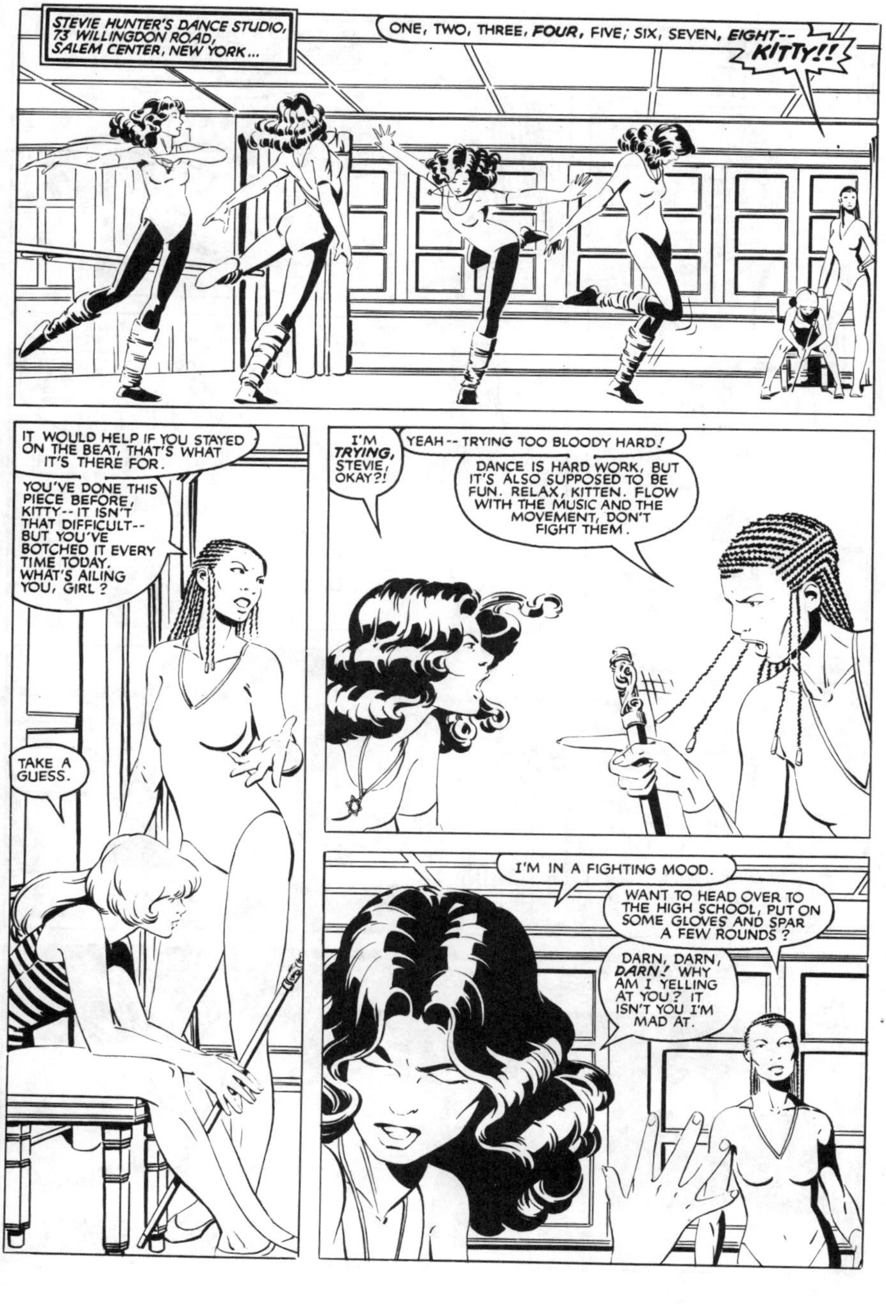
STEVIE HUNTER'S DANCE STUDIO, 73 WILLINGDON ROAD, SALEM CENTER, NEW YORK...
ONE, TWO, THREE, FOUR, FIVE; SIX, SEVEN, EIGHT--
KITTY!!
IT WOULD HELP IF YOU STAYED ON THE BEAT, THAT'S WHAT IT'S THERE FOR.
YOU'VE DONE THIS PIECE BEFORE, KITTY-- IT ISN'T THAT DIFFICULT-- BUT YOU'VE BOTCHED IT EVERY TIME TODAY. WHAT'S AILING YOU, GIRL?
TAKE A GUESS.
I'M TRYING, STEVIE, OKAY?!
YEAH--TRYING TOO BLOODY HARD!
DANCE IS HARD WORK, BUT IT'S ALSO SUPPOSED TO BE FUN. RELAX, KITTEN. FLOW WITH THE MUSIC AND THE MOVEMENT, DON'T FIGHT THEM.
I'M IN A FIGHTING MOOD.
WANT TO HEAD OVER TO THE HIGH SCHOOL, PUT ON SOME GLOVES AND SPAR A FEW ROUNDS?
DARN, DARN, DARN! WHY AM I YELLING AT YOU? IT ISN'T YOU I'M MAD AT.

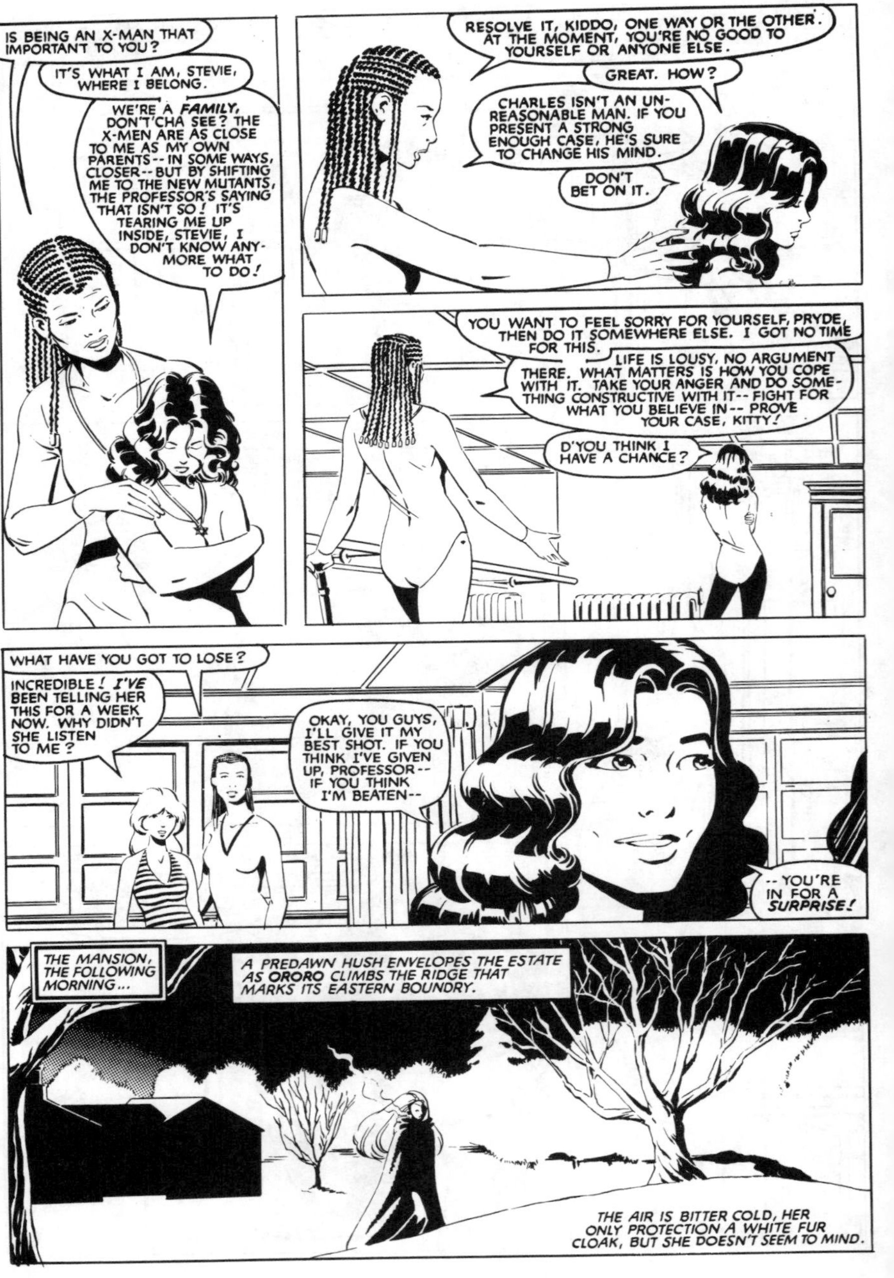

IS BEING AN X-MAN THAT IMPORTANT TO YOU?
IT'S WHAT I AM, STEVIE, WHERE I BELONG.
WE'RE A FAMILY, DON'T'CHA SEE? THE X-MEN ARE AS CLOSE TO ME AS MY OWN PARENTS-- IN SOME WAYS, CLOSER-- BUT BY SHIFTING ME TO THE NEW MUTANTS, THE PROFESSOR'S SAYING THAT ISN'T SO! IT'S TEARING ME UP INSIDE, STEVIE, I DON'T KNOW ANYMORE WHAT TO DO!
RESOLVE IT, KIDDO, ONE WAY OR THE OTHER. AT THE MOMENT, YOU'RE NO GOOD TO YOURSELF OR ANYONE ELSE.
GREAT. HOW?
CHARLES ISN'T AN UNREASONABLE MAN. IF YOU PRESENT A STRONG ENOUGH CASE, HE'S SURE TO CHANGE HIS MIND.
DON'T BET ON IT.
YOU WANT TO FEEL SORRY FOR YOURSELF, PRYDE, THEN DO IT SOMEWHERE ELSE. I GOT NO TIME FOR THIS.
LIFE IS LOUSY, NO ARGUMENT THERE. WHAT MATTERS IS HOW YOU COPE WITH IT. TAKE YOUR ANGER AND DO SOMETHING CONSTRUCTIVE WITH IT-- FIGHT FOR WHAT YOU BELIEVE IN-- PROVE YOUR CASE, KITTY!
D'YOU THINK I HAVE A CHANCE?
WHAT HAVE YOU GOT TO LOSE?
INCREDIBLE! I'VE BEEN TELLING HER THIS FOR A WEEK NOW. WHY DIDN'T SHE LISTEN TO ME?
OKAY, YOU GUYS, I'LL GIVE IT MY BEST SHOT. IF YOU THINK I'VE GIVEN UP, PROFESSOR-- IF YOU THINK I'M BEATEN--
-- YOU'RE IN FOR A SURPRISE!
THE MANSION, THE FOLLOWING MORNING...
A PREDAWN HUSH ENVELOPES THE ESTATE AS ORORO CLIMBS THE RIDGE THAT MARKS ITS EASTERN BOUNDRY.
THE AIR IS BITTER COLD, HER ONLY PROTECTION A WHITE FUR CLOAK, BUT SHE DOESN'T SEEM TO MIND.

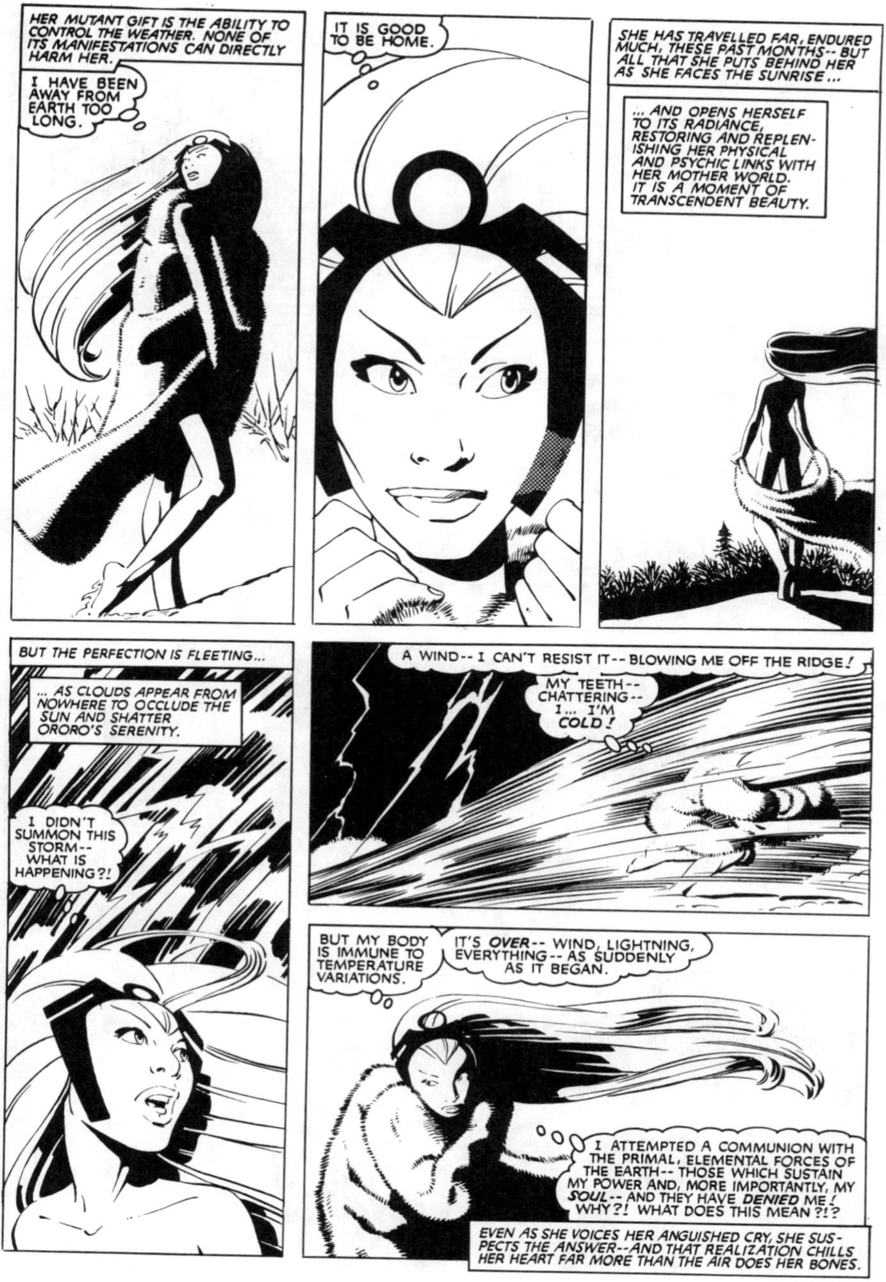
HER MUTANT GIFT IS THE ABILITY TO CONTROL THE WEATHER. NONE OF ITS MANIFESTATIONS CAN DIRECTLY HARM HER.
I HAVE BEEN AWAY FROM EARTH TOO LONG.
IT IS GOOD TO BE HOME.
SHE HAS TRAVELLED FAR, ENDURED MUCH, THESE PAST MONTHS-- BUT ALL THAT SHE PUTS BEHIND HER AS SHE FACES THE SUNRISE...
... AND OPENS HERSELF TO ITS RADIANCE, RESTORING AND REPLENISHING HER PHYSICAL AND PSYCHIC LINKS WITH HER MOTHER WORLD. IT IS A MOMENT OF TRANSCENDENT BEAUTY.
BUT THE PERFECTION IS FLEETING...
... AS CLOUDS APPEAR FROM NOWHERE TO OCCLUDE THE SUN AND SHATTER ORORO'S SERENITY.
I DIDN'T SUMMON THIS STORM-- WHAT IS HAPPENING?!
A WIND-- I CAN'T RESIST IT-- BLOWING ME OFF THE RIDGE!
MY TEETH-- CHATTERING-- I... I'M COLD!
BUT MY BODY IS IMMUNE TO TEMPERATURE VARIATIONS.
IT'S OVER-- WIND, LIGHTNING, EVERYTHING-- AS SUDDENLY AS IT BEGAN.
I ATTEMPTED A COMMUNION WITH THE PRIMAL, ELEMENTAL FORCES OF THE EARTH-- THOSE WHICH SUSTAIN MY POWER AND, MORE IMPORTANTLY, MY SOUL-- AND THEY HAVE DENIED ME! WHY?! WHAT DOES THIS MEAN?!?
EVEN AS SHE VOICES HER ANGUISHED CRY, SHE SUSPECTS THE ANSWER--AND THAT REALIZATION CHILLS HER HEART FAR MORE THAN THE AIR DOES HER BONES.

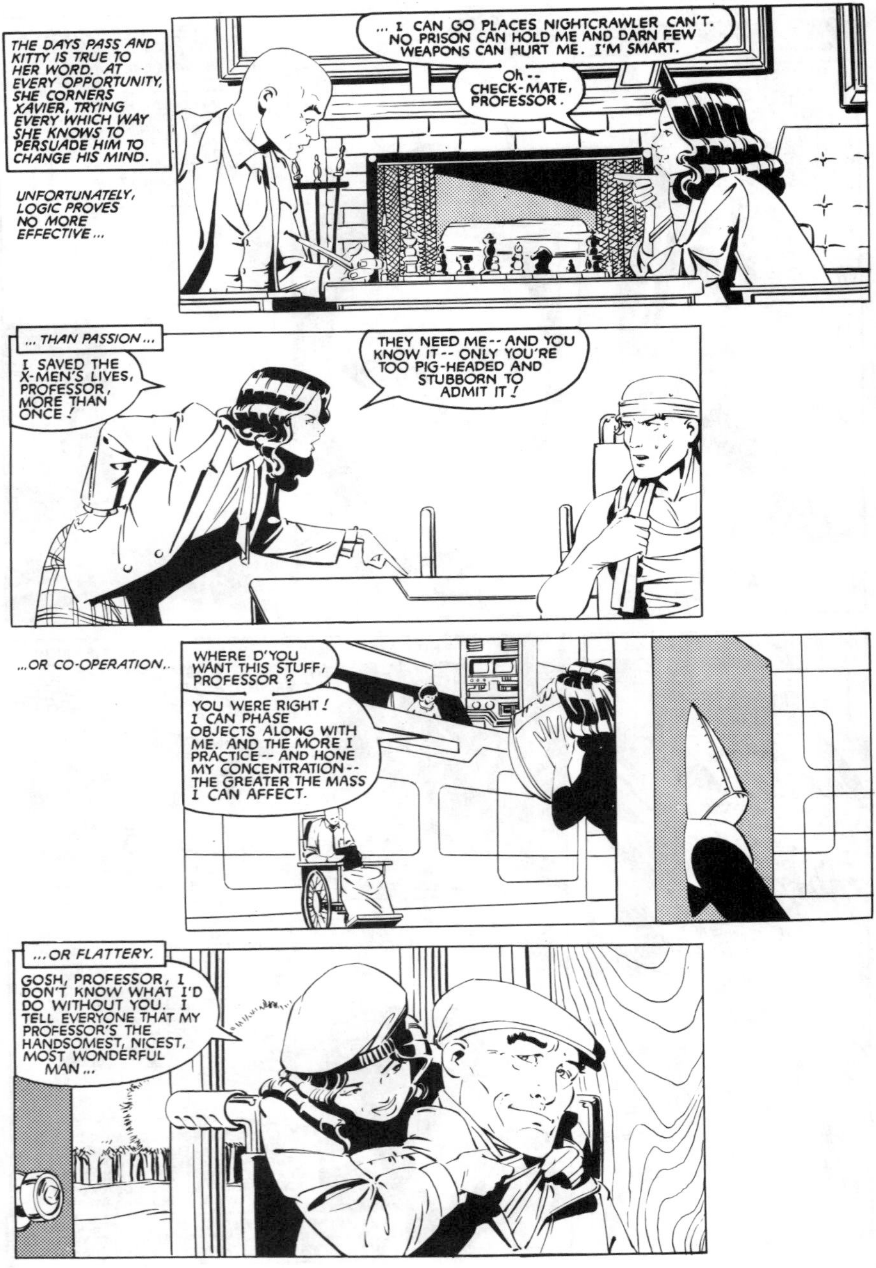
THE DAYS PASS AND KITTY IS TRUE TO HER WORD. AT EVERY OPPORTUNITY, SHE CORNERS XAVIER, TRYING EVERY WHICH WAY SHE KNOWS TO PERSUADE HIM TO CHANGE HIS MIND.
UNFORTUNATELY, LOGIC PROVES NO MORE EFFECTIVE...
... I CAN GO PLACES NIGHTCRAWLER CAN'T. NO PRISON CAN HOLD ME AND DARN FEW WEAPONS CAN HURT ME. I'M SMART.
Oh -- CHECK-MATE, PROFESSOR.
... THAN PASSION...
I SAVED THE X-MEN'S LIVES, PROFESSOR, MORE THAN ONCE!
THEY NEED ME -- AND YOU KNOW IT -- ONLY YOU'RE TOO PIG-HEADED AND STUBBORN TO ADMIT IT!
...OR CO-OPERATION..
WHERE D'YOU WANT THIS STUFF, PROFESSOR?
YOU WERE RIGHT! I CAN PHASE OBJECTS ALONG WITH ME. AND THE MORE I PRACTICE -- AND HONE MY CONCENTRATION -- THE GREATER THE MASS I CAN AFFECT.
...OR FLATTERY.
GOSH, PROFESSOR, I DON'T KNOW WHAT I'D DO WITHOUT YOU. I TELL EVERYONE THAT MY PROFESSOR'S THE HANDSOMEST, NICEST, MOST WONDERFUL MAN...

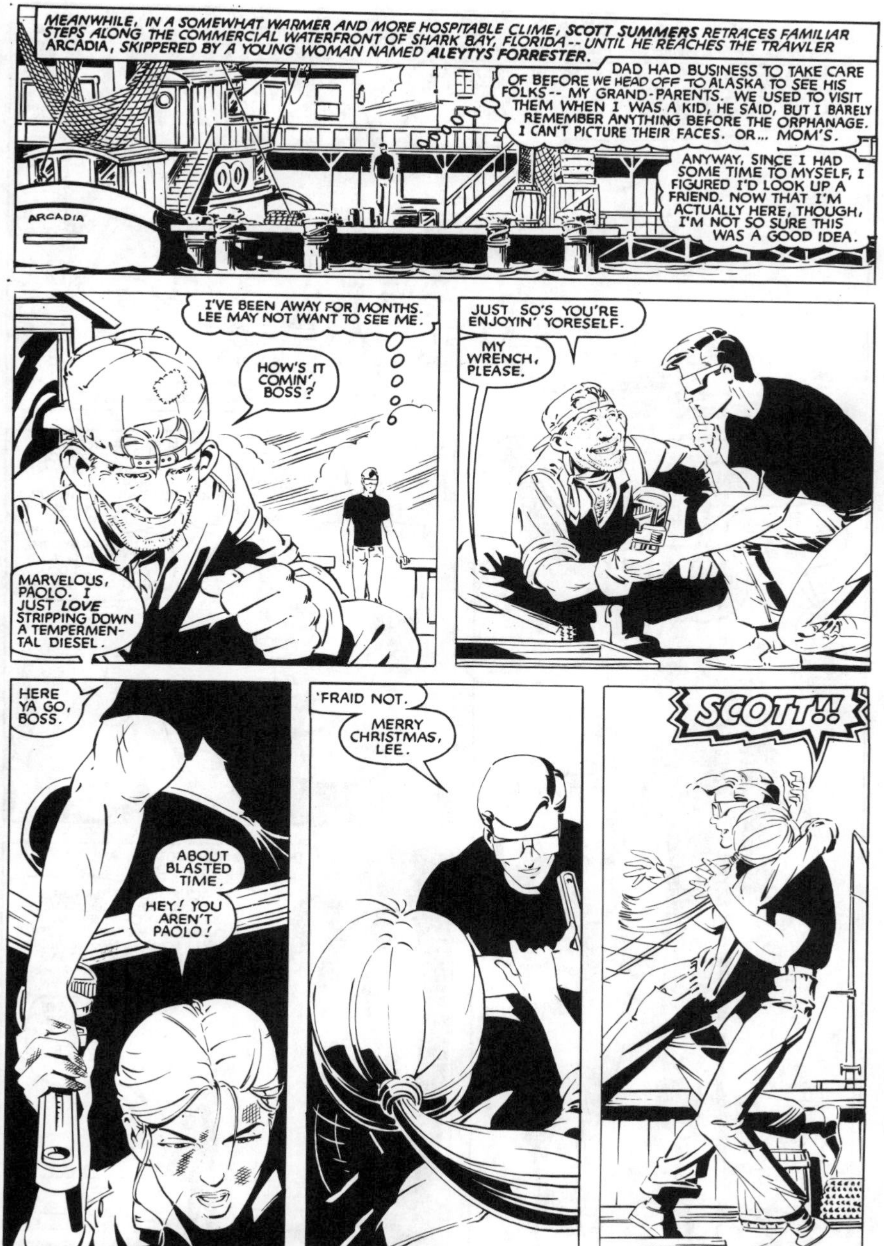
MEANWHILE, IN A SOMEWHAT WARMER AND MORE HOSPITABLE CLIME, SCOTT SUMMERS RETRACES FAMILIAR STEPS ALONG THE COMMERCIAL WATERFRONT OF SHARK BAY, FLORIDA -- UNTIL HE REACHES THE TRAWLER ARCADIA, SKIPPERED BY A YOUNG WOMAN NAMED ALEYTYS FORRESTER.
DAD HAD BUSINESS TO TAKE CARE OF BEFORE WE HEAD OFF TO ALASKA TO SEE HIS FOLKS -- MY GRAND-PARENTS. WE USED TO VISIT THEM WHEN I WAS A KID, HE SAID, BUT I BARELY REMEMBER ANYTHING BEFORE THE ORPHANAGE. I CAN'T PICTURE THEIR FACES. OR... MOM'S.
ANYWAY, SINCE I HAD SOME TIME TO MYSELF, I FIGURED I'D LOOK UP A FRIEND. NOW THAT I'M ACTUALLY HERE, THOUGH, I'M NOT SO SURE THIS WAS A GOOD IDEA.
ARCADIA
I'VE BEEN AWAY FOR MONTHS. LEE MAY NOT WANT TO SEE ME.
HOW'S IT COMIN', BOSS?
MARVELOUS, PAOLO. I JUST LOVE STRIPPING DOWN A TEMPERMENTAL DIESEL.
JUST SO'S YOU'RE ENJOYIN' YORESELF.
MY WRENCH, PLEASE.
HERE YA GO, BOSS.
ABOUT BLASTED TIME.
HEY! YOU AREN'T PAOLO!
'FRAID NOT.
MERRY CHRISTMAS, LEE.
SCOTT!!

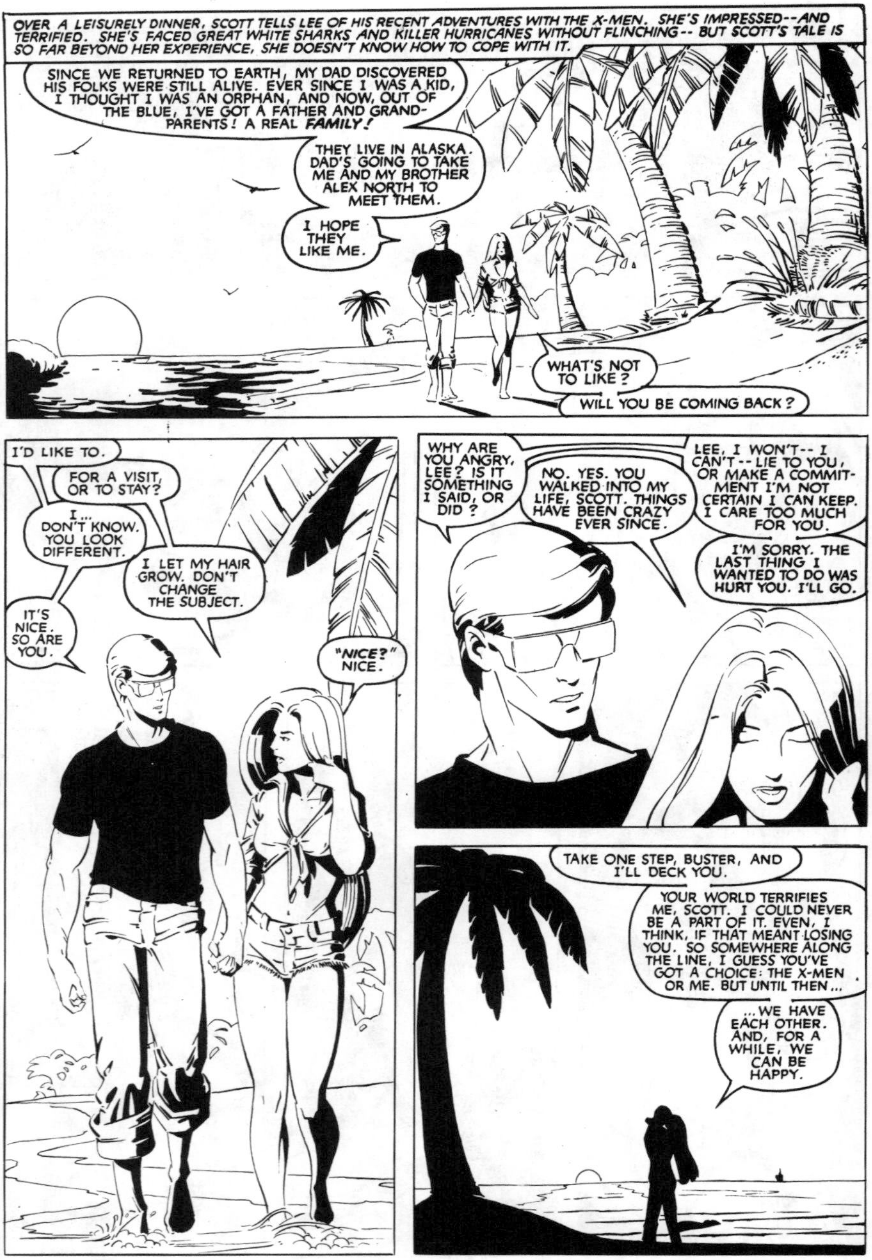
OVER A LEISURELY DINNER, SCOTT TELLS LEE OF HIS RECENT ADVENTURES WITH THE X-MEN. SHE'S IMPRESSED--AND TERRIFIED. SHE'S FACED GREAT WHITE SHARKS AND KILLER HURRICANES WITHOUT FLINCHING-- BUT SCOTT'S TALE IS SO FAR BEYOND HER EXPERIENCE, SHE DOESN'T KNOW HOW TO COPE WITH IT.
SINCE WE RETURNED TO EARTH, MY DAD DISCOVERED HIS FOLKS WERE STILL ALIVE. EVER SINCE I WAS A KID, I THOUGHT I WAS AN ORPHAN, AND NOW, OUT OF THE BLUE, I'VE GOT A FATHER AND GRAND-PARENTS! A REAL FAMILY!
THEY LIVE IN ALASKA. DAD'S GOING TO TAKE ME AND MY BROTHER ALEX NORTH TO MEET THEM.
I HOPE THEY LIKE ME.
WHAT'S NOT TO LIKE?
WILL YOU BE COMING BACK?
I'D LIKE TO.
FOR A VISIT, OR TO STAY?
I... DON'T KNOW. YOU LOOK DIFFERENT.
I LET MY HAIR GROW. DON'T CHANGE THE SUBJECT.
IT'S NICE. SO ARE YOU.
"NICE?" NICE.
WHY ARE YOU ANGRY, LEE? IS IT SOMETHING I SAID, OR DID?
NO. YES. YOU WALKED INTO MY LIFE, SCOTT. THINGS HAVE BEEN CRAZY EVER SINCE.
LEE, I WON'T-- I CAN'T -- LIE TO YOU, OR MAKE A COMMIT-MENT I'M NOT CERTAIN I CAN KEEP. I CARE TOO MUCH FOR YOU.
I'M SORRY. THE LAST THING I WANTED TO DO WAS HURT YOU. I'LL GO.
TAKE ONE STEP, BUSTER, AND I'LL DECK YOU.
YOUR WORLD TERRIFIES ME, SCOTT. I COULD NEVER BE A PART OF IT. EVEN, I THINK, IF THAT MEANT LOSING YOU. SO SOMEWHERE ALONG THE LINE, I GUESS YOU'VE GOT A CHOICE: THE X-MEN OR ME. BUT UNTIL THEN...
...WE HAVE EACH OTHER. AND, FOR A WHILE, WE CAN BE HAPPY.

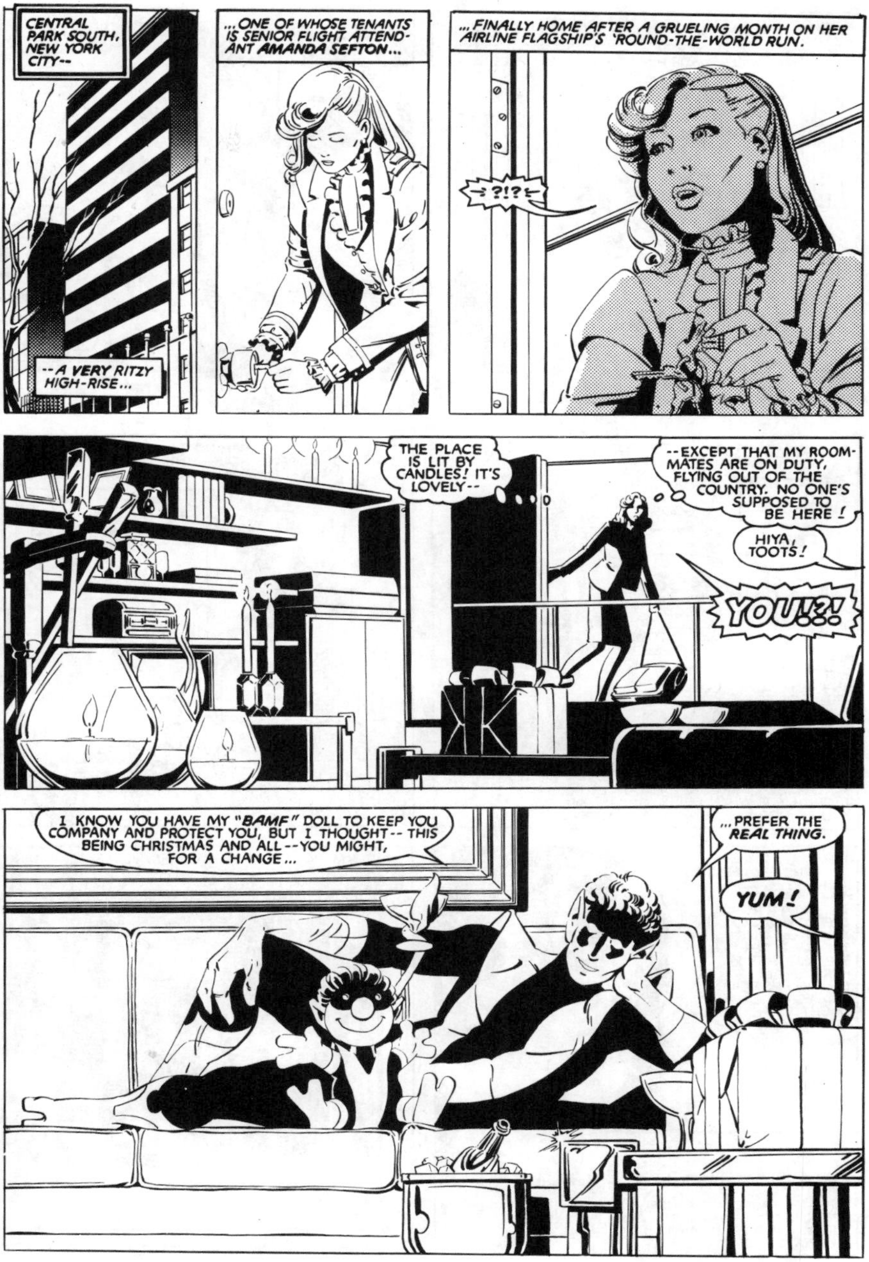
CENTRAL PARK SOUTH, NEW YORK CITY--
--A VERY RITZY HIGH-RISE...
...ONE OF WHOSE TENANTS IS SENIOR FLIGHT ATTENDANT AMANDA SEFTON...
...FINALLY HOME AFTER A GRUELING MONTH ON HER AIRLINE FLAGSHIP'S 'ROUND-THE-WORLD RUN.
?!?
THE PLACE IS LIT BY CANDLES! IT'S LOVELY--
--EXCEPT THAT MY ROOMMATES ARE ON DUTY, FLYING OUT OF THE COUNTRY. NO ONE'S SUPPOSED TO BE HERE!
HIYA, TOOTS!
YOU!?!
I KNOW YOU HAVE MY "BAMF" DOLL TO KEEP YOU COMPANY AND PROTECT YOU, BUT I THOUGHT-- THIS BEING CHRISTMAS AND ALL--YOU MIGHT, FOR A CHANGE...
...PREFER THE REAL THING.
YUM!

XAVIER'S SCHOOL... HARD AS A ROCK, THICK AS A BRICK-- I'LL **NEVER** PERSUADE HIM.

I'VE TRIED EVERY-THING! I DON'T KNOW WHAT TO DO NEXT. I'LL PROBABLY BE STUCK IN THE X-BABIES 'TIL I'M ANCIENT!

KATYA!

Hmnh?

NOK! NOK! NOK!

PETER! ILLYANA!

HI, GUYS, WHAT'CHA DOIN'-- **BRRRR!!**

IT'S **COLD!**

PUT ON A COAT, THEN, SILLY GOOSE.

WE ARE OFF TO CHOP SOME FIRE-WOOD. WOULD YOU LIKE TO COME ALONG?

NNNNAH-- I'VE STILL GOT HOME-WORK. IF I LET MY GRADES SLIP, IT'LL BE ONE MORE EXCUSE FOR THE PROFESSOR TO KEEP ME OUT OF THE X-MEN. I'LL MULL SOME CIDER, THOUGH, FOR WHEN YOU'RE DONE.

THAT'LL BE GREAT! SEE YOU LATER!

YEAH. 'BYE!

I'M SO FAR BEHIND ON MY STUDIES--'CAUSE OF BOPPING 'ROUND THE UNIVERSE WITH THE X-MEN -- I WONDER IF I'LL EVER CATCH UP.

THAT'S THE TROUBLE WITH BEING A GENIUS-- EVERYBODY EXPECTS YOU TO PRODUCE. BETWEEN REGULAR SCHOOL AND MY TRAINING SESSIONS WITH THE PROFESSOR AND DANCE CLASS, IT'S A MIRACLE I'VE MANAGED THIS LONG.

the legion of cats quiche

WHAT AM I THINKING-- THAT THE PROFESSOR'S RIGHT?!

I'D BETTER RUN THE **HOMESCAN** PROGRAM THROUGH THE COMPUTER, TO SEE WHO ELSE IS HERE. IF I'M BREWING HOT CIDER AND MUNCHIES, I OUGHT TO INCLUDE EVERYONE.

WHAT'S THIS--?!? I REGISTER PROFESSOR XAVIER AND LILANDRA IN HIS STUDY-- AND PETER AND ILLYANA IN THE WOODS--

--BUT I'M PICKING UP AN ANOMALY IN THE LOWER MAINTENANCE TUNNELS. IT ISN'T A GLITCH IN THE SYSTEM ...

...IT'S SOMETHING THE SENSORS AREN'T EQUIPPED TO IDENTIFY.

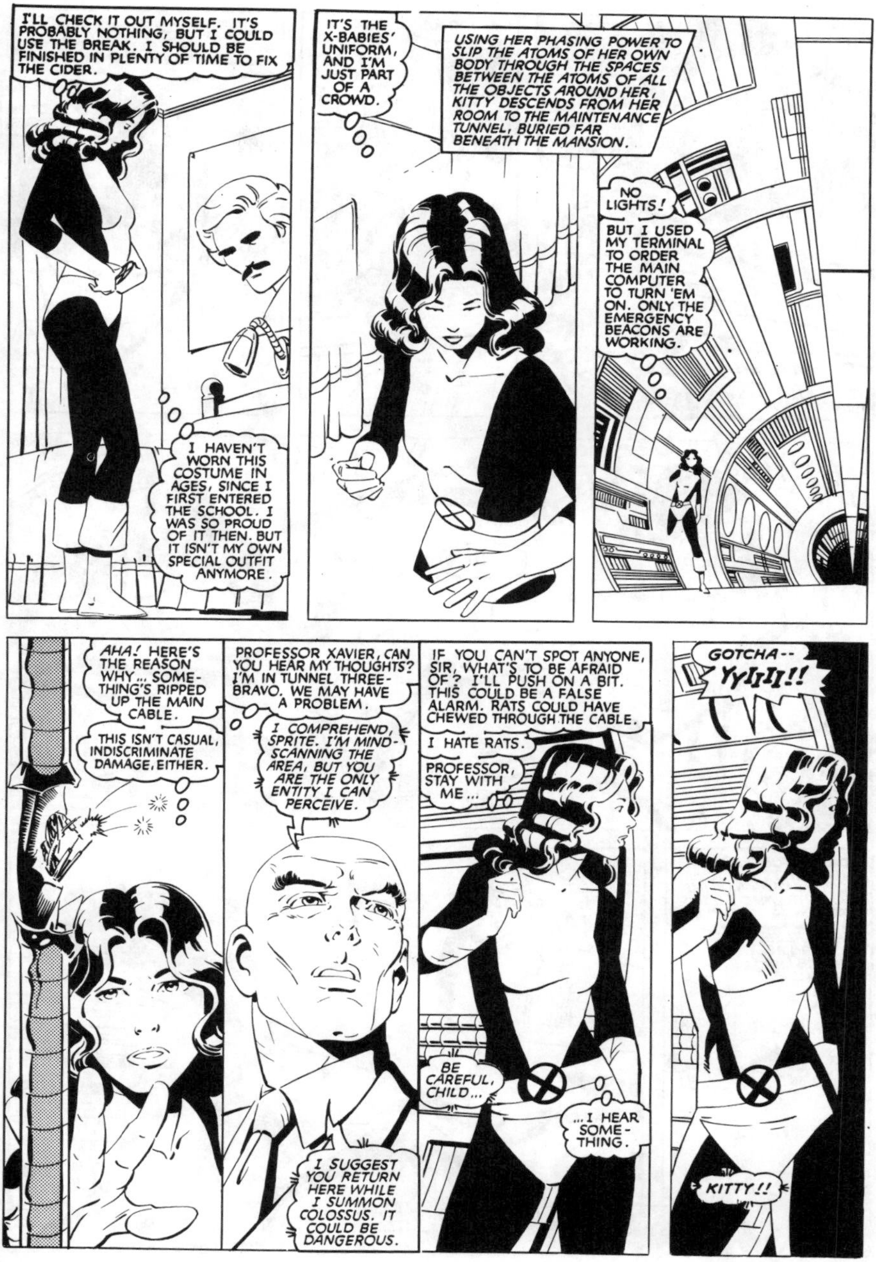
I'LL CHECK IT OUT MYSELF. IT'S PROBABLY NOTHING, BUT I COULD USE THE BREAK. I SHOULD BE FINISHED IN PLENTY OF TIME TO FIX THE CIDER.
I HAVEN'T WORN THIS COSTUME IN AGES, SINCE I FIRST ENTERED THE SCHOOL. I WAS SO PROUD OF IT THEN. BUT IT ISN'T MY OWN SPECIAL OUTFIT ANYMORE.
IT'S THE X-BABIES' UNIFORM, AND I'M JUST PART OF A CROWD.
USING HER PHASING POWER TO SLIP THE ATOMS OF HER OWN BODY THROUGH THE SPACES BETWEEN THE ATOMS OF ALL THE OBJECTS AROUND HER, KITTY DESCENDS FROM HER ROOM TO THE MAINTENANCE TUNNEL, BURIED FAR BENEATH THE MANSION.
NO LIGHTS!
BUT I USED MY TERMINAL TO ORDER THE MAIN COMPUTER TO TURN 'EM ON. ONLY THE EMERGENCY BEACONS ARE WORKING.
AHA! HERE'S THE REASON WHY... SOMETHING'S RIPPED UP THE MAIN CABLE.
THIS ISN'T CASUAL, INDISCRIMINATE DAMAGE, EITHER.
PROFESSOR XAVIER, CAN YOU HEAR MY THOUGHTS? I'M IN TUNNEL THREE-BRAVO. WE MAY HAVE A PROBLEM.
I COMPREHEND, SPRITE. I'M MIND-SCANNING THE AREA, BUT YOU ARE THE ONLY ENTITY I CAN PERCEIVE.
I SUGGEST YOU RETURN HERE WHILE I SUMMON COLOSSUS. IT COULD BE DANGEROUS.
IF YOU CAN'T SPOT ANYONE, SIR, WHAT'S TO BE AFRAID OF? I'LL PUSH ON A BIT. THIS COULD BE A FALSE ALARM. RATS COULD HAVE CHEWED THROUGH THE CABLE.
I HATE RATS.
PROFESSOR, STAY WITH ME...
BE CAREFUL, CHILD...
...I HEAR SOMETHING.
GOTCHA--
YYIIII!!
KITTY!!

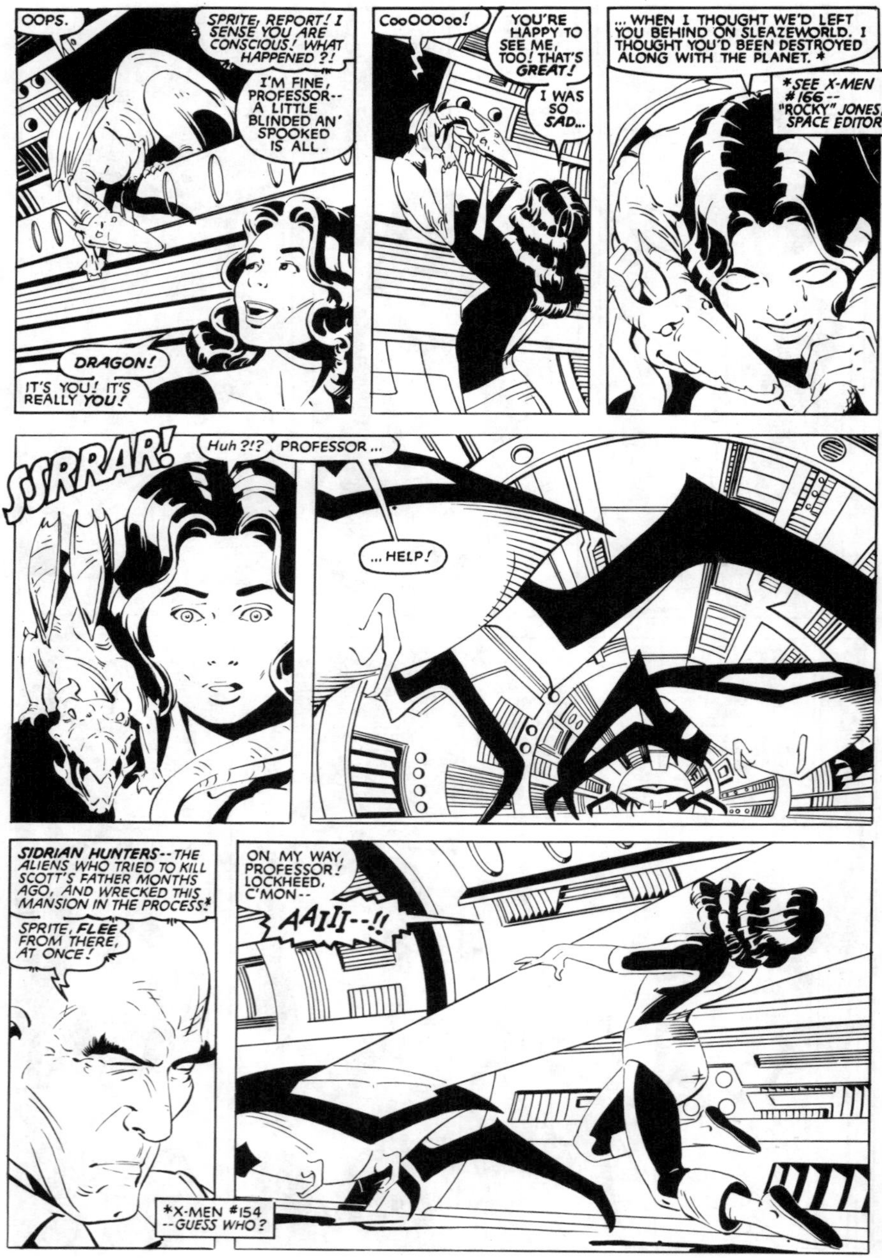

OOPS.
SPRITE, REPORT! I SENSE YOU ARE CONSCIOUS! WHAT HAPPENED?!
I'M FINE, PROFESSOR-- A LITTLE BLINDED AN' SPOOKED IS ALL.
DRAGON!
IT'S YOU! IT'S REALLY YOU!
CooOOOoo!
YOU'RE HAPPY TO SEE ME, TOO! THAT'S GREAT!
I WAS SO SAD...
...WHEN I THOUGHT WE'D LEFT YOU BEHIND ON SLEAZEWORLD. I THOUGHT YOU'D BEEN DESTROYED ALONG WITH THE PLANET.*
*SEE X-MEN #166-- "ROCKY" JONES, SPACE EDITOR.
SSRRAR!
Huh?!?
PROFESSOR...
...HELP!
SIDRIAN HUNTERS--THE ALIENS WHO TRIED TO KILL SCOTT'S FATHER MONTHS AGO, AND WRECKED THIS MANSION IN THE PROCESS!*
SPRITE, FLEE FROM THERE, AT ONCE!
*X-MEN #154 --GUESS WHO?
ON MY WAY, PROFESSOR! LOCKHEED, C'MON--
AAIII--!!

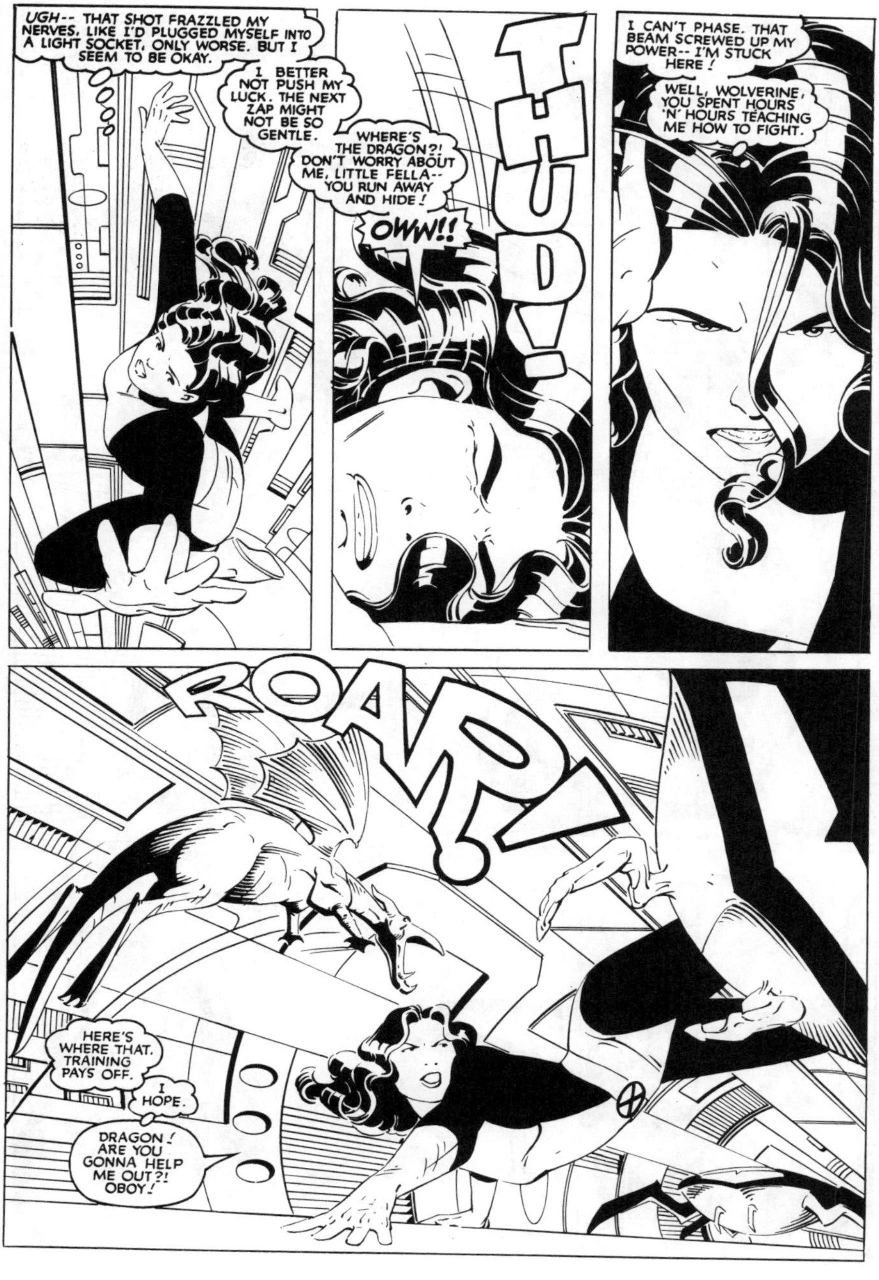
UGH-- THAT SHOT FRAZZLED MY NERVES, LIKE I'D PLUGGED MYSELF INTO A LIGHT SOCKET, ONLY WORSE. BUT I SEEM TO BE OKAY.
I BETTER NOT PUSH MY LUCK. THE NEXT ZAP MIGHT NOT BE SO GENTLE.
WHERE'S THE DRAGON?! DON'T WORRY ABOUT ME, LITTLE FELLA-- YOU RUN AWAY AND HIDE!
OWW!!
THUD!
I CAN'T PHASE. THAT BEAM SCREWED UP MY POWER-- I'M STUCK HERE!
WELL, WOLVERINE, YOU SPENT HOURS 'N' HOURS TEACHING ME HOW TO FIGHT.
ROAR!
HERE'S WHERE THAT. TRAINING PAYS OFF.
I HOPE.
DRAGON! ARE YOU GONNA HELP ME OUT?! OBOY!

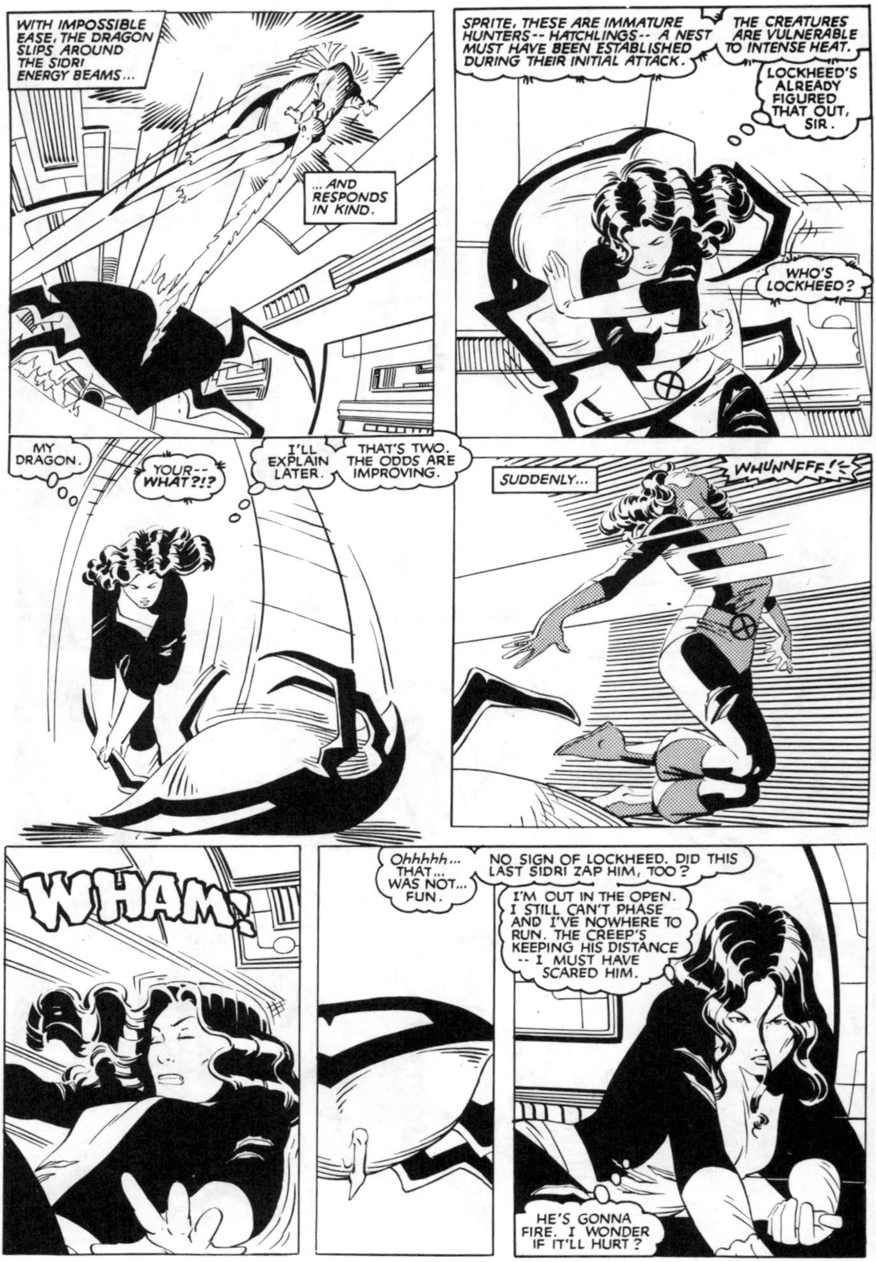

WITH IMPOSSIBLE EASE, THE DRAGON SLIPS AROUND THE SIDRI ENERGY BEAMS...
...AND RESPONDS IN KIND.
SPRITE, THESE ARE IMMATURE HUNTERS-- HATCHLINGS-- A NEST MUST HAVE BEEN ESTABLISHED DURING THEIR INITIAL ATTACK.
THE CREATURES ARE VULNERABLE TO INTENSE HEAT.
LOCKHEED'S ALREADY FIGURED THAT OUT, SIR.
WHO'S LOCKHEED?
MY DRAGON.
YOUR-- WHAT?!?
I'LL EXPLAIN LATER.
THAT'S TWO. THE ODDS ARE IMPROVING.
SUDDENLY...
WHUNNFFF!
WHAM!
Ohhhhh... THAT... WAS NOT... FUN.
NO SIGN OF LOCKHEED. DID THIS LAST SIDRI ZAP HIM, TOO?
I'M OUT IN THE OPEN. I STILL CAN'T PHASE AND I'VE NOWHERE TO RUN. THE CREEP'S KEEPING HIS DISTANCE -- I MUST HAVE SCARED HIM.
HE'S GONNA FIRE. I WONDER IF IT'LL HURT?

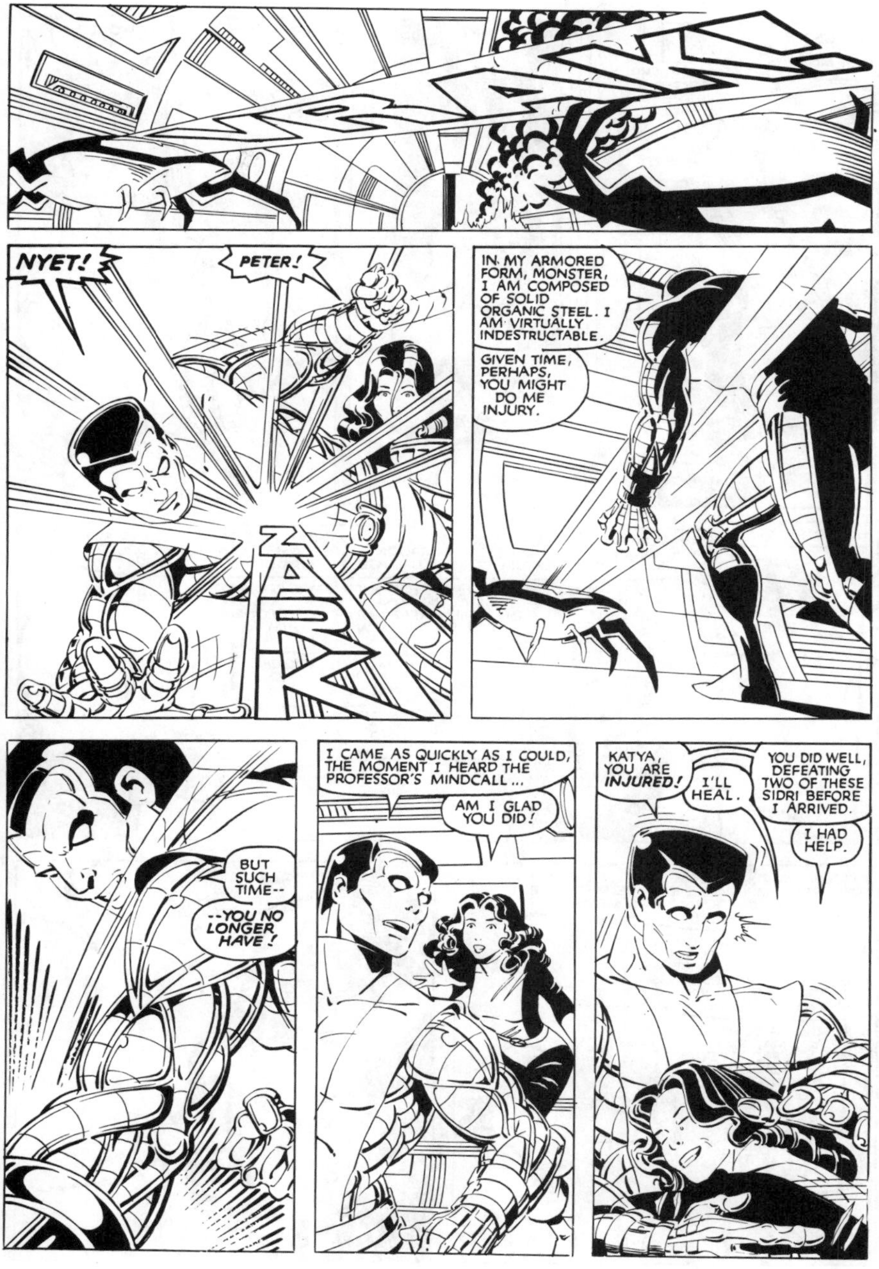
NYET!
PETER!
ZARK
IN MY ARMORED FORM, MONSTER, I AM COMPOSED OF SOLID ORGANIC STEEL. I AM VIRTUALLY INDESTRUCTABLE.
GIVEN TIME, PERHAPS, YOU MIGHT DO ME INJURY.
BUT SUCH TIME--
--YOU NO LONGER HAVE!
I CAME AS QUICKLY AS I COULD, THE MOMENT I HEARD THE PROFESSOR'S MINDCALL...
AM I GLAD YOU DID!
KATYA, YOU ARE INJURED!
I'LL HEAL.
YOU DID WELL, DEFEATING TWO OF THESE SIDRI BEFORE I ARRIVED.
I HAD HELP.

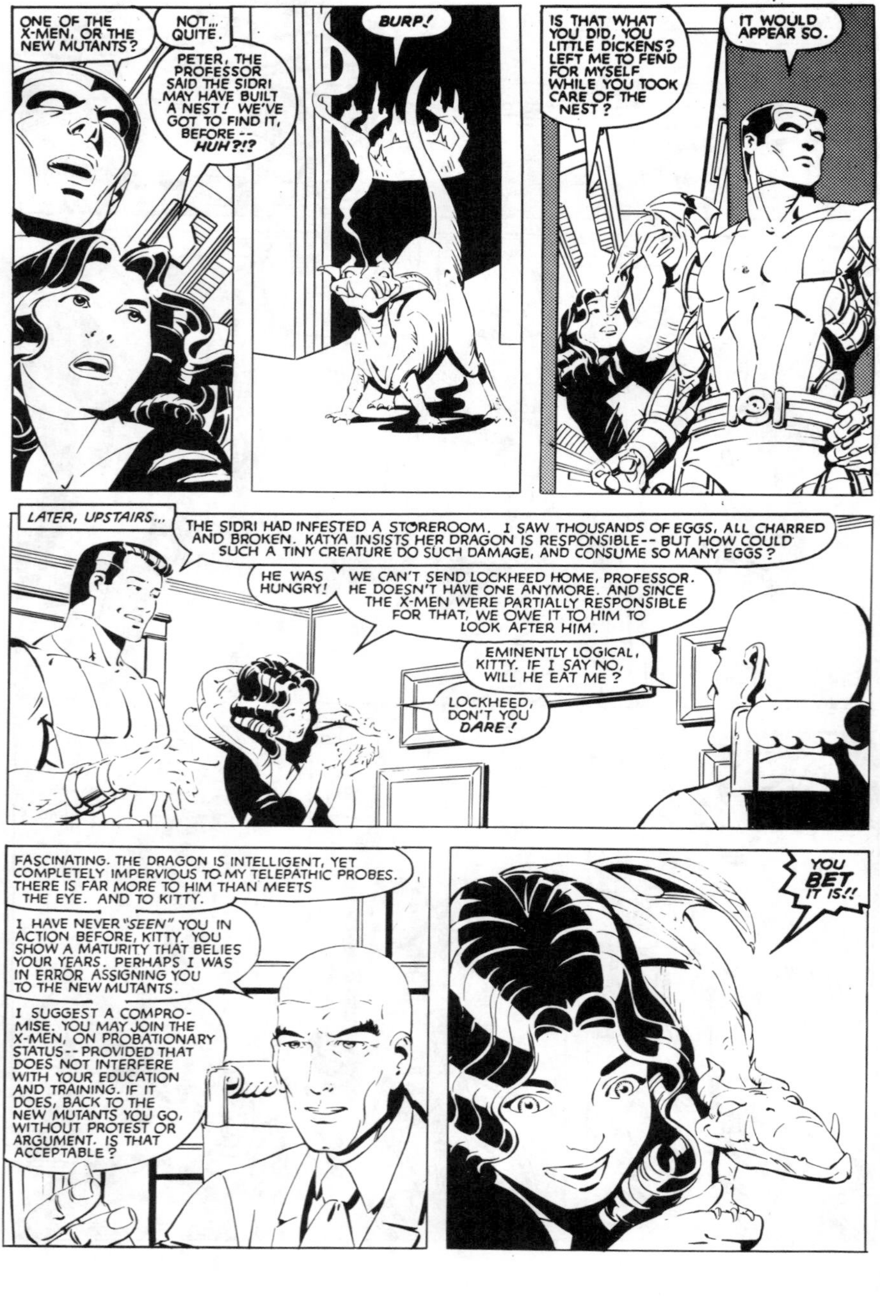
ONE OF THE X-MEN, OR THE NEW MUTANTS?
NOT... QUITE.
PETER, THE PROFESSOR SAID THE SIDRI MAY HAVE BUILT A NEST! WE'VE GOT TO FIND IT, BEFORE -- HUH?!?
BURP!
IS THAT WHAT YOU DID, YOU LITTLE DICKENS? LEFT ME TO FEND FOR MYSELF WHILE YOU TOOK CARE OF THE NEST?
IT WOULD APPEAR SO.
LATER, UPSTAIRS...
THE SIDRI HAD INFESTED A STOREROOM. I SAW THOUSANDS OF EGGS, ALL CHARRED AND BROKEN. KATYA INSISTS HER DRAGON IS RESPONSIBLE-- BUT HOW COULD SUCH A TINY CREATURE DO SUCH DAMAGE, AND CONSUME SO MANY EGGS?
HE WAS HUNGRY!
WE CAN'T SEND LOCKHEED HOME, PROFESSOR. HE DOESN'T HAVE ONE ANYMORE. AND SINCE THE X-MEN WERE PARTIALLY RESPONSIBLE FOR THAT, WE OWE IT TO HIM TO LOOK AFTER HIM.
EMINENTLY LOGICAL, KITTY. IF I SAY NO, WILL HE EAT ME?
LOCKHEED, DON'T YOU DARE!
FASCINATING. THE DRAGON IS INTELLIGENT, YET COMPLETELY IMPERVIOUS TO MY TELEPATHIC PROBES. THERE IS FAR MORE TO HIM THAN MEETS THE EYE. AND TO KITTY.
I HAVE NEVER "SEEN" YOU IN ACTION BEFORE, KITTY. YOU SHOW A MATURITY THAT BELIES YOUR YEARS. PERHAPS I WAS IN ERROR ASSIGNING YOU TO THE NEW MUTANTS.
I SUGGEST A COMPROMISE. YOU MAY JOIN THE X-MEN, ON PROBATIONARY STATUS-- PROVIDED THAT DOES NOT INTERFERE WITH YOUR EDUCATION AND TRAINING. IF IT DOES, BACK TO THE NEW MUTANTS YOU GO, WITHOUT PROTEST OR ARGUMENT. IS THAT ACCEPTABLE?
YOU BET IT IS!!

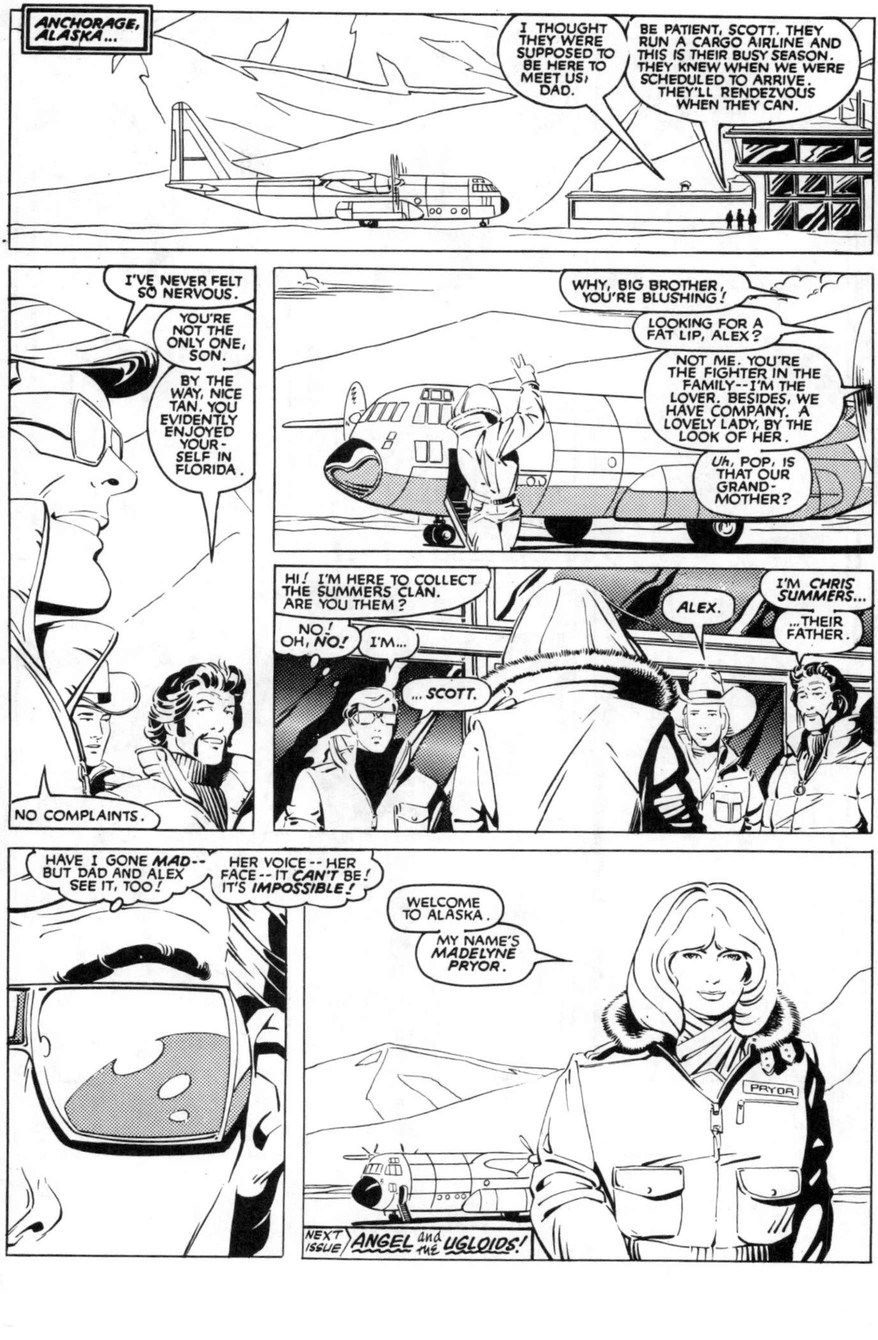
ANCHORAGE, ALASKA...
I THOUGHT THEY WERE SUPPOSED TO BE HERE TO MEET US, DAD.
BE PATIENT, SCOTT. THEY RUN A CARGO AIRLINE AND THIS IS THEIR BUSY SEASON. THEY KNEW WHEN WE WERE SCHEDULED TO ARRIVE. THEY'LL RENDEZVOUS WHEN THEY CAN.
I'VE NEVER FELT SO NERVOUS.
YOU'RE NOT THE ONLY ONE, SON.
BY THE WAY, NICE TAN. YOU EVIDENTLY ENJOYED YOURSELF IN FLORIDA.
NO COMPLAINTS.
WHY, BIG BROTHER, YOU'RE BLUSHING!
LOOKING FOR A FAT LIP, ALEX?
NOT ME. YOU'RE THE FIGHTER IN THE FAMILY--I'M THE LOVER. BESIDES, WE HAVE COMPANY. A LOVELY LADY, BY THE LOOK OF HER.
Uh, POP, IS THAT OUR GRANDMOTHER?
HI! I'M HERE TO COLLECT THE SUMMERS CLAN. ARE YOU THEM?
NO! OH, NO!
I'M...
...SCOTT.
ALEX.
I'M CHRIS SUMMERS...
...THEIR FATHER.
HAVE I GONE MAD-- BUT DAD AND ALEX SEE IT, TOO!
HER VOICE -- HER FACE -- IT CAN'T BE! IT'S IMPOSSIBLE!
WELCOME TO ALASKA.
MY NAME'S MADELYNE PRYOR.
PRYOR
NEXT ISSUE: ANGEL and the UGLOIDS!

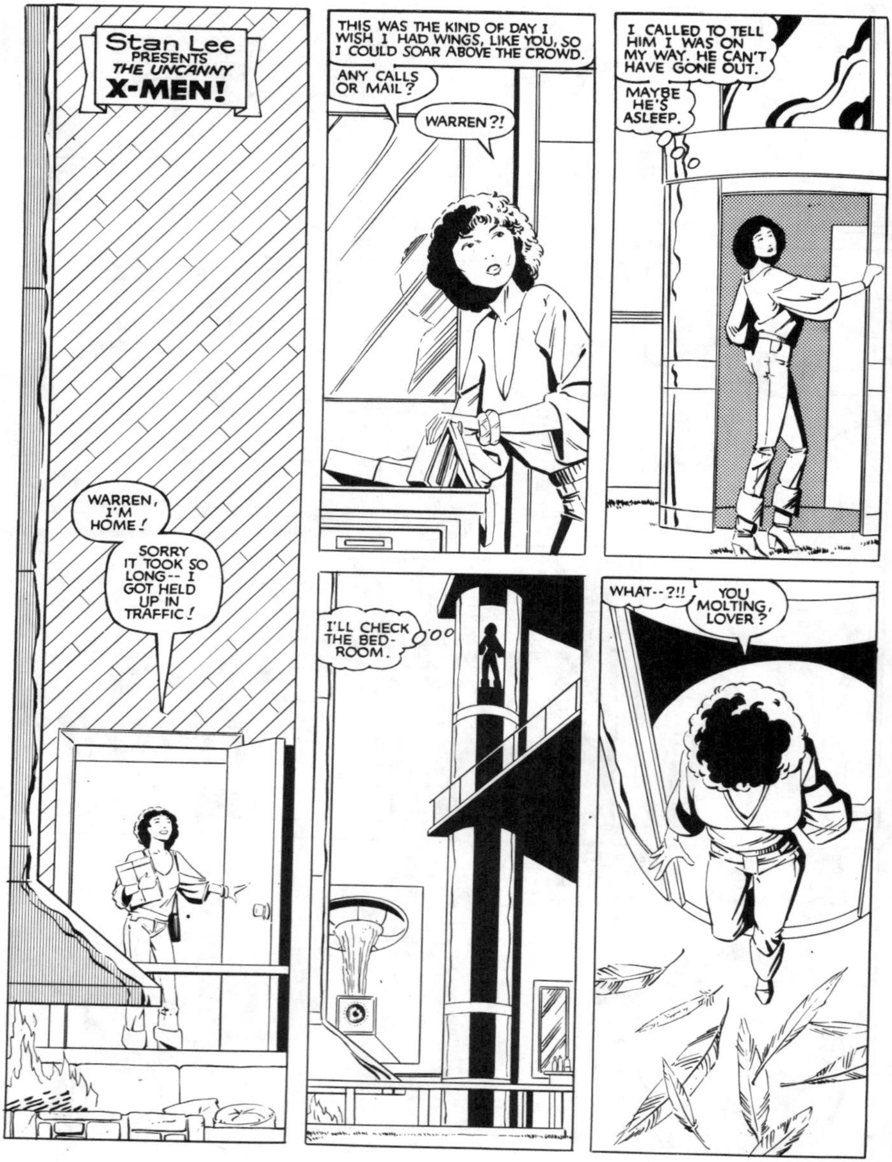
Stan Lee PRESENTS THE UNCANNY X-MEN!
WARREN, I'M HOME!
SORRY IT TOOK SO LONG-- I GOT HELD UP IN TRAFFIC!
THIS WAS THE KIND OF DAY I WISH I HAD WINGS, LIKE YOU, SO I COULD SOAR ABOVE THE CROWD.
ANY CALLS OR MAIL?
WARREN?!
I CALLED TO TELL HIM I WAS ON MY WAY. HE CAN'T HAVE GONE OUT.
MAYBE HE'S ASLEEP.
I'LL CHECK THE BED-ROOM.
WHAT--?!!
YOU MOLTING, LOVER?

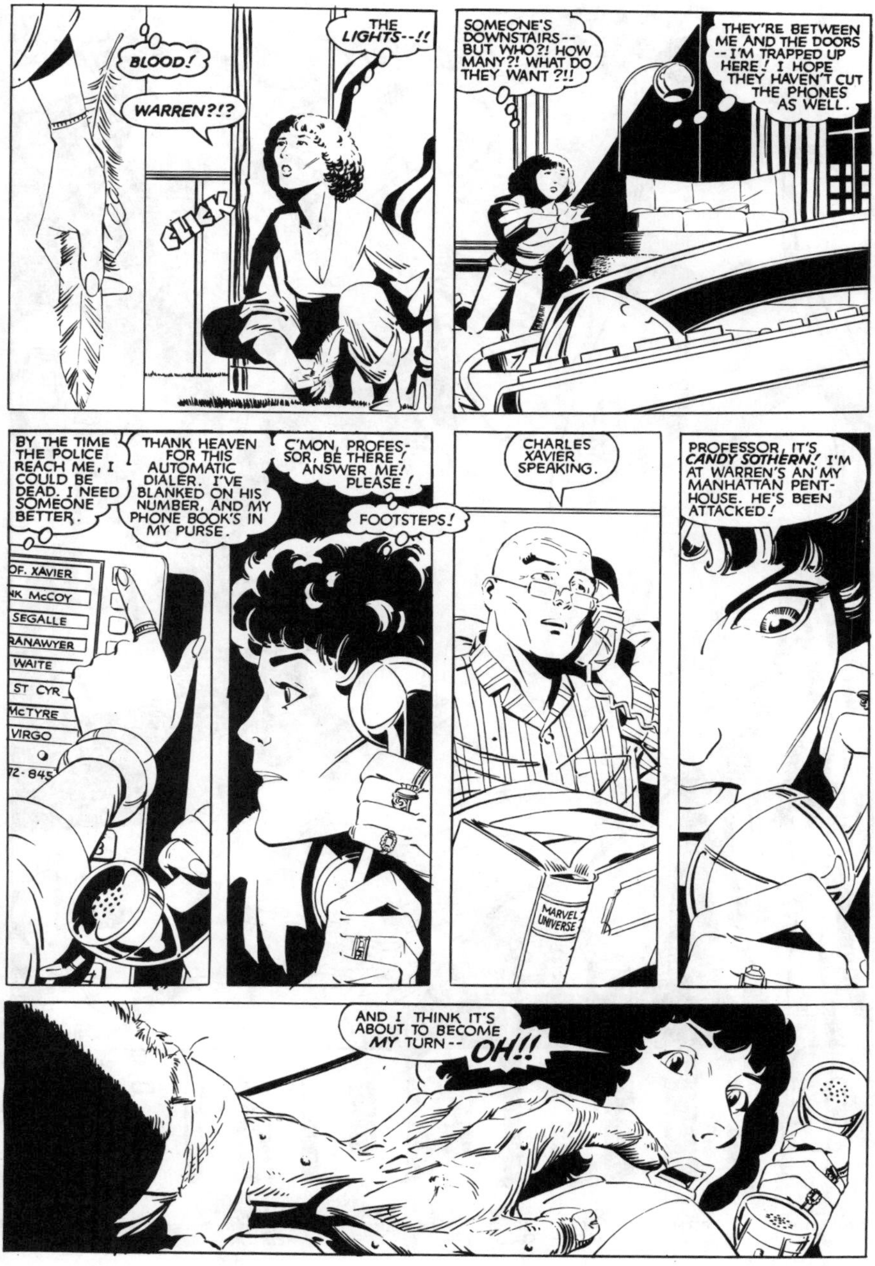
BLOOD!
WARREN?!?
CLICK
THE LIGHTS--!!
SOMEONE'S DOWNSTAIRS-- BUT WHO?! HOW MANY?! WHAT DO THEY WANT?!!
THEY'RE BETWEEN ME AND THE DOORS --I'M TRAPPED UP HERE! I HOPE THEY HAVEN'T CUT THE PHONES AS WELL.
BY THE TIME THE POLICE REACH ME, I COULD BE DEAD. I NEED SOMEONE BETTER.
THANK HEAVEN FOR THIS AUTOMATIC DIALER. I'VE BLANKED ON HIS NUMBER, AND MY PHONE BOOK'S IN MY PURSE.
OF. XAVIER
NK McCOY
SEGALLE
RANAWYER
WAITE
ST CYR
McTYRE
VIRGO
72-845
C'MON, PROFESSOR, BE THERE! ANSWER ME! PLEASE!
FOOTSTEPS!
CHARLES XAVIER SPEAKING.
MARVEL UNIVERSE
PROFESSOR, IT'S CANDY SOTHERN! I'M AT WARREN'S AN' MY MANHATTAN PENTHOUSE. HE'S BEEN ATTACKED!
AND I THINK IT'S ABOUT TO BECOME MY TURN-- OH!!

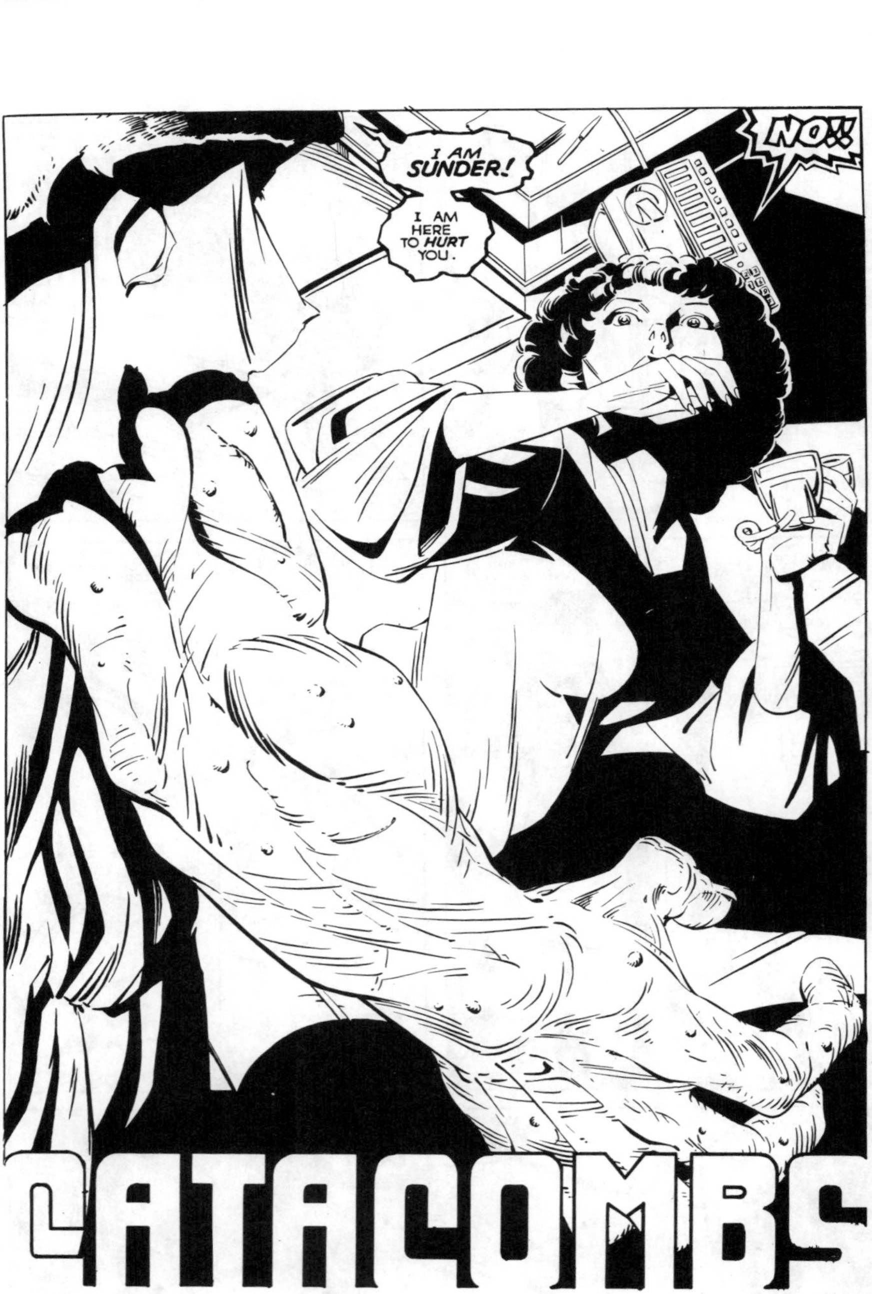
I AM SUNDER!
I AM HERE TO HURT YOU.
NO!!
CATACOMBS

CHRIS CLAREMONT *WRITER* · PAUL SMITH *PENCILLER* · BOB WIACEK *INKER* · BOB SHAREN *COLORIST* · TOM ORZECHOWSKI *LETTERER* · LOUISE JONES *EDITOR* · JIM SHOOTER *EDITOR-IN-CHIEF*

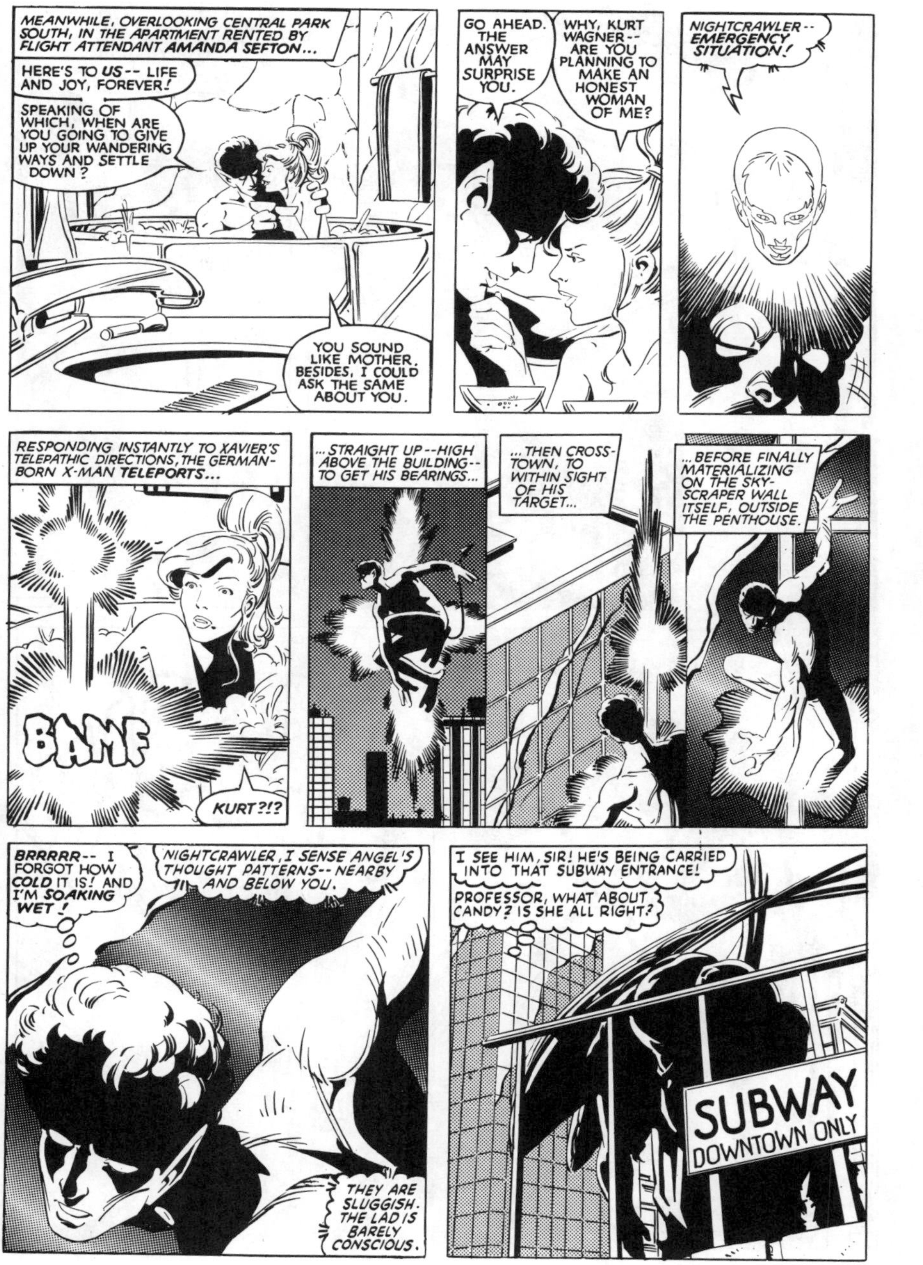

MEANWHILE, OVERLOOKING CENTRAL PARK SOUTH, IN THE APARTMENT RENTED BY FLIGHT ATTENDANT AMANDA SEFTON...
HERE'S TO US -- LIFE AND JOY, FOREVER!
SPEAKING OF WHICH, WHEN ARE YOU GOING TO GIVE UP YOUR WANDERING WAYS AND SETTLE DOWN?
YOU SOUND LIKE MOTHER. BESIDES, I COULD ASK THE SAME ABOUT YOU.
WHY, KURT WAGNER -- ARE YOU PLANNING TO MAKE AN HONEST WOMAN OF ME?
GO AHEAD. THE ANSWER MAY SURPRISE YOU.
NIGHTCRAWLER -- EMERGENCY SITUATION!
RESPONDING INSTANTLY TO XAVIER'S TELEPATHIC DIRECTIONS, THE GERMAN-BORN X-MAN TELEPORTS...
BAMF
KURT?!?
...STRAIGHT UP -- HIGH ABOVE THE BUILDING -- TO GET HIS BEARINGS...
...THEN CROSS-TOWN, TO WITHIN SIGHT OF HIS TARGET...
...BEFORE FINALLY MATERIALIZING ON THE SKY-SCRAPER WALL ITSELF, OUTSIDE THE PENTHOUSE.
BRRRRR -- I FORGOT HOW COLD IT IS! AND I'M SOAKING WET!
NIGHTCRAWLER, I SENSE ANGEL'S THOUGHT PATTERNS -- NEARBY AND BELOW YOU.
THEY ARE SLUGGISH. THE LAD IS BARELY CONSCIOUS.
I SEE HIM, SIR! HE'S BEING CARRIED INTO THAT SUBWAY ENTRANCE!
PROFESSOR, WHAT ABOUT CANDY? IS SHE ALL RIGHT?
SUBWAY
DOWNTOWN ONLY

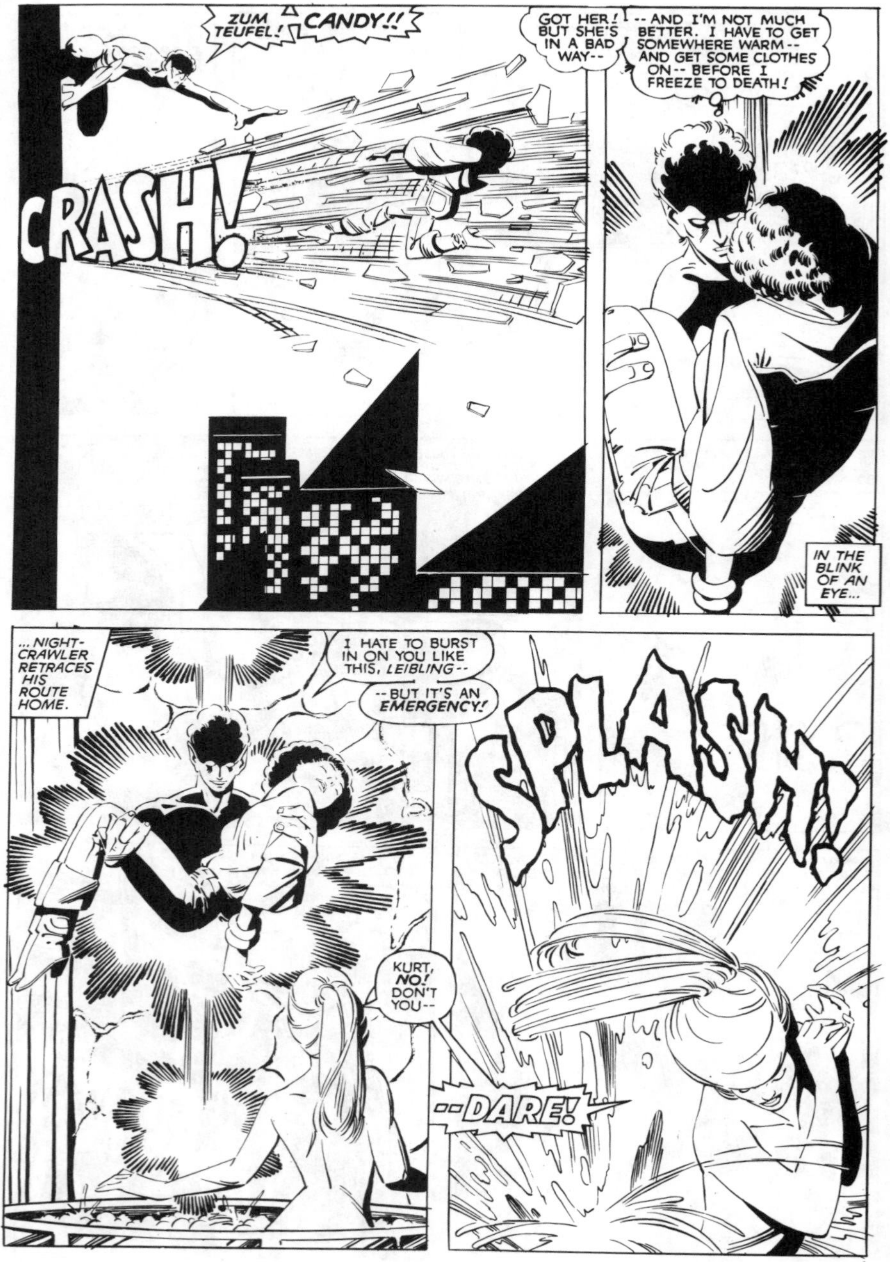
ZUM TEUFEL!
CANDY!!
CRASH!
GOT HER! BUT SHE'S IN A BAD WAY--
--AND I'M NOT MUCH BETTER. I HAVE TO GET SOMEWHERE WARM-- AND GET SOME CLOTHES ON-- BEFORE I FREEZE TO DEATH!
IN THE BLINK OF AN EYE...
...NIGHT-CRAWLER RETRACES HIS ROUTE HOME.
I HATE TO BURST IN ON YOU LIKE THIS, LEIBLING--
--BUT IT'S AN EMERGENCY!
KURT, NO! DON'T YOU--
SPLASH!
--DARE!

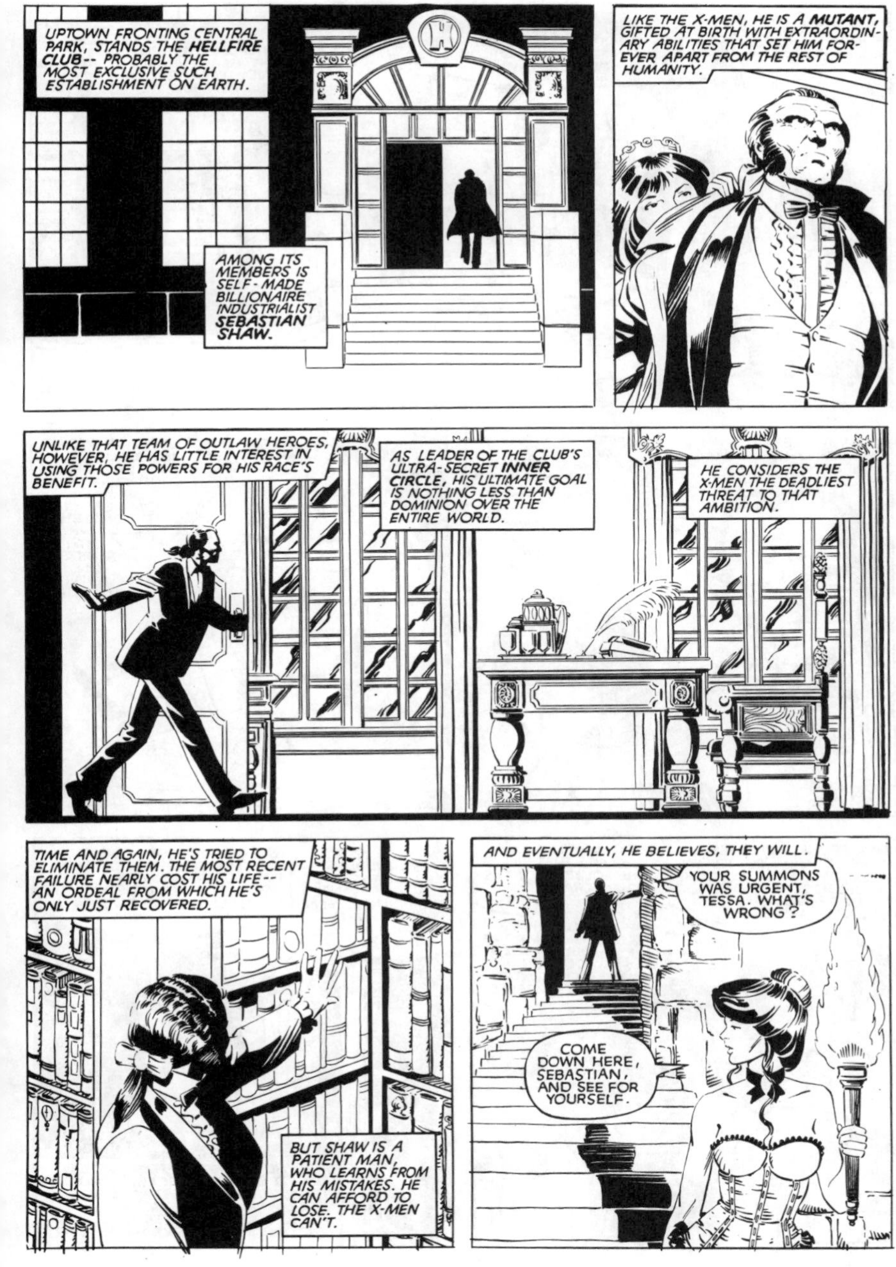
UPTOWN FRONTING CENTRAL PARK, STANDS THE HELLFIRE CLUB-- PROBABLY THE MOST EXCLUSIVE SUCH ESTABLISHMENT ON EARTH.
AMONG ITS MEMBERS IS SELF-MADE BILLIONAIRE INDUSTRIALIST SEBASTIAN SHAW.
LIKE THE X-MEN, HE IS A MUTANT, GIFTED AT BIRTH WITH EXTRAORDINARY ABILITIES THAT SET HIM FOREVER APART FROM THE REST OF HUMANITY.
UNLIKE THAT TEAM OF OUTLAW HEROES, HOWEVER, HE HAS LITTLE INTEREST IN USING THOSE POWERS FOR HIS RACE'S BENEFIT.
AS LEADER OF THE CLUB'S ULTRA-SECRET INNER CIRCLE, HIS ULTIMATE GOAL IS NOTHING LESS THAN DOMINION OVER THE ENTIRE WORLD.
HE CONSIDERS THE X-MEN THE DEADLIEST THREAT TO THAT AMBITION.
TIME AND AGAIN, HE'S TRIED TO ELIMINATE THEM. THE MOST RECENT FAILURE NEARLY COST HIS LIFE-- AN ORDEAL FROM WHICH HE'S ONLY JUST RECOVERED.
BUT SHAW IS A PATIENT MAN, WHO LEARNS FROM HIS MISTAKES. HE CAN AFFORD TO LOSE. THE X-MEN CAN'T.
AND EVENTUALLY, HE BELIEVES, THEY WILL.
YOUR SUMMONS WAS URGENT, TESSA. WHAT'S WRONG?
COME DOWN HERE, SEBASTIAN, AND SEE FOR YOURSELF.

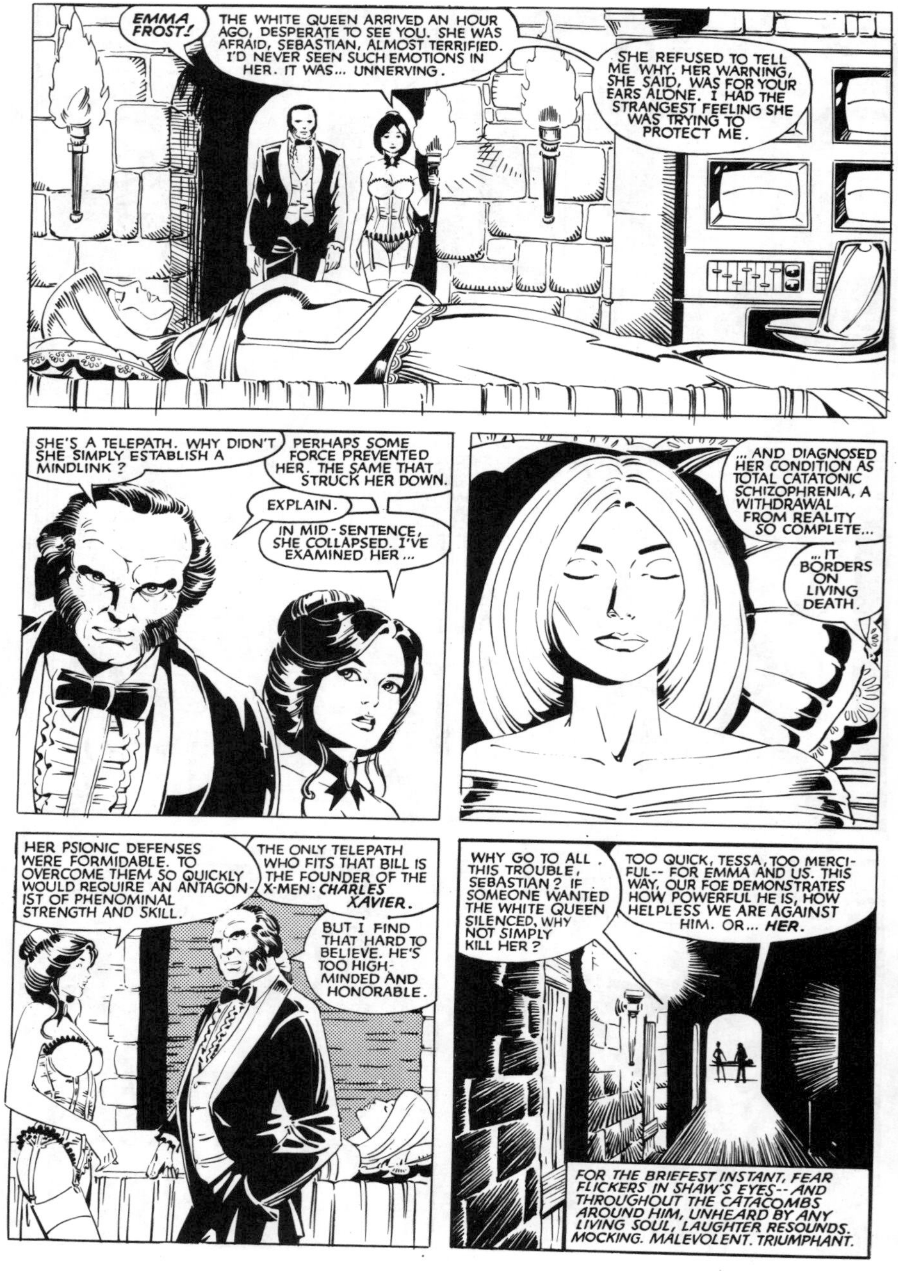
EMMA FROST!
THE WHITE QUEEN ARRIVED AN HOUR AGO, DESPERATE TO SEE YOU. SHE WAS AFRAID, SEBASTIAN, ALMOST TERRIFIED. I'D NEVER SEEN SUCH EMOTIONS IN HER. IT WAS... UNNERVING.
SHE REFUSED TO TELL ME WHY. HER WARNING, SHE SAID, WAS FOR YOUR EARS ALONE. I HAD THE STRANGEST FEELING SHE WAS TRYING TO PROTECT ME.
SHE'S A TELEPATH. WHY DIDN'T SHE SIMPLY ESTABLISH A MINDLINK?
PERHAPS SOME FORCE PREVENTED HER. THE SAME THAT STRUCK HER DOWN.
EXPLAIN.
IN MID-SENTENCE, SHE COLLAPSED. I'VE EXAMINED HER...
... AND DIAGNOSED HER CONDITION AS TOTAL CATATONIC SCHIZOPHRENIA, A WITHDRAWAL FROM REALITY SO COMPLETE...
... IT BORDERS ON LIVING DEATH.
HER PSIONIC DEFENSES WERE FORMIDABLE. TO OVERCOME THEM SO QUICKLY WOULD REQUIRE AN ANTAGONIST OF PHENOMINAL STRENGTH AND SKILL.
THE ONLY TELEPATH WHO FITS THAT BILL IS THE FOUNDER OF THE X-MEN: CHARLES XAVIER.
BUT I FIND THAT HARD TO BELIEVE. HE'S TOO HIGH-MINDED AND HONORABLE.
WHY GO TO ALL THIS TROUBLE, SEBASTIAN? IF SOMEONE WANTED THE WHITE QUEEN SILENCED, WHY NOT SIMPLY KILL HER?
TOO QUICK, TESSA, TOO MERCIFUL-- FOR EMMA AND US. THIS WAY, OUR FOE DEMONSTRATES HOW POWERFUL HE IS, HOW HELPLESS WE ARE AGAINST HIM. OR... HER.
FOR THE BRIEFEST INSTANT, FEAR FLICKERS IN SHAW'S EYES-- AND THROUGHOUT THE CATACOMBS AROUND HIM, UNHEARD BY ANY LIVING SOUL, LAUGHTER RESOUNDS. MOCKING. MALEVOLENT. TRIUMPHANT.

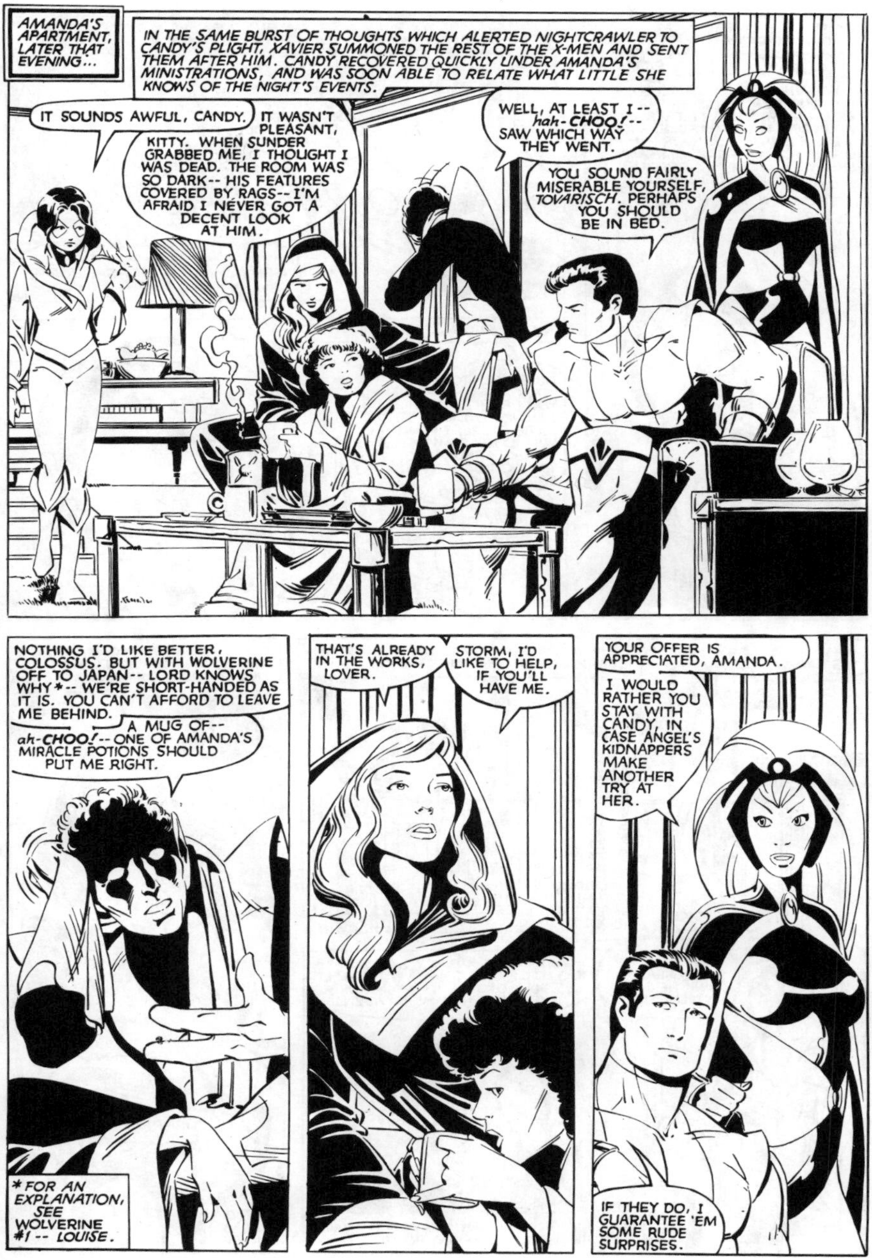

AMANDA'S APARTMENT, LATER THAT EVENING...
IN THE SAME BURST OF THOUGHTS WHICH ALERTED NIGHTCRAWLER TO CANDY'S PLIGHT, XAVIER SUMMONED THE REST OF THE X-MEN AND SENT THEM AFTER HIM. CANDY RECOVERED QUICKLY UNDER AMANDA'S MINISTRATIONS, AND WAS SOON ABLE TO RELATE WHAT LITTLE SHE KNOWS OF THE NIGHT'S EVENTS.
IT SOUNDS AWFUL, CANDY.
IT WASN'T PLEASANT, KITTY. WHEN SUNDER GRABBED ME, I THOUGHT I WAS DEAD. THE ROOM WAS SO DARK-- HIS FEATURES COVERED BY RAGS-- I'M AFRAID I NEVER GOT A DECENT LOOK AT HIM.
WELL, AT LEAST I -- hah-CHOO! -- SAW WHICH WAY THEY WENT.
YOU SOUND FAIRLY MISERABLE YOURSELF, TOVARISCH. PERHAPS YOU SHOULD BE IN BED.
NOTHING I'D LIKE BETTER, COLOSSUS. BUT WITH WOLVERINE OFF TO JAPAN-- LORD KNOWS WHY*-- WE'RE SHORT-HANDED AS IT IS. YOU CAN'T AFFORD TO LEAVE ME BEHIND.
A MUG OF-- ah-CHOO! -- ONE OF AMANDA'S MIRACLE POTIONS SHOULD PUT ME RIGHT.
*FOR AN EXPLANATION, SEE WOLVERINE #1 -- LOUISE.
THAT'S ALREADY IN THE WORKS, LOVER.
STORM, I'D LIKE TO HELP, IF YOU'LL HAVE ME.
YOUR OFFER IS APPRECIATED, AMANDA.
I WOULD RATHER YOU STAY WITH CANDY, IN CASE ANGEL'S KIDNAPPERS MAKE ANOTHER TRY AT HER.
IF THEY DO, I GUARANTEE 'EM SOME RUDE SURPRISES.

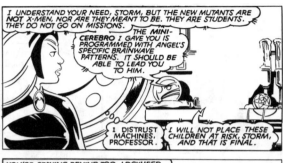

PROFESSOR, CAN YOU READ MY THOUGHTS?

PERFECTLY, STORM.

WE ARE READY TO PROCEED, BUT OUR TASK WOULD BE FAR EASIER IF WE HAD A TRACKER. SINCE WOLVERINE IS UNAVAILABLE, MIGHT WE USE *RAHNE SINCLAIR*? IN HER LUPINE FORM-- AS *WOLFSBANE*-- SHE WOULD HAVE NO TROUBLE FOLLOWING ANGEL'S TRAIL.

I UNDERSTAND YOUR NEED, STORM, BUT THE NEW MUTANTS ARE *NOT* X-MEN, NOR ARE THEY MEANT TO BE. THEY ARE STUDENTS. THEY DO NOT GO ON MISSIONS.

THE MINI-CEREBRO I GAVE YOU IS PROGRAMMED WITH ANGEL'S SPECIFIC BRAINWAVE PATTERNS. IT SHOULD BE ABLE TO LEAD YOU TO HIM.

I DISTRUST MACHINES, PROFESSOR.

I WILL NOT PLACE THESE CHILDREN AT RISK, STORM, AND THAT IS FINAL.

YOU'RE STAYING BEHIND TOO, LOCKHEED.

GRRRRRRRR!

HUSH UP! DON'T YOU GROWL AT ME, YOU DRAGON YOU. I'M NOT DOING THIS TO BE CRUEL, I WANT YOU TO HELP AMANDA PROTECT CANDY. WILL YOU DO THAT FOR ME, PLEASE, THERE'S A GOOD LOCKHEED?

≥ PFUI! ≤

WAS THAT *DA* OR *NYET*, KATYA-- YES OR NO?

IF YOU ASK ME, PETS SHOULD KNOW THEIR PLACE AND DO AS THEY'RE TOLD.

I WONDER IF LOCKHEED FEELS THAT WAY ABOUT US.

DON'T WORRY, KITTY. MY MOM TAUGHT ME ALL ABOUT THE CARE AND FEEDING OF DRAGONS.

PURR*RRRR*!

GOOD LUCK, X-MEN.

WOW! ORORO, D'YOU REALLY THINK HE'S THAT INTELLIGENT?

WHO CAN SAY, KITTEN? WE KNOW TOO LITTLE ABOUT HIM-- NOT EVEN IF HE'S FULL GROWN, AN INFANT, OR ANYWHERE IN BETWEEN.

HE'S BEEN FED AN' EV'RYTHING, AMANDA. HE SHOULDN'T BE ANY BOTHER.

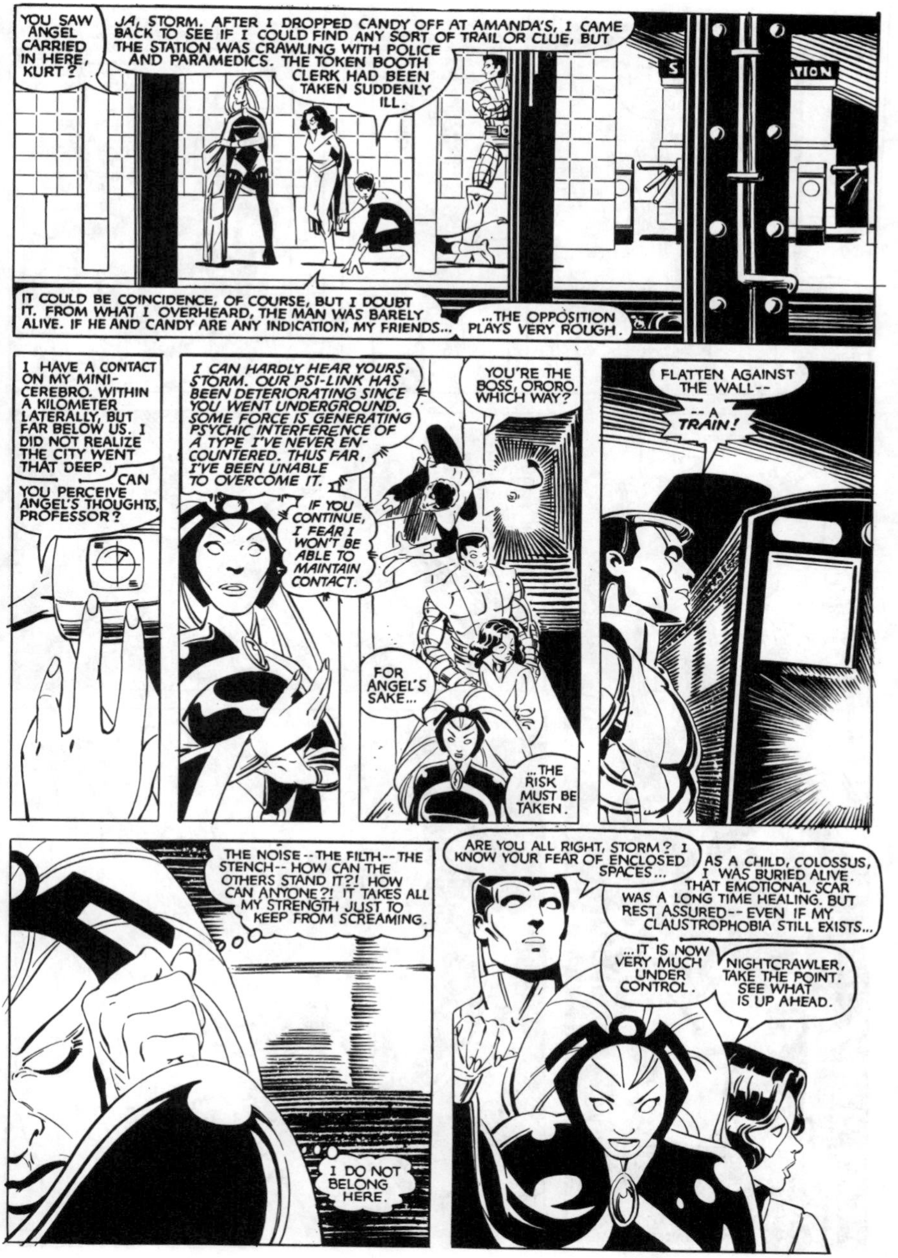
YOU SAW ANGEL CARRIED IN HERE, KURT?
JA, STORM. AFTER I DROPPED CANDY OFF AT AMANDA'S, I CAME BACK TO SEE IF I COULD FIND ANY SORT OF TRAIL OR CLUE, BUT THE STATION WAS CRAWLING WITH POLICE AND PARAMEDICS. THE TOKEN BOOTH CLERK HAD BEEN TAKEN SUDDENLY ILL.
IT COULD BE COINCIDENCE, OF COURSE, BUT I DOUBT IT. FROM WHAT I OVERHEARD, THE MAN WAS BARELY ALIVE. IF HE AND CANDY ARE ANY INDICATION, MY FRIENDS...
...THE OPPOSITION PLAYS VERY ROUGH.
I HAVE A CONTACT ON MY MINI-CEREBRO. WITHIN A KILOMETER LATERALLY, BUT FAR BELOW US. I DID NOT REALIZE THE CITY WENT THAT DEEP.
CAN YOU PERCEIVE ANGEL'S THOUGHTS, PROFESSOR?
I CAN HARDLY HEAR YOURS, STORM. OUR PSI-LINK HAS BEEN DETERIORATING SINCE YOU WENT UNDERGROUND. SOME FORCE IS GENERATING PSYCHIC INTERFERENCE OF A TYPE I'VE NEVER ENCOUNTERED. THUS FAR, I'VE BEEN UNABLE TO OVERCOME IT.
IF YOU CONTINUE, I FEAR I WON'T BE ABLE TO MAINTAIN CONTACT.
YOU'RE THE BOSS, ORORO. WHICH WAY?
FOR ANGEL'S SAKE...
...THE RISK MUST BE TAKEN.
FLATTEN AGAINST THE WALL--
--A TRAIN!
THE NOISE--THE FILTH--THE STENCH--HOW CAN THE OTHERS STAND IT?! HOW CAN ANYONE?! IT TAKES ALL MY STRENGTH JUST TO KEEP FROM SCREAMING.
I DO NOT BELONG HERE.
ARE YOU ALL RIGHT, STORM? I KNOW YOUR FEAR OF ENCLOSED SPACES...
AS A CHILD, COLOSSUS, I WAS BURIED ALIVE. THAT EMOTIONAL SCAR WAS A LONG TIME HEALING. BUT REST ASSURED--EVEN IF MY CLAUSTROPHOBIA STILL EXISTS...
...IT IS NOW VERY MUCH UNDER CONTROL.
NIGHTCRAWLER, TAKE THE POINT. SEE WHAT IS UP AHEAD.

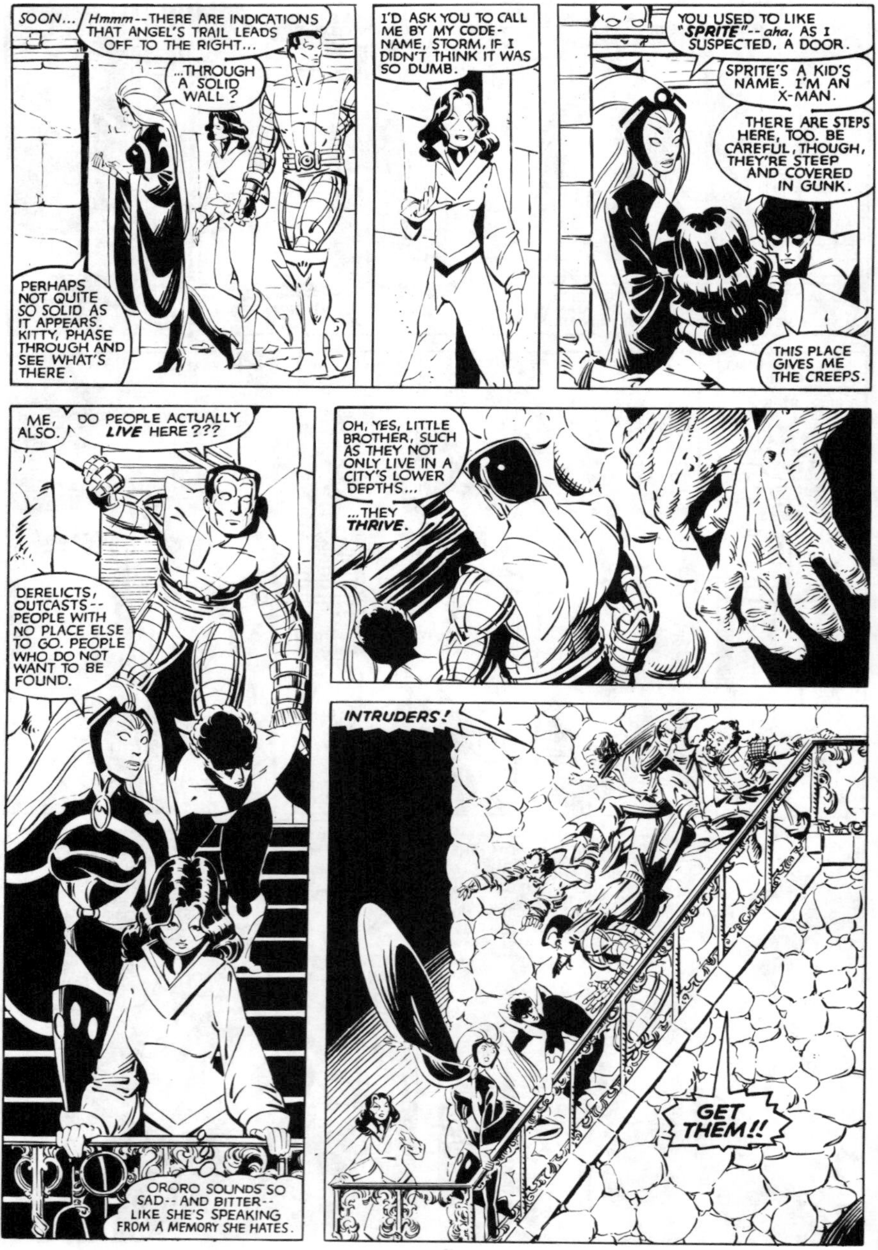

SOON...
Hmmm--THERE ARE INDICATIONS THAT ANGEL'S TRAIL LEADS OFF TO THE RIGHT...
...THROUGH A SOLID WALL?
PERHAPS NOT QUITE SO SOLID AS IT APPEARS. KITTY, PHASE THROUGH AND SEE WHAT'S THERE.
I'D ASK YOU TO CALL ME BY MY CODE-NAME, STORM, IF I DIDN'T THINK IT WAS SO DUMB.
YOU USED TO LIKE "SPRITE"--aha, AS I SUSPECTED, A DOOR.
SPRITE'S A KID'S NAME. I'M AN X-MAN.
THERE ARE STEPS HERE, TOO. BE CAREFUL, THOUGH, THEY'RE STEEP AND COVERED IN GUNK.
THIS PLACE GIVES ME THE CREEPS.
ME, ALSO.
DO PEOPLE ACTUALLY LIVE HERE???
DERELICTS, OUTCASTS--PEOPLE WITH NO PLACE ELSE TO GO. PEOPLE WHO DO NOT WANT TO BE FOUND.
ORORO SOUNDS SO SAD--AND BITTER--LIKE SHE'S SPEAKING FROM A MEMORY SHE HATES.
OH, YES, LITTLE BROTHER, SUCH AS THEY NOT ONLY LIVE IN A CITY'S LOWER DEPTHS...
...THEY THRIVE.
INTRUDERS!
GET THEM!!

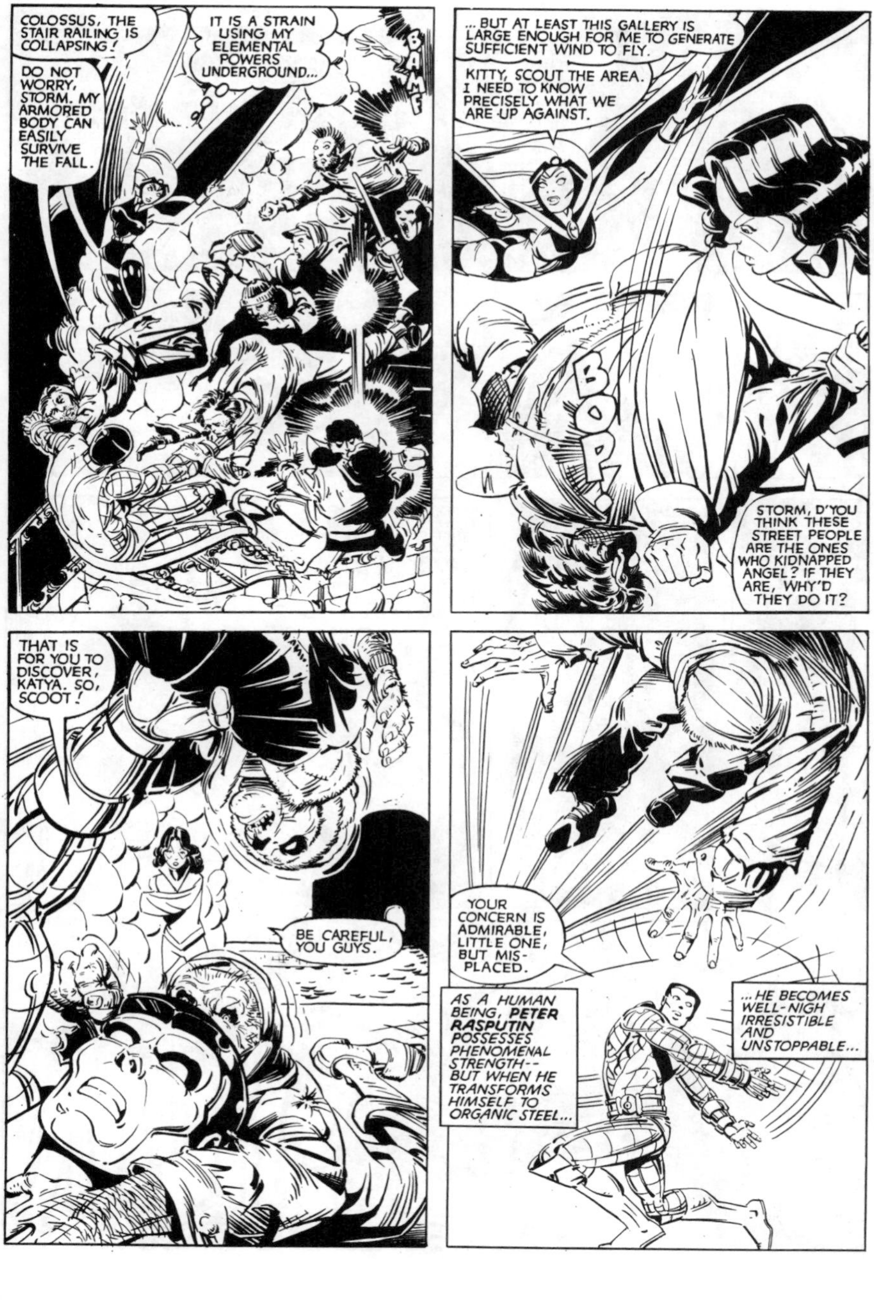
COLOSSUS, THE STAIR RAILING IS COLLAPSING!
IT IS A STRAIN USING MY ELEMENTAL POWERS UNDERGROUND...
DO NOT WORRY, STORM. MY ARMORED BODY CAN EASILY SURVIVE THE FALL.
BAMF
...BUT AT LEAST THIS GALLERY IS LARGE ENOUGH FOR ME TO GENERATE SUFFICIENT WIND TO FLY.
KITTY, SCOUT THE AREA. I NEED TO KNOW PRECISELY WHAT WE ARE UP AGAINST.
BOP!
STORM, D'YOU THINK THESE STREET PEOPLE ARE THE ONES WHO KIDNAPPED ANGEL? IF THEY ARE, WHY'D THEY DO IT?
THAT IS FOR YOU TO DISCOVER, KATYA. SO, SCOOT!
BE CAREFUL, YOU GUYS.
YOUR CONCERN IS ADMIRABLE, LITTLE ONE, BUT MIS-PLACED.
AS A HUMAN BEING, PETER RASPUTIN POSSESSES PHENOMENAL STRENGTH-- BUT WHEN HE TRANSFORMS HIMSELF TO ORGANIC STEEL...
...HE BECOMES WELL-NIGH IRRESISTIBLE AND UNSTOPPABLE...

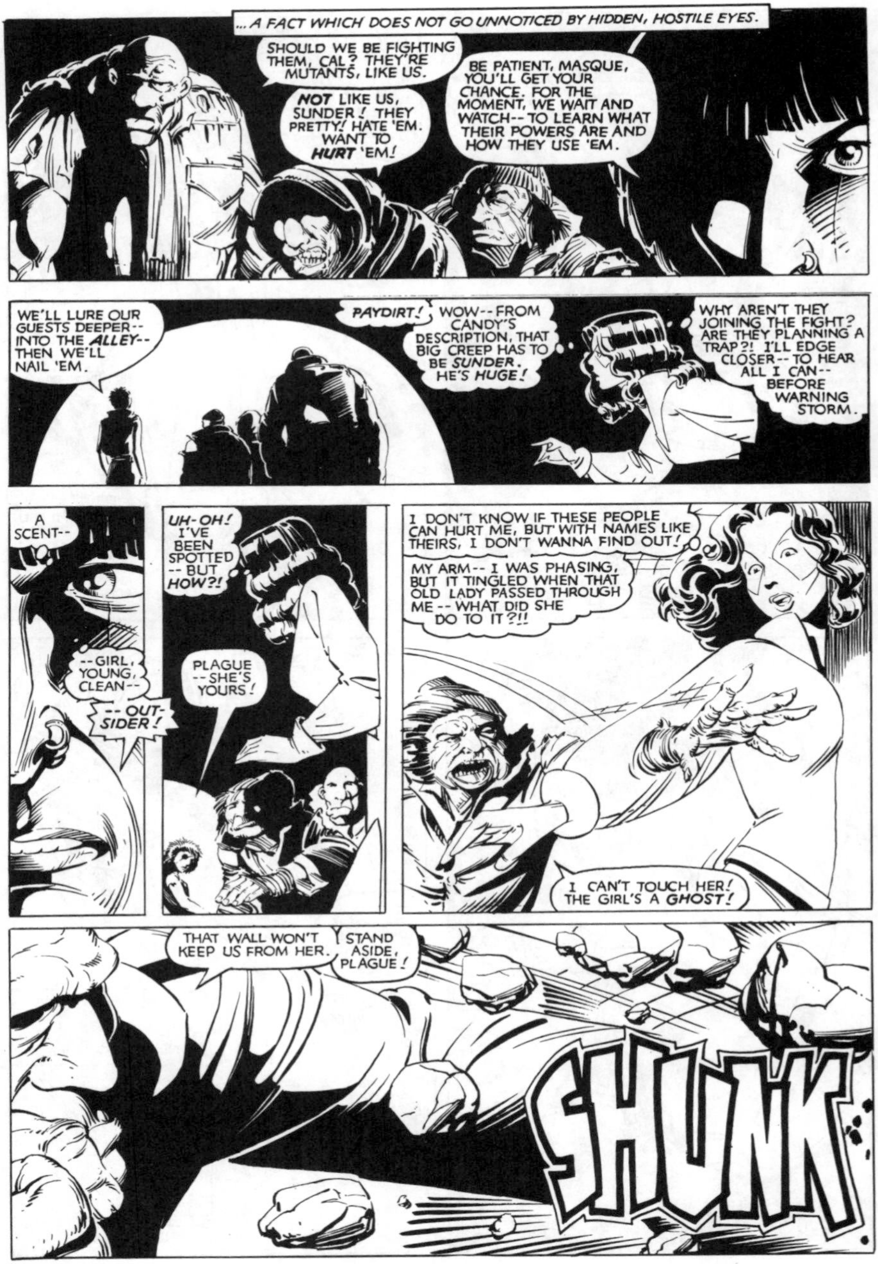
...A FACT WHICH DOES NOT GO UNNOTICED BY HIDDEN, HOSTILE EYES.
SHOULD WE BE FIGHTING THEM, CAL? THEY'RE MUTANTS, LIKE US.
NOT LIKE US, SUNDER! THEY PRETTY! HATE 'EM. WANT TO HURT 'EM!
BE PATIENT, MASQUE, YOU'LL GET YOUR CHANCE. FOR THE MOMENT, WE WAIT AND WATCH-- TO LEARN WHAT THEIR POWERS ARE AND HOW THEY USE 'EM.
WE'LL LURE OUR GUESTS DEEPER-- INTO THE ALLEY-- THEN WE'LL NAIL 'EM.
PAYDIRT!
WOW--FROM CANDY'S DESCRIPTION, THAT BIG CREEP HAS TO BE SUNDER. HE'S HUGE!
WHY AREN'T THEY JOINING THE FIGHT? ARE THEY PLANNING A TRAP?! I'LL EDGE CLOSER-- TO HEAR ALL I CAN-- BEFORE WARNING STORM.
A SCENT--
--GIRL, YOUNG, CLEAN--
--OUT-SIDER!
UH-OH! I'VE BEEN SPOTTED --BUT HOW?!
PLAGUE --SHE'S YOURS!
I DON'T KNOW IF THESE PEOPLE CAN HURT ME, BUT WITH NAMES LIKE THEIRS, I DON'T WANNA FIND OUT!
MY ARM-- I WAS PHASING, BUT IT TINGLED WHEN THAT OLD LADY PASSED THROUGH ME -- WHAT DID SHE DO TO IT?!!
I CAN'T TOUCH HER! THE GIRL'S A GHOST!
THAT WALL WON'T KEEP US FROM HER.
STAND ASIDE, PLAGUE!
SHUNK

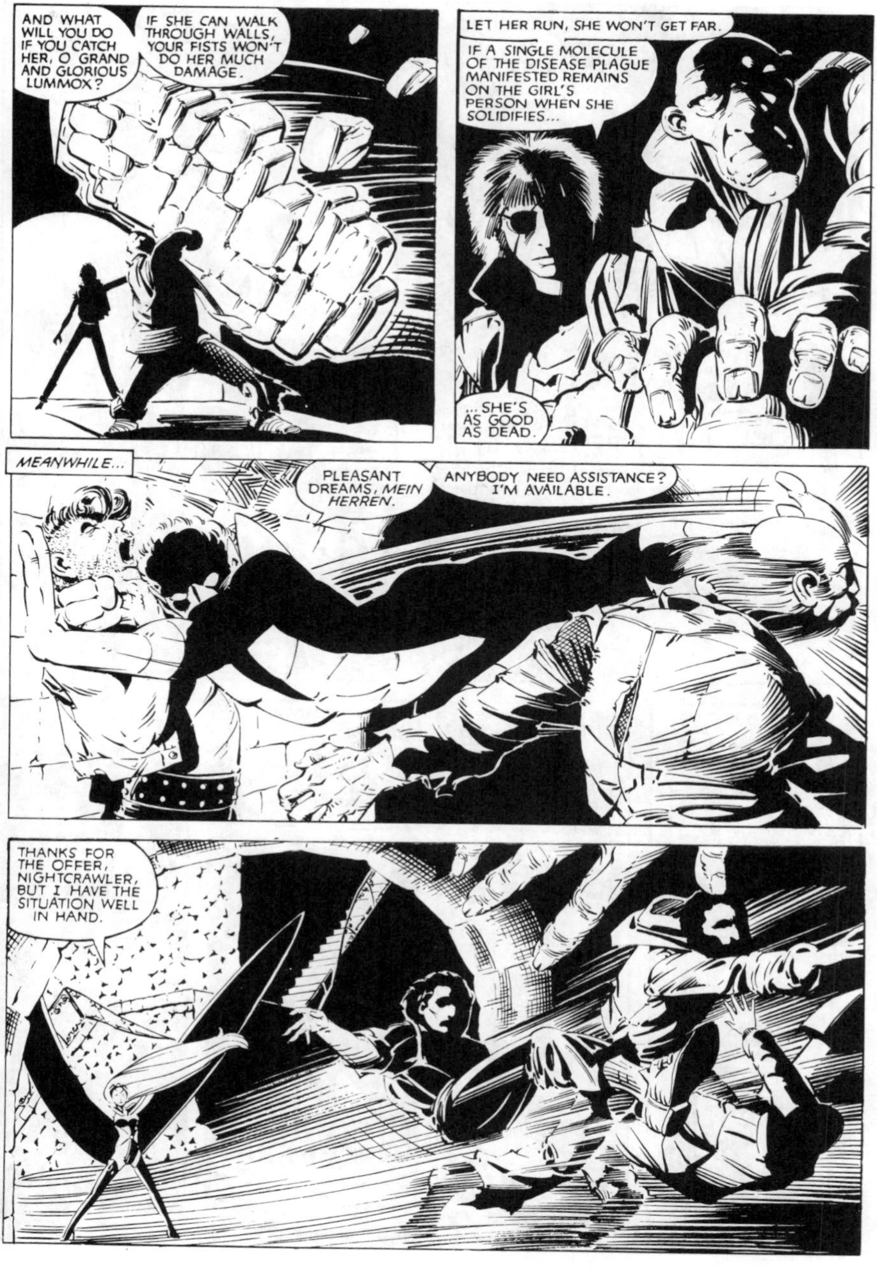
AND WHAT WILL YOU DO IF YOU CATCH HER, O GRAND AND GLORIOUS LUMMOX?
IF SHE CAN WALK THROUGH WALLS, YOUR FISTS WON'T DO HER MUCH DAMAGE.
LET HER RUN, SHE WON'T GET FAR.
IF A SINGLE MOLECULE OF THE DISEASE PLAGUE MANIFESTED REMAINS ON THE GIRL'S PERSON WHEN SHE SOLIDIFIES...
...SHE'S AS GOOD AS DEAD.
MEANWHILE...
PLEASANT DREAMS, MEIN HERREN.
ANYBODY NEED ASSISTANCE? I'M AVAILABLE.
THANKS FOR THE OFFER, NIGHTCRAWLER, BUT I HAVE THE SITUATION WELL IN HAND.

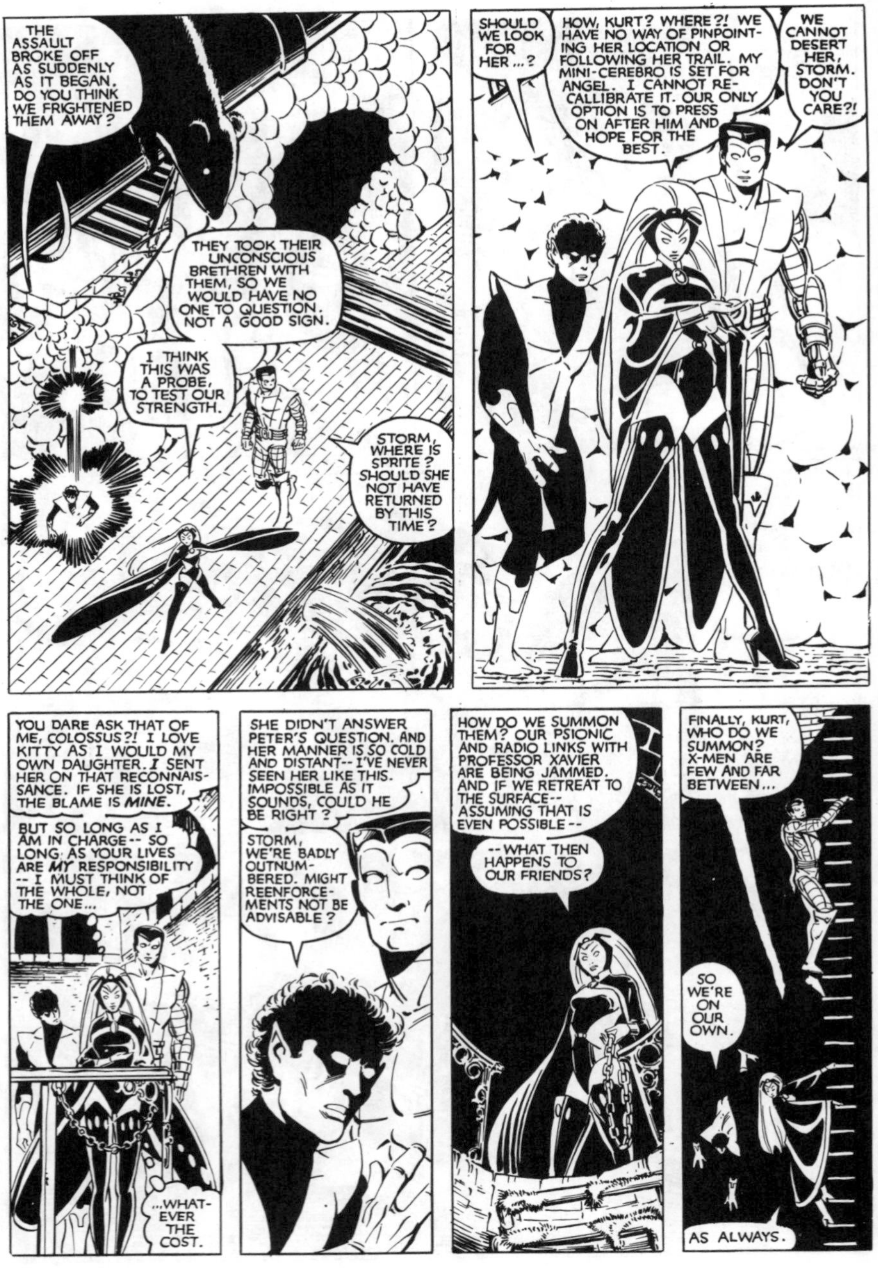
THE ASSAULT BROKE OFF AS SUDDENLY AS IT BEGAN. DO YOU THINK WE FRIGHTENED THEM AWAY?
THEY TOOK THEIR UNCONSCIOUS BRETHREN WITH THEM, SO WE WOULD HAVE NO ONE TO QUESTION. NOT A GOOD SIGN.
I THINK THIS WAS A PROBE, TO TEST OUR STRENGTH.
STORM, WHERE IS SPRITE? SHOULD SHE NOT HAVE RETURNED BY THIS TIME?
SHOULD WE LOOK FOR HER...?
HOW, KURT? WHERE?! WE HAVE NO WAY OF PINPOINTING HER LOCATION OR FOLLOWING HER TRAIL. MY MINI-CEREBRO IS SET FOR ANGEL. I CANNOT RECALLIBRATE IT. OUR ONLY OPTION IS TO PRESS ON AFTER HIM AND HOPE FOR THE BEST.
WE CANNOT DESERT HER, STORM. DON'T YOU CARE?!
YOU DARE ASK THAT OF ME, COLOSSUS?! I LOVE KITTY AS I WOULD MY OWN DAUGHTER. I SENT HER ON THAT RECONNAISSANCE. IF SHE IS LOST, THE BLAME IS MINE.
BUT SO LONG AS I AM IN CHARGE-- SO LONG AS YOUR LIVES ARE MY RESPONSIBILITY -- I MUST THINK OF THE WHOLE, NOT THE ONE...
...WHATEVER THE COST.
SHE DIDN'T ANSWER PETER'S QUESTION. AND HER MANNER IS SO COLD AND DISTANT-- I'VE NEVER SEEN HER LIKE THIS. IMPOSSIBLE AS IT SOUNDS, COULD HE BE RIGHT?
STORM, WE'RE BADLY OUTNUMBERED. MIGHT REENFORCEMENTS NOT BE ADVISABLE?
HOW DO WE SUMMON THEM? OUR PSIONIC AND RADIO LINKS WITH PROFESSOR XAVIER ARE BEING JAMMED. AND IF WE RETREAT TO THE SURFACE-- ASSUMING THAT IS EVEN POSSIBLE--
--WHAT THEN HAPPENS TO OUR FRIENDS?
FINALLY, KURT, WHO DO WE SUMMON? X-MEN ARE FEW AND FAR BETWEEN...
SO WE'RE ON OUR OWN.
AS ALWAYS.

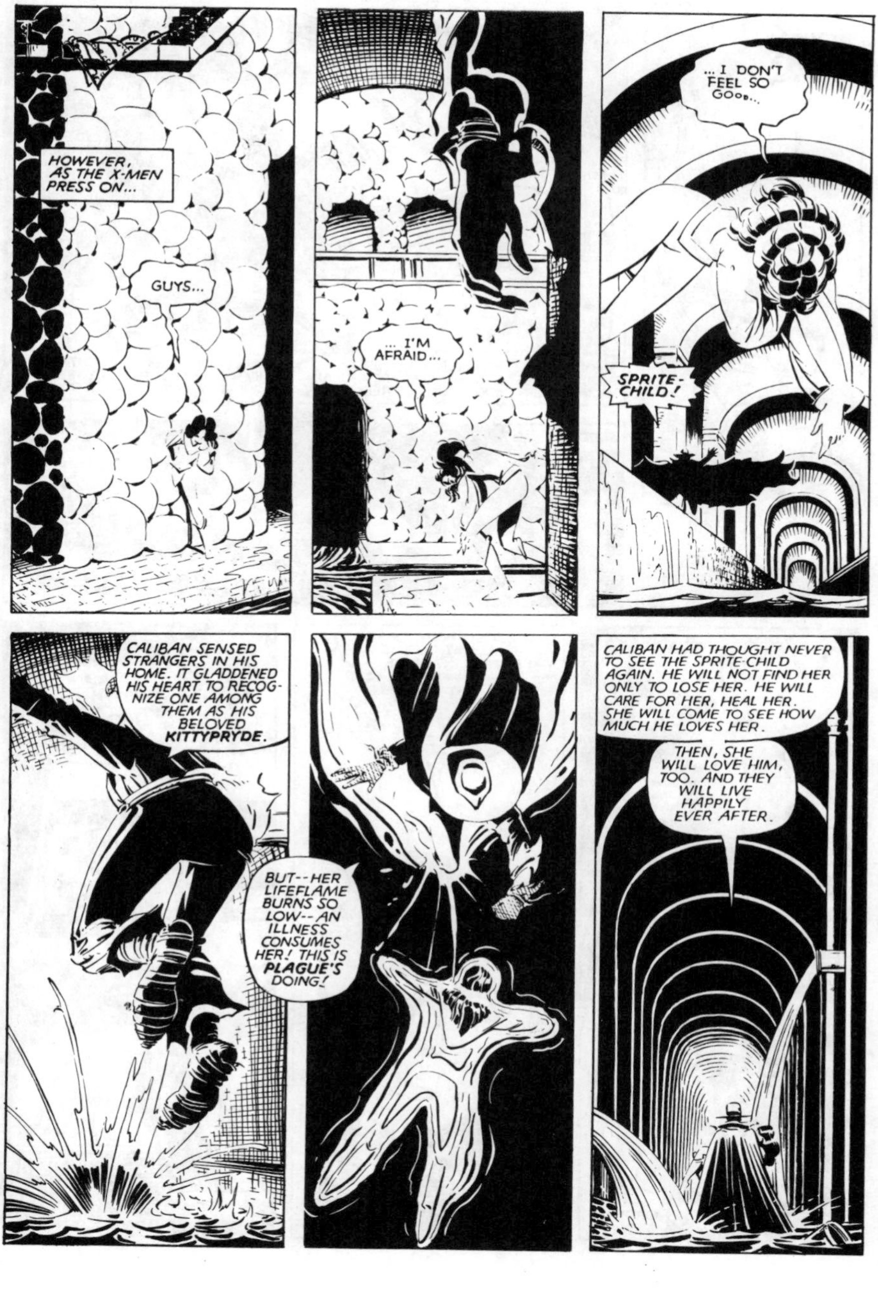
HOWEVER, AS THE X-MEN PRESS ON...
GUYS...
... I'M AFRAID...
... I DON'T FEEL SO GOOD...
SPRITE-CHILD!
CALIBAN SENSED STRANGERS IN HIS HOME. IT GLADDENED HIS HEART TO RECOGNIZE ONE AMONG THEM AS HIS BELOVED KITTYPRYDE.
BUT--HER LIFEFLAME BURNS SO LOW--AN ILLNESS CONSUMES HER! THIS IS PLAGUE'S DOING!
CALIBAN HAD THOUGHT NEVER TO SEE THE SPRITE-CHILD AGAIN. HE WILL NOT FIND HER ONLY TO LOSE HER. HE WILL CARE FOR HER, HEAL HER. SHE WILL COME TO SEE HOW MUCH HE LOVES HER.
THEN, SHE WILL LOVE HIM, TOO. AND THEY WILL LIVE HAPPILY EVER AFTER.

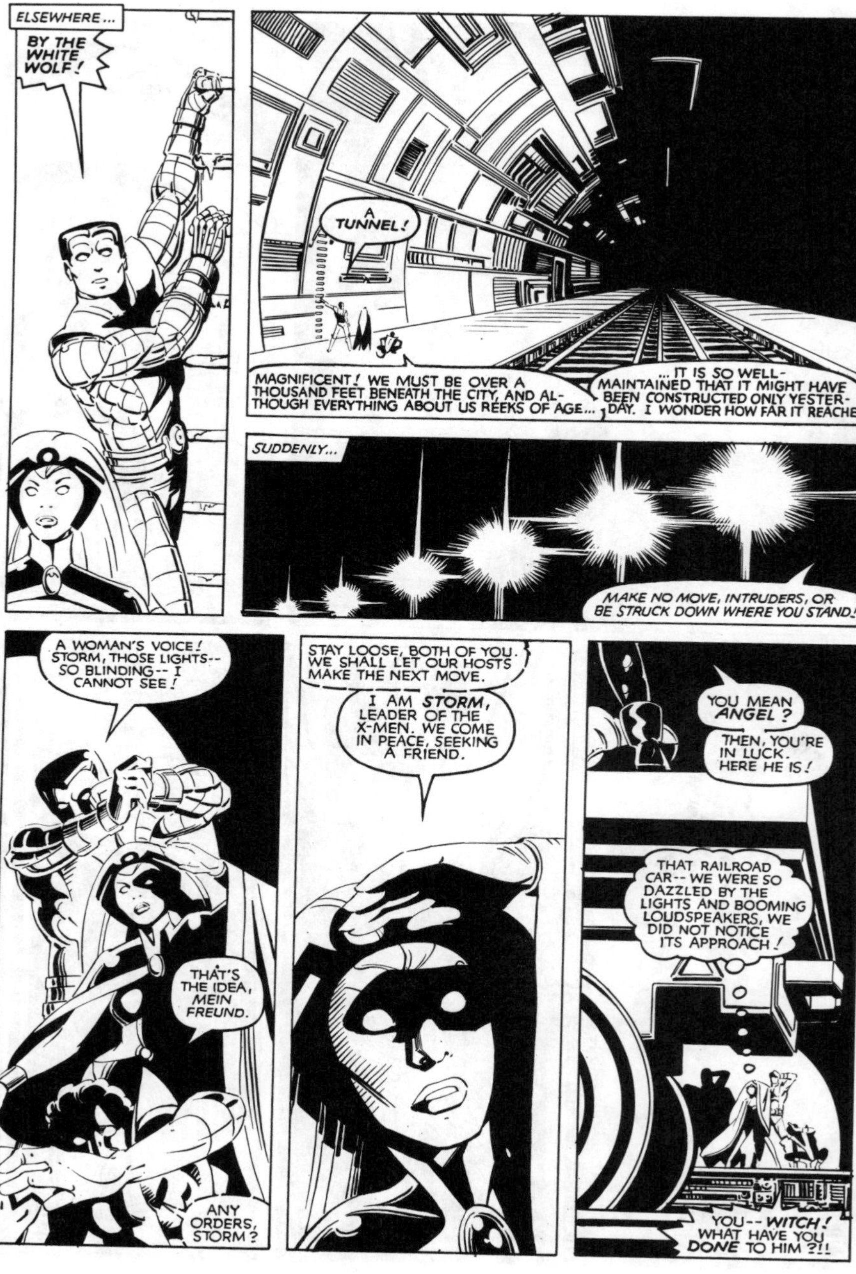

ELSEWHERE...
BY THE WHITE WOLF!
A TUNNEL!
MAGNIFICENT! WE MUST BE OVER A THOUSAND FEET BENEATH THE CITY, AND ALTHOUGH EVERYTHING ABOUT US REEKS OF AGE...
... IT IS SO WELL-MAINTAINED THAT IT MIGHT HAVE BEEN CONSTRUCTED ONLY YESTERDAY. I WONDER HOW FAR IT REACHES.
SUDDENLY...
MAKE NO MOVE, INTRUDERS, OR BE STRUCK DOWN WHERE YOU STAND!
A WOMAN'S VOICE! STORM, THOSE LIGHTS-- SO BLINDING-- I CANNOT SEE!
THAT'S THE IDEA, MEIN FREUND.
ANY ORDERS, STORM?
STAY LOOSE, BOTH OF YOU. WE SHALL LET OUR HOSTS MAKE THE NEXT MOVE.
I AM STORM, LEADER OF THE X-MEN. WE COME IN PEACE, SEEKING A FRIEND.
YOU MEAN ANGEL?
THEN, YOU'RE IN LUCK. HERE HE IS!
THAT RAILROAD CAR-- WE WERE SO DAZZLED BY THE LIGHTS AND BOOMING LOUDSPEAKERS, WE DID NOT NOTICE ITS APPROACH!
YOU-- WITCH! WHAT HAVE YOU DONE TO HIM?!!

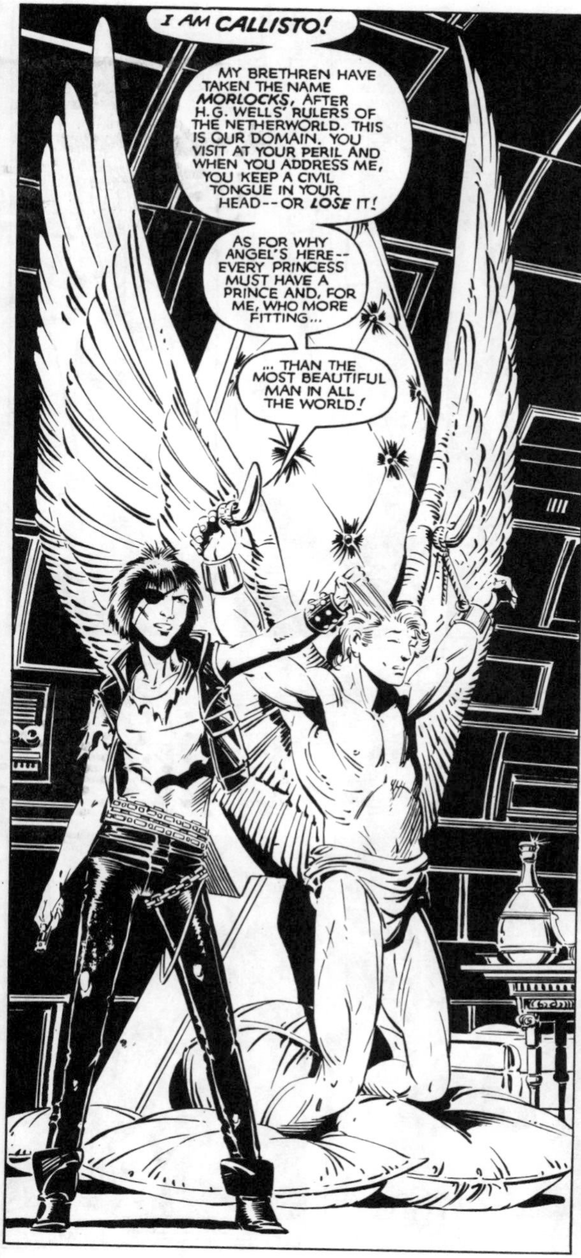
I AM CALLISTO!
MY BRETHREN HAVE TAKEN THE NAME MORLOCKS, AFTER H.G. WELLS' RULERS OF THE NETHERWORLD. THIS IS OUR DOMAIN. YOU VISIT AT YOUR PERIL AND WHEN YOU ADDRESS ME, YOU KEEP A CIVIL TONGUE IN YOUR HEAD--OR LOSE IT!
AS FOR WHY ANGEL'S HERE--EVERY PRINCESS MUST HAVE A PRINCE AND, FOR ME, WHO MORE FITTING...
... THAN THE MOST BEAUTIFUL MAN IN ALL THE WORLD!

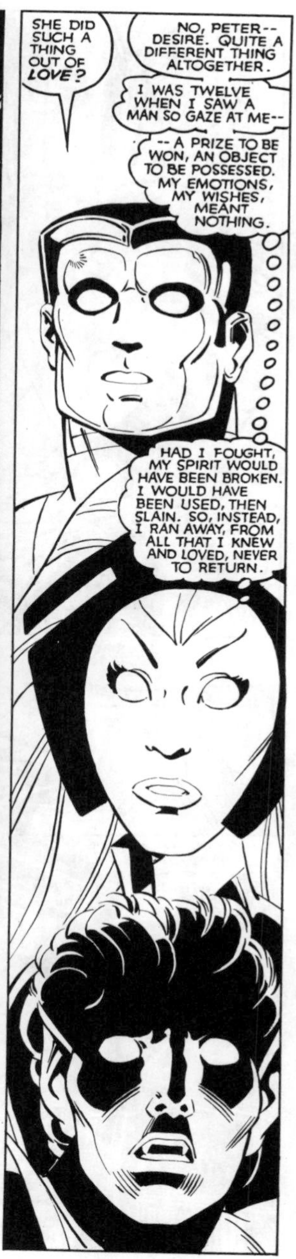
SHE DID SUCH A THING OUT OF LOVE?
NO, PETER--DESIRE. QUITE A DIFFERENT THING ALTOGETHER.
I WAS TWELVE WHEN I SAW A MAN SO GAZE AT ME--
--A PRIZE TO BE WON, AN OBJECT TO BE POSSESSED. MY EMOTIONS, MY WISHES, MEANT NOTHING.
HAD I FOUGHT, MY SPIRIT WOULD HAVE BEEN BROKEN. I WOULD HAVE BEEN USED, THEN SLAIN. SO, INSTEAD, I RAN AWAY, FROM ALL THAT I KNEW AND LOVED, NEVER TO RETURN.

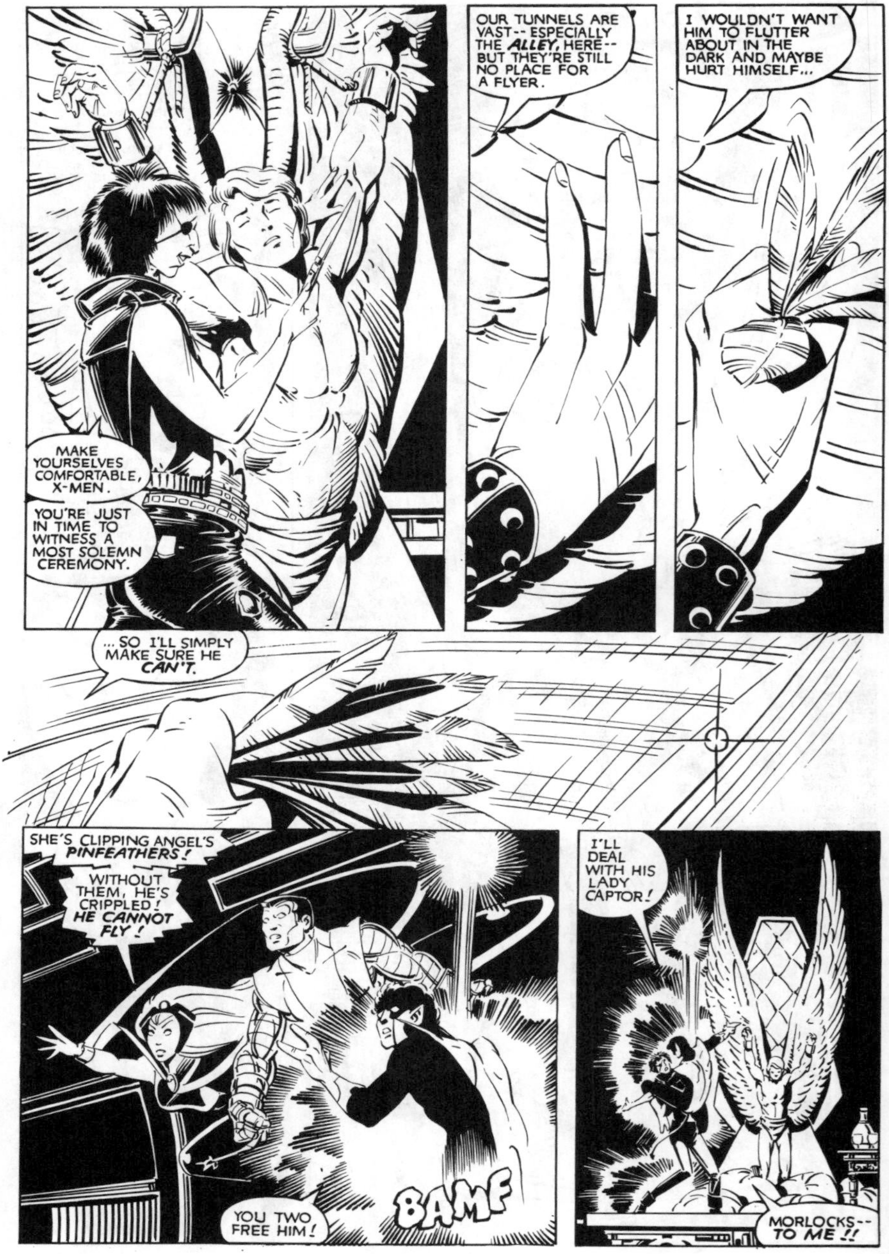
MAKE YOURSELVES COMFORTABLE, X-MEN.
YOU'RE JUST IN TIME TO WITNESS A MOST SOLEMN CEREMONY.
OUR TUNNELS ARE VAST-- ESPECIALLY THE ALLEY, HERE-- BUT THEY'RE STILL NO PLACE FOR A FLYER.
I WOULDN'T WANT HIM TO FLUTTER ABOUT IN THE DARK AND MAYBE HURT HIMSELF...
...SO I'LL SIMPLY MAKE SURE HE CAN'T.
SHE'S CLIPPING ANGEL'S PINFEATHERS!
WITHOUT THEM, HE'S CRIPPLED! HE CANNOT FLY!
YOU TWO FREE HIM!
BAMF
I'LL DEAL WITH HIS LADY CAPTOR!
MORLOCKS-- TO ME!!

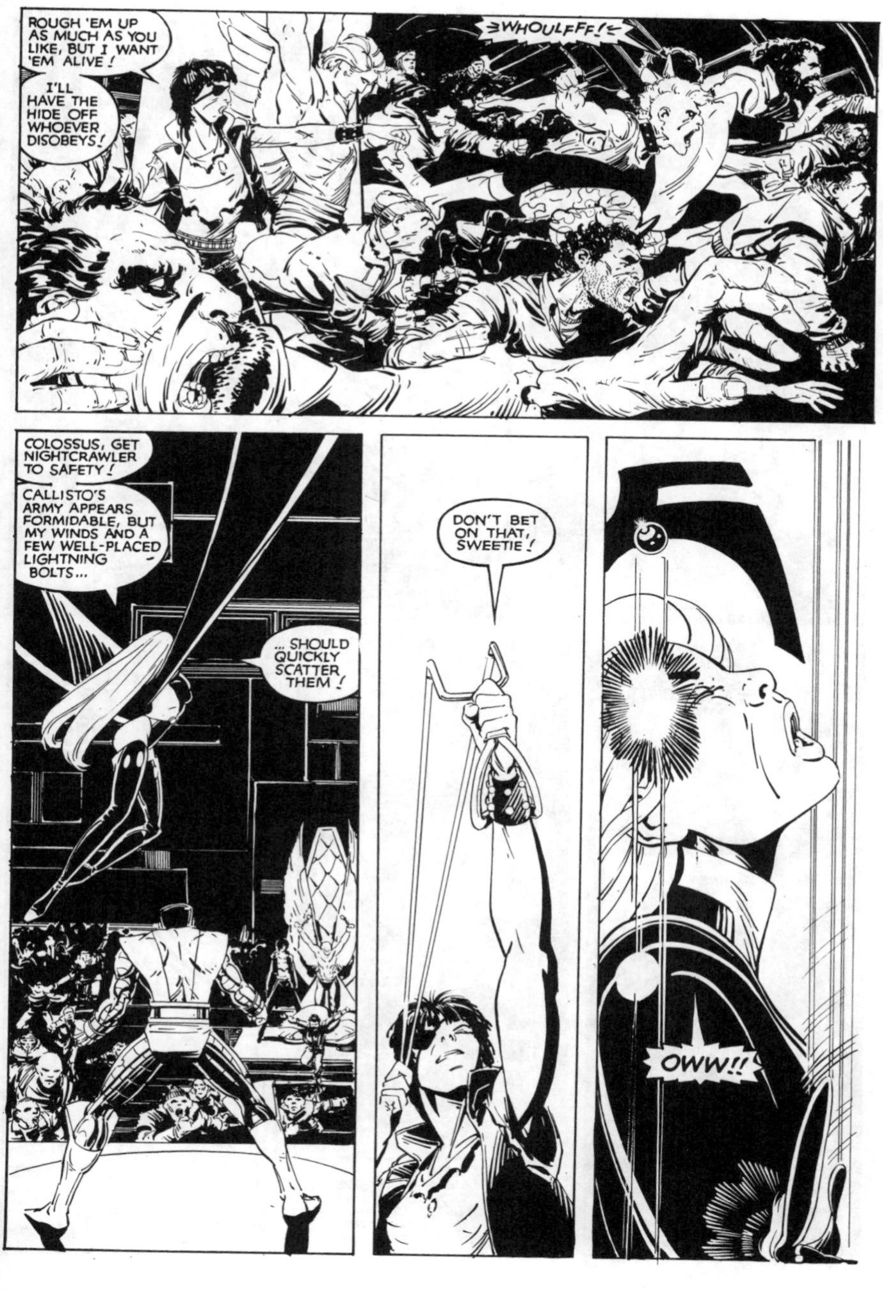
ROUGH 'EM UP AS MUCH AS YOU LIKE, BUT I WANT 'EM ALIVE!
I'LL HAVE THE HIDE OFF WHOEVER DISOBEYS!
WHOULFFF!
COLOSSUS, GET NIGHTCRAWLER TO SAFETY!
CALLISTO'S ARMY APPEARS FORMIDABLE, BUT MY WINDS AND A FEW WELL-PLACED LIGHTNING BOLTS...
...SHOULD QUICKLY SCATTER THEM!
DON'T BET ON THAT, SWEETIE!
OWW!!

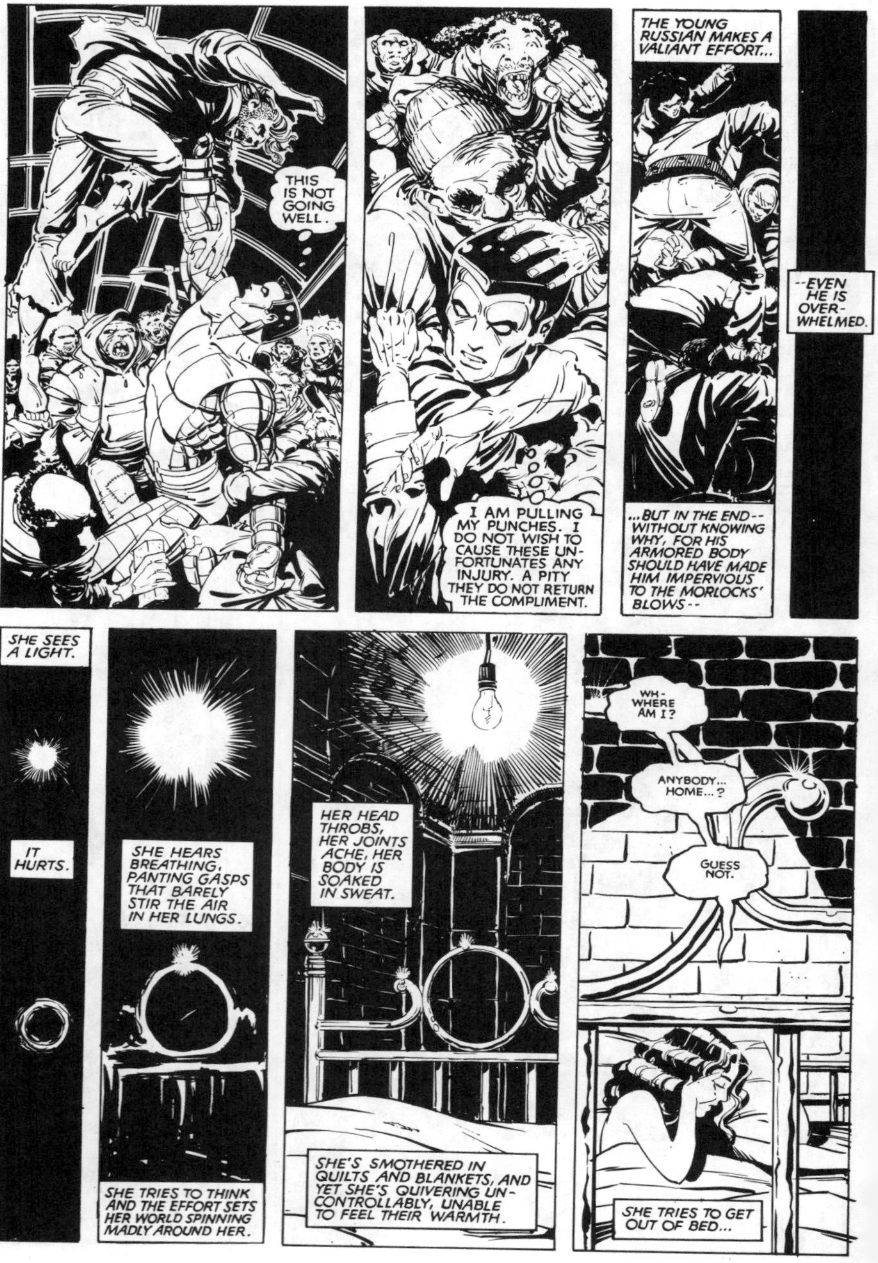
THIS IS NOT GOING WELL.
I AM PULLING MY PUNCHES. I DO NOT WISH TO CAUSE THESE UNFORTUNATES ANY INJURY. A PITY THEY DO NOT RETURN THE COMPLIMENT.
THE YOUNG RUSSIAN MAKES A VALIANT EFFORT...
...BUT IN THE END--WITHOUT KNOWING WHY, FOR HIS ARMORED BODY SHOULD HAVE MADE HIM IMPERVIOUS TO THE MORLOCKS' BLOWS--
--EVEN HE IS OVERWHELMED.
SHE SEES A LIGHT.
IT HURTS.
SHE HEARS BREATHING, PANTING GASPS THAT BARELY STIR THE AIR IN HER LUNGS.
SHE TRIES TO THINK AND THE EFFORT SETS HER WORLD SPINNING MADLY AROUND HER.
HER HEAD THROBS, HER JOINTS ACHE, HER BODY IS SOAKED IN SWEAT.
SHE'S SMOTHERED IN QUILTS AND BLANKETS, AND YET SHE'S QUIVERING UNCONTROLLABLY, UNABLE TO FEEL THEIR WARMTH.
WH-WHERE AM I?
ANYBODY... HOME...?
GUESS NOT.
...
SHE TRIES TO GET OUT OF BED...

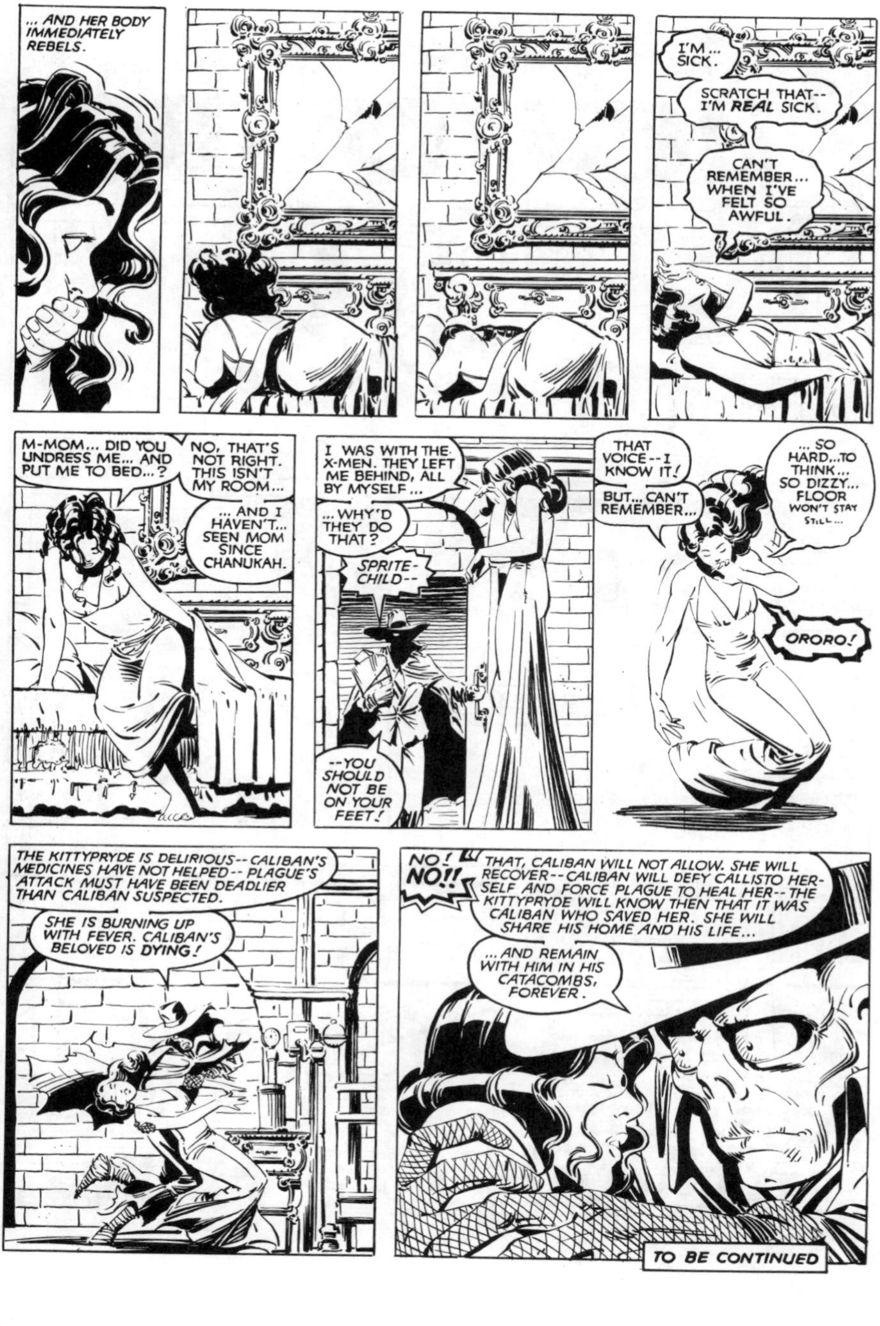

... AND HER BODY IMMEDIATELY REBELS.
I'M... SICK.
SCRATCH THAT-- I'M REAL SICK.
CAN'T REMEMBER... WHEN I'VE FELT SO AWFUL.
M-MOM... DID YOU UNDRESS ME... AND PUT ME TO BED...?
NO, THAT'S NOT RIGHT. THIS ISN'T MY ROOM...
... AND I HAVEN'T... SEEN MOM SINCE CHANUKAH.
I WAS WITH THE X-MEN. THEY LEFT ME BEHIND, ALL BY MYSELF...
... WHY'D THEY DO THAT?
SPRITE-CHILD--
--YOU SHOULD NOT BE ON YOUR FEET!
THAT VOICE--I KNOW IT!
BUT... CAN'T REMEMBER...
... SO HARD...TO THINK... SO DIZZY... FLOOR WON'T STAY STILL...
ORORO!
THE KITTYPRYDE IS DELIRIOUS--CALIBAN'S MEDICINES HAVE NOT HELPED--PLAGUE'S ATTACK MUST HAVE BEEN DEADLIER THAN CALIBAN SUSPECTED.
SHE IS BURNING UP WITH FEVER. CALIBAN'S BELOVED IS DYING!
NO! NO!!
THAT, CALIBAN WILL NOT ALLOW. SHE WILL RECOVER--CALIBAN WILL DEFY CALLISTO HERSELF AND FORCE PLAGUE TO HEAL HER--THE KITTYPRYDE WILL KNOW THEN THAT IT WAS CALIBAN WHO SAVED HER. SHE WILL SHARE HIS HOME AND HIS LIFE...
... AND REMAIN WITH HIM IN HIS CATACOMBS, FOREVER.
TO BE CONTINUED

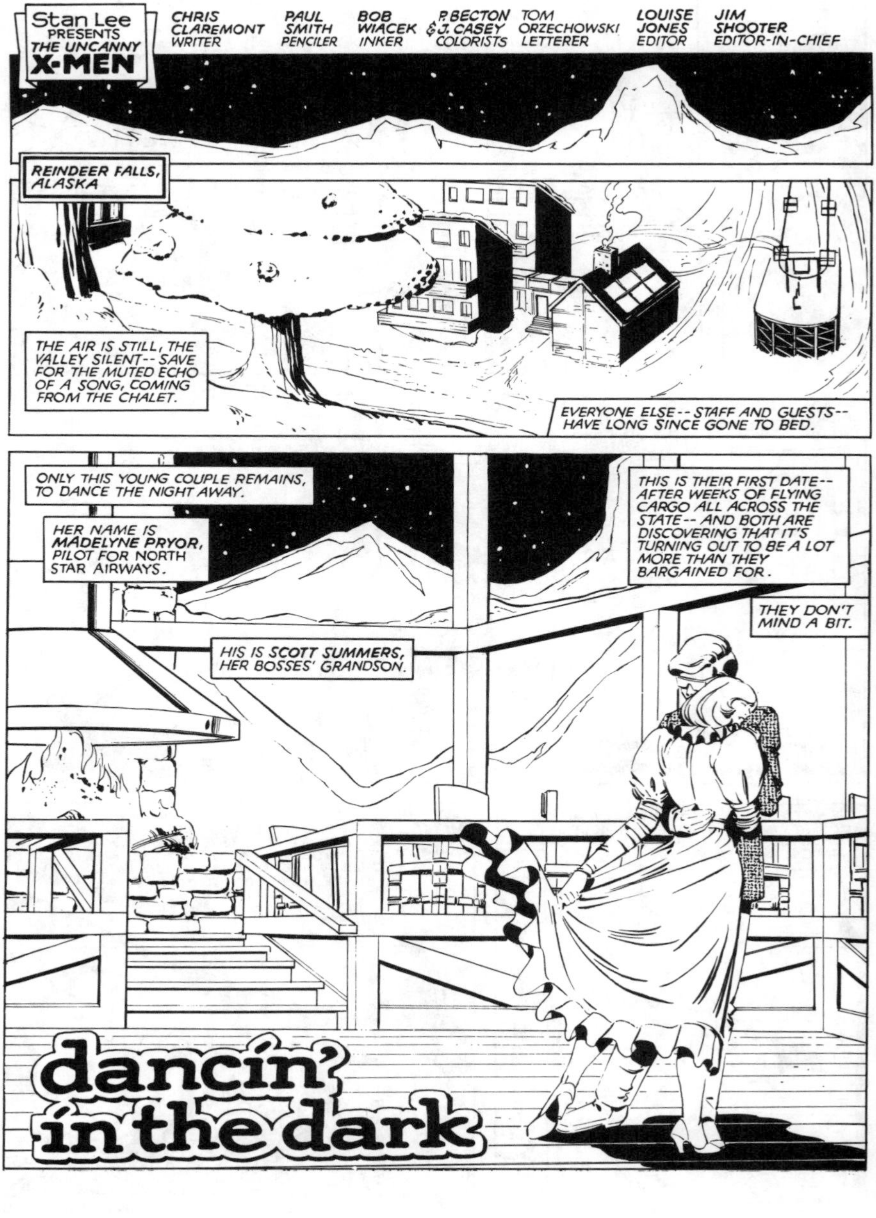
Stan Lee PRESENTS THE UNCANNY X-MEN
CHRIS CLAREMONT WRITER
PAUL SMITH PENCILER
BOB WIACEK INKER
P. BECTON & J. CASEY COLORISTS
TOM ORZECHOWSKI LETTERER
LOUISE JONES EDITOR
JIM SHOOTER EDITOR-IN-CHIEF
REINDEER FALLS, ALASKA
THE AIR IS STILL, THE VALLEY SILENT-- SAVE FOR THE MUTED ECHO OF A SONG, COMING FROM THE CHALET.
EVERYONE ELSE-- STAFF AND GUESTS-- HAVE LONG SINCE GONE TO BED.
ONLY THIS YOUNG COUPLE REMAINS, TO DANCE THE NIGHT AWAY.
HER NAME IS MADELYNE PRYOR, PILOT FOR NORTH STAR AIRWAYS.
THIS IS THEIR FIRST DATE-- AFTER WEEKS OF FLYING CARGO ALL ACROSS THE STATE-- AND BOTH ARE DISCOVERING THAT IT'S TURNING OUT TO BE A LOT MORE THAN THEY BARGAINED FOR.
THEY DON'T MIND A BIT.
HIS IS SCOTT SUMMERS, HER BOSSES' GRANDSON.
dancín' ín the dark

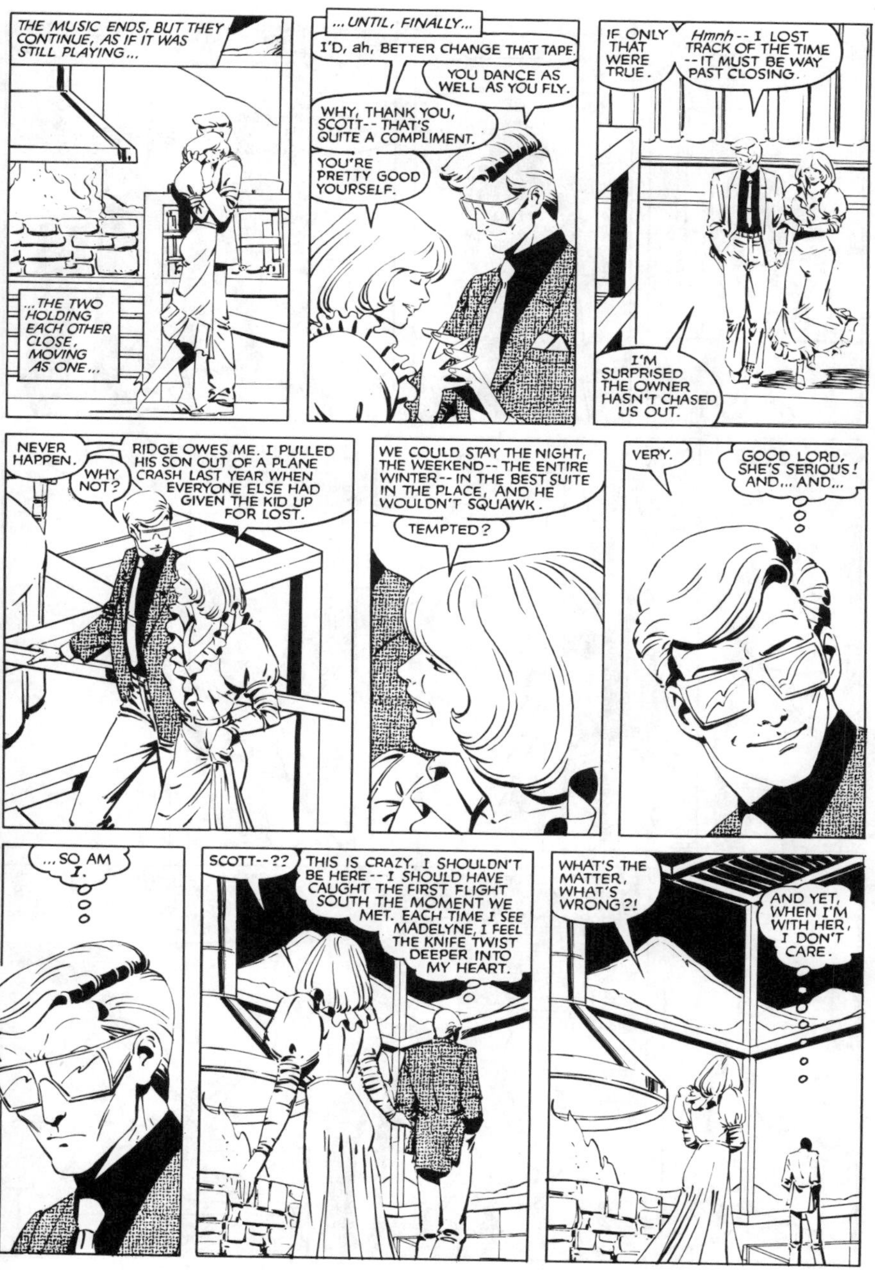
THE MUSIC ENDS, BUT THEY CONTINUE, AS IF IT WAS STILL PLAYING...
...THE TWO HOLDING EACH OTHER CLOSE, MOVING AS ONE...
...UNTIL, FINALLY...
I'D, ah, BETTER CHANGE THAT TAPE.
YOU DANCE AS WELL AS YOU FLY.
WHY, THANK YOU, SCOTT-- THAT'S QUITE A COMPLIMENT.
YOU'RE PRETTY GOOD YOURSELF.
IF ONLY THAT WERE TRUE.
Hmnh -- I LOST TRACK OF THE TIME -- IT MUST BE WAY PAST CLOSING.
I'M SURPRISED THE OWNER HASN'T CHASED US OUT.
NEVER HAPPEN.
WHY NOT?
RIDGE OWES ME. I PULLED HIS SON OUT OF A PLANE CRASH LAST YEAR WHEN EVERYONE ELSE HAD GIVEN THE KID UP FOR LOST.
WE COULD STAY THE NIGHT, THE WEEKEND-- THE ENTIRE WINTER-- IN THE BEST SUITE IN THE PLACE, AND HE WOULDN'T SQUAWK.
TEMPTED?
VERY.
GOOD LORD, SHE'S SERIOUS! AND... AND...
...SO AM I.
SCOTT--??
THIS IS CRAZY. I SHOULDN'T BE HERE-- I SHOULD HAVE CAUGHT THE FIRST FLIGHT SOUTH THE MOMENT WE MET. EACH TIME I SEE MADELYNE, I FEEL THE KNIFE TWIST DEEPER INTO MY HEART.
WHAT'S THE MATTER, WHAT'S WRONG?!
AND YET, WHEN I'M WITH HER, I DON'T CARE.

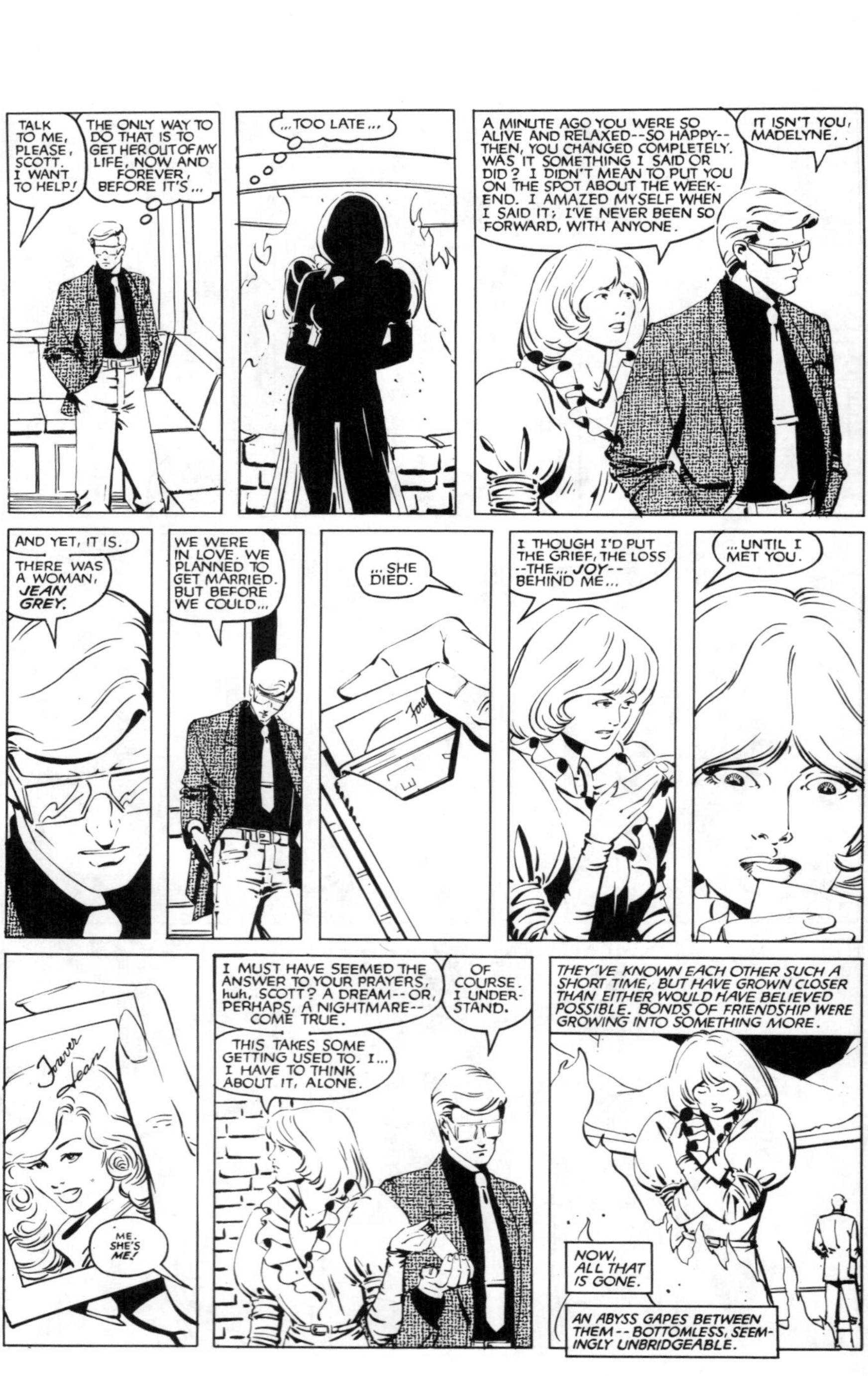
TALK TO ME, PLEASE, SCOTT. I WANT TO HELP!
THE ONLY WAY TO DO THAT IS TO GET HER OUT OF MY LIFE, NOW AND FOREVER, BEFORE IT'S...
...TOO LATE...
A MINUTE AGO YOU WERE SO ALIVE AND RELAXED--SO HAPPY--THEN, YOU CHANGED COMPLETELY. WAS IT SOMETHING I SAID OR DID? I DIDN'T MEAN TO PUT YOU ON THE SPOT ABOUT THE WEEK-END. I AMAZED MYSELF WHEN I SAID IT; I'VE NEVER BEEN SO FORWARD, WITH ANYONE.
IT ISN'T YOU, MADELYNE.
AND YET, IT IS.
THERE WAS A WOMAN, JEAN GREY.
WE WERE IN LOVE. WE PLANNED TO GET MARRIED. BUT BEFORE WE COULD...
...SHE DIED.
I THOUGH I'D PUT THE GRIEF, THE LOSS --THE... JOY-- BEHIND ME...
...UNTIL I MET YOU.
Forever Jean
ME. SHE'S ME!
I MUST HAVE SEEMED THE ANSWER TO YOUR PRAYERS, huh, SCOTT? A DREAM--OR, PERHAPS, A NIGHTMARE--COME TRUE.
OF COURSE. I UNDER-STAND.
THIS TAKES SOME GETTING USED TO. I... I HAVE TO THINK ABOUT IT, ALONE.
THEY'VE KNOWN EACH OTHER SUCH A SHORT TIME, BUT HAVE GROWN CLOSER THAN EITHER WOULD HAVE BELIEVED POSSIBLE. BONDS OF FRIENDSHIP WERE GROWING INTO SOMETHING MORE.
NOW, ALL THAT IS GONE.
AN ABYSS GAPES BETWEEN THEM--BOTTOMLESS, SEEM-INGLY UNBRIDGEABLE.

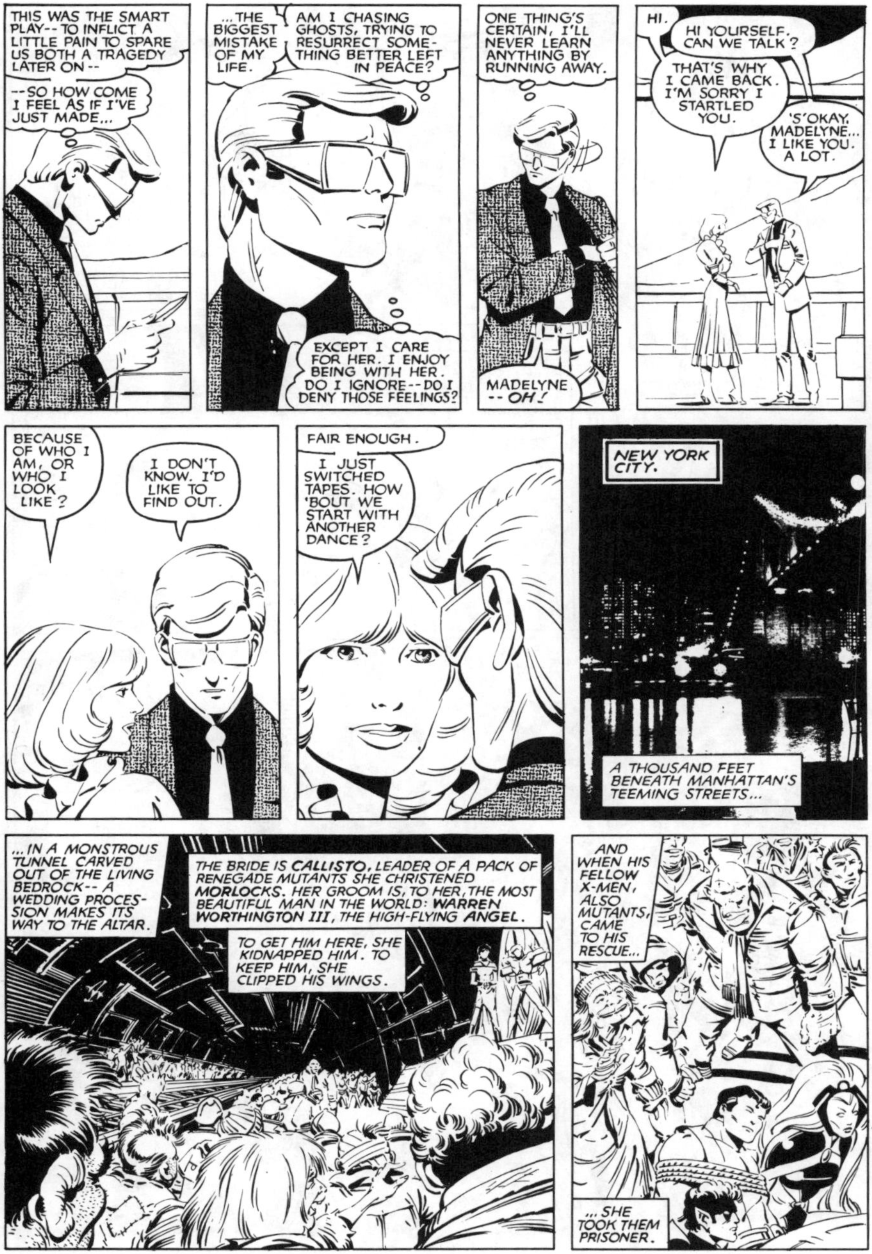
THIS WAS THE SMART PLAY-- TO INFLICT A LITTLE PAIN TO SPARE US BOTH A TRAGEDY LATER ON--
--SO HOW COME I FEEL AS IF I'VE JUST MADE...
...THE BIGGEST MISTAKE OF MY LIFE.
AM I CHASING GHOSTS, TRYING TO RESURRECT SOMETHING BETTER LEFT IN PEACE?
EXCEPT I CARE FOR HER. I ENJOY BEING WITH HER. DO I IGNORE--DO I DENY THOSE FEELINGS?
ONE THING'S CERTAIN, I'LL NEVER LEARN ANYTHING BY RUNNING AWAY.
MADELYNE --OH!
HI.
HI YOURSELF. CAN WE TALK?
THAT'S WHY I CAME BACK. I'M SORRY I STARTLED YOU.
'S'OKAY, MADELYNE... I LIKE YOU. A LOT.
BECAUSE OF WHO I AM, OR WHO I LOOK LIKE?
I DON'T KNOW. I'D LIKE TO FIND OUT.
FAIR ENOUGH.
I JUST SWITCHED TAPES. HOW 'BOUT WE START WITH ANOTHER DANCE?
NEW YORK CITY.
A THOUSAND FEET BENEATH MANHATTAN'S TEEMING STREETS...
...IN A MONSTROUS TUNNEL CARVED OUT OF THE LIVING BEDROCK-- A WEDDING PROCESSION MAKES ITS WAY TO THE ALTAR.
THE BRIDE IS CALLISTO, LEADER OF A PACK OF RENEGADE MUTANTS SHE CHRISTENED MORLOCKS. HER GROOM IS, TO HER, THE MOST BEAUTIFUL MAN IN THE WORLD: WARREN WORTHINGTON III, THE HIGH-FLYING ANGEL.
TO GET HIM HERE, SHE KIDNAPPED HIM. TO KEEP HIM, SHE CLIPPED HIS WINGS.
AND WHEN HIS FELLOW X-MEN, ALSO MUTANTS, CAME TO HIS RESCUE...
...SHE TOOK THEM PRISONER.

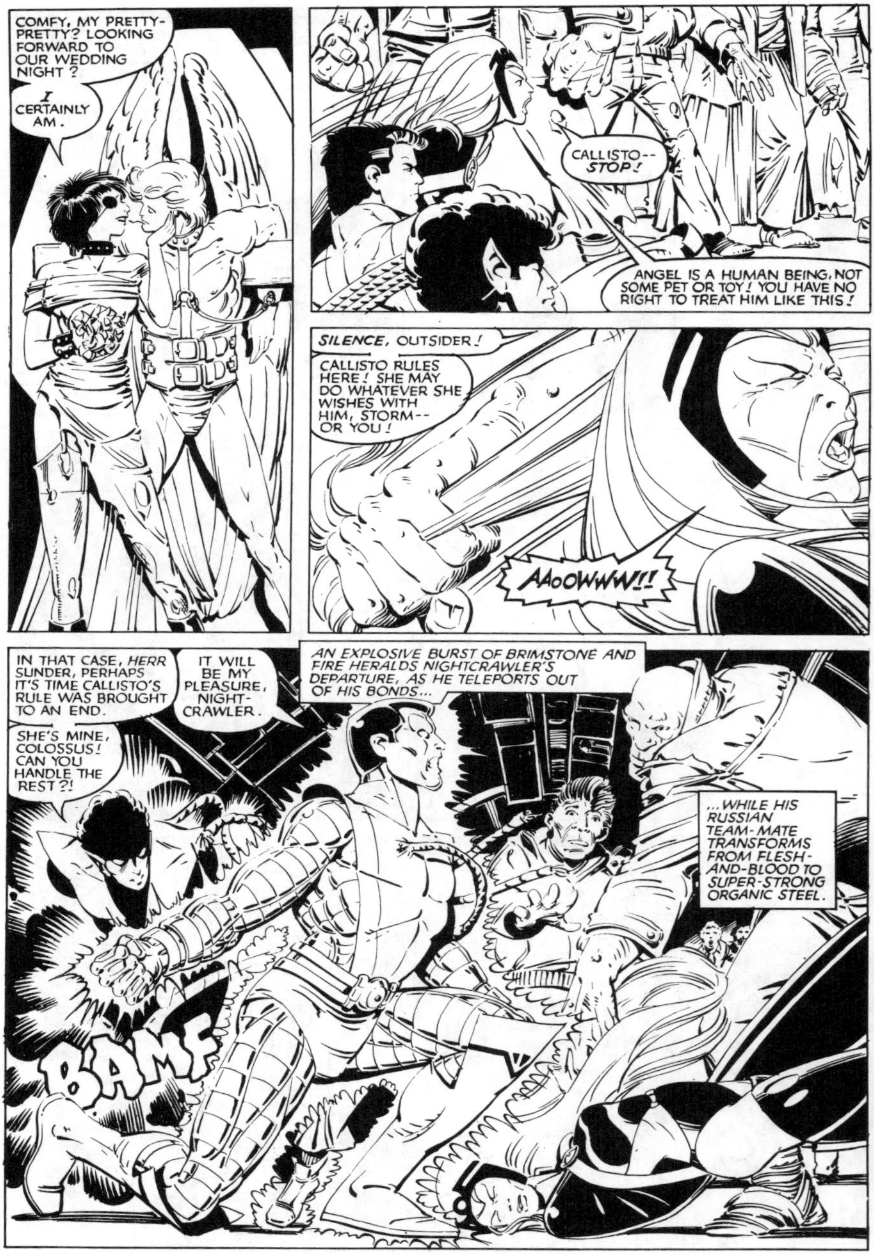
COMFY, MY PRETTY-PRETTY? LOOKING FORWARD TO OUR WEDDING NIGHT?
I CERTAINLY AM.
CALLISTO-- STOP!
ANGEL IS A HUMAN BEING, NOT SOME PET OR TOY! YOU HAVE NO RIGHT TO TREAT HIM LIKE THIS!
SILENCE, OUTSIDER!
CALLISTO RULES HERE! SHE MAY DO WHATEVER SHE WISHES WITH HIM, STORM-- OR YOU!
AAOOWWW!!
IN THAT CASE, HERR SUNDER, PERHAPS IT'S TIME CALLISTO'S RULE WAS BROUGHT TO AN END.
IT WILL BE MY PLEASURE, NIGHT-CRAWLER.
SHE'S MINE, COLOSSUS! CAN YOU HANDLE THE REST?!
AN EXPLOSIVE BURST OF BRIMSTONE AND FIRE HERALDS NIGHTCRAWLER'S DEPARTURE, AS HE TELEPORTS OUT OF HIS BONDS...
...WHILE HIS RUSSIAN TEAM-MATE TRANSFORMS FROM FLESH-AND-BLOOD TO SUPER-STRONG ORGANIC STEEL.
BAMF

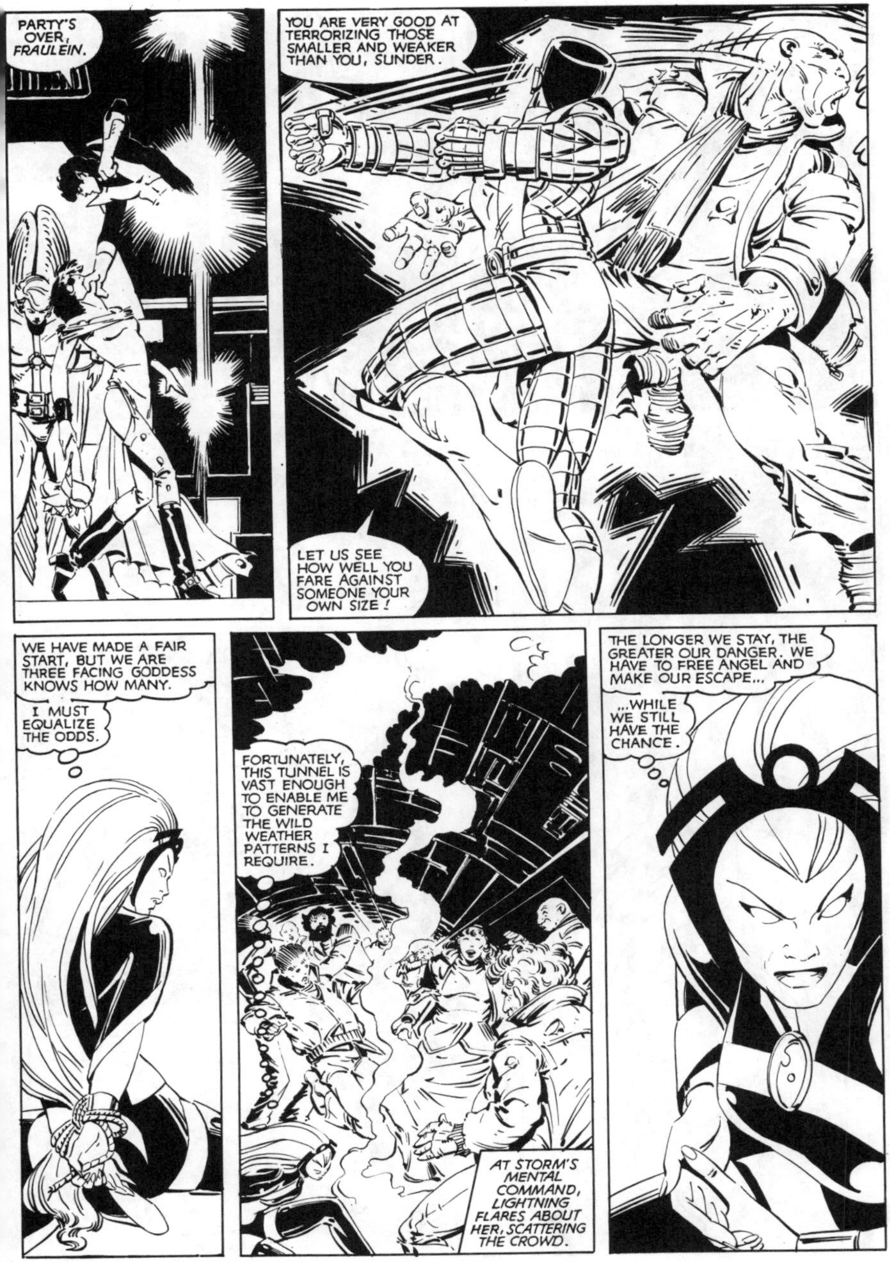
PARTY'S OVER, FRAULEIN.
YOU ARE VERY GOOD AT TERRORIZING THOSE SMALLER AND WEAKER THAN YOU, SUNDER.
LET US SEE HOW WELL YOU FARE AGAINST SOMEONE YOUR OWN SIZE!
WE HAVE MADE A FAIR START, BUT WE ARE THREE FACING GODDESS KNOWS HOW MANY.
I MUST EQUALIZE THE ODDS.
FORTUNATELY, THIS TUNNEL IS VAST ENOUGH TO ENABLE ME TO GENERATE THE WILD WEATHER PATTERNS I REQUIRE.
AT STORM'S MENTAL COMMAND, LIGHTNING FLARES ABOUT HER, SCATTERING THE CROWD.
THE LONGER WE STAY, THE GREATER OUR DANGER. WE HAVE TO FREE ANGEL AND MAKE OUR ESCAPE...
...WHILE WE STILL HAVE THE CHANCE.

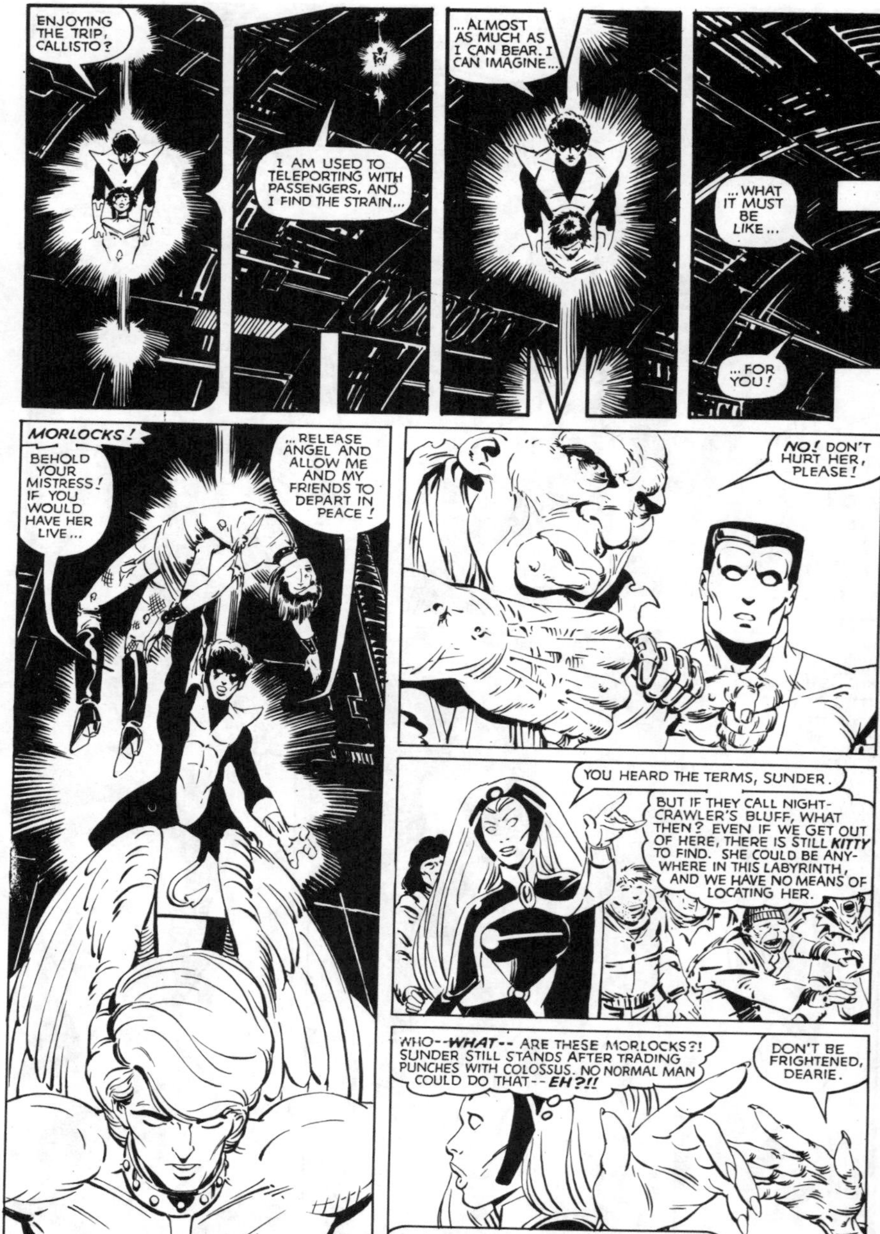
ENJOYING THE TRIP, CALLISTO?
I AM USED TO TELEPORTING WITH PASSENGERS, AND I FIND THE STRAIN...
...ALMOST AS MUCH AS I CAN BEAR. I CAN IMAGINE...
...WHAT IT MUST BE LIKE...
...FOR YOU!
BAMF
MORLOCKS!
BEHOLD YOUR MISTRESS! IF YOU WOULD HAVE HER LIVE...
...RELEASE ANGEL AND ALLOW ME AND MY FRIENDS TO DEPART IN PEACE!
NO! DON'T HURT HER, PLEASE!
YOU HEARD THE TERMS, SUNDER.
BUT IF THEY CALL NIGHT-CRAWLER'S BLUFF, WHAT THEN? EVEN IF WE GET OUT OF HERE, THERE IS STILL KITTY TO FIND. SHE COULD BE ANY-WHERE IN THIS LABYRINTH, AND WE HAVE NO MEANS OF LOCATING HER.
WHO--WHAT--ARE THESE MORLOCKS?! SUNDER STILL STANDS AFTER TRADING PUNCHES WITH COLOSSUS. NO NORMAL MAN COULD DO THAT--EH?!!
DON'T BE FRIGHTENED, DEARIE.
WHAT HARM COULD A LITTLE OLD LADY DO...

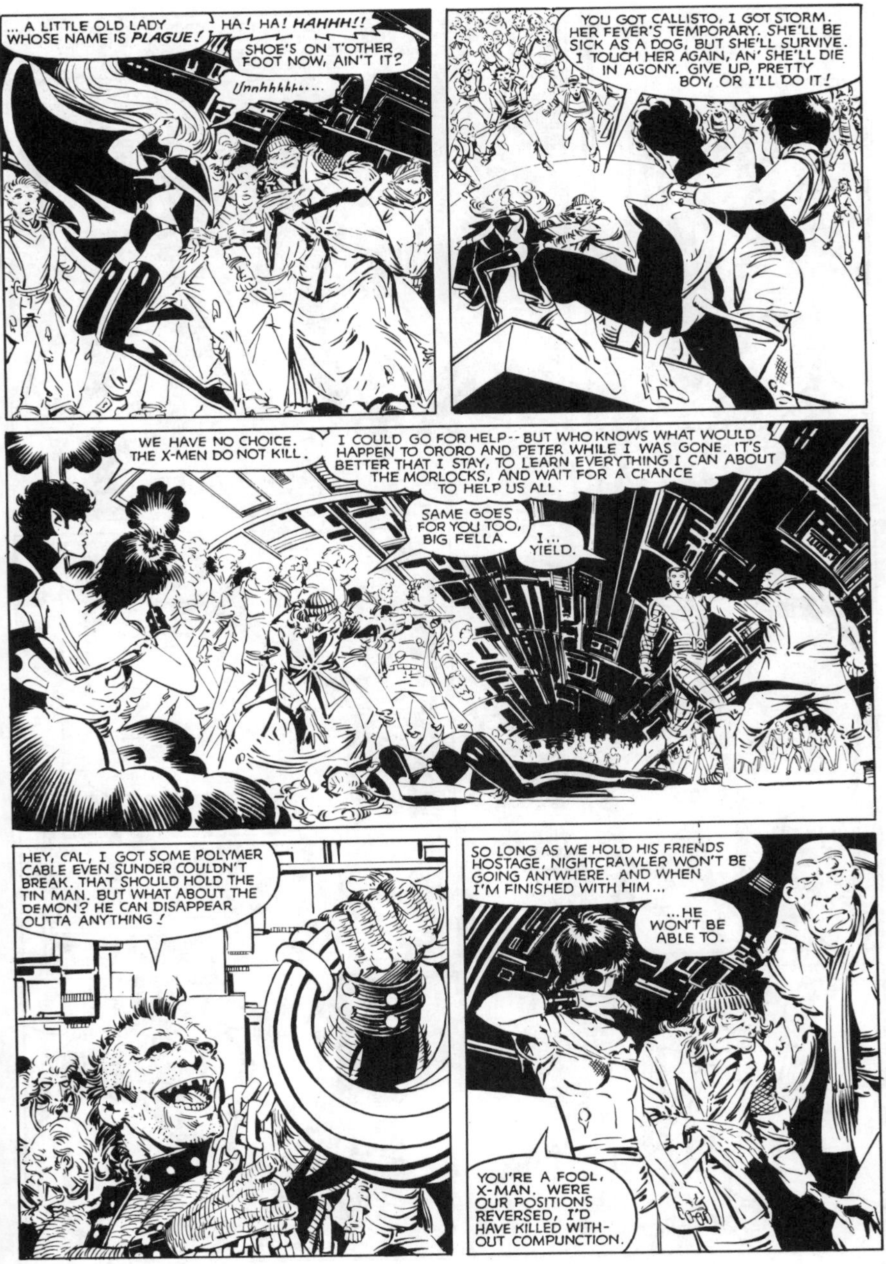

... A LITTLE OLD LADY WHOSE NAME IS *PLAGUE*!
HA! HA! *HAHHH!!*
SHOE'S ON T'OTHER FOOT NOW, AIN'T IT?
Unnhhhhhh....
YOU GOT CALLISTO, I GOT STORM. HER FEVER'S TEMPORARY. SHE'LL BE SICK AS A DOG, BUT SHE'LL SURVIVE. I TOUCH HER AGAIN, AN' SHE'LL DIE IN AGONY. GIVE UP, PRETTY BOY, OR I'LL DO IT!
WE HAVE NO CHOICE. THE X-MEN DO NOT KILL.
I COULD GO FOR HELP-- BUT WHO KNOWS WHAT WOULD HAPPEN TO ORORO AND PETER WHILE I WAS GONE. IT'S BETTER THAT I STAY, TO LEARN EVERYTHING I CAN ABOUT THE MORLOCKS, AND WAIT FOR A CHANCE TO HELP US ALL.
SAME GOES FOR YOU TOO, BIG FELLA.
I... YIELD.
HEY, CAL, I GOT SOME POLYMER CABLE EVEN SUNDER COULDN'T BREAK. THAT SHOULD HOLD THE TIN MAN. BUT WHAT ABOUT THE DEMON? HE CAN DISAPPEAR OUTTA ANYTHING!
SO LONG AS WE HOLD HIS FRIENDS HOSTAGE, NIGHTCRAWLER WON'T BE GOING ANYWHERE. AND WHEN I'M FINISHED WITH HIM...
...HE WON'T BE ABLE TO.
YOU'RE A FOOL, X-MAN. WERE OUR POSITIONS REVERSED, I'D HAVE KILLED WITH-OUT COMPUNCTION.

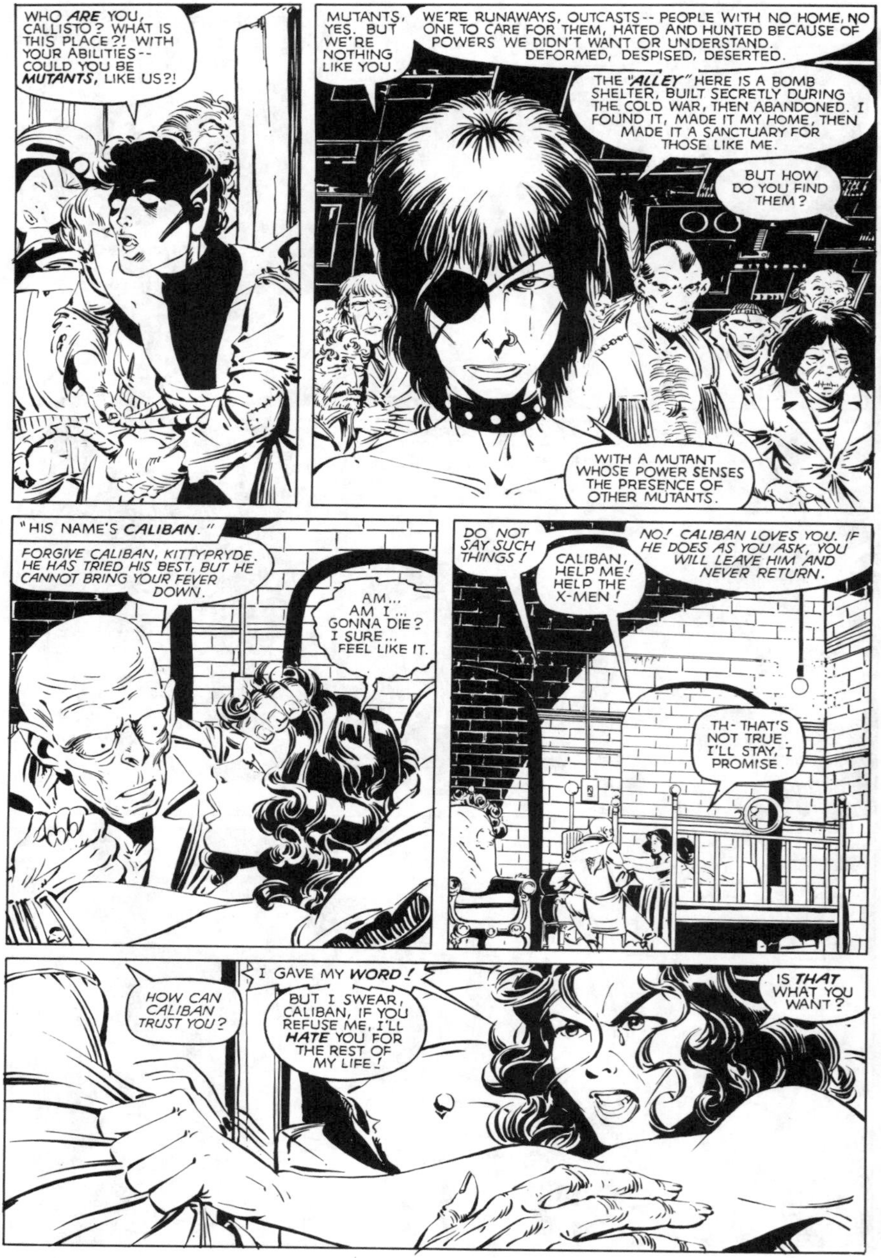
WHO ARE YOU, CALLISTO? WHAT IS THIS PLACE?! WITH YOUR ABILITIES-- COULD YOU BE MUTANTS, LIKE US?!
MUTANTS, YES. BUT WE'RE NOTHING LIKE YOU.
WE'RE RUNAWAYS, OUTCASTS-- PEOPLE WITH NO HOME, NO ONE TO CARE FOR THEM, HATED AND HUNTED BECAUSE OF POWERS WE DIDN'T WANT OR UNDERSTAND. DEFORMED, DESPISED, DESERTED.
THE "ALLEY" HERE IS A BOMB SHELTER, BUILT SECRETLY DURING THE COLD WAR, THEN ABANDONED. I FOUND IT, MADE IT MY HOME, THEN MADE IT A SANCTUARY FOR THOSE LIKE ME.
BUT HOW DO YOU FIND THEM?
WITH A MUTANT WHOSE POWER SENSES THE PRESENCE OF OTHER MUTANTS.
"HIS NAME'S CALIBAN."
FORGIVE CALIBAN, KITTYPRYDE. HE HAS TRIED HIS BEST, BUT HE CANNOT BRING YOUR FEVER DOWN.
AM... AM I... GONNA DIE? I SURE... FEEL LIKE IT.
DO NOT SAY SUCH THINGS!
CALIBAN, HELP ME! HELP THE X-MEN!
NO! CALIBAN LOVES YOU. IF HE DOES AS YOU ASK, YOU WILL LEAVE HIM AND NEVER RETURN.
TH- THAT'S NOT TRUE. I'LL STAY, I PROMISE.
HOW CAN CALIBAN TRUST YOU?
I GAVE MY WORD!
BUT I SWEAR, CALIBAN, IF YOU REFUSE ME, I'LL HATE YOU FOR THE REST OF MY LIFE!
IS THAT WHAT YOU WANT?

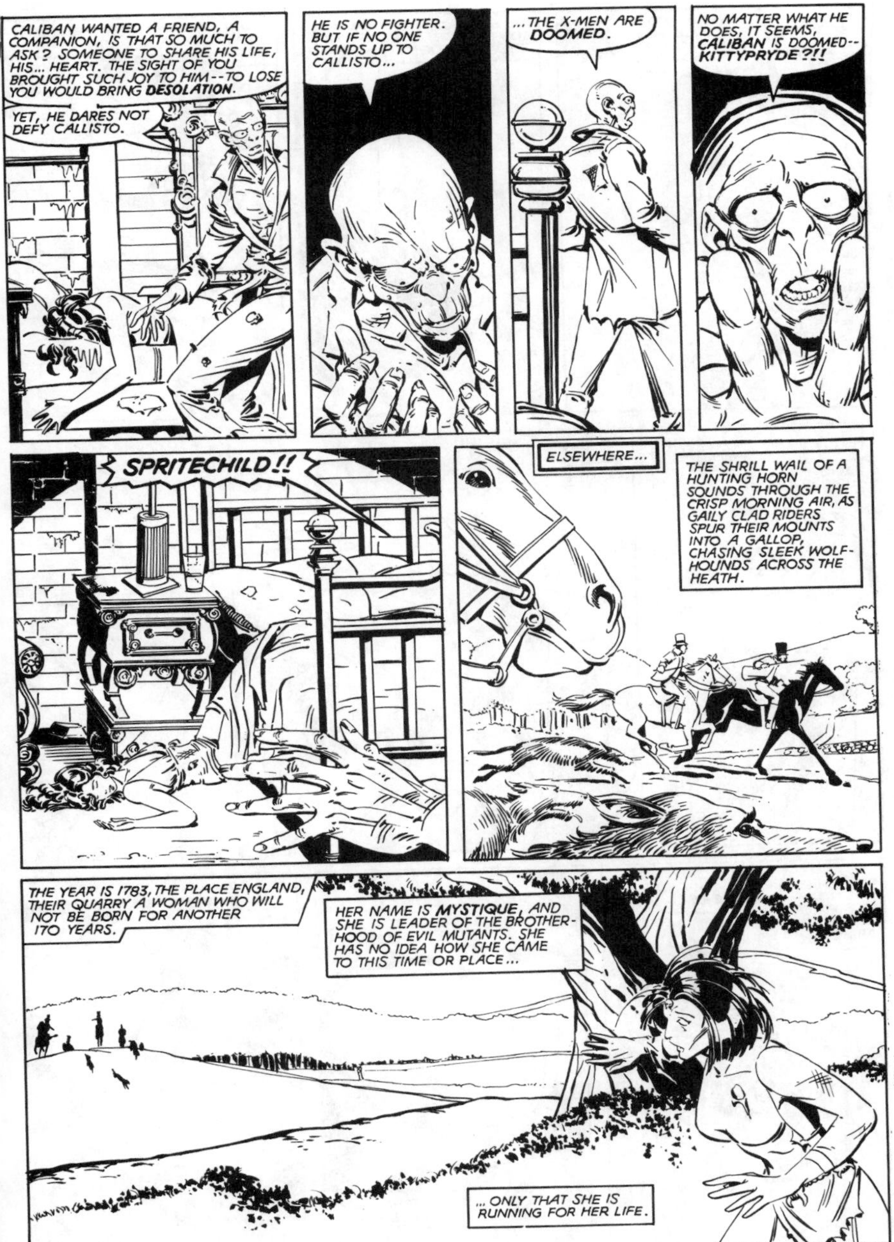
CALIBAN WANTED A FRIEND, A COMPANION, IS THAT SO MUCH TO ASK? SOMEONE TO SHARE HIS LIFE, HIS... HEART. THE SIGHT OF YOU BROUGHT SUCH JOY TO HIM--TO LOSE YOU WOULD BRING DESOLATION.
YET, HE DARES NOT DEFY CALLISTO.
HE IS NO FIGHTER. BUT IF NO ONE STANDS UP TO CALLISTO...
...THE X-MEN ARE DOOMED.
NO MATTER WHAT HE DOES, IT SEEMS, CALIBAN IS DOOMED--KITTYPRYDE?!!
SPRITECHILD!!
ELSEWHERE...
THE SHRILL WAIL OF A HUNTING HORN SOUNDS THROUGH THE CRISP MORNING AIR, AS GAILY CLAD RIDERS SPUR THEIR MOUNTS INTO A GALLOP, CHASING SLEEK WOLF-HOUNDS ACROSS THE HEATH.
THE YEAR IS 1783, THE PLACE ENGLAND, THEIR QUARRY A WOMAN WHO WILL NOT BE BORN FOR ANOTHER 170 YEARS.
HER NAME IS MYSTIQUE, AND SHE IS LEADER OF THE BROTHERHOOD OF EVIL MUTANTS. SHE HAS NO IDEA HOW SHE CAME TO THIS TIME OR PLACE...
...ONLY THAT SHE IS RUNNING FOR HER LIFE.

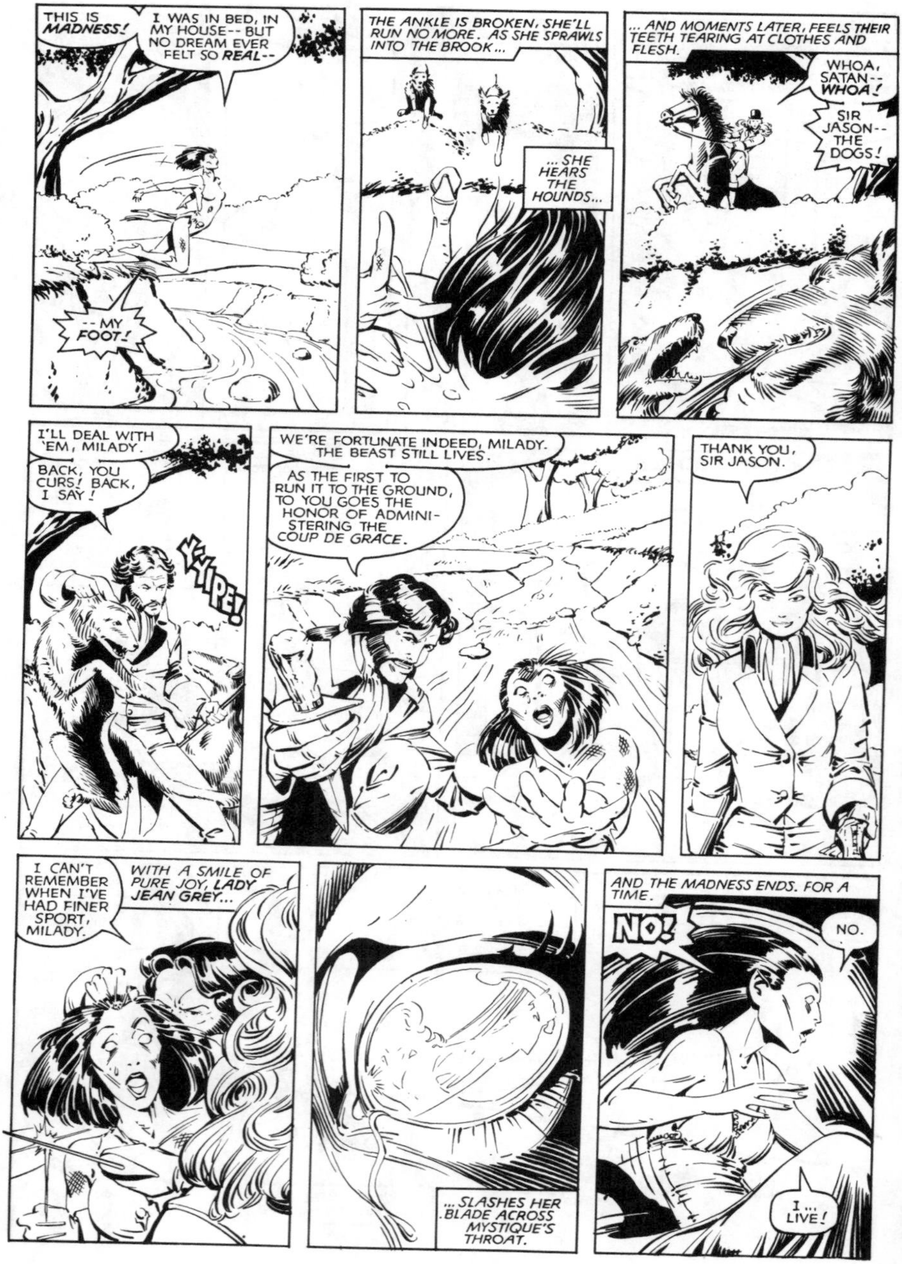
THIS IS MADNESS!
I WAS IN BED, IN MY HOUSE-- BUT NO DREAM EVER FELT SO REAL--
--MY FOOT!
THE ANKLE IS BROKEN, SHE'LL RUN NO MORE. AS SHE SPRAWLS INTO THE BROOK...
...SHE HEARS THE HOUNDS...
...AND MOMENTS LATER, FEELS THEIR TEETH TEARING AT CLOTHES AND FLESH.
WHOA, SATAN-- WHOA!
SIR JASON-- THE DOGS!
I'LL DEAL WITH 'EM, MILADY.
BACK, YOU CURS! BACK, I SAY!
YYIPE!
WE'RE FORTUNATE INDEED, MILADY. THE BEAST STILL LIVES.
AS THE FIRST TO RUN IT TO THE GROUND, TO YOU GOES THE HONOR OF ADMINI-STERING THE COUP DE GRACE.
THANK YOU, SIR JASON.
I CAN'T REMEMBER WHEN I'VE HAD FINER SPORT, MILADY.
WITH A SMILE OF PURE JOY, LADY JEAN GREY...
...SLASHES HER BLADE ACROSS MYSTIQUE'S THROAT.
AND THE MADNESS ENDS. FOR A TIME.
NO!
NO.
I... LIVE!

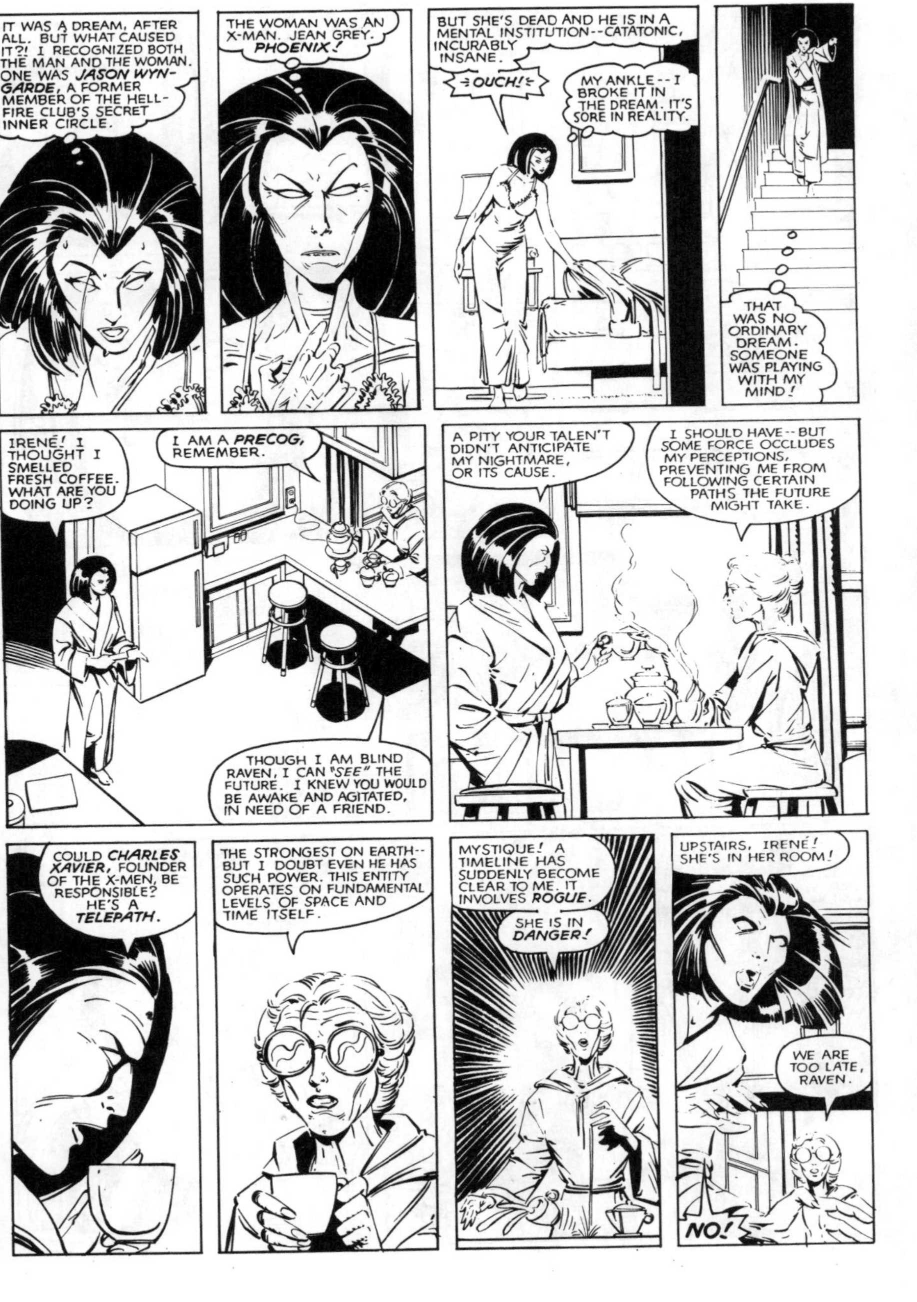
IT WAS A DREAM, AFTER ALL. BUT WHAT CAUSED IT?! I RECOGNIZED BOTH THE MAN AND THE WOMAN. ONE WAS JASON WYNGARDE, A FORMER MEMBER OF THE HELLFIRE CLUB'S SECRET INNER CIRCLE.
THE WOMAN WAS AN X-MAN. JEAN GREY. PHOENIX!
BUT SHE'S DEAD AND HE IS IN A MENTAL INSTITUTION--CATATONIC, INCURABLY INSANE.
OUCH!
MY ANKLE--I BROKE IT IN THE DREAM. IT'S SORE IN REALITY.
THAT WAS NO ORDINARY DREAM. SOMEONE WAS PLAYING WITH MY MIND!
IRENÉ! I THOUGHT I SMELLED FRESH COFFEE. WHAT ARE YOU DOING UP?
I AM A PRECOG, REMEMBER.
THOUGH I AM BLIND RAVEN, I CAN "SEE" THE FUTURE. I KNEW YOU WOULD BE AWAKE AND AGITATED, IN NEED OF A FRIEND.
A PITY YOUR TALEN'T DIDN'T ANTICIPATE MY NIGHTMARE, OR ITS CAUSE.
I SHOULD HAVE--BUT SOME FORCE OCCLUDES MY PERCEPTIONS, PREVENTING ME FROM FOLLOWING CERTAIN PATHS THE FUTURE MIGHT TAKE.
COULD CHARLES XAVIER, FOUNDER OF THE X-MEN, BE RESPONSIBLE? HE'S A TELEPATH.
THE STRONGEST ON EARTH--BUT I DOUBT EVEN HE HAS SUCH POWER. THIS ENTITY OPERATES ON FUNDAMENTAL LEVELS OF SPACE AND TIME ITSELF.
MYSTIQUE! A TIMELINE HAS SUDDENLY BECOME CLEAR TO ME. IT INVOLVES ROGUE.
SHE IS IN DANGER!
UPSTAIRS, IRENÉ! SHE'S IN HER ROOM!
WE ARE TOO LATE, RAVEN.
NO!

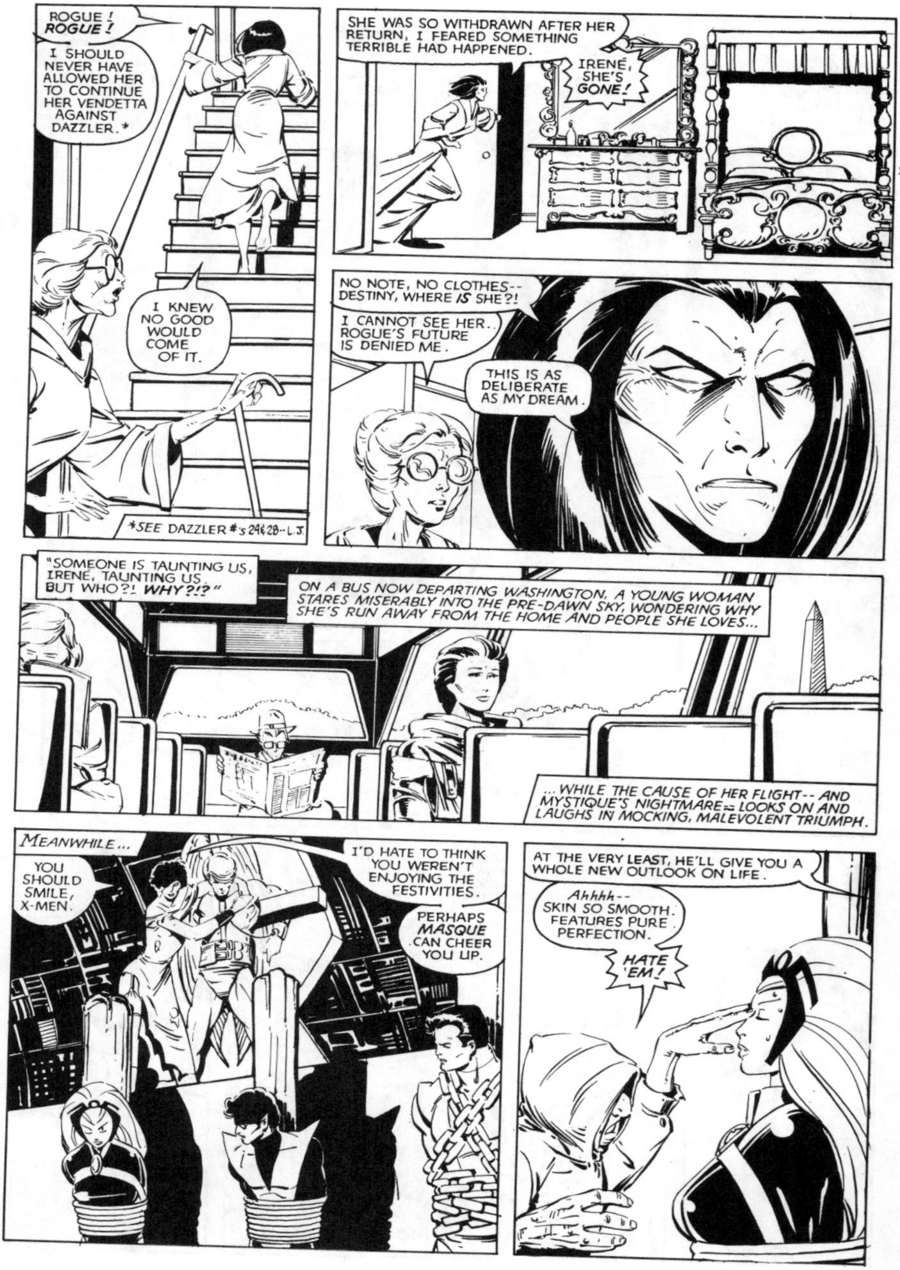
ROGUE! ROGUE!
I SHOULD NEVER HAVE ALLOWED HER TO CONTINUE HER VENDETTA AGAINST DAZZLER.*
I KNEW NO GOOD WOULD COME OF IT.
*SEE DAZZLER #'s 24 & 28 -- L.J.
SHE WAS SO WITHDRAWN AFTER HER RETURN, I FEARED SOMETHING TERRIBLE HAD HAPPENED.
IRENE, SHE'S GONE!
NO NOTE, NO CLOTHES-- DESTINY, WHERE IS SHE?!
I CANNOT SEE HER.. ROGUE'S FUTURE IS DENIED ME.
THIS IS AS DELIBERATE AS MY DREAM.
"SOMEONE IS TAUNTING US, IRENE, TAUNTING US. BUT WHO?! WHY?!?"
ON A BUS NOW DEPARTING WASHINGTON, A YOUNG WOMAN STARES MISERABLY INTO THE PRE-DAWN SKY, WONDERING WHY SHE'S RUN AWAY FROM THE HOME AND PEOPLE SHE LOVES...
...WHILE THE CAUSE OF HER FLIGHT-- AND MYSTIQUE'S NIGHTMARE-- LOOKS ON AND LAUGHS IN MOCKING, MALEVOLENT TRIUMPH.
MEANWHILE...
YOU SHOULD SMILE, X-MEN.
I'D HATE TO THINK YOU WEREN'T ENJOYING THE FESTIVITIES.
PERHAPS MASQUE CAN CHEER YOU UP.
AT THE VERY LEAST, HE'LL GIVE YOU A WHOLE NEW OUTLOOK ON LIFE.
Ahhhh-- SKIN SO SMOOTH. FEATURES PURE PERFECTION.
HATE 'EM!

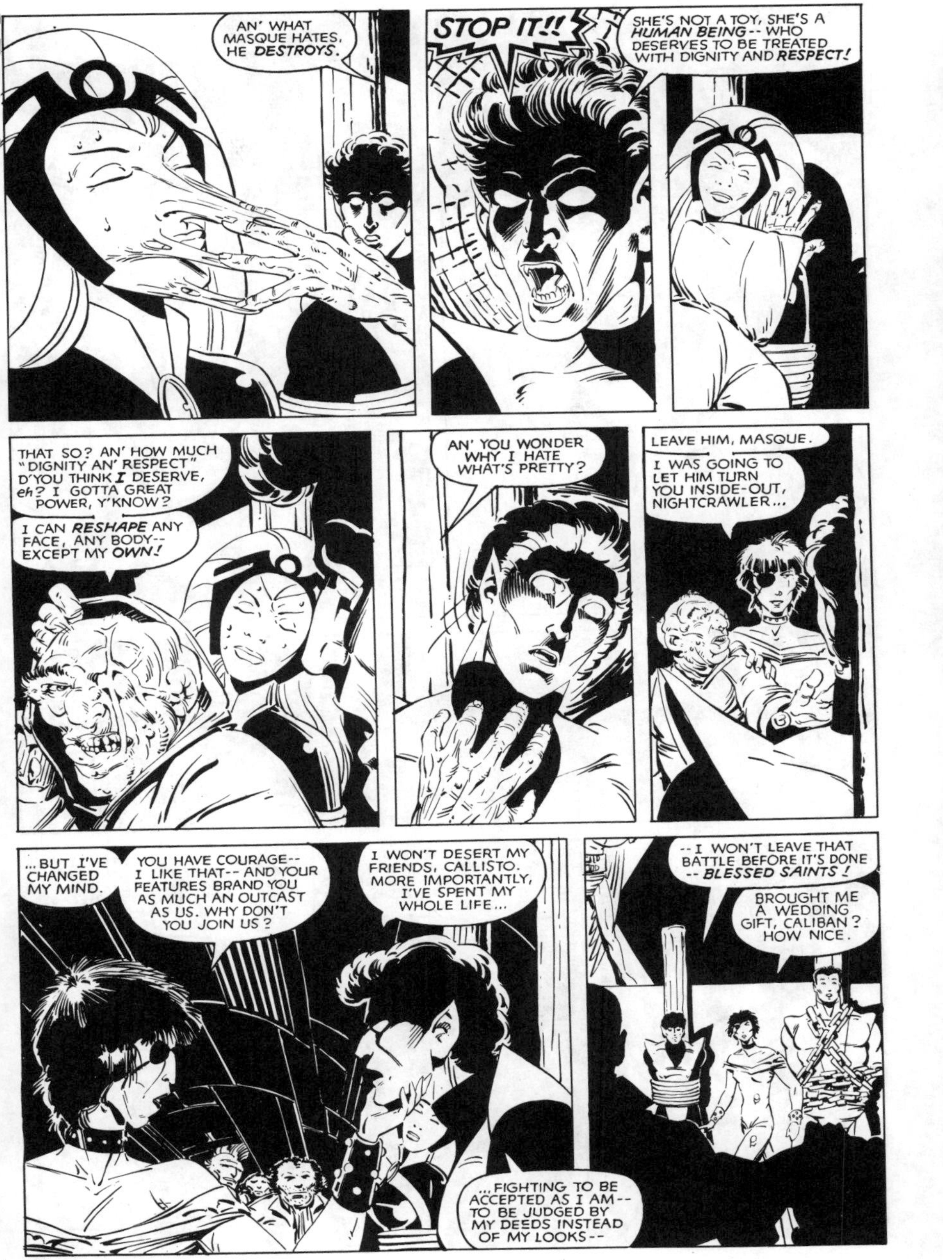
AN' WHAT MASQUE HATES, HE DESTROYS.
STOP IT!!
SHE'S NOT A TOY, SHE'S A HUMAN BEING-- WHO DESERVES TO BE TREATED WITH DIGNITY AND RESPECT!
THAT SO? AN' HOW MUCH "DIGNITY AN' RESPECT" D'YOU THINK I DESERVE, eh? I GOTTA GREAT POWER, Y'KNOW?
I CAN RESHAPE ANY FACE, ANY BODY-- EXCEPT MY OWN!
AN' YOU WONDER WHY I HATE WHAT'S PRETTY?
LEAVE HIM, MASQUE.
I WAS GOING TO LET HIM TURN YOU INSIDE-OUT, NIGHTCRAWLER...
...BUT I'VE CHANGED MY MIND.
YOU HAVE COURAGE-- I LIKE THAT-- AND YOUR FEATURES BRAND YOU AS MUCH AN OUTCAST AS US. WHY DON'T YOU JOIN US?
I WON'T DESERT MY FRIENDS, CALLISTO. MORE IMPORTANTLY, I'VE SPENT MY WHOLE LIFE...
...FIGHTING TO BE ACCEPTED AS I AM-- TO BE JUDGED BY MY DEEDS INSTEAD OF MY LOOKS--
--I WON'T LEAVE THAT BATTLE BEFORE IT'S DONE -- BLESSED SAINTS!
BROUGHT ME A WEDDING GIFT, CALIBAN? HOW NICE.

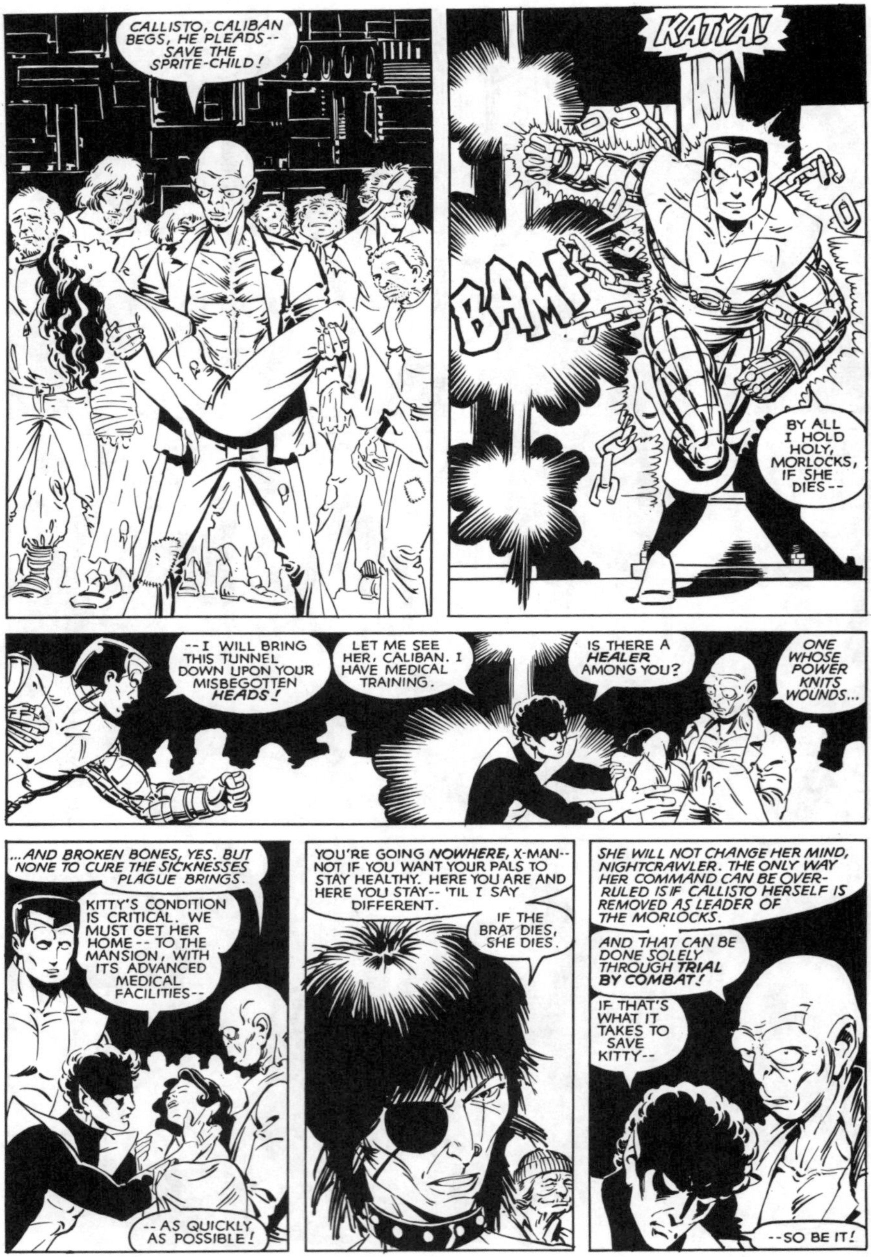
CALLISTO, CALIBAN BEGS, HE PLEADS-- SAVE THE SPRITE-CHILD!
KATYA!
BAMF
BY ALL I HOLD HOLY, MORLOCKS, IF SHE DIES--
--I WILL BRING THIS TUNNEL DOWN UPON YOUR MISBEGOTTEN HEADS!
LET ME SEE HER, CALIBAN. I HAVE MEDICAL TRAINING.
IS THERE A HEALER AMONG YOU?
ONE WHOSE POWER KNITS WOUNDS...
...AND BROKEN BONES, YES. BUT NONE TO CURE THE SICKNESSES PLAGUE BRINGS.
KITTY'S CONDITION IS CRITICAL. WE MUST GET HER HOME--TO THE MANSION, WITH ITS ADVANCED MEDICAL FACILITIES--
--AS QUICKLY AS POSSIBLE!
YOU'RE GOING NOWHERE, X-MAN--NOT IF YOU WANT YOUR PALS TO STAY HEALTHY. HERE YOU ARE AND HERE YOU STAY--'TIL I SAY DIFFERENT.
IF THE BRAT DIES, SHE DIES.
SHE WILL NOT CHANGE HER MIND, NIGHTCRAWLER. THE ONLY WAY HER COMMAND CAN BE OVER-RULED IS IF CALLISTO HERSELF IS REMOVED AS LEADER OF THE MORLOCKS.
AND THAT CAN BE DONE SOLELY THROUGH TRIAL BY COMBAT!
IF THAT'S WHAT IT TAKES TO SAVE KITTY--
--SO BE IT!

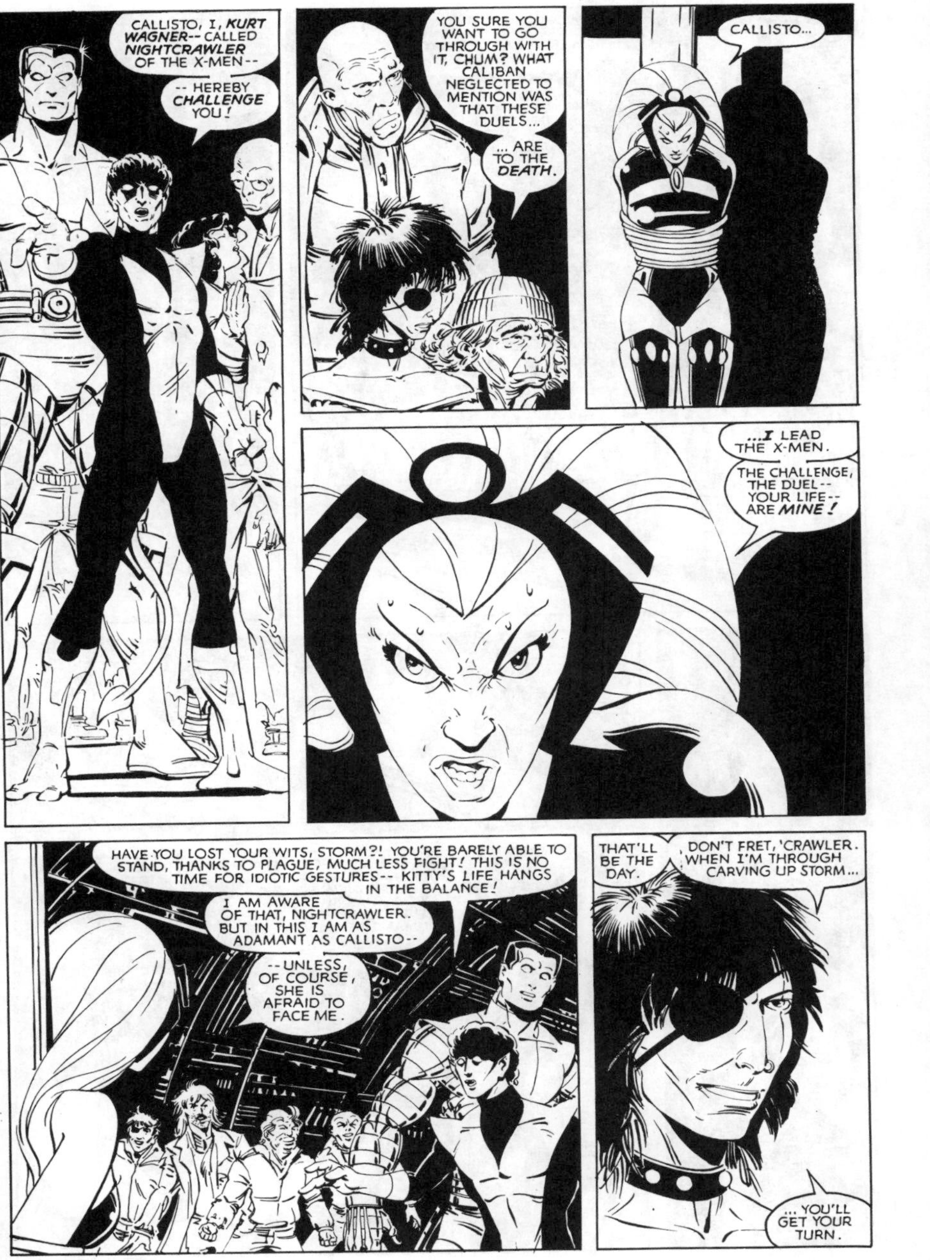
CALLISTO, I, KURT WAGNER-- CALLED NIGHTCRAWLER OF THE X-MEN--
-- HEREBY CHALLENGE YOU!
YOU SURE YOU WANT TO GO THROUGH WITH IT, CHUM? WHAT CALIBAN NEGLECTED TO MENTION WAS THAT THESE DUELS...
... ARE TO THE DEATH.
CALLISTO...
...I LEAD THE X-MEN.
THE CHALLENGE, THE DUEL-- YOUR LIFE-- ARE MINE!
HAVE YOU LOST YOUR WITS, STORM?! YOU'RE BARELY ABLE TO STAND, THANKS TO PLAGUE, MUCH LESS FIGHT! THIS IS NO TIME FOR IDIOTIC GESTURES-- KITTY'S LIFE HANGS IN THE BALANCE!
I AM AWARE OF THAT, NIGHTCRAWLER. BUT IN THIS I AM AS ADAMANT AS CALLISTO--
--UNLESS, OF COURSE, SHE IS AFRAID TO FACE ME.
THAT'LL BE THE DAY.
DON'T FRET, 'CRAWLER. WHEN I'M THROUGH CARVING UP STORM...
... YOU'LL GET YOUR TURN.

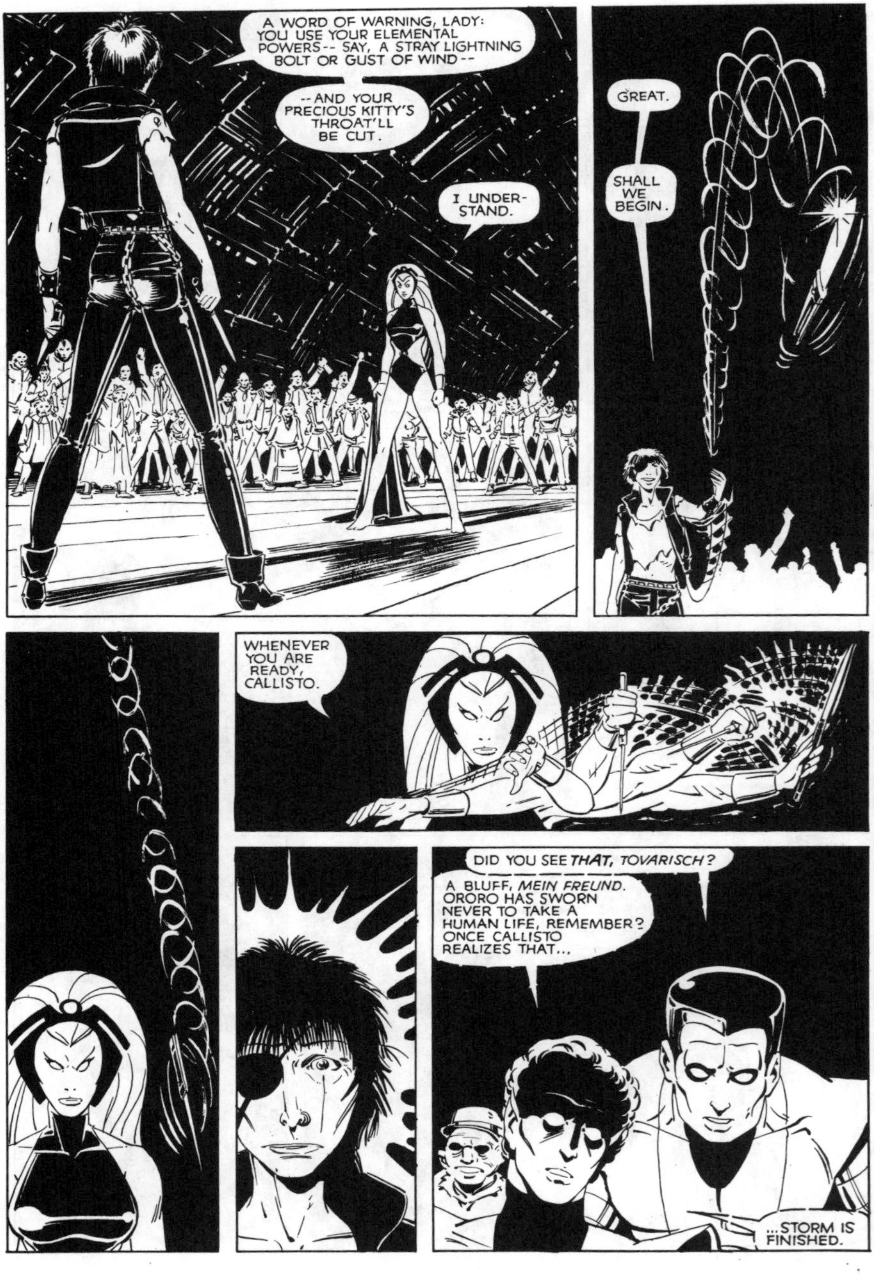
A WORD OF WARNING, LADY: YOU USE YOUR ELEMENTAL POWERS-- SAY, A STRAY LIGHTNING BOLT OR GUST OF WIND--
--AND YOUR PRECIOUS KITTY'S THROAT'LL BE CUT.
I UNDER-STAND.
GREAT.
SHALL WE BEGIN.
WHENEVER YOU ARE READY, CALLISTO.
DID YOU SEE THAT, TOVARISCH?
A BLUFF, MEIN FREUND. ORORO HAS SWORN NEVER TO TAKE A HUMAN LIFE, REMEMBER? ONCE CALLISTO REALIZES THAT...
...STORM IS FINISHED.

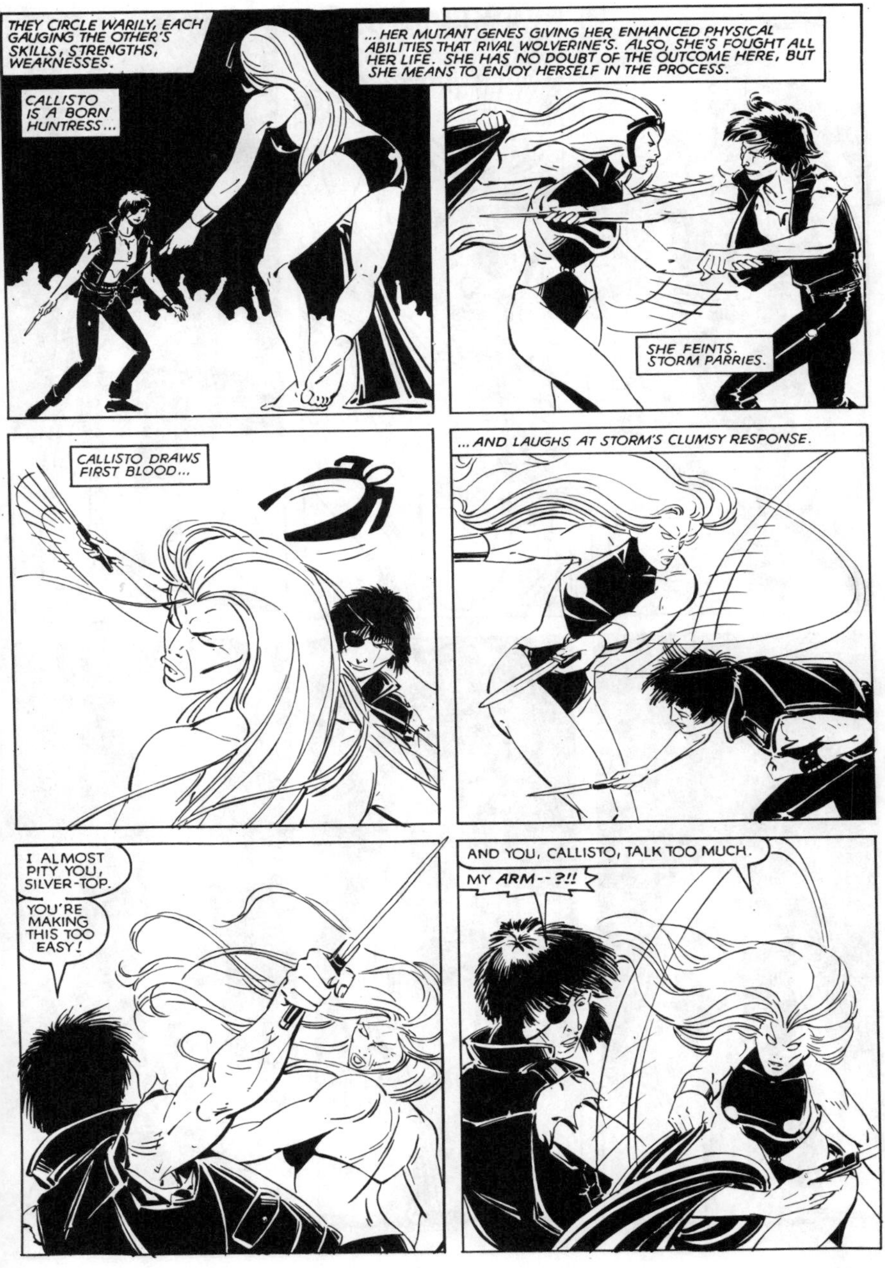
THEY CIRCLE WARILY, EACH GAUGING THE OTHER'S SKILLS, STRENGTHS, WEAKNESSES.
CALLISTO IS A BORN HUNTRESS...
...HER MUTANT GENES GIVING HER ENHANCED PHYSICAL ABILITIES THAT RIVAL WOLVERINE'S. ALSO, SHE'S FOUGHT ALL HER LIFE. SHE HAS NO DOUBT OF THE OUTCOME HERE, BUT SHE MEANS TO ENJOY HERSELF IN THE PROCESS.
SHE FEINTS. STORM PARRIES.
CALLISTO DRAWS FIRST BLOOD...
...AND LAUGHS AT STORM'S CLUMSY RESPONSE.
I ALMOST PITY YOU, SILVER-TOP.
YOU'RE MAKING THIS TOO EASY!
AND YOU, CALLISTO, TALK TOO MUCH.
MY ARM--?!!

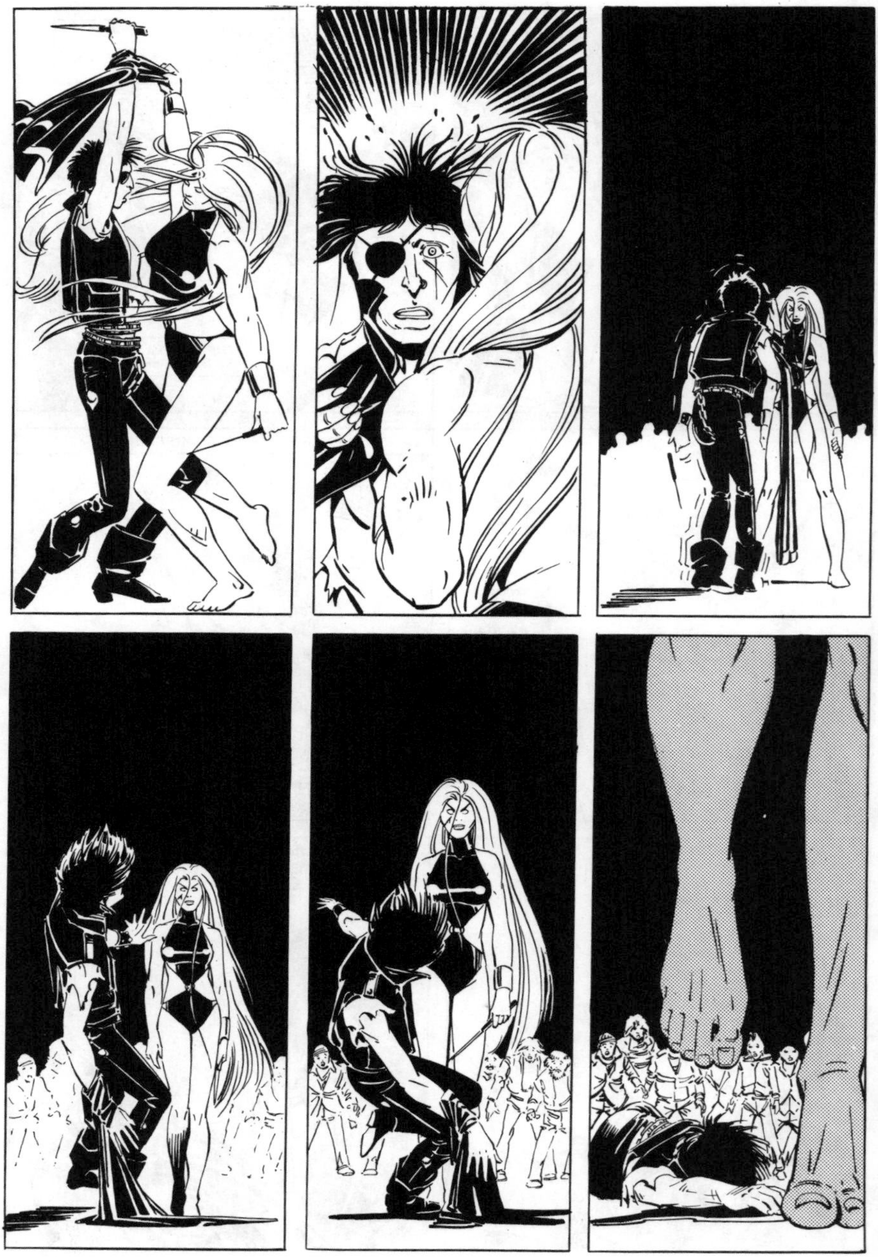

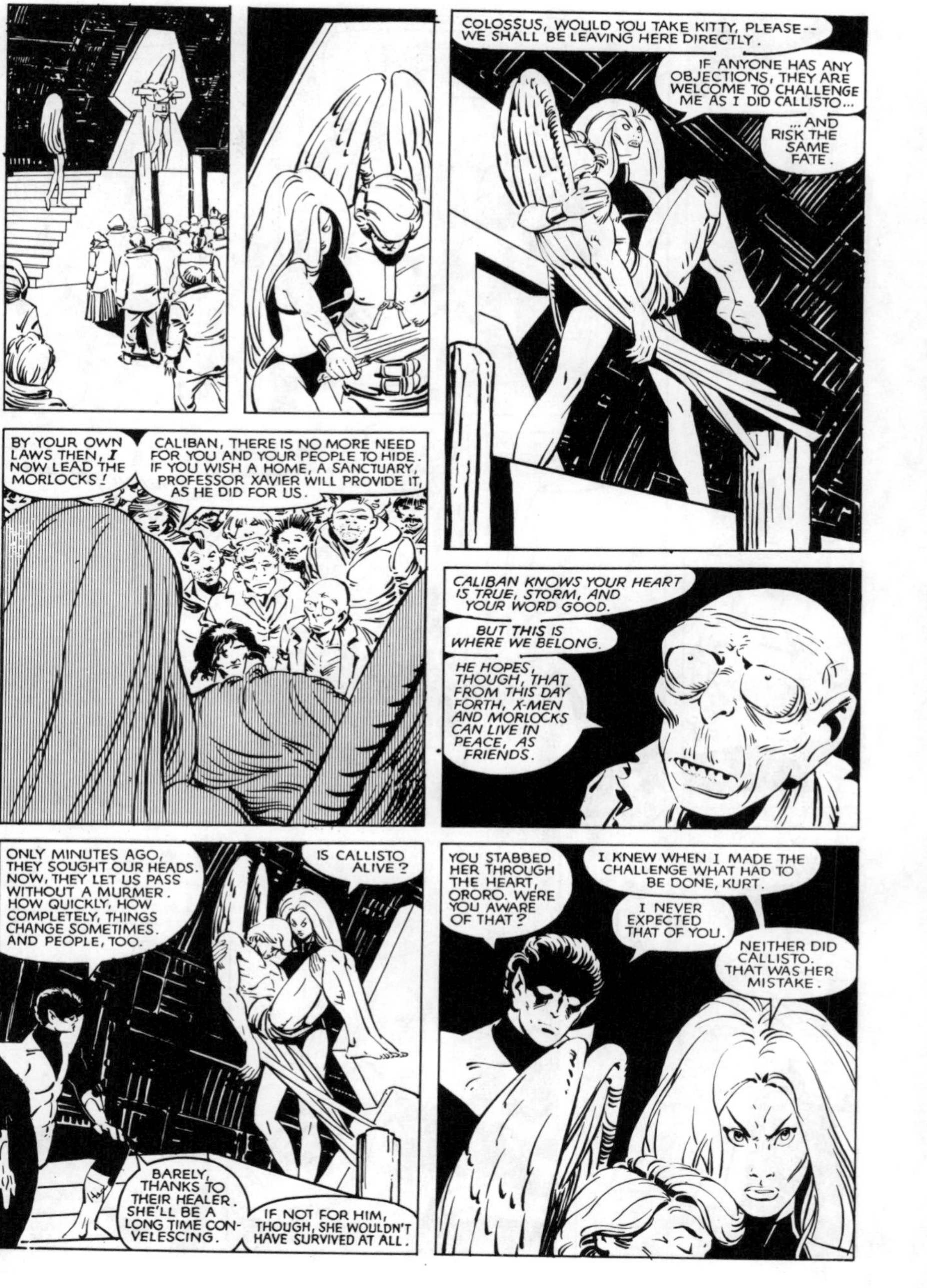
COLOSSUS, WOULD YOU TAKE KITTY, PLEASE-- WE SHALL BE LEAVING HERE DIRECTLY.
IF ANYONE HAS ANY OBJECTIONS, THEY ARE WELCOME TO CHALLENGE ME AS I DID CALLISTO...
...AND RISK THE SAME FATE.
BY YOUR OWN LAWS THEN, I NOW LEAD THE MORLOCKS!
CALIBAN, THERE IS NO MORE NEED FOR YOU AND YOUR PEOPLE TO HIDE. IF YOU WISH A HOME, A SANCTUARY, PROFESSOR XAVIER WILL PROVIDE IT, AS HE DID FOR US.
CALIBAN KNOWS YOUR HEART IS TRUE, STORM, AND YOUR WORD GOOD.
BUT THIS IS WHERE WE BELONG.
HE HOPES, THOUGH, THAT FROM THIS DAY FORTH, X-MEN AND MORLOCKS CAN LIVE IN PEACE, AS FRIENDS.
ONLY MINUTES AGO, THEY SOUGHT OUR HEADS. NOW, THEY LET US PASS WITHOUT A MURMER. HOW QUICKLY, HOW COMPLETELY, THINGS CHANGE SOMETIMES. AND PEOPLE, TOO.
IS CALLISTO ALIVE?
BARELY, THANKS TO THEIR HEALER. SHE'LL BE A LONG TIME CON-VELESCING.
IF NOT FOR HIM, THOUGH, SHE WOULDN'T HAVE SURVIVED AT ALL.
YOU STABBED HER THROUGH THE HEART, ORORO. WERE YOU AWARE OF THAT?
I KNEW WHEN I MADE THE CHALLENGE WHAT HAD TO BE DONE, KURT.
I NEVER EXPECTED THAT OF YOU.
NEITHER DID CALLISTO. THAT WAS HER MISTAKE.

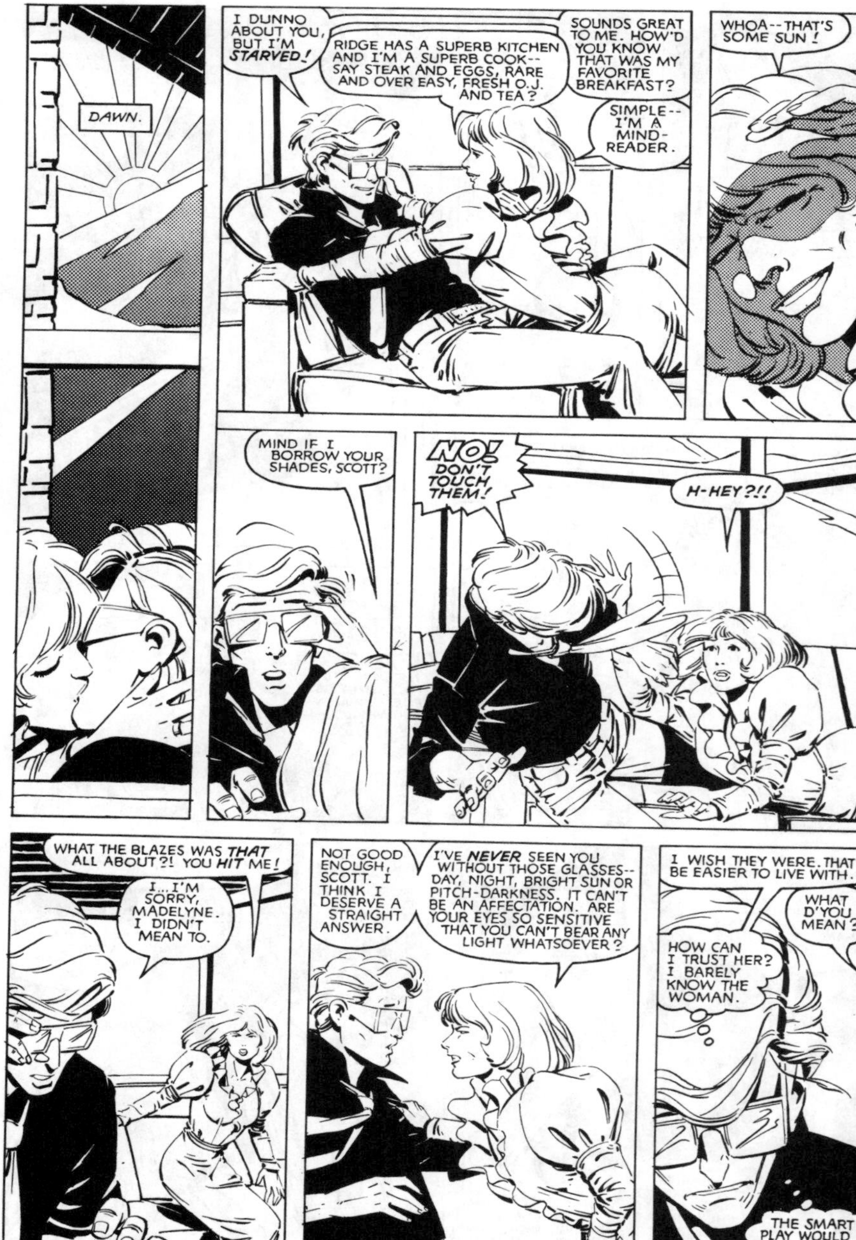
DAWN.
I DUNNO ABOUT YOU, BUT I'M STARVED!
RIDGE HAS A SUPERB KITCHEN AND I'M A SUPERB COOK-- SAY STEAK AND EGGS, RARE AND OVER EASY, FRESH O.J. AND TEA?
SOUNDS GREAT TO ME. HOW'D YOU KNOW THAT WAS MY FAVORITE BREAKFAST?
SIMPLE-- I'M A MIND-READER.
WHOA--THAT'S SOME SUN!
MIND IF I BORROW YOUR SHADES, SCOTT?
NO! DON'T TOUCH THEM!
H-HEY?!!
WHAT THE BLAZES WAS THAT ALL ABOUT?! YOU HIT ME!
I...I'M SORRY, MADELYNE. I DIDN'T MEAN TO.
NOT GOOD ENOUGH, SCOTT. I THINK I DESERVE A STRAIGHT ANSWER.
I'VE NEVER SEEN YOU WITHOUT THOSE GLASSES-- DAY, NIGHT, BRIGHT SUN OR PITCH-DARKNESS. IT CAN'T BE AN AFFECTATION. ARE YOUR EYES SO SENSITIVE THAT YOU CAN'T BEAR ANY LIGHT WHATSOEVER?
I WISH THEY WERE. THAT'D BE EASIER TO LIVE WITH.
WHAT D'YOU MEAN?
HOW CAN I TRUST HER? I BARELY KNOW THE WOMAN.
THE SMART PLAY WOULD BE TO LIE.

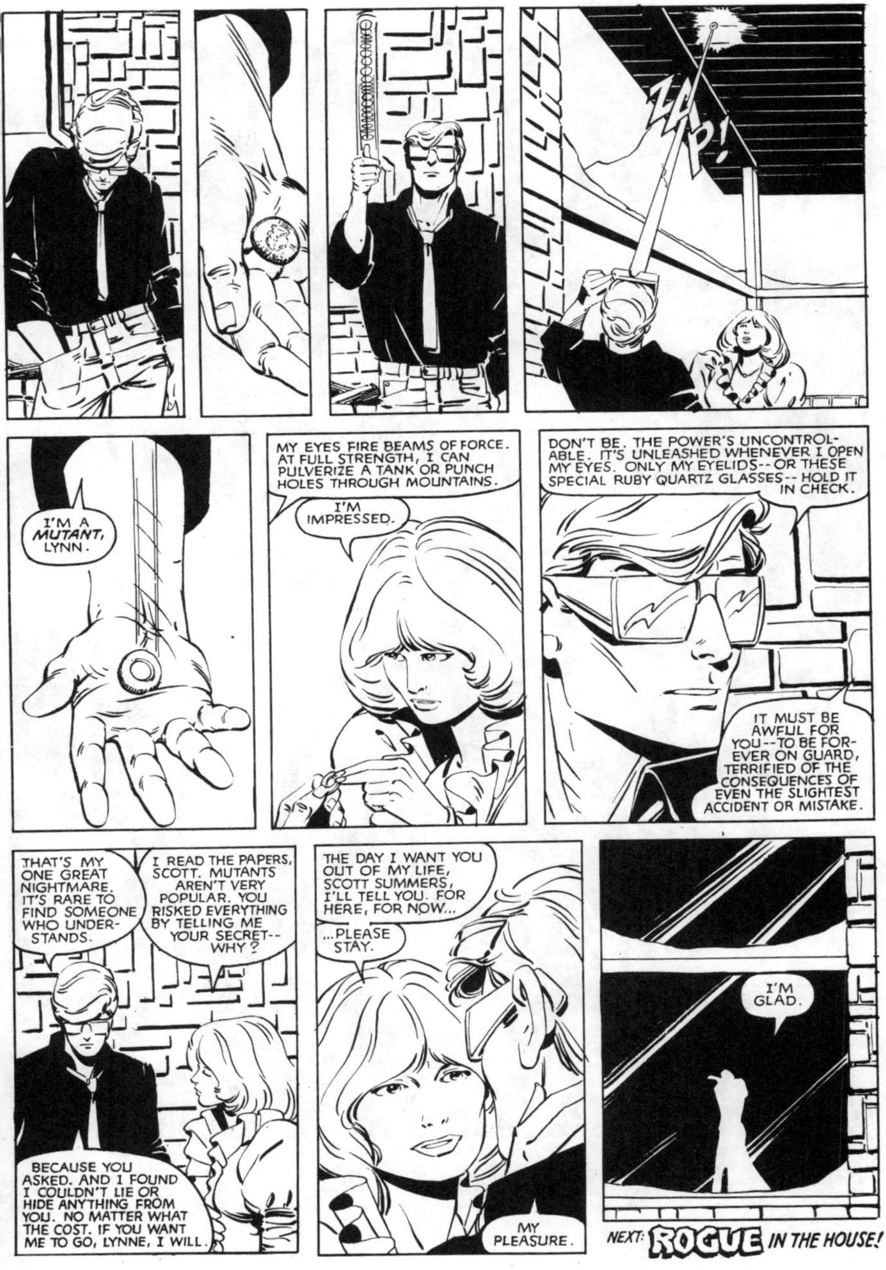
ZZAP!
I'M A MUTANT, LYNN.
MY EYES FIRE BEAMS OF FORCE. AT FULL STRENGTH, I CAN PULVERIZE A TANK OR PUNCH HOLES THROUGH MOUNTAINS.
I'M IMPRESSED.
DON'T BE. THE POWER'S UNCONTROLLABLE. IT'S UNLEASHED WHENEVER I OPEN MY EYES. ONLY MY EYELIDS-- OR THESE SPECIAL RUBY QUARTZ GLASSES-- HOLD IT IN CHECK.
IT MUST BE AWFUL FOR YOU--TO BE FOREVER ON GUARD, TERRIFIED OF THE CONSEQUENCES OF EVEN THE SLIGHTEST ACCIDENT OR MISTAKE.
THAT'S MY ONE GREAT NIGHTMARE. IT'S RARE TO FIND SOMEONE WHO UNDERSTANDS.
I READ THE PAPERS, SCOTT. MUTANTS AREN'T VERY POPULAR. YOU RISKED EVERYTHING BY TELLING ME YOUR SECRET-- WHY?
BECAUSE YOU ASKED. AND I FOUND I COULDN'T LIE OR HIDE ANYTHING FROM YOU. NO MATTER WHAT THE COST. IF YOU WANT ME TO GO, LYNNE, I WILL.
THE DAY I WANT YOU OUT OF MY LIFE, SCOTT SUMMERS, I'LL TELL YOU. FOR HERE, FOR NOW...
...PLEASE STAY.
MY PLEASURE.
I'M GLAD.

NEXT: ROGUE IN THE HOUSE!

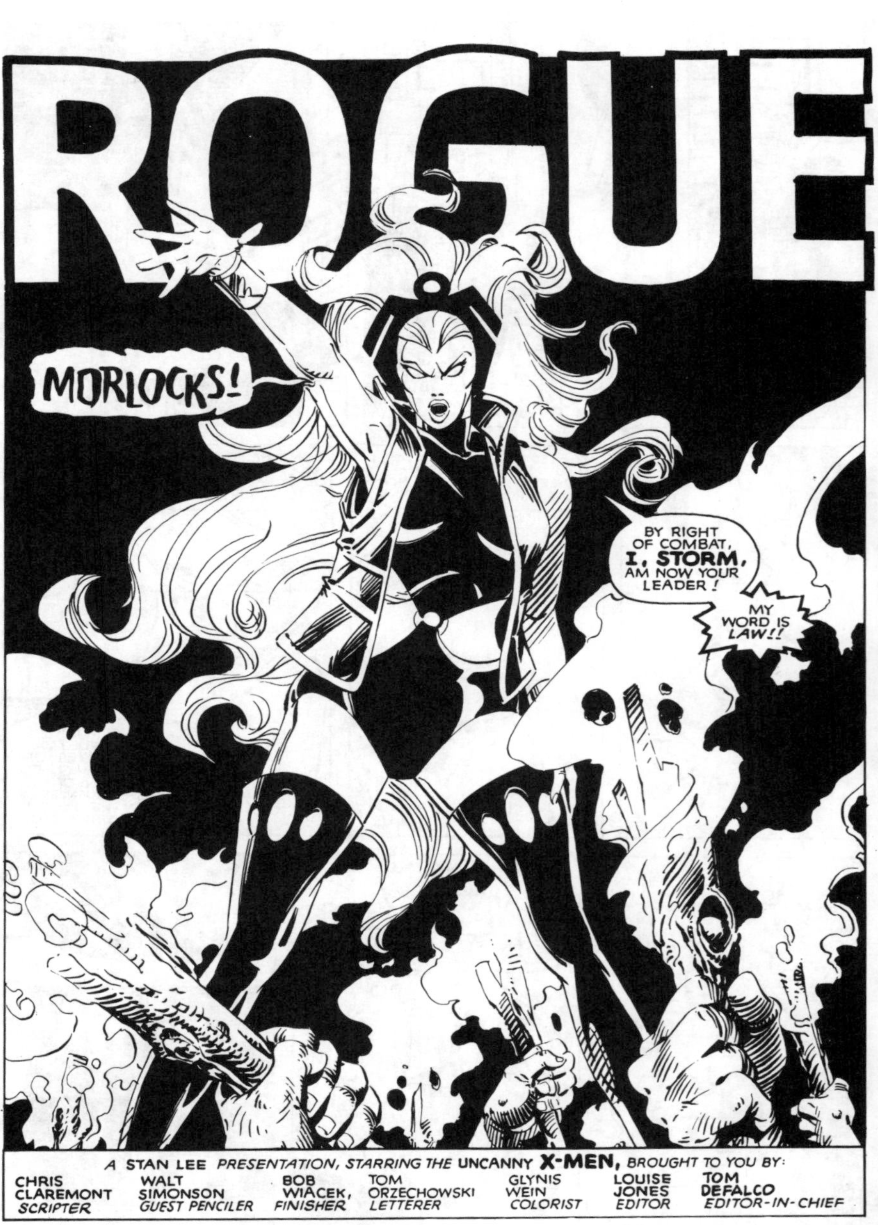
ROGUE
MORLOCKS!
BY RIGHT OF COMBAT, I, STORM, AM NOW YOUR LEADER!
MY WORD IS LAW!!
A STAN LEE PRESENTATION, STARRING THE UNCANNY X-MEN, BROUGHT TO YOU BY:
CHRIS CLAREMONT SCRIPTER
WALT SIMONSON GUEST PENCILER
BOB WIACEK, FINISHER
TOM ORZECHOWSKI LETTERER
GLYNIS WEIN COLORIST
LOUISE JONES EDITOR
TOM DEFALCO EDITOR-IN-CHIEF

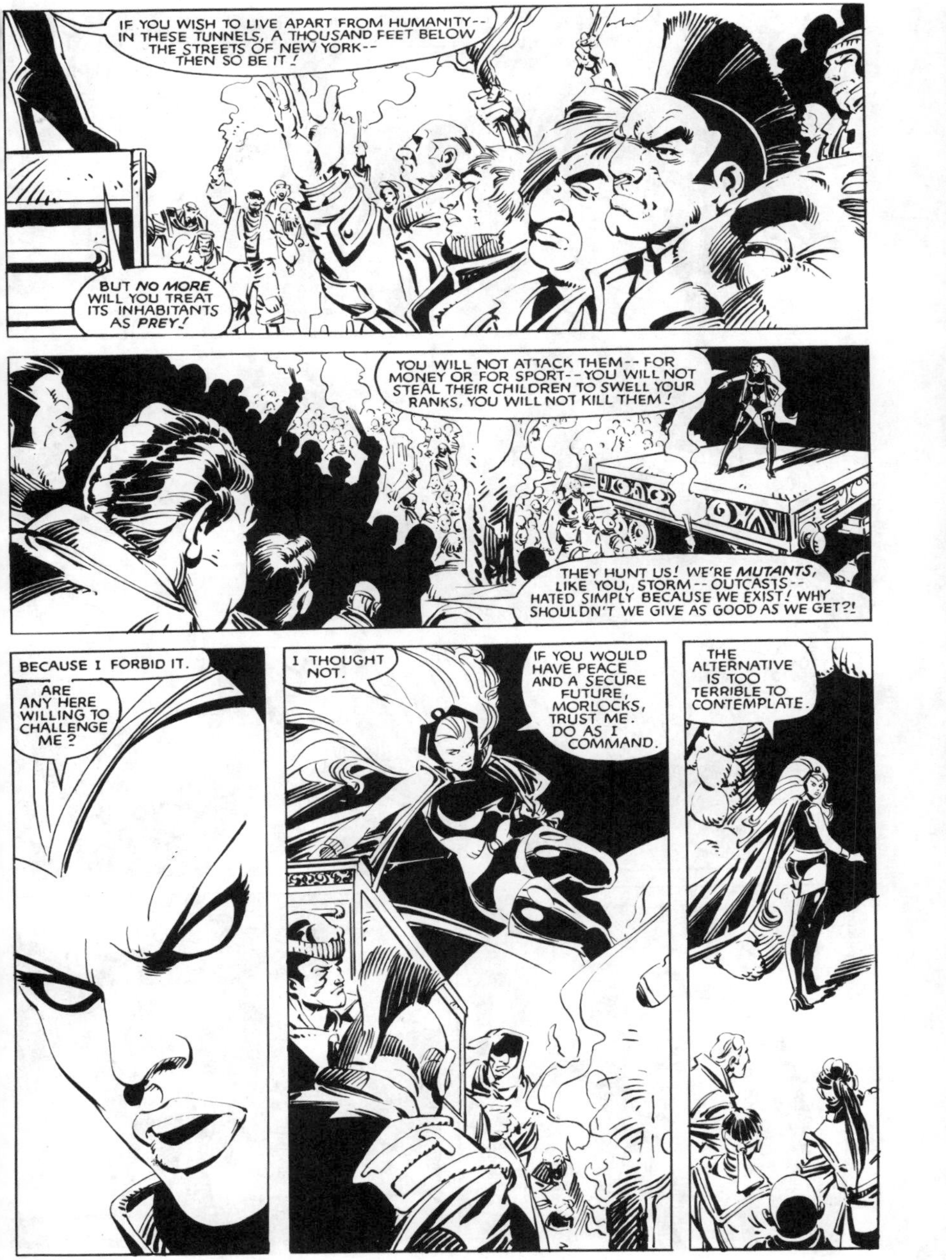
IF YOU WISH TO LIVE APART FROM HUMANITY-- IN THESE TUNNELS, A THOUSAND FEET BELOW THE STREETS OF NEW YORK-- THEN SO BE IT!
BUT NO MORE WILL YOU TREAT ITS INHABITANTS AS PREY!
YOU WILL NOT ATTACK THEM-- FOR MONEY OR FOR SPORT--YOU WILL NOT STEAL THEIR CHILDREN TO SWELL YOUR RANKS, YOU WILL NOT KILL THEM!
THEY HUNT US! WE'RE MUTANTS, LIKE YOU, STORM--OUTCASTS-- HATED SIMPLY BECAUSE WE EXIST! WHY SHOULDN'T WE GIVE AS GOOD AS WE GET?!
BECAUSE I FORBID IT.
ARE ANY HERE WILLING TO CHALLENGE ME?
I THOUGHT NOT.
IF YOU WOULD HAVE PEACE AND A SECURE FUTURE, MORLOCKS, TRUST ME. DO AS I COMMAND.
THE ALTERNATIVE IS TOO TERRIBLE TO CONTEMPLATE.

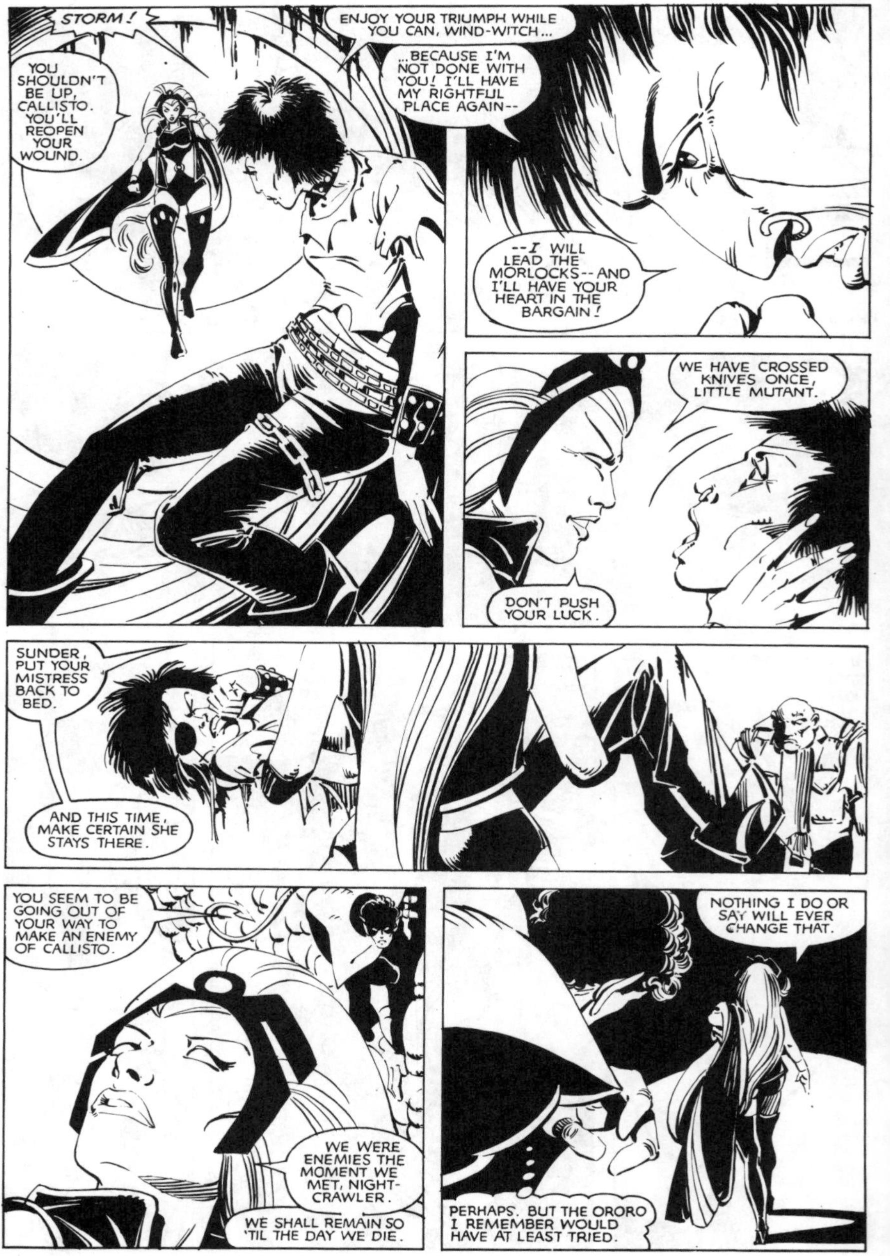
STORM!
YOU SHOULDN'T BE UP, CALLISTO. YOU'LL REOPEN YOUR WOUND.
ENJOY YOUR TRIUMPH WHILE YOU CAN, WIND-WITCH...
...BECAUSE I'M NOT DONE WITH YOU! I'LL HAVE MY RIGHTFUL PLACE AGAIN--
--I WILL LEAD THE MORLOCKS--AND I'LL HAVE YOUR HEART IN THE BARGAIN!
WE HAVE CROSSED KNIVES ONCE, LITTLE MUTANT.
DON'T PUSH YOUR LUCK.
SUNDER, PUT YOUR MISTRESS BACK TO BED.
AND THIS TIME, MAKE CERTAIN SHE STAYS THERE.
YOU SEEM TO BE GOING OUT OF YOUR WAY TO MAKE AN ENEMY OF CALLISTO.
WE WERE ENEMIES THE MOMENT WE MET, NIGHT-CRAWLER.
WE SHALL REMAIN SO 'TIL THE DAY WE DIE.
NOTHING I DO OR SAY WILL EVER CHANGE THAT.
PERHAPS. BUT THE ORORO I REMEMBER WOULD HAVE AT LEAST TRIED.

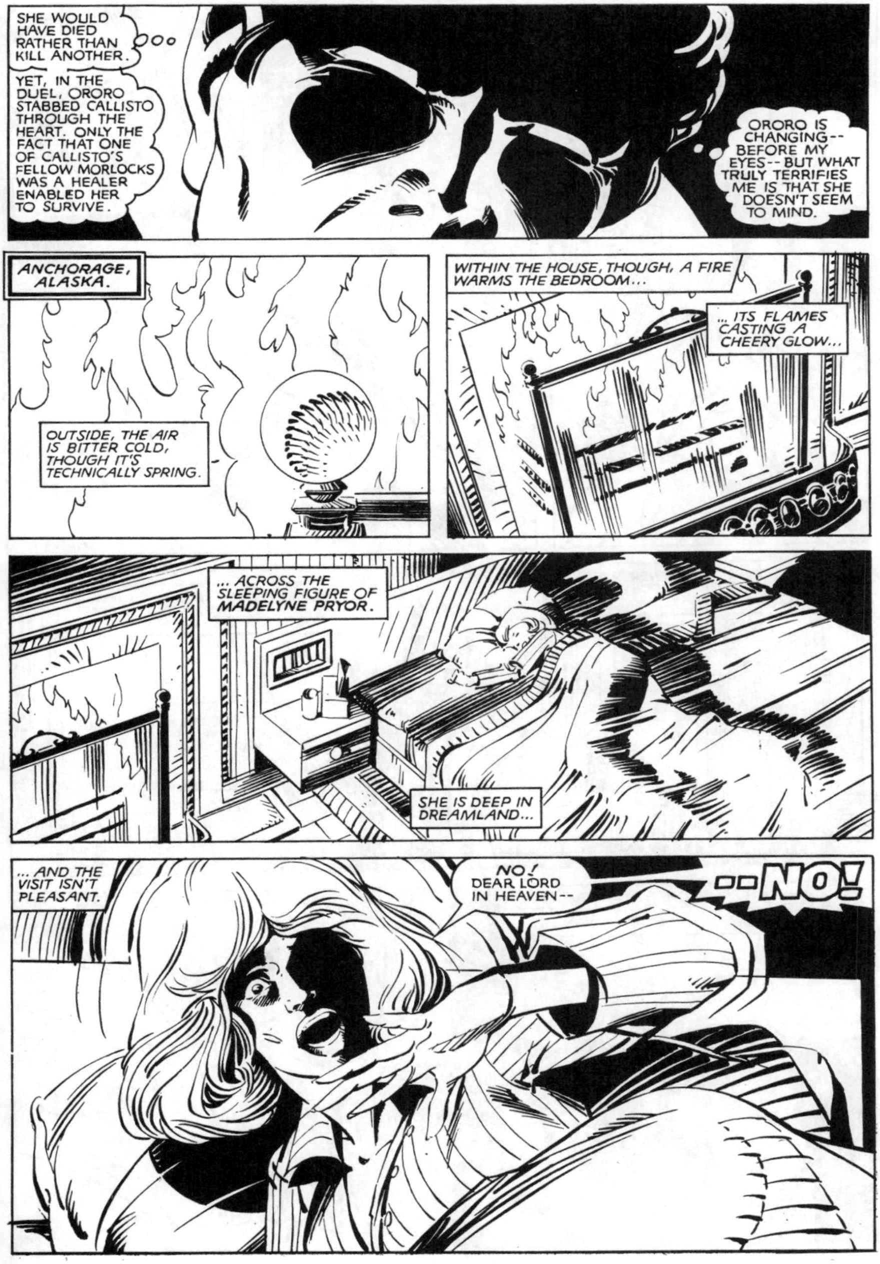
SHE WOULD HAVE DIED RATHER THAN KILL ANOTHER.
YET, IN THE DUEL, ORORO STABBED CALLISTO THROUGH THE HEART. ONLY THE FACT THAT ONE OF CALLISTO'S FELLOW MORLOCKS WAS A HEALER ENABLED HER TO SURVIVE.
ORORO IS CHANGING-- BEFORE MY EYES-- BUT WHAT TRULY TERRIFIES ME IS THAT SHE DOESN'T SEEM TO MIND.
ANCHORAGE, ALASKA.
OUTSIDE, THE AIR IS BITTER COLD, THOUGH IT'S TECHNICALLY SPRING.
WITHIN THE HOUSE, THOUGH, A FIRE WARMS THE BEDROOM...
... ITS FLAMES CASTING A CHEERY GLOW...
... ACROSS THE SLEEPING FIGURE OF MADELYNE PRYOR.
SHE IS DEEP IN DREAMLAND...
... AND THE VISIT ISN'T PLEASANT.
NO! DEAR LORD IN HEAVEN--
--NO!

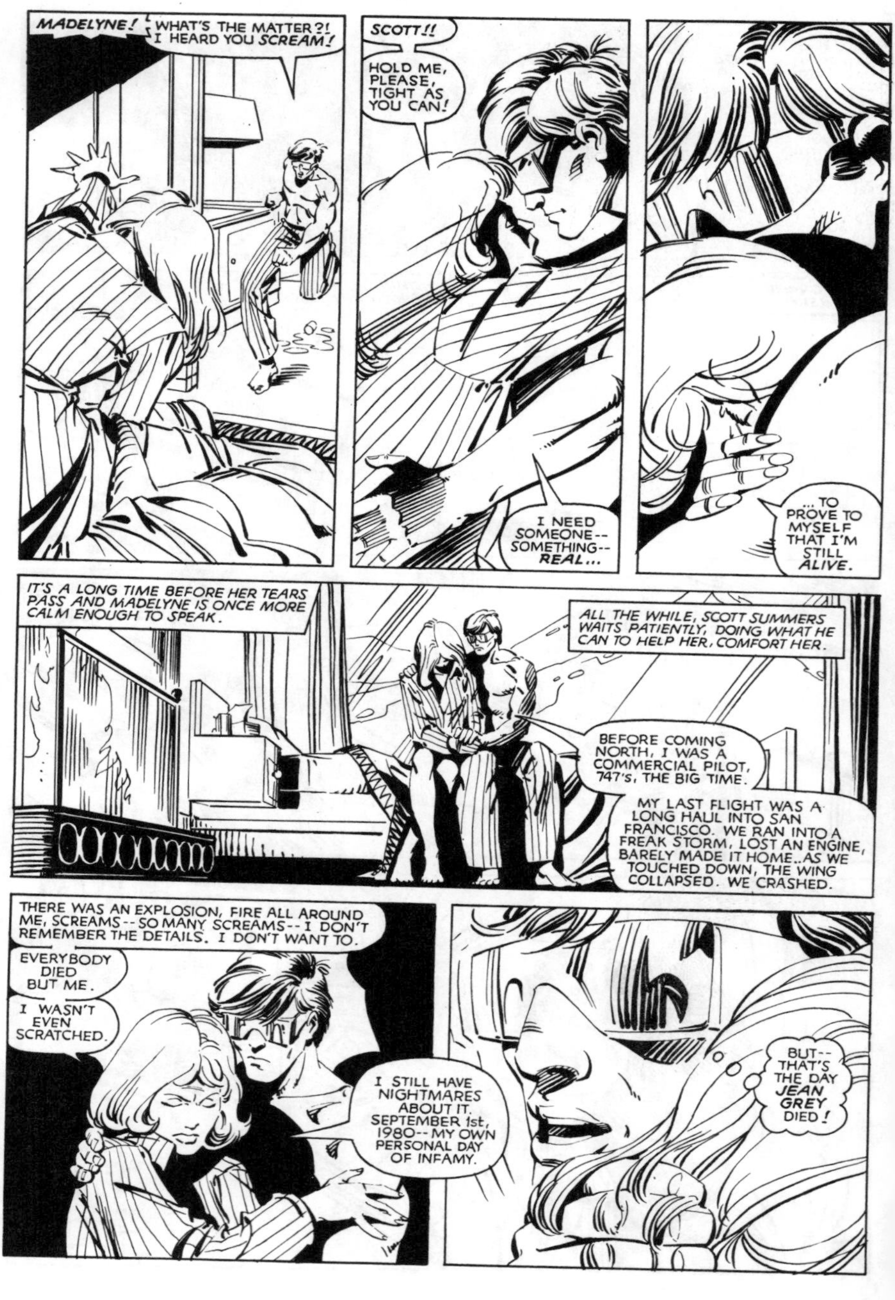

MADELYNE!
WHAT'S THE MATTER?! I HEARD YOU SCREAM!
SCOTT!!
HOLD ME, PLEASE, TIGHT AS YOU CAN!
I NEED SOMEONE-- SOMETHING-- REAL...
...TO PROVE TO MYSELF THAT I'M STILL ALIVE.
IT'S A LONG TIME BEFORE HER TEARS PASS AND MADELYNE IS ONCE MORE CALM ENOUGH TO SPEAK.
ALL THE WHILE, SCOTT SUMMERS WAITS PATIENTLY, DOING WHAT HE CAN TO HELP HER, COMFORT HER.
BEFORE COMING NORTH, I WAS A COMMERCIAL PILOT, 747'S, THE BIG TIME.
MY LAST FLIGHT WAS A LONG HAUL INTO SAN FRANCISCO. WE RAN INTO A FREAK STORM, LOST AN ENGINE, BARELY MADE IT HOME..AS WE TOUCHED DOWN, THE WING COLLAPSED. WE CRASHED.
THERE WAS AN EXPLOSION, FIRE ALL AROUND ME, SCREAMS-- SO MANY SCREAMS-- I DON'T REMEMBER THE DETAILS. I DON'T WANT TO.
EVERYBODY DIED BUT ME.
I WASN'T EVEN SCRATCHED.
I STILL HAVE NIGHTMARES ABOUT IT. SEPTEMBER 1st, 1980-- MY OWN PERSONAL DAY OF INFAMY.
BUT-- THAT'S THE DAY JEAN GREY DIED!

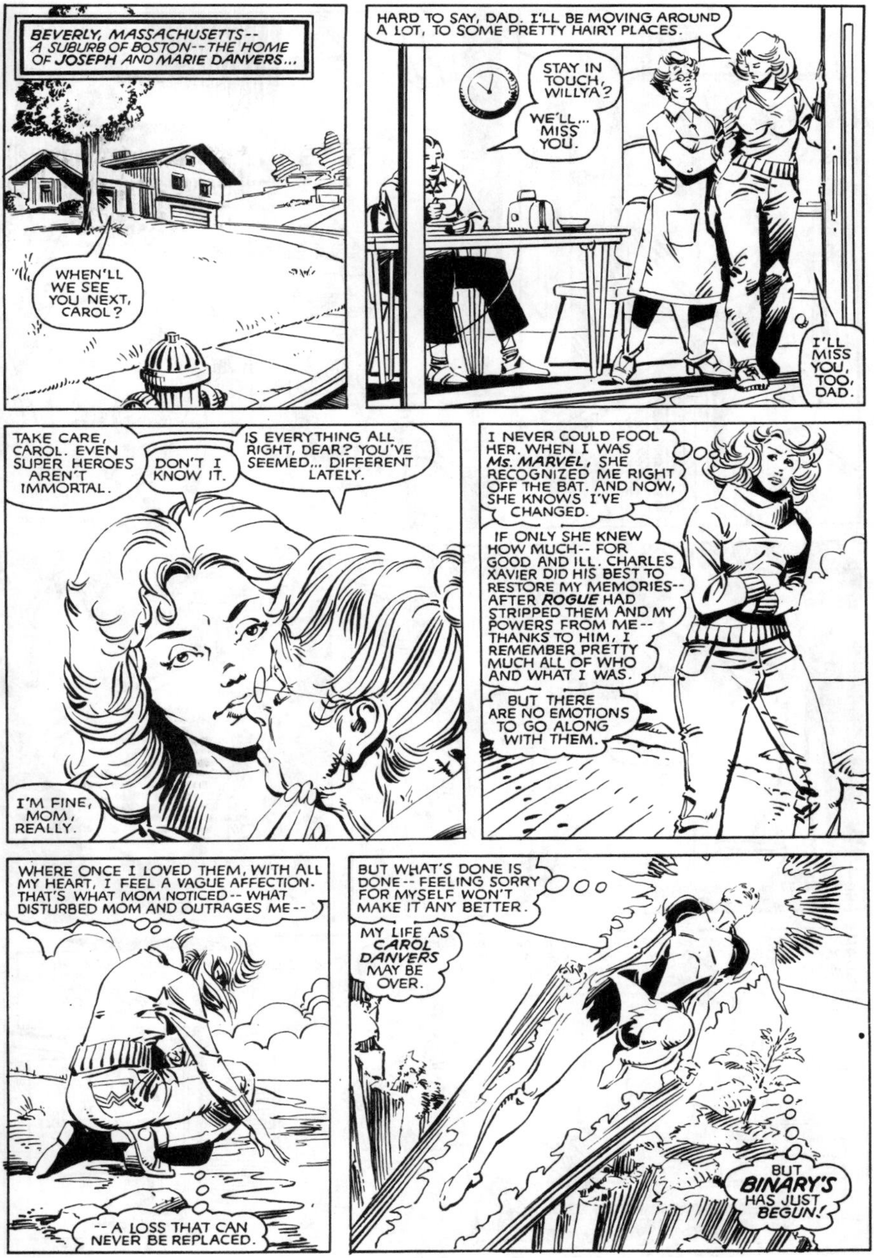
BEVERLY, MASSACHUSETTS-- A SUBURB OF BOSTON-- THE HOME OF JOSEPH AND MARIE DANVERS...
WHEN'LL WE SEE YOU NEXT, CAROL?
HARD TO SAY, DAD. I'LL BE MOVING AROUND A LOT, TO SOME PRETTY HAIRY PLACES.
STAY IN TOUCH, WILLYA?
WE'LL... MISS YOU.
I'LL MISS YOU, TOO, DAD.
TAKE CARE, CAROL. EVEN SUPER HEROES AREN'T IMMORTAL.
DON'T I KNOW IT.
IS EVERYTHING ALL RIGHT, DEAR? YOU'VE SEEMED... DIFFERENT LATELY.
I'M FINE, MOM, REALLY.
I NEVER COULD FOOL HER. WHEN I WAS Ms. MARVEL, SHE RECOGNIZED ME RIGHT OFF THE BAT. AND NOW, SHE KNOWS I'VE CHANGED.
IF ONLY SHE KNEW HOW MUCH-- FOR GOOD AND ILL. CHARLES XAVIER DID HIS BEST TO RESTORE MY MEMORIES-- AFTER ROGUE HAD STRIPPED THEM AND MY POWERS FROM ME-- THANKS TO HIM, I REMEMBER PRETTY MUCH ALL OF WHO AND WHAT I WAS.
BUT THERE ARE NO EMOTIONS TO GO ALONG WITH THEM.
WHERE ONCE I LOVED THEM, WITH ALL MY HEART, I FEEL A VAGUE AFFECTION. THAT'S WHAT MOM NOTICED-- WHAT DISTURBED MOM AND OUTRAGES ME--
-- A LOSS THAT CAN NEVER BE REPLACED.
BUT WHAT'S DONE IS DONE-- FEELING SORRY FOR MYSELF WON'T MAKE IT ANY BETTER.
MY LIFE AS CAROL DANVERS MAY BE OVER.
BUT BINARY'S HAS JUST BEGUN!

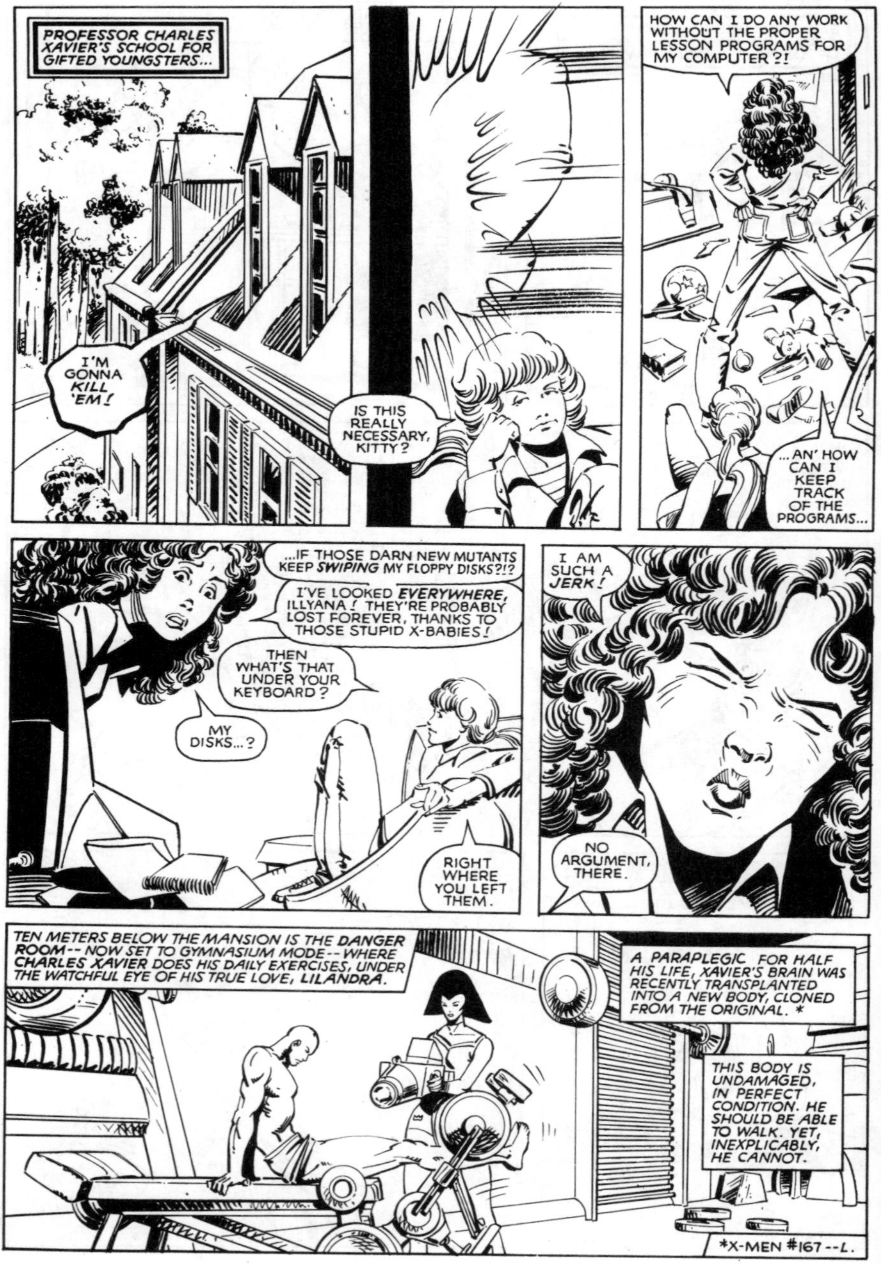

PROFESSOR CHARLES XAVIER'S SCHOOL FOR GIFTED YOUNGSTERS...
I'M GONNA KILL 'EM!
IS THIS REALLY NECESSARY, KITTY?
HOW CAN I DO ANY WORK WITHOUT THE PROPER LESSON PROGRAMS FOR MY COMPUTER?!
...AN' HOW CAN I KEEP TRACK OF THE PROGRAMS...
...IF THOSE DARN NEW MUTANTS KEEP SWIPING MY FLOPPY DISKS?!?
I'VE LOOKED EVERYWHERE, ILLYANA! THEY'RE PROBABLY LOST FOREVER, THANKS TO THOSE STUPID X-BABIES!
THEN WHAT'S THAT UNDER YOUR KEYBOARD?
MY DISKS...?
RIGHT WHERE YOU LEFT THEM.
I AM SUCH A JERK!
NO ARGUMENT, THERE.
TEN METERS BELOW THE MANSION IS THE DANGER ROOM--NOW SET TO GYMNASIUM MODE--WHERE CHARLES XAVIER DOES HIS DAILY EXERCISES, UNDER THE WATCHFUL EYE OF HIS TRUE LOVE, LILANDRA.
A PARAPLEGIC FOR HALF HIS LIFE, XAVIER'S BRAIN WAS RECENTLY TRANSPLANTED INTO A NEW BODY, CLONED FROM THE ORIGINAL. *
THIS BODY IS UNDAMAGED, IN PERFECT CONDITION. HE SHOULD BE ABLE TO WALK. YET, INEXPLICABLY, HE CANNOT.
*X-MEN #167 --L.

NO MORE, LIL, I BEG YOU!

PROBLEMS?

WHEN I USE MY LEGS, THE PSYCHO-SOMATIC PAIN I FEEL INHIBITS MY PSIONIC POWERS, ESPECIALLY MY ABILITY TO SCREEN OUT OTHER PEOPLE'S THOUGHTS.

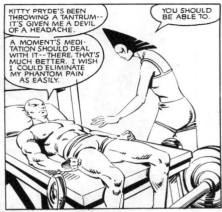

KITTY PRYDE'S BEEN THROWING A TANTRUM-- IT'S GIVEN ME A DEVIL OF A HEADACHE.

YOU SHOULD BE ABLE TO.

A MOMENT'S MEDI-TATION SHOULD DEAL WITH IT--THERE, THAT'S MUCH BETTER. I WISH I COULD ELIMINATE MY PHANTOM PAIN AS EASILY.

YOU ARE, AFTER ALL, THE STRONGEST MUTANT MIND ON EARTH... AMONG OTHER THINGS.

UPSTAIRS, IN THE KITCHEN, ANOTHER OF XAVIER'S STUDENTS, *PIOTR NIKOLIEVITCH RASPUTIN*, PONDERS THE COMPLEX MYSTERIES AND INHERENT CONTRADICTIONS...

... OF A COOKBOOK.

WHAT DO YOU SUGGEST?

WE COULD PLAY DOCTOR.

LILANDRA!

SERIOUSLY, CHARLES, I WOULD LIKE TO GIVE YOU A THOROUGH EXAMI-NATION. PERHAPS YOUR CONDITION ISN'T PSYCHIC IN NATURE, BUT *PHYSICAL*.

EGGS, BACON, CREAM, BUTTER, SPICES-- SLICE, BEAT, MIX, BAKE-- AND IN HALF AN HOUR: *QUICHE LORRAINE*. IT LOOKS SIMPLE ENOUGH.

COLOSSUS, WE HAVE A VISITOR.

AT ONCE, PROFESSOR.

I FELT THE PROFESSOR'S FATIGUE THROUGH HIS THOUGHT PROJECTION. I HOPE HE IS NOT PUSHING HIMSELF TOO HARD.

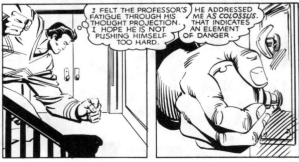

HE ADDRESSED ME AS *COLOSSUS*. THAT INDICATES AN ELEMENT OF DANGER.

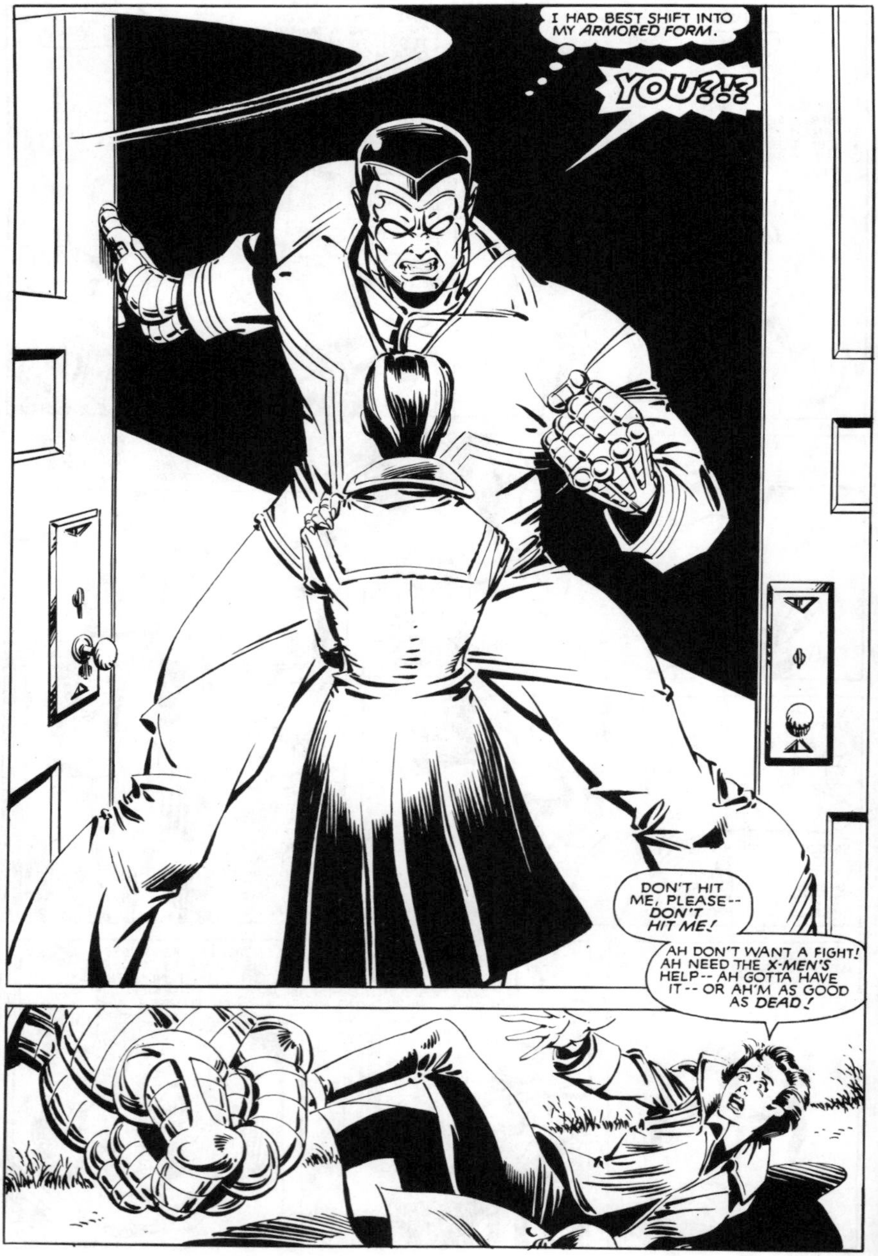
I HAD BEST SHIFT INTO MY ARMORED FORM.
YOU?!?
DON'T HIT ME, PLEASE-- DON'T HIT ME!
AH DON'T WANT A FIGHT! AH NEED THE X-MEN'S HELP-- AH GOTTA HAVE IT-- OR AH'M AS GOOD AS DEAD!

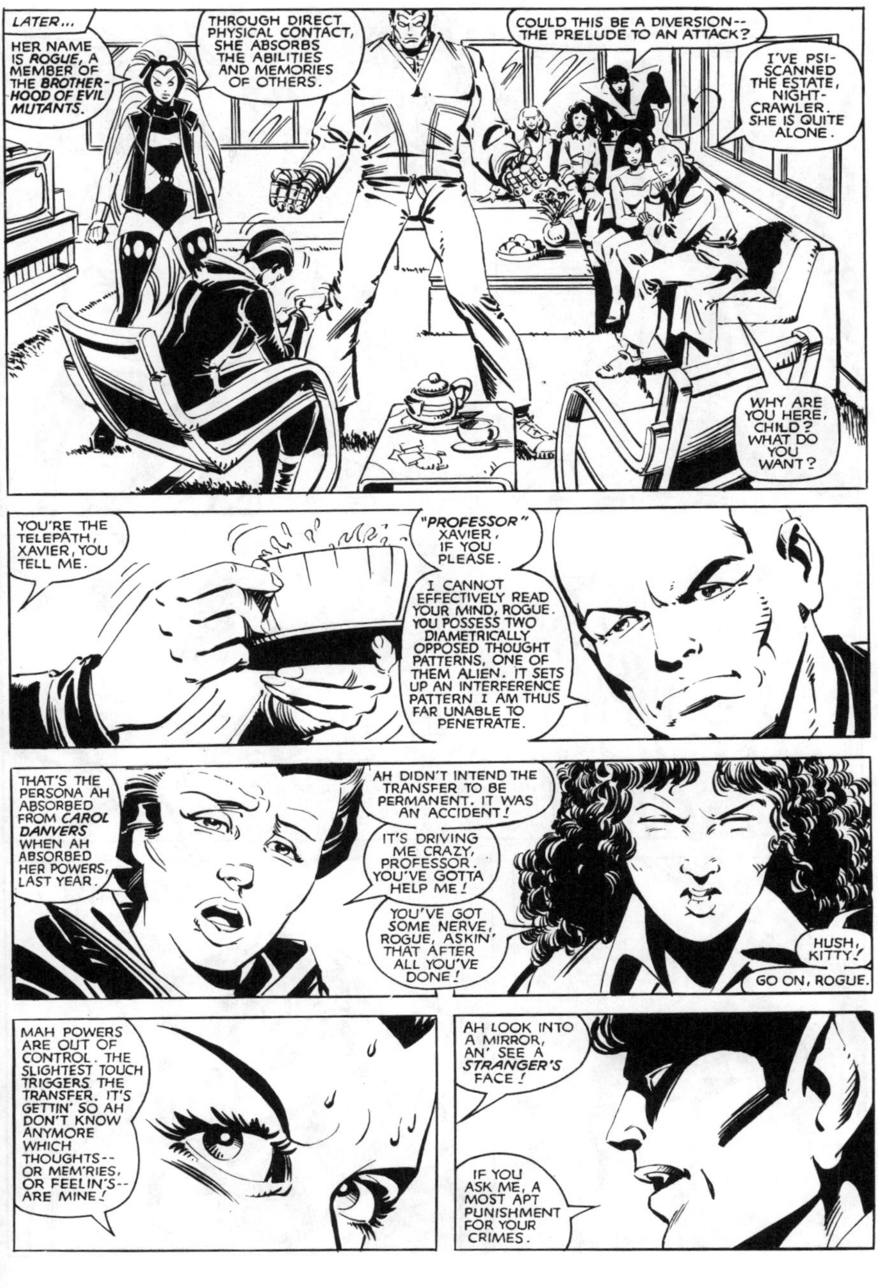
LATER...
HER NAME IS ROGUE, A MEMBER OF THE BROTHERHOOD OF EVIL MUTANTS.
THROUGH DIRECT PHYSICAL CONTACT, SHE ABSORBS THE ABILITIES AND MEMORIES OF OTHERS.
COULD THIS BE A DIVERSION-- THE PRELUDE TO AN ATTACK?
I'VE PSI-SCANNED THE ESTATE, NIGHT-CRAWLER. SHE IS QUITE ALONE.
WHY ARE YOU HERE, CHILD? WHAT DO YOU WANT?
YOU'RE THE TELEPATH, XAVIER, YOU TELL ME.
"PROFESSOR" XAVIER, IF YOU PLEASE.
I CANNOT EFFECTIVELY READ YOUR MIND, ROGUE. YOU POSSESS TWO DIAMETRICALLY OPPOSED THOUGHT PATTERNS, ONE OF THEM ALIEN. IT SETS UP AN INTERFERENCE PATTERN I AM THUS FAR UNABLE TO PENETRATE.
THAT'S THE PERSONA AH ABSORBED FROM CAROL DANVERS WHEN AH ABSORBED HER POWERS, LAST YEAR.
AH DIDN'T INTEND THE TRANSFER TO BE PERMANENT. IT WAS AN ACCIDENT!
IT'S DRIVING ME CRAZY, PROFESSOR. YOU'VE GOTTA HELP ME!
YOU'VE GOT SOME NERVE, ROGUE, ASKIN' THAT AFTER ALL YOU'VE DONE!
HUSH, KITTY!
GO ON, ROGUE.
MAH POWERS ARE OUT OF CONTROL. THE SLIGHTEST TOUCH TRIGGERS THE TRANSFER. IT'S GETTIN' SO AH DON'T KNOW ANYMORE WHICH THOUGHTS-- OR MEM'RIES, OR FEELIN'S-- ARE MINE!
AH LOOK INTO A MIRROR, AN' SEE A STRANGER'S FACE!
IF YOU ASK ME, A MOST APT PUNISHMENT FOR YOUR CRIMES.

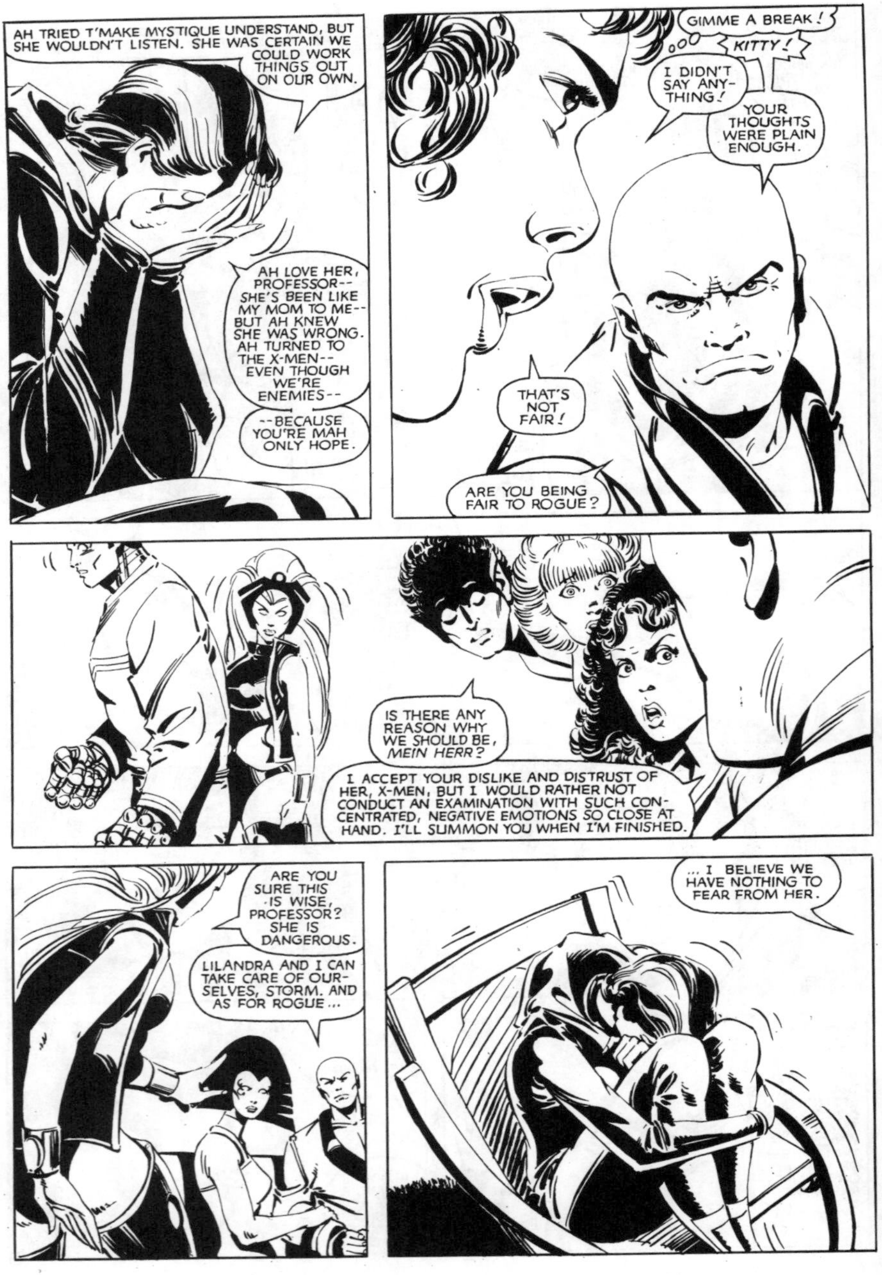
AH TRIED T'MAKE MYSTIQUE UNDERSTAND, BUT SHE WOULDN'T LISTEN. SHE WAS CERTAIN WE COULD WORK THINGS OUT ON OUR OWN.
AH LOVE HER, PROFESSOR-- SHE'S BEEN LIKE MY MOM TO ME-- BUT AH KNEW SHE WAS WRONG. AH TURNED TO THE X-MEN-- EVEN THOUGH WE'RE ENEMIES--
--BECAUSE YOU'RE MAH ONLY HOPE.
GIMME A BREAK!
KITTY!
I DIDN'T SAY ANY-THING!
YOUR THOUGHTS WERE PLAIN ENOUGH.
THAT'S NOT FAIR!
ARE YOU BEING FAIR TO ROGUE?
IS THERE ANY REASON WHY WE SHOULD BE, MEIN HERR?
I ACCEPT YOUR DISLIKE AND DISTRUST OF HER, X-MEN, BUT I WOULD RATHER NOT CONDUCT AN EXAMINATION WITH SUCH CON-CENTRATED, NEGATIVE EMOTIONS SO CLOSE AT HAND. I'LL SUMMON YOU WHEN I'M FINISHED.
ARE YOU SURE THIS IS WISE, PROFESSOR? SHE IS DANGEROUS.
LILANDRA AND I CAN TAKE CARE OF OUR-SELVES, STORM. AND AS FOR ROGUE...
... I BELIEVE WE HAVE NOTHING TO FEAR FROM HER.

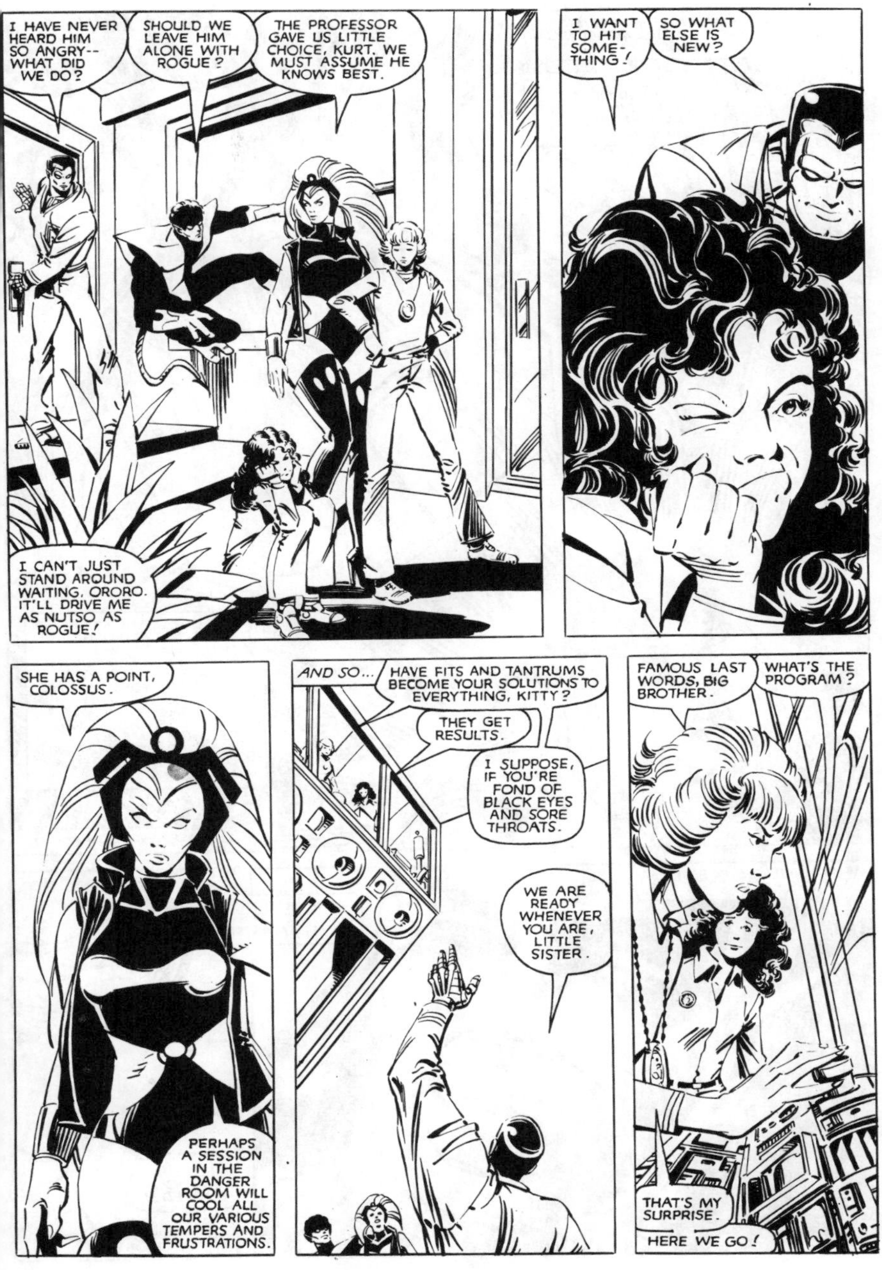
I HAVE NEVER HEARD HIM SO ANGRY-- WHAT DID WE DO?
SHOULD WE LEAVE HIM ALONE WITH ROGUE?
THE PROFESSOR GAVE US LITTLE CHOICE, KURT. WE MUST ASSUME HE KNOWS BEST.
I CAN'T JUST STAND AROUND WAITING, ORORO. IT'LL DRIVE ME AS NUTSO AS ROGUE!
I WANT TO HIT SOME-THING!
SO WHAT ELSE IS NEW?
SHE HAS A POINT, COLOSSUS.
PERHAPS A SESSION IN THE DANGER ROOM WILL COOL ALL OUR VARIOUS TEMPERS AND FRUSTRATIONS.
AND SO...
HAVE FITS AND TANTRUMS BECOME YOUR SOLUTIONS TO EVERYTHING, KITTY?
THEY GET RESULTS.
I SUPPOSE, IF YOU'RE FOND OF BLACK EYES AND SORE THROATS.
WE ARE READY WHENEVER YOU ARE, LITTLE SISTER.
FAMOUS LAST WORDS, BIG BROTHER.
WHAT'S THE PROGRAM?
THAT'S MY SURPRISE.
HERE WE GO!

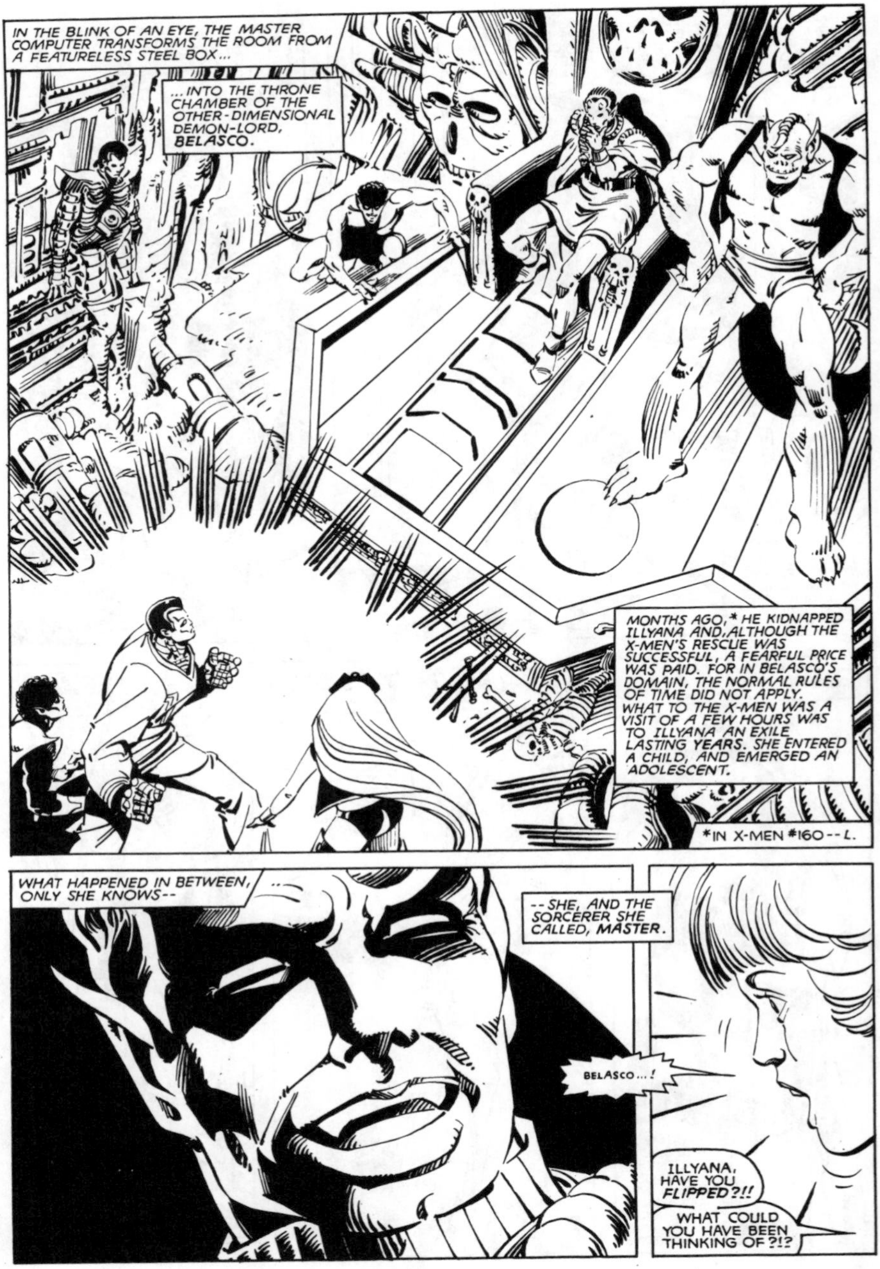
IN THE BLINK OF AN EYE, THE MASTER COMPUTER TRANSFORMS THE ROOM FROM A FEATURELESS STEEL BOX...
...INTO THE THRONE CHAMBER OF THE OTHER-DIMENSIONAL DEMON-LORD, BELASCO.
MONTHS AGO,* HE KIDNAPPED ILLYANA AND, ALTHOUGH THE X-MEN'S RESCUE WAS SUCCESSFUL, A FEARFUL PRICE WAS PAID. FOR IN BELASCO'S DOMAIN, THE NORMAL RULES OF TIME DID NOT APPLY. WHAT TO THE X-MEN WAS A VISIT OF A FEW HOURS WAS TO ILLYANA AN EXILE LASTING YEARS. SHE ENTERED A CHILD, AND EMERGED AN ADOLESCENT.
*IN X-MEN #160--L.
WHAT HAPPENED IN BETWEEN, ONLY SHE KNOWS--
--SHE, AND THE SORCERER SHE CALLED, MASTER.
BELASCO...!
ILLYANA, HAVE YOU FLIPPED?!!
WHAT COULD YOU HAVE BEEN THINKING OF?!?

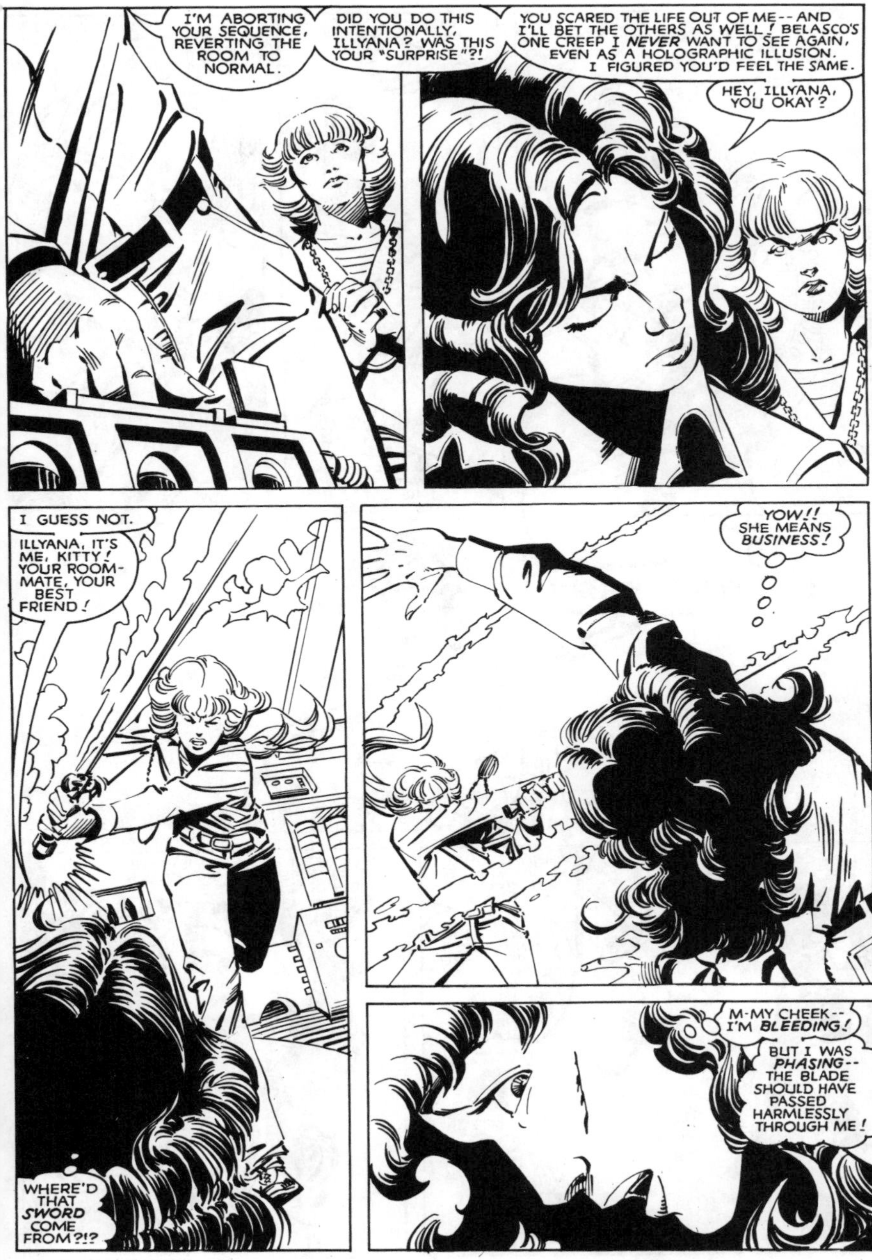
I'M ABORTING YOUR SEQUENCE, REVERTING THE ROOM TO NORMAL.
DID YOU DO THIS INTENTIONALLY, ILLYANA? WAS THIS YOUR "SURPRISE"?!
YOU SCARED THE LIFE OUT OF ME-- AND I'LL BET THE OTHERS AS WELL! BELASCO'S ONE CREEP I NEVER WANT TO SEE AGAIN, EVEN AS A HOLOGRAPHIC ILLUSION. I FIGURED YOU'D FEEL THE SAME.
HEY, ILLYANA, YOU OKAY?
I GUESS NOT.
ILLYANA, IT'S ME, KITTY! YOUR ROOMMATE, YOUR BEST FRIEND!
WHERE'D THAT SWORD COME FROM?!?
YOW!! SHE MEANS BUSINESS!
M-MY CHEEK-- I'M BLEEDING!
BUT I WAS PHASING-- THE BLADE SHOULD HAVE PASSED HARMLESSLY THROUGH ME!

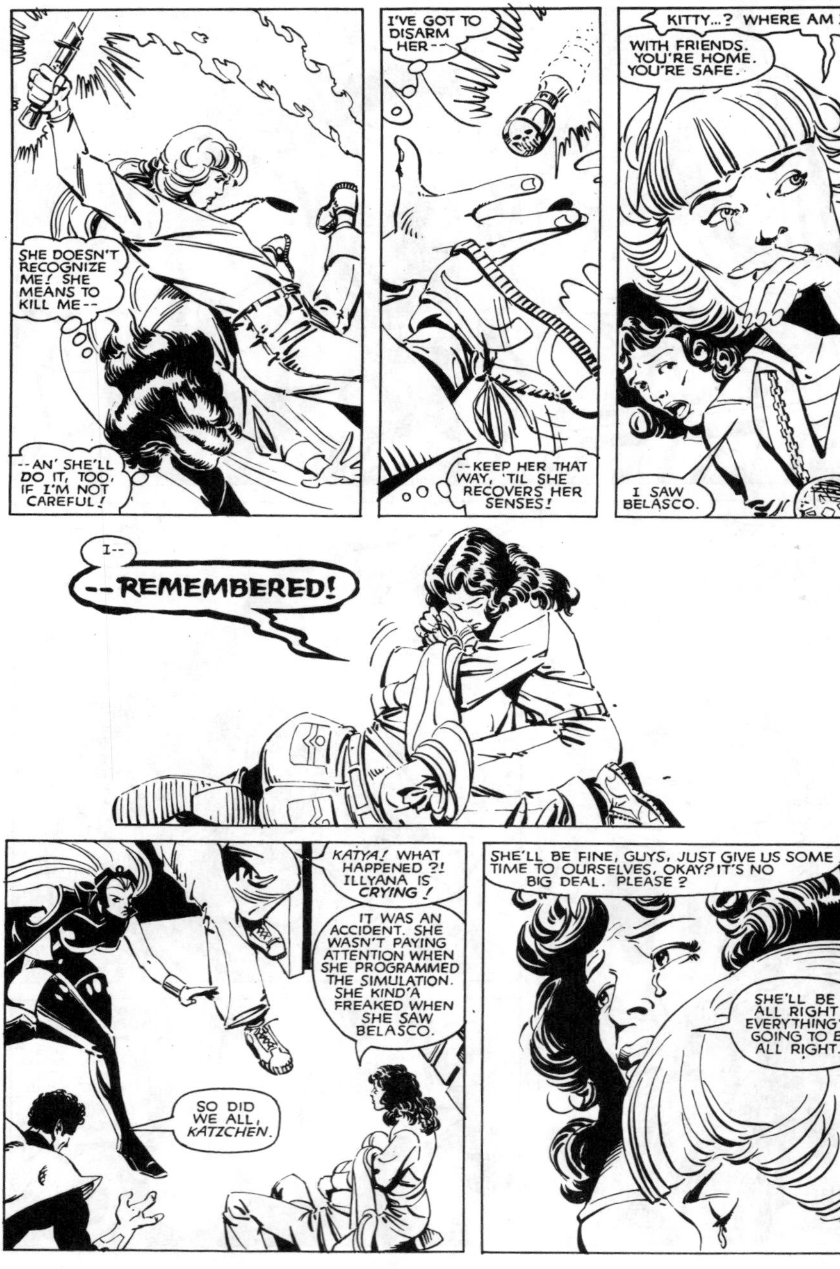
SHE DOESN'T RECOGNIZE ME! SHE MEANS TO KILL ME--
--AN' SHE'LL DO IT, TOO, IF I'M NOT CAREFUL!
I'VE GOT TO DISARM HER--
--KEEP HER THAT WAY, 'TIL SHE RECOVERS HER SENSES!
KITTY...? WHERE AM I?
WITH FRIENDS. YOU'RE HOME. YOU'RE SAFE.
I SAW BELASCO.
I--
--REMEMBERED!
KATYA! WHAT HAPPENED?! ILLYANA IS CRYING!
IT WAS AN ACCIDENT. SHE WASN'T PAYING ATTENTION WHEN SHE PROGRAMMED THE SIMULATION. SHE KIND'A FREAKED WHEN SHE SAW BELASCO.
SO DID WE ALL, KATZCHEN.
SHE'LL BE FINE, GUYS, JUST GIVE US SOME TIME TO OURSELVES, OKAY? IT'S NO BIG DEAL. PLEASE?
SHE'LL BE ALL RIGHT. EVERYTHING'S GOING TO BE ALL RIGHT.

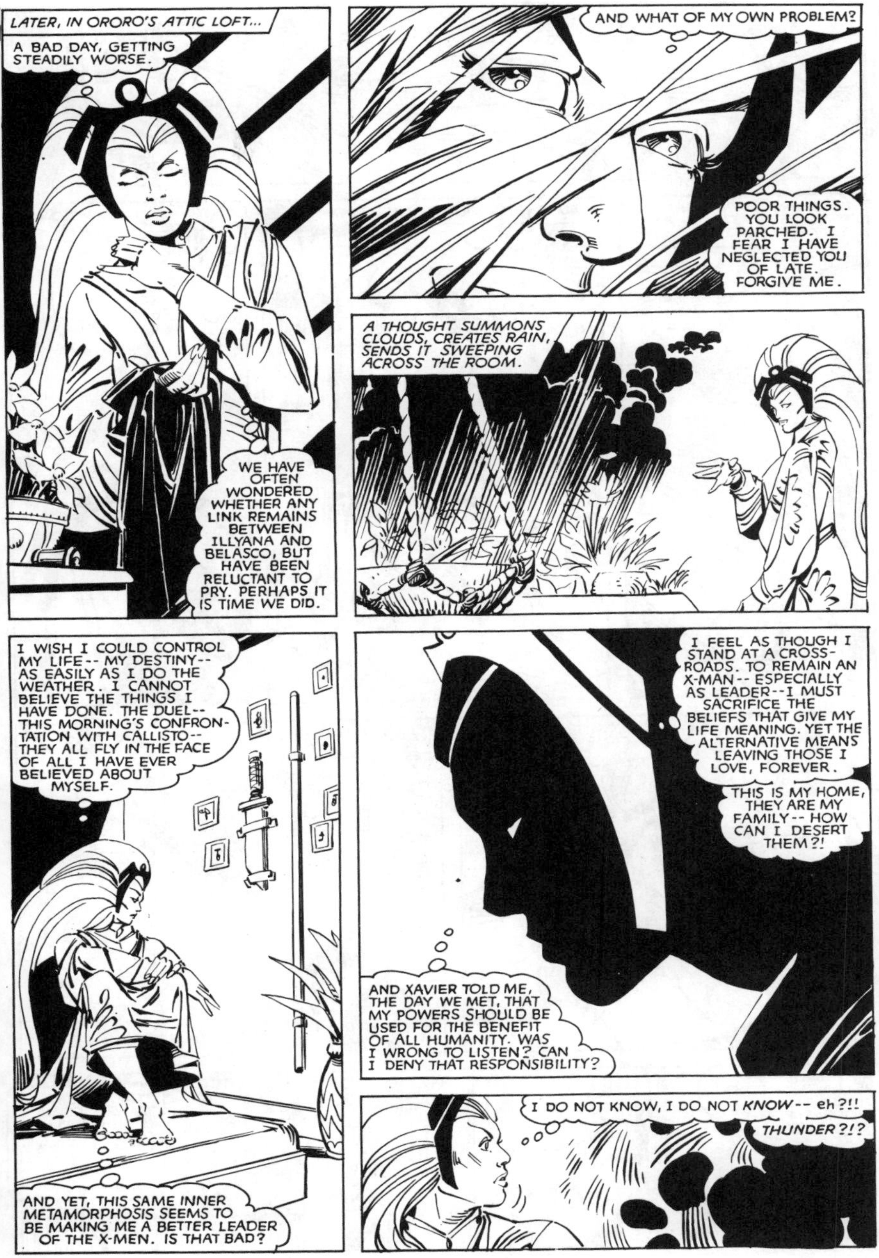
LATER, IN ORORO'S ATTIC LOFT...
A BAD DAY, GETTING STEADILY WORSE.
WE HAVE OFTEN WONDERED WHETHER ANY LINK REMAINS BETWEEN ILLYANA AND BELASCO, BUT HAVE BEEN RELUCTANT TO PRY. PERHAPS IT IS TIME WE DID.
AND WHAT OF MY OWN PROBLEM?
POOR THINGS. YOU LOOK PARCHED. I FEAR I HAVE NEGLECTED YOU OF LATE. FORGIVE ME.
A THOUGHT SUMMONS CLOUDS, CREATES RAIN, SENDS IT SWEEPING ACROSS THE ROOM.
I WISH I COULD CONTROL MY LIFE-- MY DESTINY-- AS EASILY AS I DO THE WEATHER. I CANNOT BELIEVE THE THINGS I HAVE DONE. THE DUEL-- THIS MORNING'S CONFRONTATION WITH CALLISTO-- THEY ALL FLY IN THE FACE OF ALL I HAVE EVER BELIEVED ABOUT MYSELF.
AND YET, THIS SAME INNER METAMORPHOSIS SEEMS TO BE MAKING ME A BETTER LEADER OF THE X-MEN. IS THAT BAD?
I FEEL AS THOUGH I STAND AT A CROSSROADS. TO REMAIN AN X-MAN-- ESPECIALLY AS LEADER--I MUST SACRIFICE THE BELIEFS THAT GIVE MY LIFE MEANING. YET THE ALTERNATIVE MEANS LEAVING THOSE I LOVE, FOREVER.
THIS IS MY HOME, THEY ARE MY FAMILY-- HOW CAN I DESERT THEM?!
AND XAVIER TOLD ME, THE DAY WE MET, THAT MY POWERS SHOULD BE USED FOR THE BENEFIT OF ALL HUMANITY. WAS I WRONG TO LISTEN? CAN I DENY THAT RESPONSIBILITY?
I DO NOT KNOW, I DO NOT KNOW-- eh?!!
THUNDER?!?

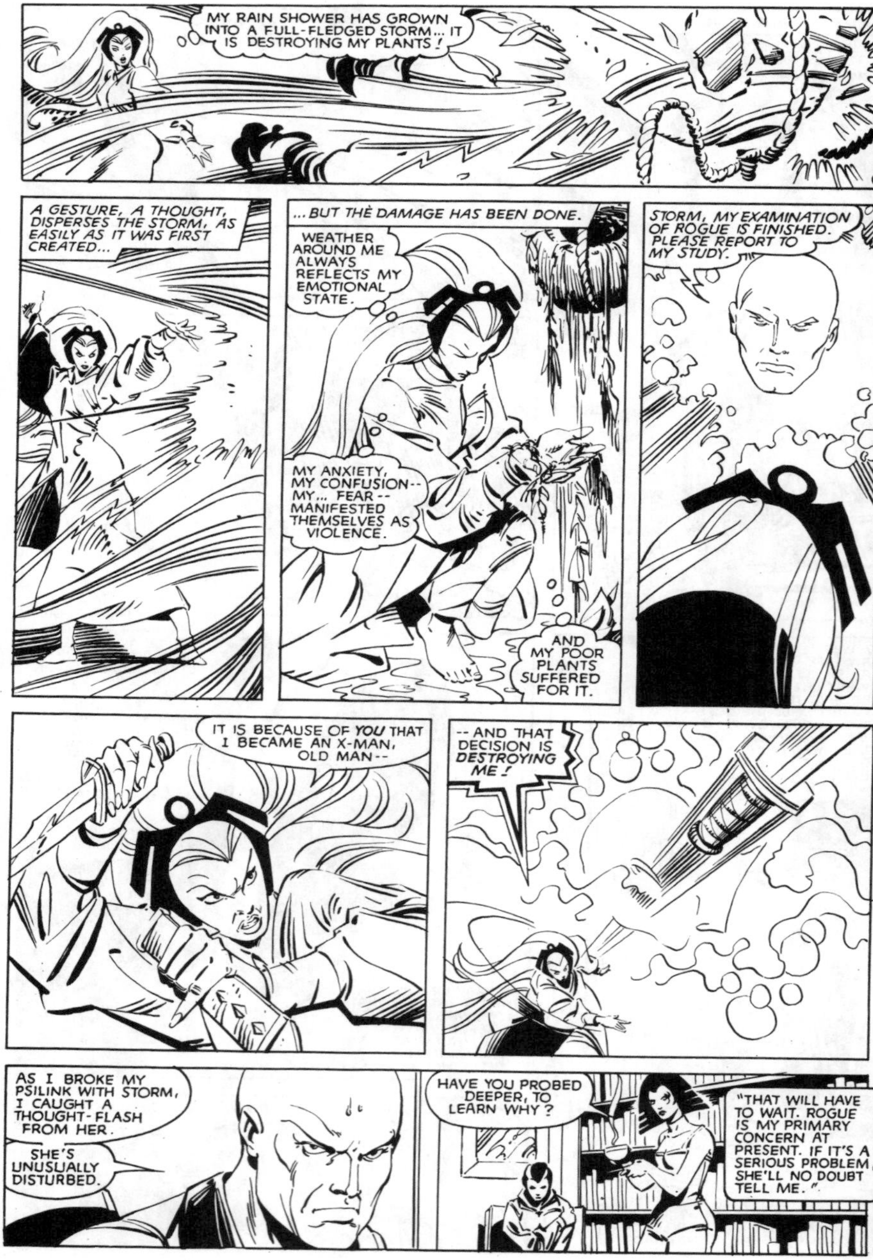
MY RAIN SHOWER HAS GROWN INTO A FULL-FLEDGED STORM... IT IS DESTROYING MY PLANTS!
A GESTURE, A THOUGHT, DISPERSES THE STORM, AS EASILY AS IT WAS FIRST CREATED...
...BUT THE DAMAGE HAS BEEN DONE.
WEATHER AROUND ME ALWAYS REFLECTS MY EMOTIONAL STATE.
MY ANXIETY, MY CONFUSION-- MY... FEAR-- MANIFESTED THEMSELVES AS VIOLENCE.
AND MY POOR PLANTS SUFFERED FOR IT.
STORM, MY EXAMINATION OF ROGUE IS FINISHED. PLEASE REPORT TO MY STUDY.
IT IS BECAUSE OF YOU THAT I BECAME AN X-MAN, OLD MAN--
--AND THAT DECISION IS DESTROYING ME!
AS I BROKE MY PSILINK WITH STORM, I CAUGHT A THOUGHT-FLASH FROM HER.
SHE'S UNUSUALLY DISTURBED.
HAVE YOU PROBED DEEPER, TO LEARN WHY?
"THAT WILL HAVE TO WAIT. ROGUE IS MY PRIMARY CONCERN AT PRESENT. IF IT'S A SERIOUS PROBLEM, SHE'LL NO DOUBT TELL ME."

I'VE QUESTIONED ROGUE, AT LENGTH, AND AM CONVINCED OF BOTH HER NEED AND HER SINCERITY.

THEREFORE, I HAVE DECIDED TO ADMIT HER NOT ONLY TO THE SCHOOL...

...BUT TO THE X-MEN, AS A PROBATIONARY MEMBER...

NO.

I BEG YOUR PARDON, STORM?

I LEAD THE X-MEN, PROFESSOR. I THINK THAT ENTITLES ME TO SOME SAY IN THIS MATTER.

YOU KNOW ROGUE'S HISTORY. ARE WE EXPECTED TO FIGHT BESIDE SOMEONE WE DO NOT--*DARE NOT*--TRUST...

...WHO MIGHT BETRAY US AT ANY TIME?!

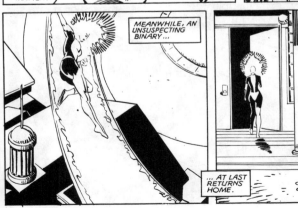

MEANWHILE, AN UNSUSPECTING BINARY...

...AT LAST RETURNS HOME.

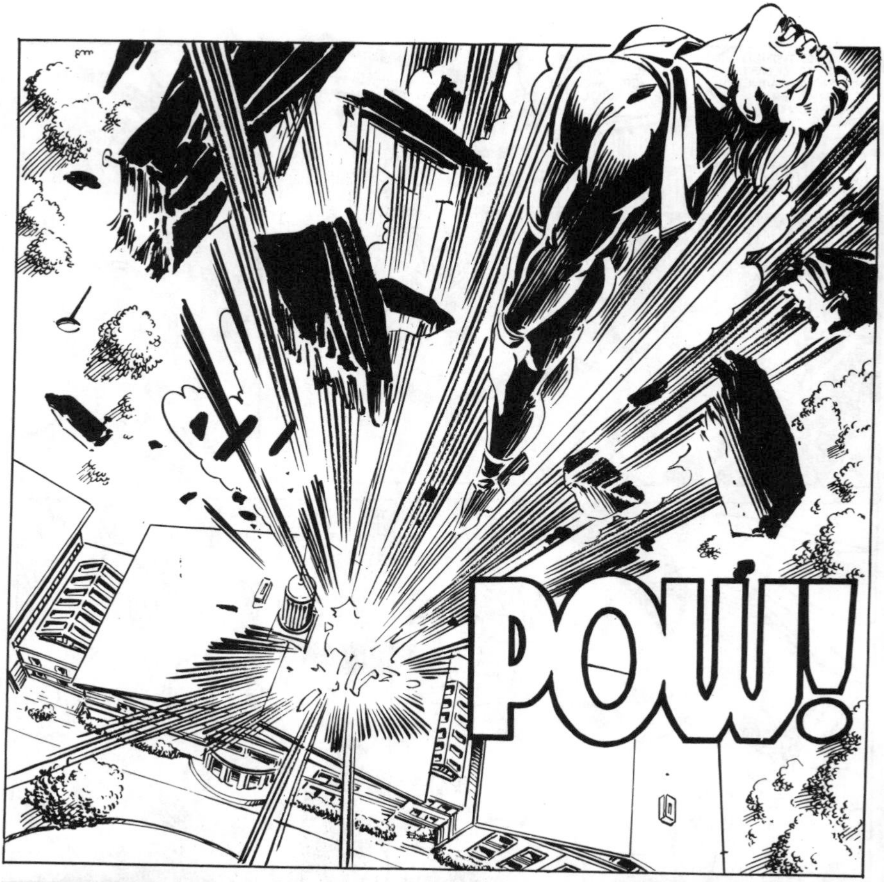
POW!

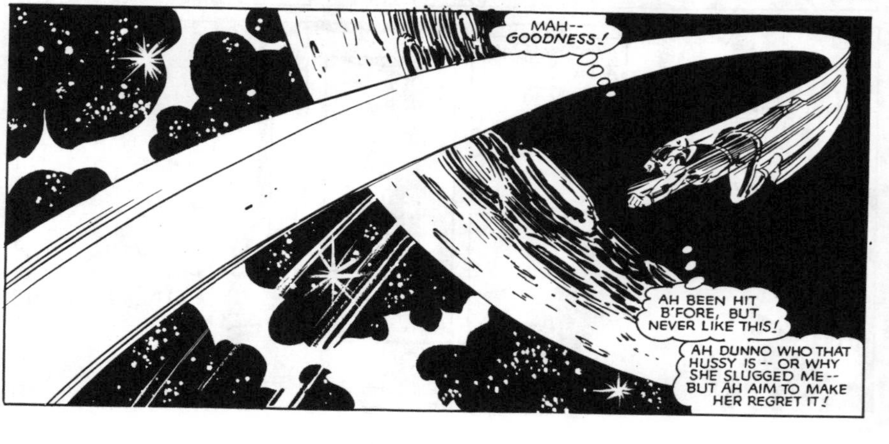
MAH-- GOODNESS!
AH BEEN HIT B'FORE, BUT NEVER LIKE THIS!
AH DUNNO WHO THAT HUSSY IS -- OR WHY SHE SLUGGED ME -- BUT AH AIM TO MAKE HER REGRET IT!

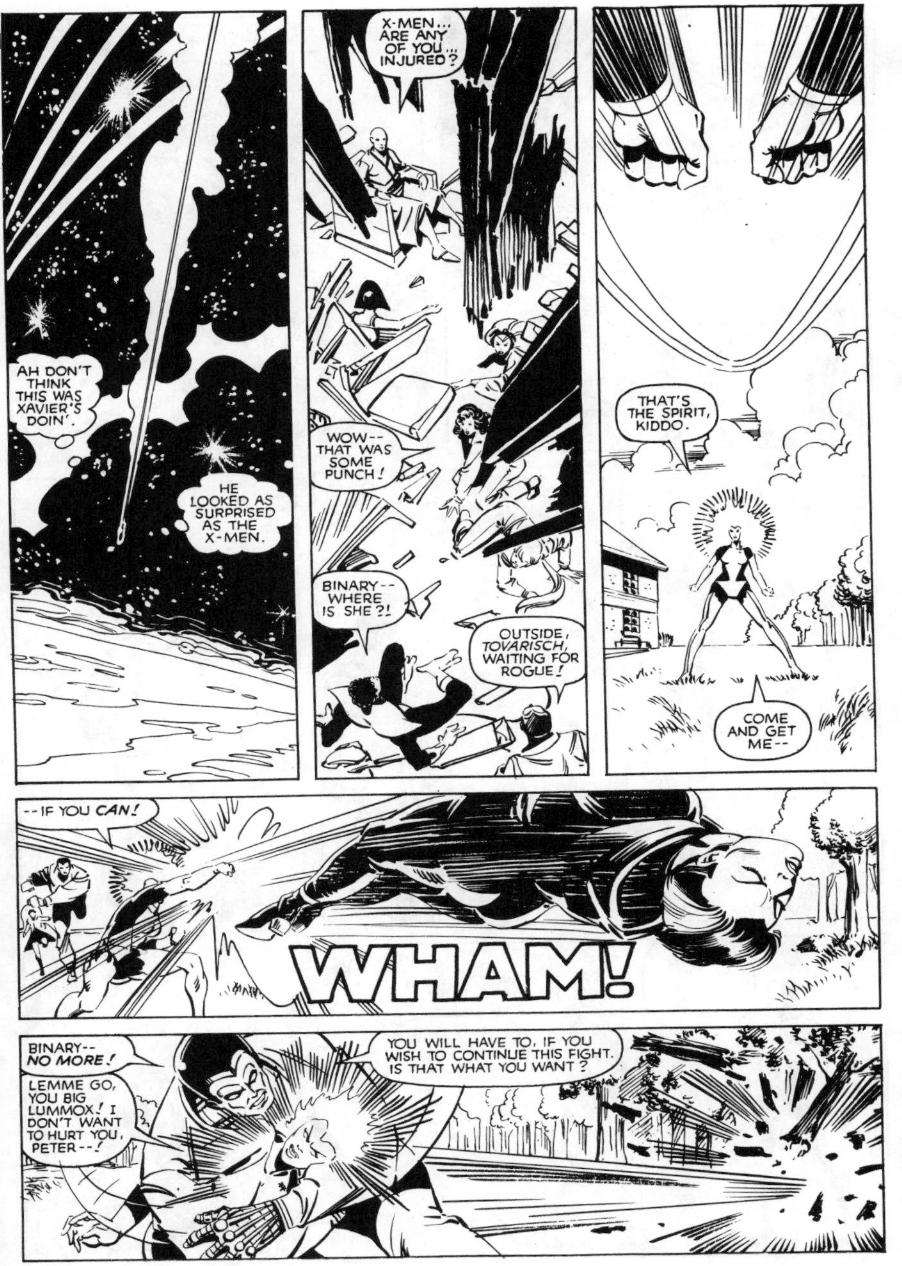
AH DON'T THINK THIS WAS XAVIER'S DOIN'.
HE LOOKED AS SURPRISED AS THE X-MEN.
X-MEN... ARE ANY OF YOU... INJURED?
WOW-- THAT WAS SOME PUNCH!
BINARY-- WHERE IS SHE?!
OUTSIDE, TOVARISCH, WAITING FOR ROGUE!
THAT'S THE SPIRIT, KIDDO.
COME AND GET ME--
--IF YOU CAN!
WHAM!
BINARY-- NO MORE!
LEMME GO, YOU BIG LUMMOX! I DON'T WANT TO HURT YOU, PETER--!
YOU WILL HAVE TO, IF YOU WISH TO CONTINUE THIS FIGHT. IS THAT WHAT YOU WANT?

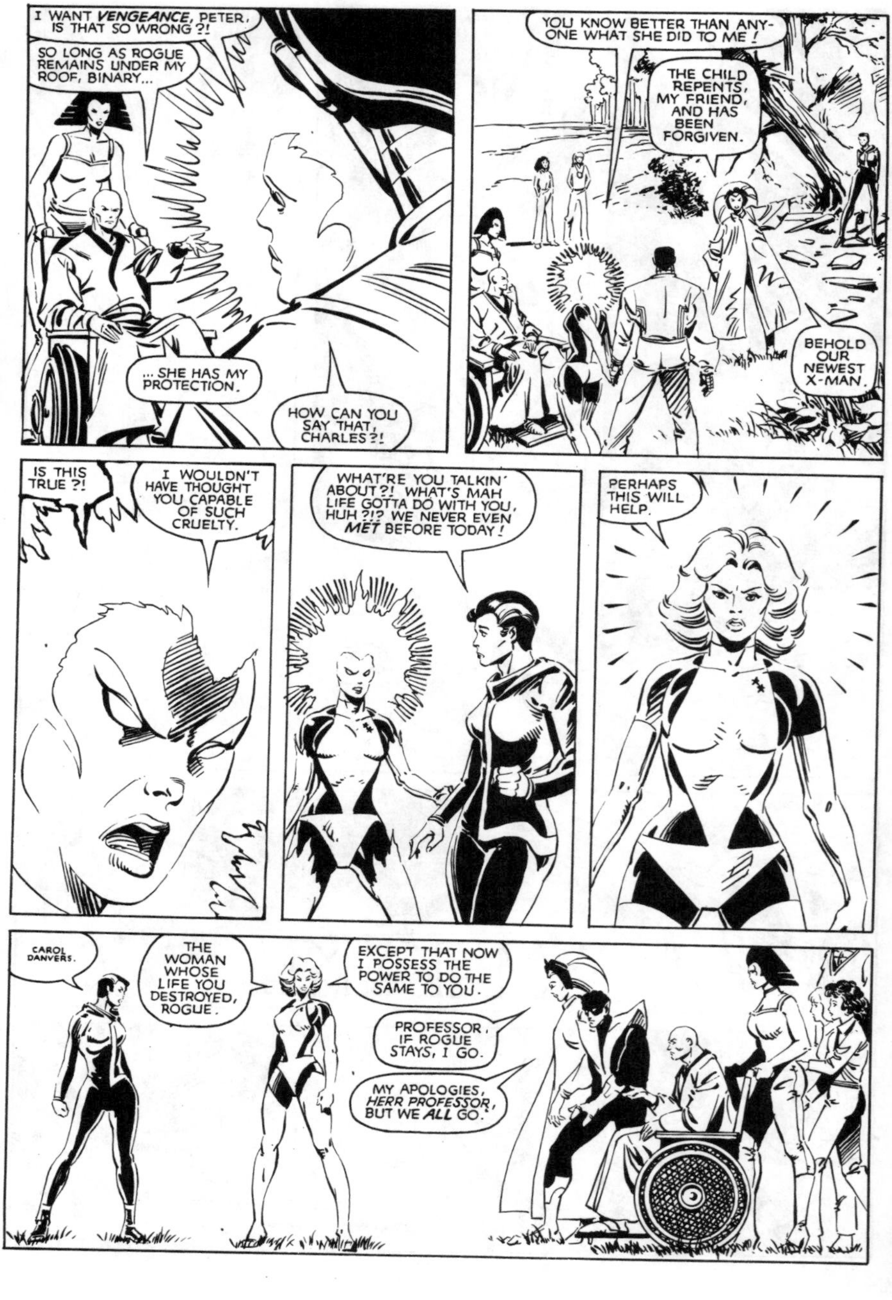
I WANT VENGEANCE, PETER, IS THAT SO WRONG?!
SO LONG AS ROGUE REMAINS UNDER MY ROOF, BINARY...
...SHE HAS MY PROTECTION.
HOW CAN YOU SAY THAT, CHARLES?!
YOU KNOW BETTER THAN ANYONE WHAT SHE DID TO ME!
THE CHILD REPENTS, MY FRIEND, AND HAS BEEN FORGIVEN.
BEHOLD OUR NEWEST X-MAN.
IS THIS TRUE?!
I WOULDN'T HAVE THOUGHT YOU CAPABLE OF SUCH CRUELTY.
WHAT'RE YOU TALKIN' ABOUT?! WHAT'S MAH LIFE GOTTA DO WITH YOU, HUH?!? WE NEVER EVEN MET BEFORE TODAY!
PERHAPS THIS WILL HELP.
CAROL DANVERS.
THE WOMAN WHOSE LIFE YOU DESTROYED, ROGUE.
EXCEPT THAT NOW I POSSESS THE POWER TO DO THE SAME TO YOU.
PROFESSOR, IF ROGUE STAYS, I GO.
MY APOLOGIES, HERR PROFESSOR, BUT WE ALL GO.

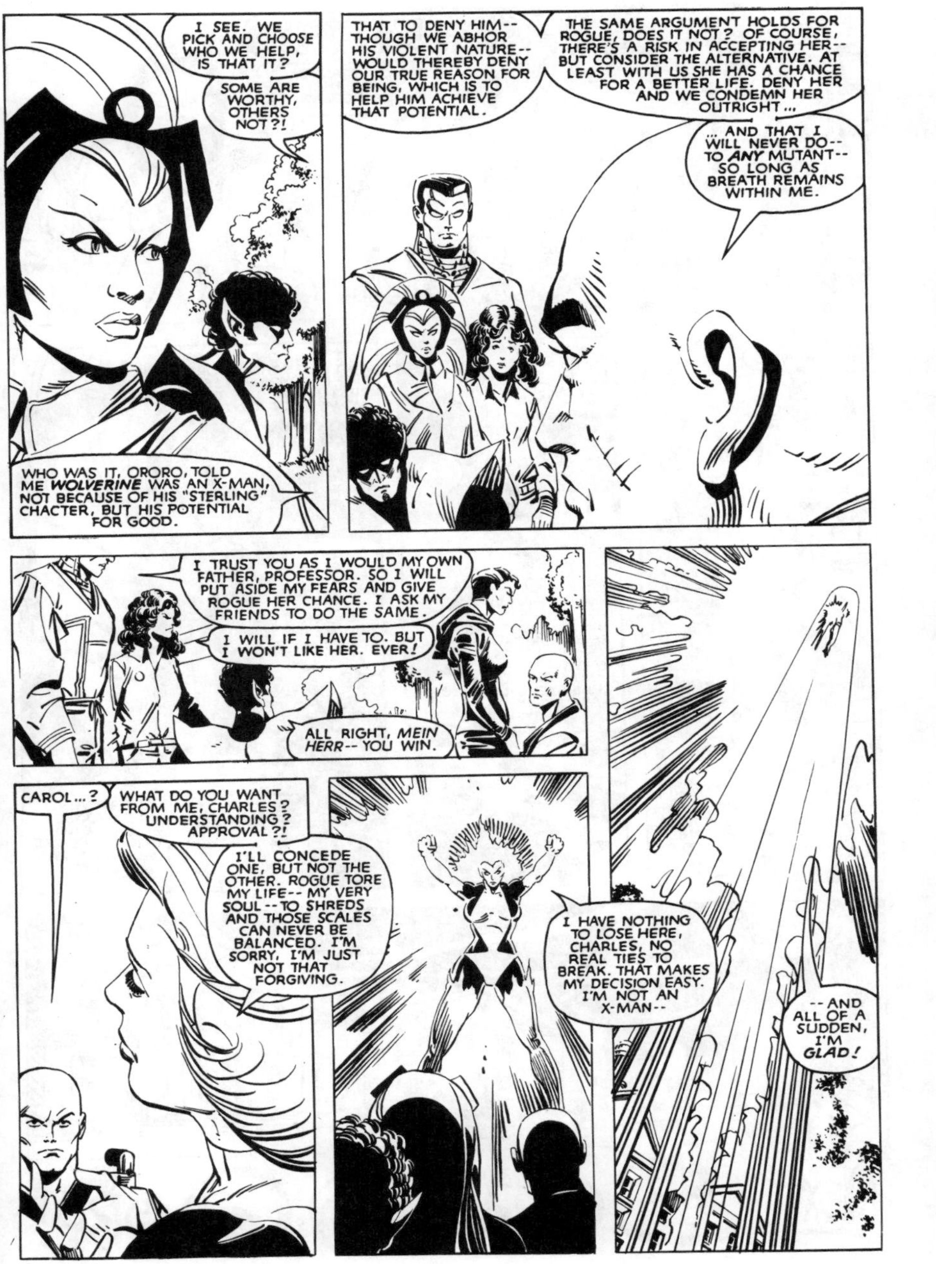
I SEE. WE PICK AND CHOOSE WHO WE HELP, IS THAT IT?
SOME ARE WORTHY, OTHERS NOT?!
WHO WAS IT, ORORO, TOLD ME WOLVERINE WAS AN X-MAN, NOT BECAUSE OF HIS "STERLING" CHACTER, BUT HIS POTENTIAL FOR GOOD.
THAT TO DENY HIM-- THOUGH WE ABHOR HIS VIOLENT NATURE-- WOULD THEREBY DENY OUR TRUE REASON FOR BEING, WHICH IS TO HELP HIM ACHIEVE THAT POTENTIAL.
THE SAME ARGUMENT HOLDS FOR ROGUE, DOES IT NOT? OF COURSE, THERE'S A RISK IN ACCEPTING HER-- BUT CONSIDER THE ALTERNATIVE. AT LEAST WITH US SHE HAS A CHANCE FOR A BETTER LIFE. DENY HER AND WE CONDEMN HER OUTRIGHT...
... AND THAT I WILL NEVER DO-- TO ANY MUTANT-- SO LONG AS BREATH REMAINS WITHIN ME.
I TRUST YOU AS I WOULD MY OWN FATHER, PROFESSOR. SO I WILL PUT ASIDE MY FEARS AND GIVE ROGUE HER CHANCE. I ASK MY FRIENDS TO DO THE SAME.
I WILL IF I HAVE TO. BUT I WON'T LIKE HER. EVER!
ALL RIGHT, MEIN HERR-- YOU WIN.
CAROL...?
WHAT DO YOU WANT FROM ME, CHARLES? UNDERSTANDING? APPROVAL?!
I'LL CONCEDE ONE, BUT NOT THE OTHER. ROGUE TORE MY LIFE-- MY VERY SOUL--TO SHREDS AND THOSE SCALES CAN NEVER BE BALANCED. I'M SORRY, I'M JUST NOT THAT FORGIVING.
I HAVE NOTHING TO LOSE HERE, CHARLES, NO REAL TIES TO BREAK. THAT MAKES MY DECISION EASY. I'M NOT AN X-MAN--
--AND ALL OF A SUDDEN, I'M GLAD!

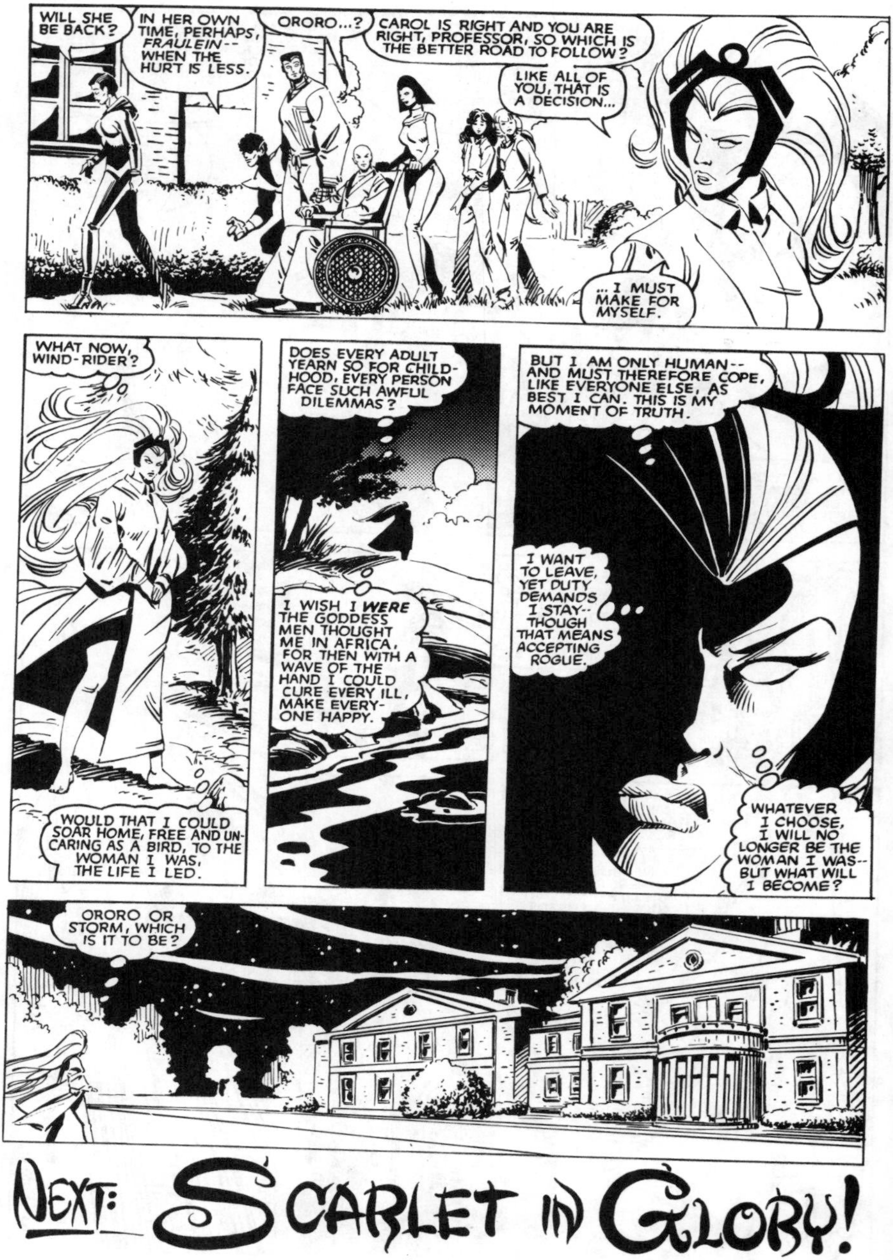
WILL SHE BE BACK?
IN HER OWN TIME, PERHAPS, FRAULEIN-- WHEN THE HURT IS LESS.
ORORO...?
CAROL IS RIGHT AND YOU ARE RIGHT, PROFESSOR, SO WHICH IS THE BETTER ROAD TO FOLLOW?
LIKE ALL OF YOU, THAT IS A DECISION...
...I MUST MAKE FOR MYSELF.
WHAT NOW, WIND-RIDER?
WOULD THAT I COULD SOAR HOME, FREE AND UNCARING AS A BIRD, TO THE WOMAN I WAS, THE LIFE I LED.
DOES EVERY ADULT YEARN SO FOR CHILDHOOD, EVERY PERSON FACE SUCH AWFUL DILEMMAS?
I WISH I WERE THE GODDESS MEN THOUGHT ME IN AFRICA, FOR THEN WITH A WAVE OF THE HAND I COULD CURE EVERY ILL, MAKE EVERYONE HAPPY.
BUT I AM ONLY HUMAN-- AND MUST THEREFORE COPE, LIKE EVERYONE ELSE, AS BEST I CAN. THIS IS MY MOMENT OF TRUTH.
I WANT TO LEAVE, YET DUTY DEMANDS I STAY-- THOUGH THAT MEANS ACCEPTING ROGUE.
WHATEVER I CHOOSE, I WILL NO LONGER BE THE WOMAN I WAS-- BUT WHAT WILL I BECOME?
ORORO OR STORM, WHICH IS IT TO BE?

NEXT: SCARLET IN GLORY!

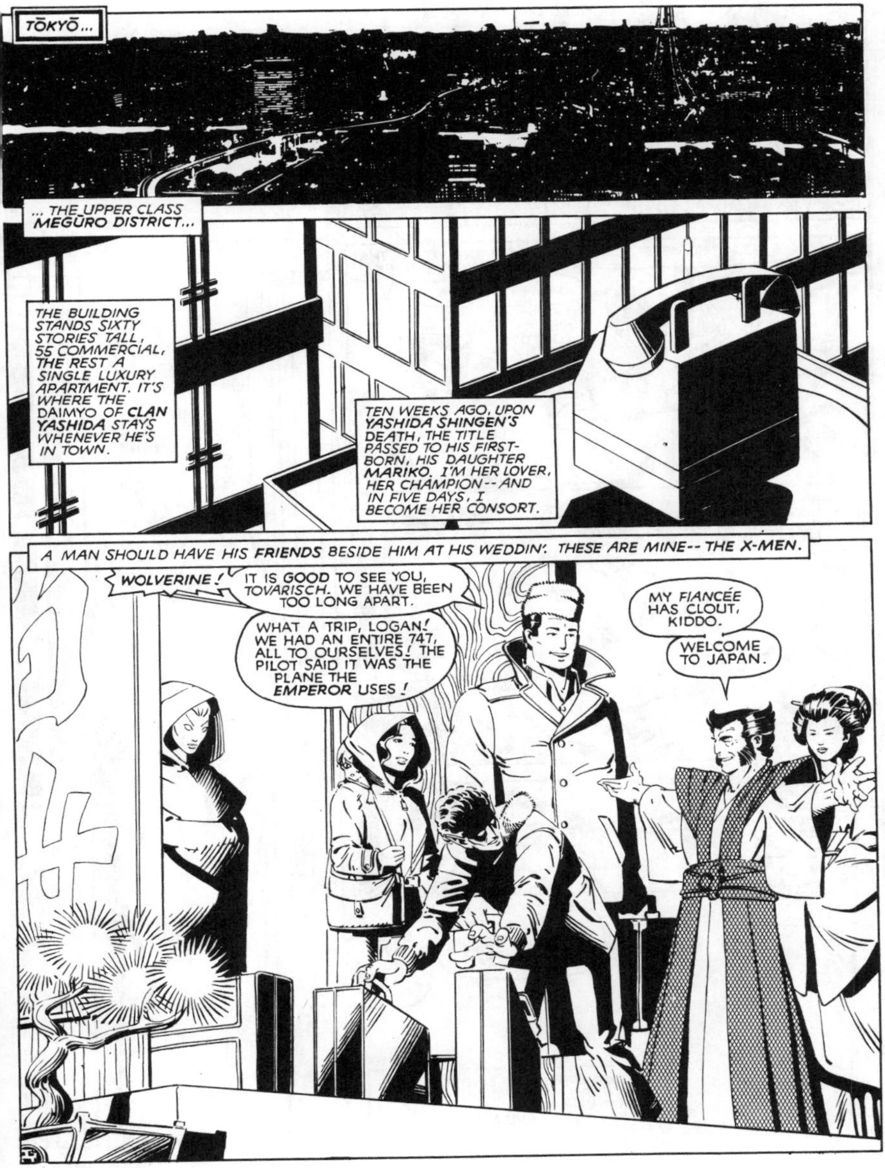
TŌKYŌ...
... THE UPPER CLASS MEGŪRO DISTRICT...
THE BUILDING STANDS SIXTY STORIES TALL, 55 COMMERCIAL, THE REST A SINGLE LUXURY APARTMENT. IT'S WHERE THE DAIMYO OF CLAN YASHIDA STAYS WHENEVER HE'S IN TOWN.
TEN WEEKS AGO, UPON YASHIDA SHINGEN'S DEATH, THE TITLE PASSED TO HIS FIRST-BORN, HIS DAUGHTER MARIKO. I'M HER LOVER, HER CHAMPION-- AND IN FIVE DAYS, I BECOME HER CONSORT.
A MAN SHOULD HAVE HIS FRIENDS BESIDE HIM AT HIS WEDDIN'. THESE ARE MINE-- THE X-MEN.
WOLVERINE!
IT IS GOOD TO SEE YOU, TOVARISCH. WE HAVE BEEN TOO LONG APART.
WHAT A TRIP, LOGAN! WE HAD AN ENTIRE 747, ALL TO OURSELVES! THE PILOT SAID IT WAS THE PLANE THE EMPEROR USES!
MY FIANCÉE HAS CLOUT, KIDDO.
WELCOME TO JAPAN.

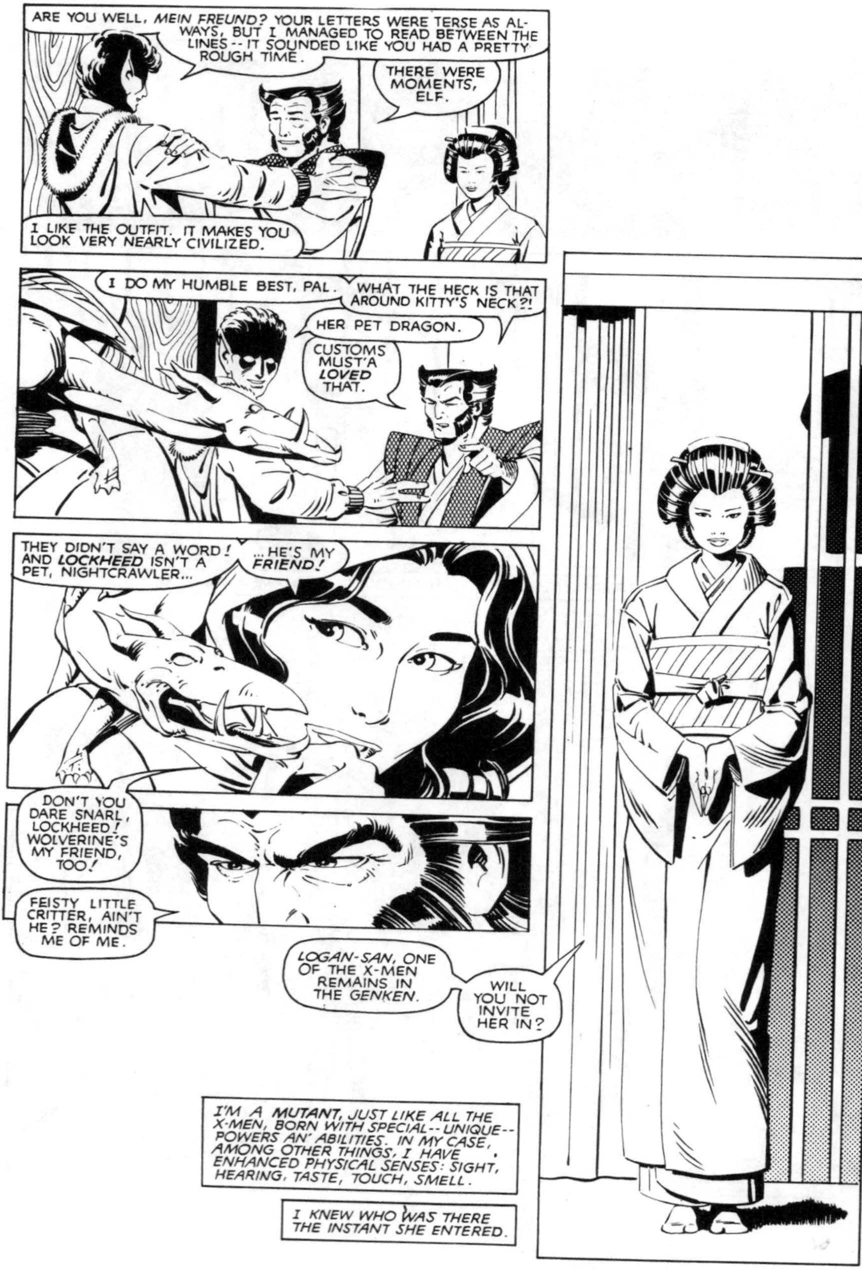
ARE YOU WELL, *MEIN FREUND?* YOUR LETTERS WERE TERSE AS ALWAYS, BUT I MANAGED TO READ BETWEEN THE LINES -- IT SOUNDED LIKE YOU HAD A PRETTY ROUGH TIME.
THERE WERE MOMENTS, ELF.
I LIKE THE OUTFIT. IT MAKES YOU LOOK VERY NEARLY CIVILIZED.
I DO MY HUMBLE BEST, PAL.
WHAT THE HECK IS THAT AROUND KITTY'S NECK?!
HER PET DRAGON.
CUSTOMS MUST'A *LOVED* THAT.
THEY DIDN'T SAY A WORD! AND *LOCKHEED* ISN'T A PET, NIGHTCRAWLER...
...HE'S MY *FRIEND!*
DON'T YOU DARE SNARL, LOCKHEED! WOLVERINE'S MY FRIEND, TOO!
FEISTY LITTLE CRITTER, AIN'T HE? REMINDS ME OF ME.
LOGAN-SAN, ONE OF THE X-MEN REMAINS IN THE *GENKEN*.
WILL YOU NOT INVITE HER IN?
*I'M A **MUTANT**, JUST LIKE ALL THE X-MEN, BORN WITH SPECIAL -- UNIQUE -- POWERS AN' ABILITIES. IN MY CASE, AMONG OTHER THINGS, I HAVE ENHANCED PHYSICAL SENSES: SIGHT, HEARING, TASTE, TOUCH, SMELL.*
I KNEW WHO WAS THERE THE INSTANT SHE ENTERED.

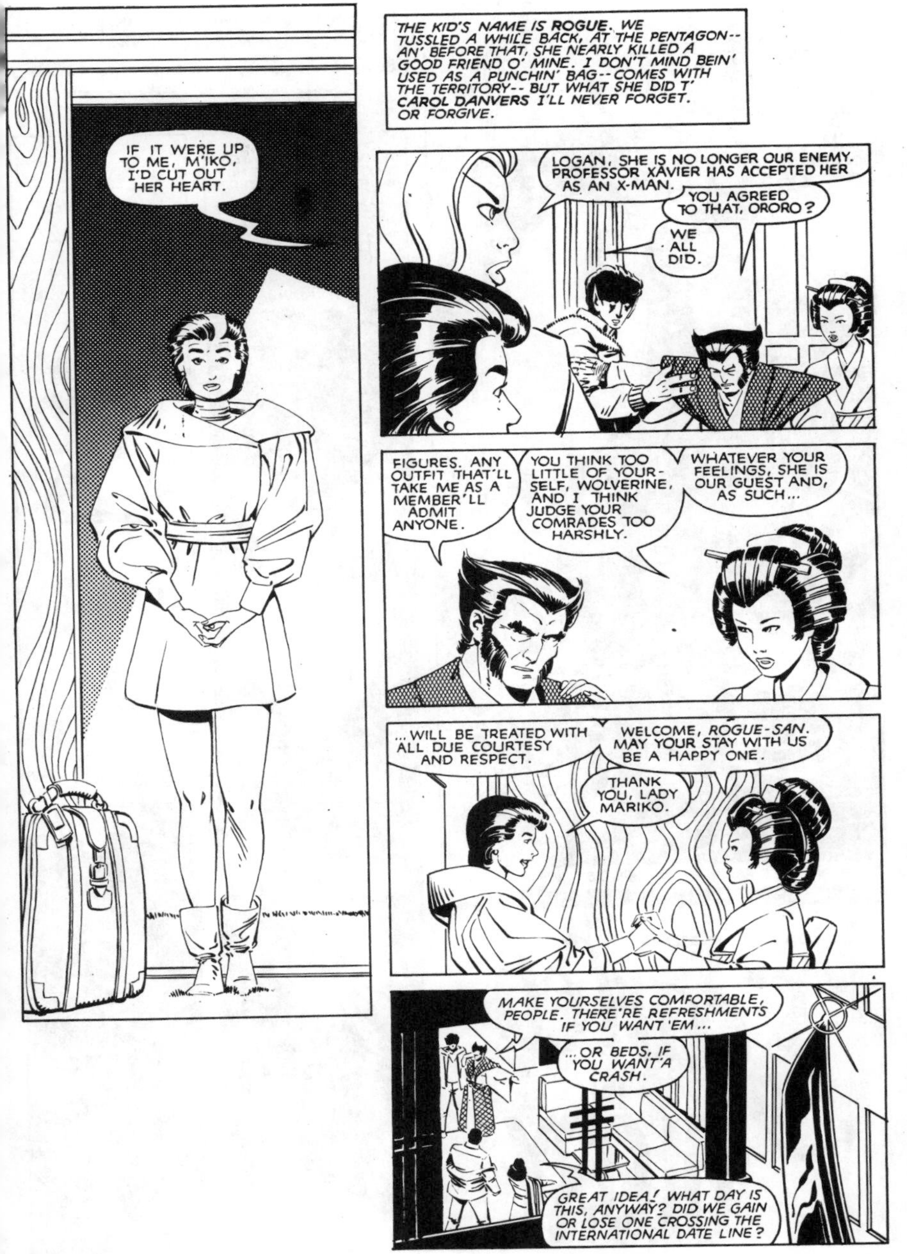
IF IT WERE UP TO ME, M'IKO, I'D CUT OUT HER HEART.
THE KID'S NAME IS ROGUE. WE TUSSLED A WHILE BACK, AT THE PENTAGON-- AN' BEFORE THAT, SHE NEARLY KILLED A GOOD FRIEND O' MINE. I DON'T MIND BEIN' USED AS A PUNCHIN' BAG-- COMES WITH THE TERRITORY-- BUT WHAT SHE DID T' CAROL DANVERS I'LL NEVER FORGET. OR FORGIVE.
LOGAN, SHE IS NO LONGER OUR ENEMY. PROFESSOR XAVIER HAS ACCEPTED HER AS AN X-MAN.
YOU AGREED TO THAT, ORORO?
WE ALL DID.
FIGURES. ANY OUTFIT THAT'LL TAKE ME AS A MEMBER'LL ADMIT ANYONE.
YOU THINK TOO LITTLE OF YOURSELF, WOLVERINE, AND I THINK JUDGE YOUR COMRADES TOO HARSHLY.
WHATEVER YOUR FEELINGS, SHE IS OUR GUEST AND, AS SUCH...
...WILL BE TREATED WITH ALL DUE COURTESY AND RESPECT.
WELCOME, ROGUE-SAN. MAY YOUR STAY WITH US BE A HAPPY ONE.
THANK YOU, LADY MARIKO.
MAKE YOURSELVES COMFORTABLE, PEOPLE. THERE'RE REFRESHMENTS IF YOU WANT 'EM...
...OR BEDS, IF YOU WANT'A CRASH.
GREAT IDEA! WHAT DAY IS THIS, ANYWAY? DID WE GAIN OR LOSE ONE CROSSING THE INTERNATIONAL DATE LINE?

CHRIS CLAREMONT *WRITER* · PAUL SMITH *PENCILER* · BOB WIACEK *INKER*

GLYNIS WEIN, *colorist* • TOM ORZECHOWSKI, *letterer*

LOUISE JONES *EDITOR* · JIM SHOOTER *EDITOR-IN-CHIEF*

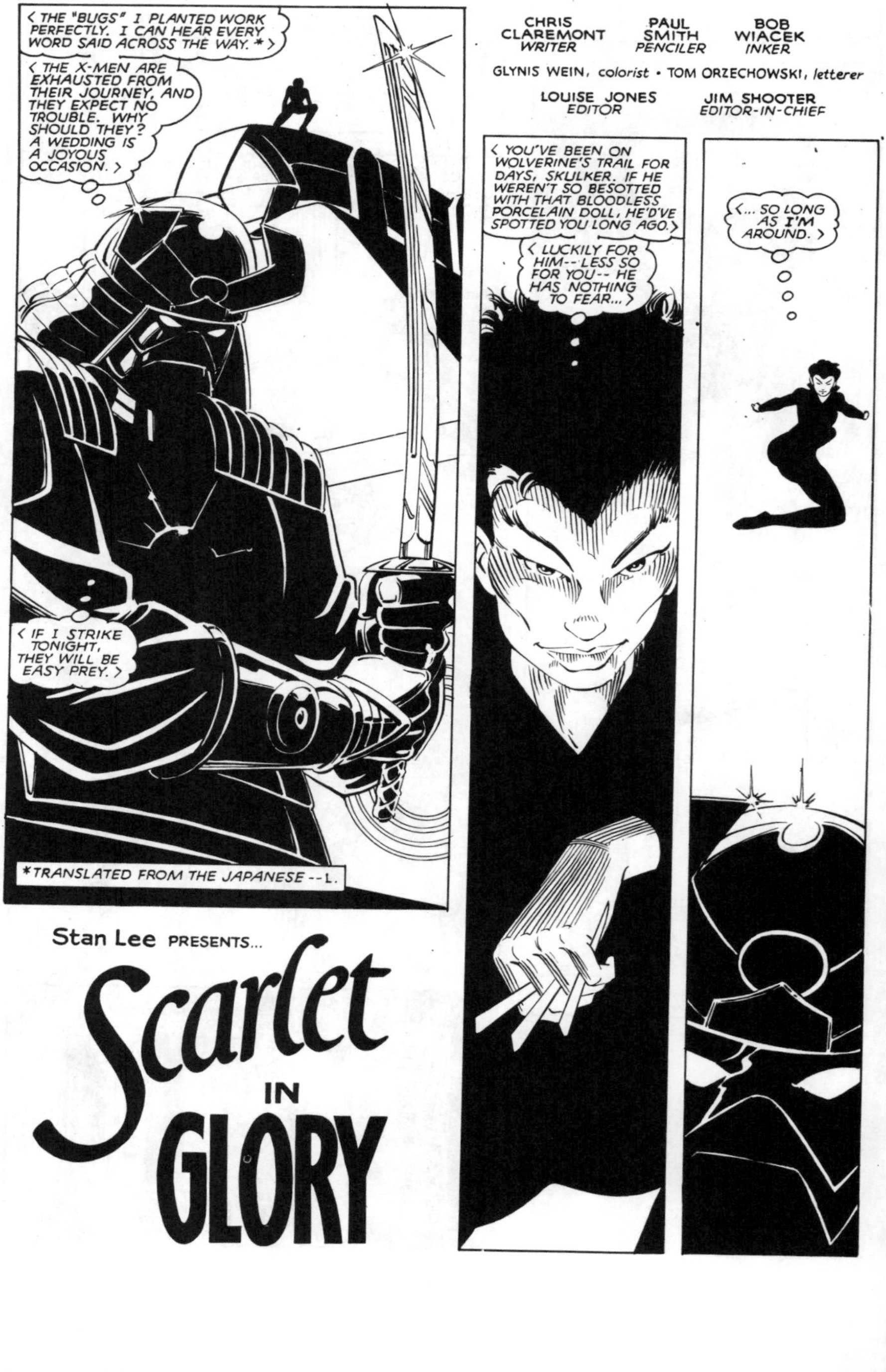

< THE "BUGS" I PLANTED WORK PERFECTLY. I CAN HEAR EVERY WORD SAID ACROSS THE WAY. * >
< THE X-MEN ARE EXHAUSTED FROM THEIR JOURNEY, AND THEY EXPECT NO TROUBLE. WHY SHOULD THEY? A WEDDING IS A JOYOUS OCCASION. >
< IF I STRIKE TONIGHT, THEY WILL BE EASY PREY. >
*TRANSLATED FROM THE JAPANESE --L.
< YOU'VE BEEN ON WOLVERINE'S TRAIL FOR DAYS, SKULKER. IF HE WEREN'T SO BESOTTED WITH THAT BLOODLESS PORCELAIN DOLL, HE'D'VE SPOTTED YOU LONG AGO. >
< LUCKILY FOR HIM-- LESS SO FOR YOU-- HE HAS NOTHING TO FEAR... >
<... SO LONG AS I'M AROUND. >

Stan Lee PRESENTS...

Scarlet IN GLORY

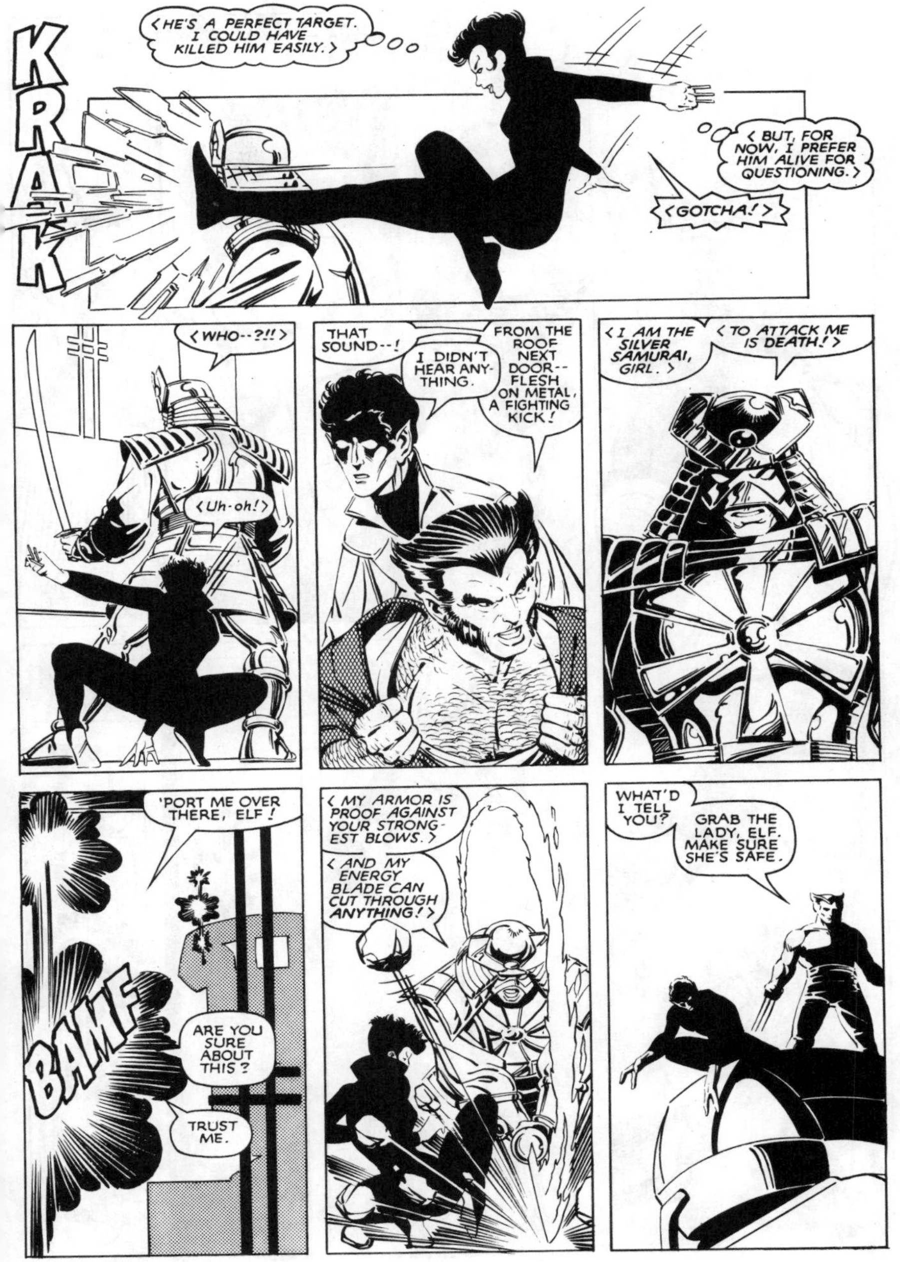

KRAK
< HE'S A PERFECT TARGET. I COULD HAVE KILLED HIM EASILY. >
< BUT, FOR NOW, I PREFER HIM ALIVE FOR QUESTIONING. >
< GOTCHA! >
< WHO--?!! >
< Uh-oh! >
THAT SOUND--!
I DIDN'T HEAR ANYTHING.
FROM THE ROOF NEXT DOOR-- FLESH ON METAL, A FIGHTING KICK!
< I AM THE SILVER SAMURAI, GIRL. >
< TO ATTACK ME IS DEATH! >
'PORT ME OVER THERE, ELF!
BAMF
ARE YOU SURE ABOUT THIS?
TRUST ME.
< MY ARMOR IS PROOF AGAINST YOUR STRONGEST BLOWS. >
< AND MY ENERGY BLADE CAN CUT THROUGH ANYTHING! >
WHAT'D I TELL YOU?
GRAB THE LADY, ELF. MAKE SURE SHE'S SAFE.

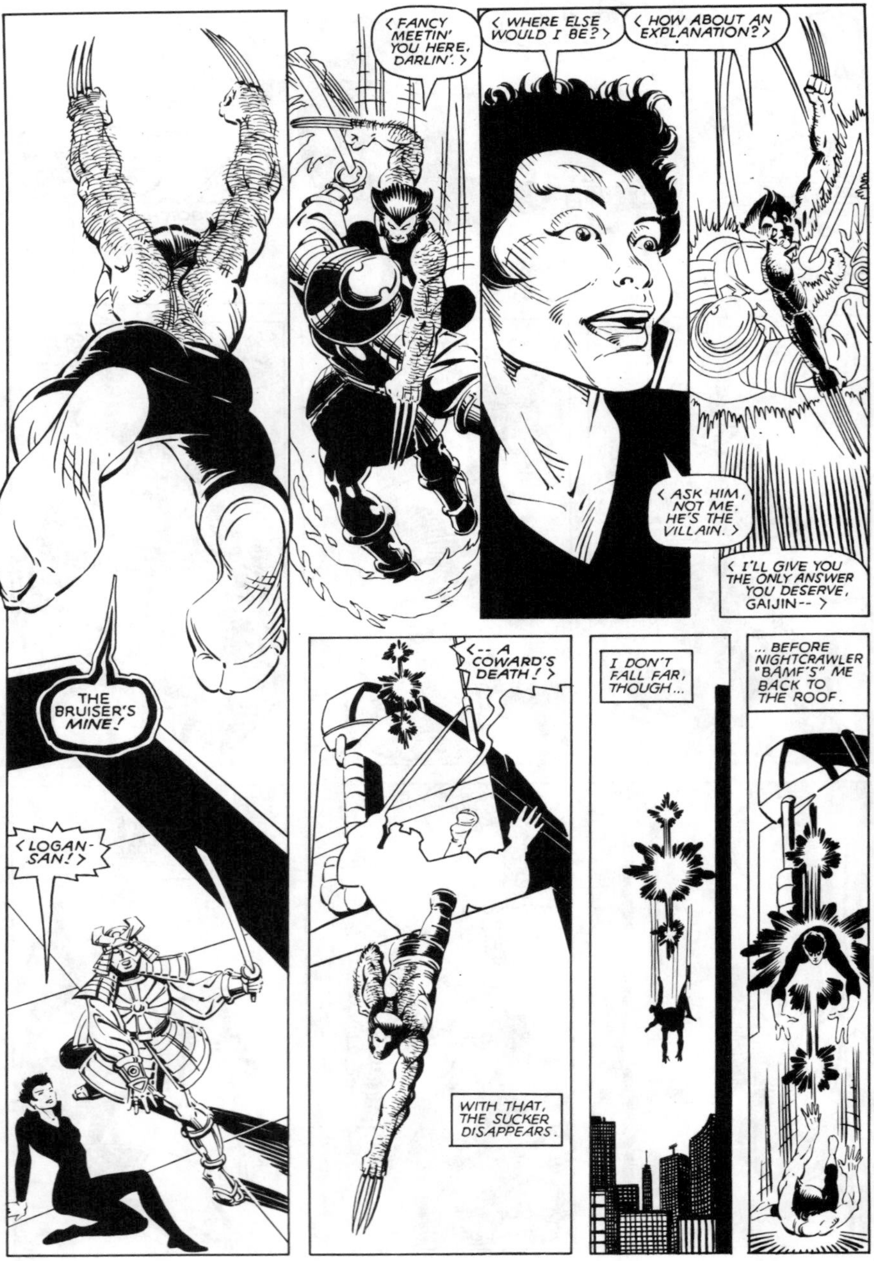

< FANCY MEETIN' YOU HERE, DARLIN'. >
< WHERE ELSE WOULD I BE? >
< HOW ABOUT AN EXPLANATION? >
< ASK HIM, NOT ME. HE'S THE VILLAIN. >
< I'LL GIVE YOU THE ONLY ANSWER YOU DESERVE, GAIJIN-- >
THE BRUISER'S MINE!
< LOGAN-SAN! >
< -- A COWARD'S DEATH! >
WITH THAT, THE SUCKER DISAPPEARS.
I DON'T FALL FAR, THOUGH...
... BEFORE NIGHTCRAWLER "BAMF'S" ME BACK TO THE ROOF.

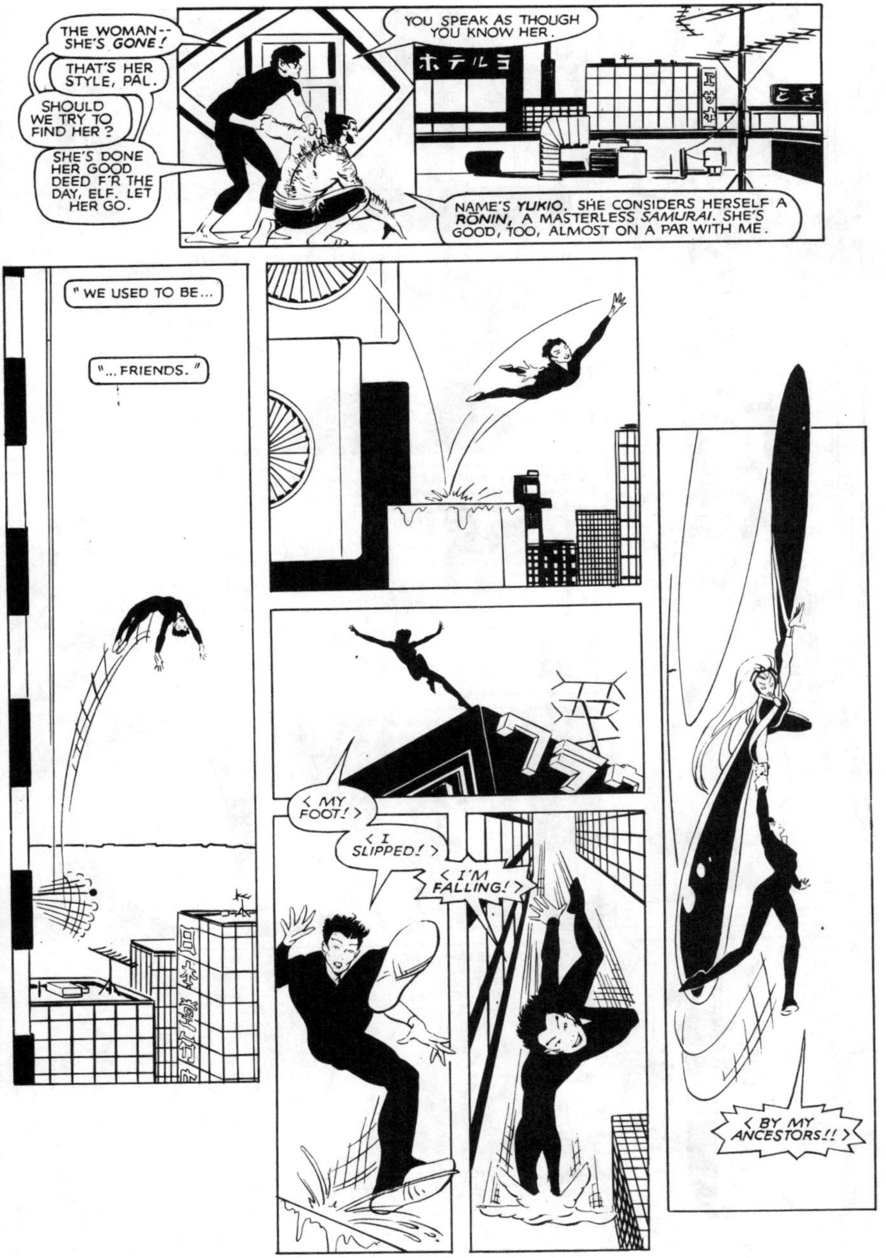
THE WOMAN-- SHE'S GONE!
THAT'S HER STYLE, PAL.
SHOULD WE TRY TO FIND HER?
SHE'S DONE HER GOOD DEED F'R THE DAY, ELF. LET HER GO.
YOU SPEAK AS THOUGH YOU KNOW HER.
NAME'S YUKIO. SHE CONSIDERS HERSELF A RŌNIN, A MASTERLESS SAMURAI. SHE'S GOOD, TOO, ALMOST ON A PAR WITH ME.
ホテルヨ
"WE USED TO BE...
"...FRIENDS."
< MY FOOT! >
< I SLIPPED! >
< I'M FALLING! >
< BY MY ANCESTORS!! >

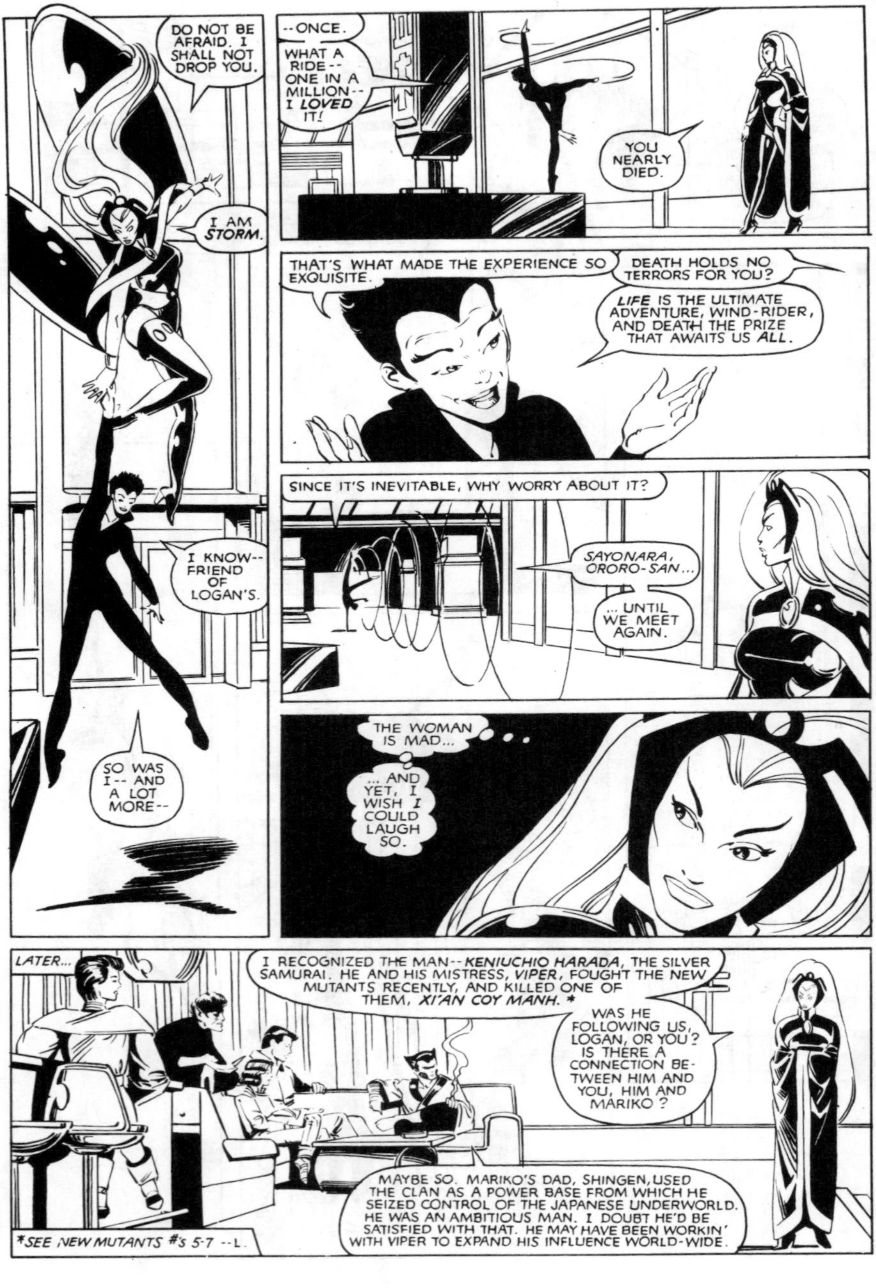
DO NOT BE AFRAID. I SHALL NOT DROP YOU.
I AM STORM.
I KNOW-- FRIEND OF LOGAN'S.
SO WAS I-- AND A LOT MORE--
--ONCE.
WHAT A RIDE-- ONE IN A MILLION-- I LOVED IT!
YOU NEARLY DIED.
THAT'S WHAT MADE THE EXPERIENCE SO EXQUISITE.
DEATH HOLDS NO TERRORS FOR YOU?
LIFE IS THE ULTIMATE ADVENTURE, WIND-RIDER, AND DEATH THE PRIZE THAT AWAITS US ALL.
SINCE IT'S INEVITABLE, WHY WORRY ABOUT IT?
SAYONARA, ORORO-SAN...
...UNTIL WE MEET AGAIN.
THE WOMAN IS MAD...
...AND YET, I WISH I COULD LAUGH SO.
LATER...
I RECOGNIZED THE MAN--KENIUCHIO HARADA, THE SILVER SAMURAI. HE AND HIS MISTRESS, VIPER, FOUGHT THE NEW MUTANTS RECENTLY, AND KILLED ONE OF THEM, XI'AN COY MANH. *
WAS HE FOLLOWING US, LOGAN, OR YOU? IS THERE A CONNECTION BETWEEN HIM AND YOU, HIM AND MARIKO?
MAYBE SO. MARIKO'S DAD, SHINGEN, USED THE CLAN AS A POWER BASE FROM WHICH HE SEIZED CONTROL OF THE JAPANESE UNDERWORLD. HE WAS AN AMBITIOUS MAN. I DOUBT HE'D BE SATISFIED WITH THAT. HE MAY HAVE BEEN WORKIN' WITH VIPER TO EXPAND HIS INFLUENCE WORLD-WIDE.
*SEE NEW MUTANTS #'s 5-7 --L.

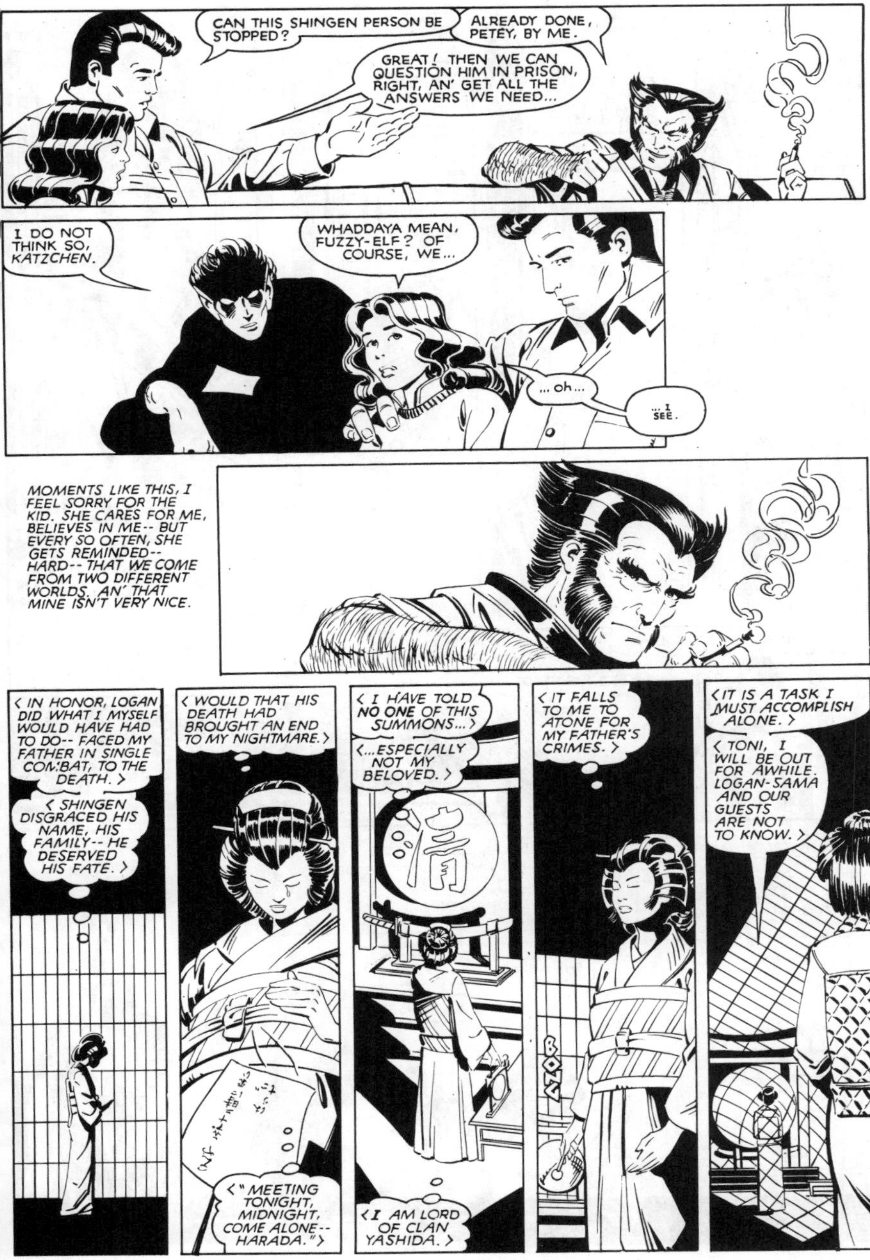

CAN THIS SHINGEN PERSON BE STOPPED?
ALREADY DONE, PETEY, BY ME.
GREAT! THEN WE CAN QUESTION HIM IN PRISON, RIGHT, AN' GET ALL THE ANSWERS WE NEED...
I DO NOT THINK SO, KATZCHEN.
WHADDAYA MEAN, FUZZY-ELF? OF COURSE, WE...
... oh ...
... I SEE.
MOMENTS LIKE THIS, I FEEL SORRY FOR THE KID. SHE CARES FOR ME, BELIEVES IN ME-- BUT EVERY SO OFTEN, SHE GETS REMINDED-- HARD-- THAT WE COME FROM TWO DIFFERENT WORLDS. AN' THAT MINE ISN'T VERY NICE.
< IN HONOR, LOGAN DID WHAT I MYSELF WOULD HAVE HAD TO DO-- FACED MY FATHER IN SINGLE COMBAT, TO THE DEATH. >
< SHINGEN DISGRACED HIS NAME, HIS FAMILY-- HE DESERVED HIS FATE. >
< WOULD THAT HIS DEATH HAD BROUGHT AN END TO MY NIGHTMARE. >
< "MEETING TONIGHT, MIDNIGHT, COME ALONE-- HARADA." >
< I HAVE TOLD NO ONE OF THIS SUMMONS... >
< ...ESPECIALLY NOT MY BELOVED. >
< I AM LORD OF CLAN YASHIDA. >
< IT FALLS TO ME TO ATONE FOR MY FATHER'S CRIMES. >
BONG
< IT IS A TASK I MUST ACCOMPLISH ALONE. >
< TONI, I WILL BE OUT FOR AWHILE. LOGAN-SAMA AND OUR GUESTS ARE NOT TO KNOW. >

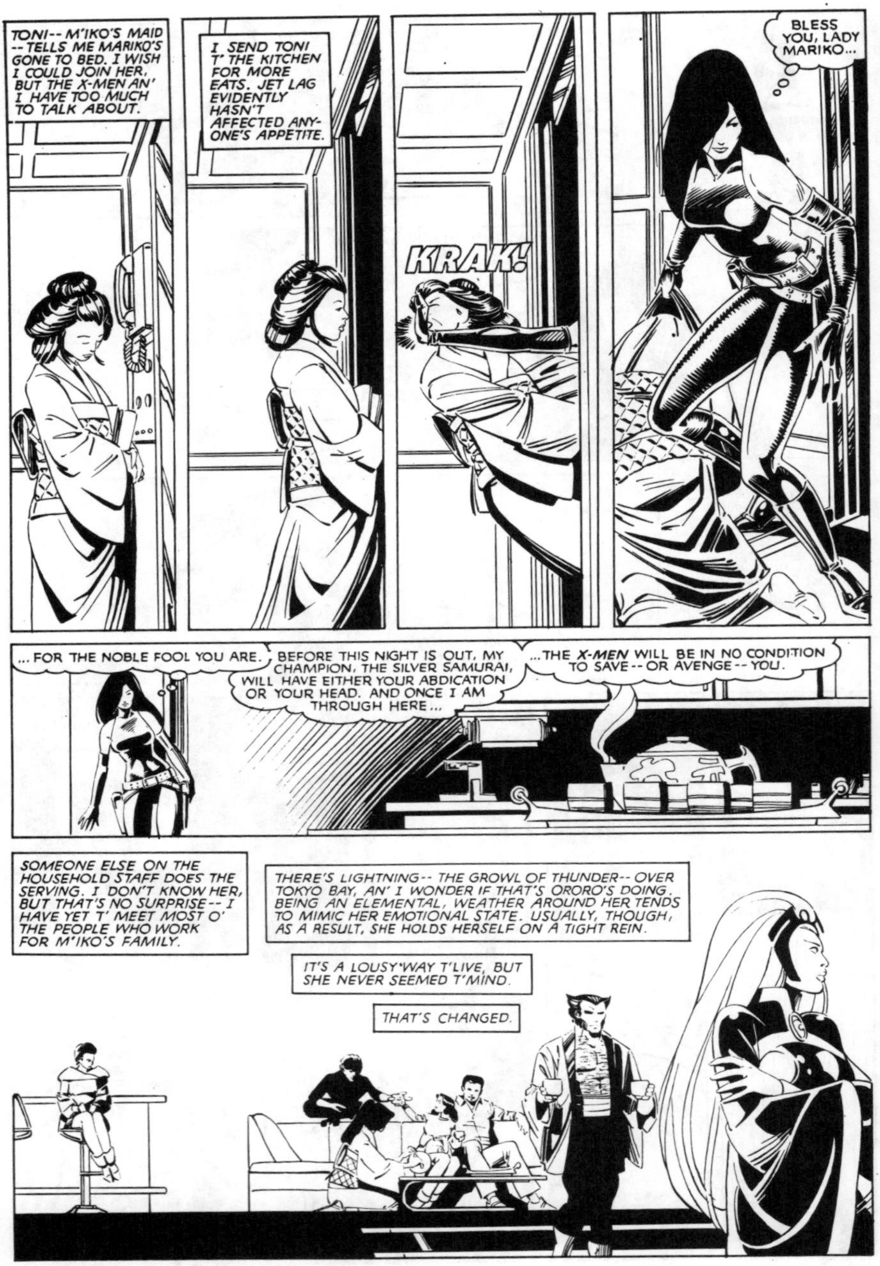

TONI-- M'IKO'S MAID --TELLS ME MARIKO'S GONE TO BED. I WISH I COULD JOIN HER, BUT THE X-MEN AN' I HAVE TOO MUCH TO TALK ABOUT.
I SEND TONI T' THE KITCHEN FOR MORE EATS. JET LAG EVIDENTLY HASN'T AFFECTED ANY-ONE'S APPETITE.
KRAK!
BLESS YOU, LADY MARIKO...
...FOR THE NOBLE FOOL YOU ARE.
BEFORE THIS NIGHT IS OUT, MY CHAMPION, THE SILVER SAMURAI, WILL HAVE EITHER YOUR ABDICATION OR YOUR HEAD. AND ONCE I AM THROUGH HERE...
...THE X-MEN WILL BE IN NO CONDITION TO SAVE--OR AVENGE--YOU.
SOMEONE ELSE ON THE HOUSEHOLD STAFF DOES THE SERVING. I DON'T KNOW HER, BUT THAT'S NO SURPRISE-- I HAVE YET T' MEET MOST O' THE PEOPLE WHO WORK FOR M'IKO'S FAMILY.
THERE'S LIGHTNING-- THE GROWL OF THUNDER-- OVER TOKYO BAY, AN' I WONDER IF THAT'S ORORO'S DOING. BEING AN ELEMENTAL, WEATHER AROUND HER TENDS TO MIMIC HER EMOTIONAL STATE. USUALLY, THOUGH, AS A RESULT, SHE HOLDS HERSELF ON A TIGHT REIN.
IT'S A LOUSY WAY T'LIVE, BUT SHE NEVER SEEMED T'MIND.
THAT'S CHANGED.

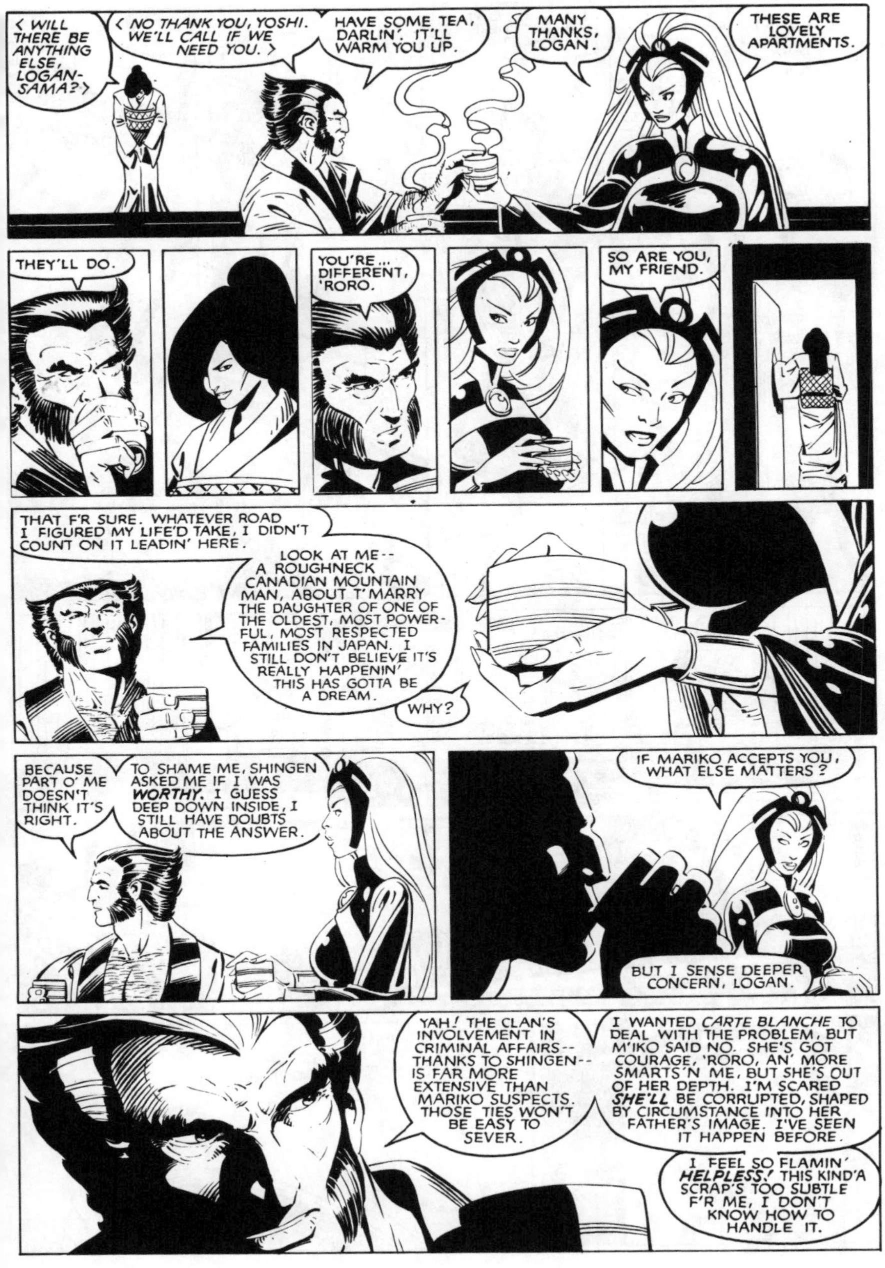

< WILL THERE BE ANYTHING ELSE, LOGAN-SAMA? >
< NO THANK YOU, YOSHI. WE'LL CALL IF WE NEED YOU. >
HAVE SOME TEA, DARLIN'. IT'LL WARM YOU UP.
MANY THANKS, LOGAN.
THESE ARE LOVELY APARTMENTS.
THEY'LL DO.
YOU'RE... DIFFERENT, 'RORO.
SO ARE YOU, MY FRIEND.
THAT F'R SURE. WHATEVER ROAD I FIGURED MY LIFE'D TAKE, I DIDN'T COUNT ON IT LEADIN' HERE.
LOOK AT ME-- A ROUGHNECK CANADIAN MOUNTAIN MAN, ABOUT T' MARRY THE DAUGHTER OF ONE OF THE OLDEST, MOST POWERFUL, MOST RESPECTED FAMILIES IN JAPAN. I STILL DON'T BELIEVE IT'S REALLY HAPPENIN' THIS HAS GOTTA BE A DREAM.
WHY?
BECAUSE PART O' ME DOESN'T THINK IT'S RIGHT.
TO SHAME ME, SHINGEN ASKED ME IF I WAS WORTHY. I GUESS DEEP DOWN INSIDE, I STILL HAVE DOUBTS ABOUT THE ANSWER.
IF MARIKO ACCEPTS YOU, WHAT ELSE MATTERS?
BUT I SENSE DEEPER CONCERN, LOGAN.
YAH! THE CLAN'S INVOLVEMENT IN CRIMINAL AFFAIRS-- THANKS TO SHINGEN-- IS FAR MORE EXTENSIVE THAN MARIKO SUSPECTS. THOSE TIES WON'T BE EASY TO SEVER.
I WANTED CARTE BLANCHE TO DEAL WITH THE PROBLEM, BUT M'IKO SAID NO. SHE'S GOT COURAGE, 'RORO, AN' MORE SMARTS 'N ME, BUT SHE'S OUT OF HER DEPTH. I'M SCARED SHE'LL BE CORRUPTED, SHAPED BY CIRCUMSTANCE INTO HER FATHER'S IMAGE. I'VE SEEN IT HAPPEN BEFORE.
I FEEL SO FLAMIN' HELPLESS! THIS KIND'A SCRAP'S TOO SUBTLE F'R ME, I DON'T KNOW HOW TO HANDLE IT.

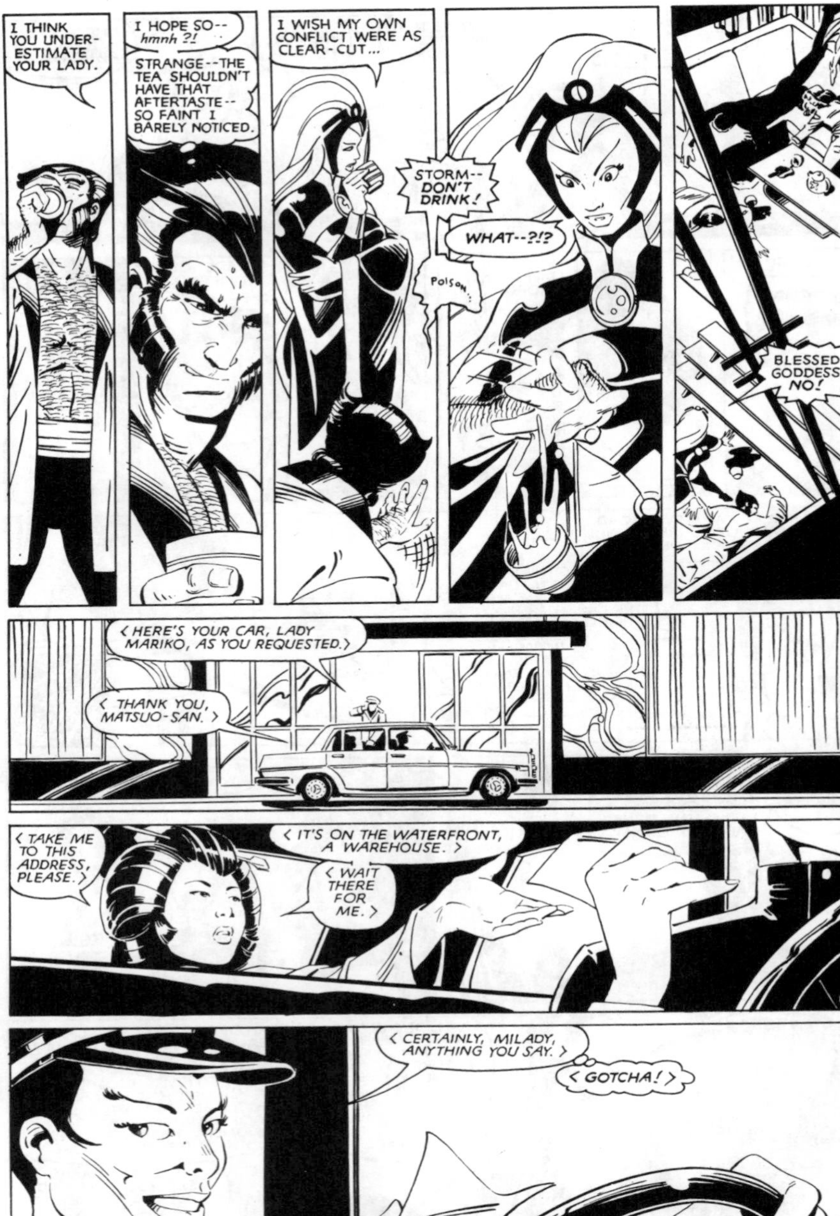
I THINK YOU UNDER-ESTIMATE YOUR LADY.
I HOPE SO-- hmnh ?!
STRANGE--THE TEA SHOULDN'T HAVE THAT AFTERTASTE-- SO FAINT I BARELY NOTICED.
I WISH MY OWN CONFLICT WERE AS CLEAR-CUT...
STORM-- DON'T DRINK!
WHAT--?!?
POISON...
BLESSED GODDESS-- NO!
< HERE'S YOUR CAR, LADY MARIKO, AS YOU REQUESTED. >
< THANK YOU, MATSUO-SAN. >
< TAKE ME TO THIS ADDRESS, PLEASE. >
< IT'S ON THE WATERFRONT, A WAREHOUSE. >
< WAIT THERE FOR ME. >
< CERTAINLY, MILADY, ANYTHING YOU SAY. >
< GOTCHA! >

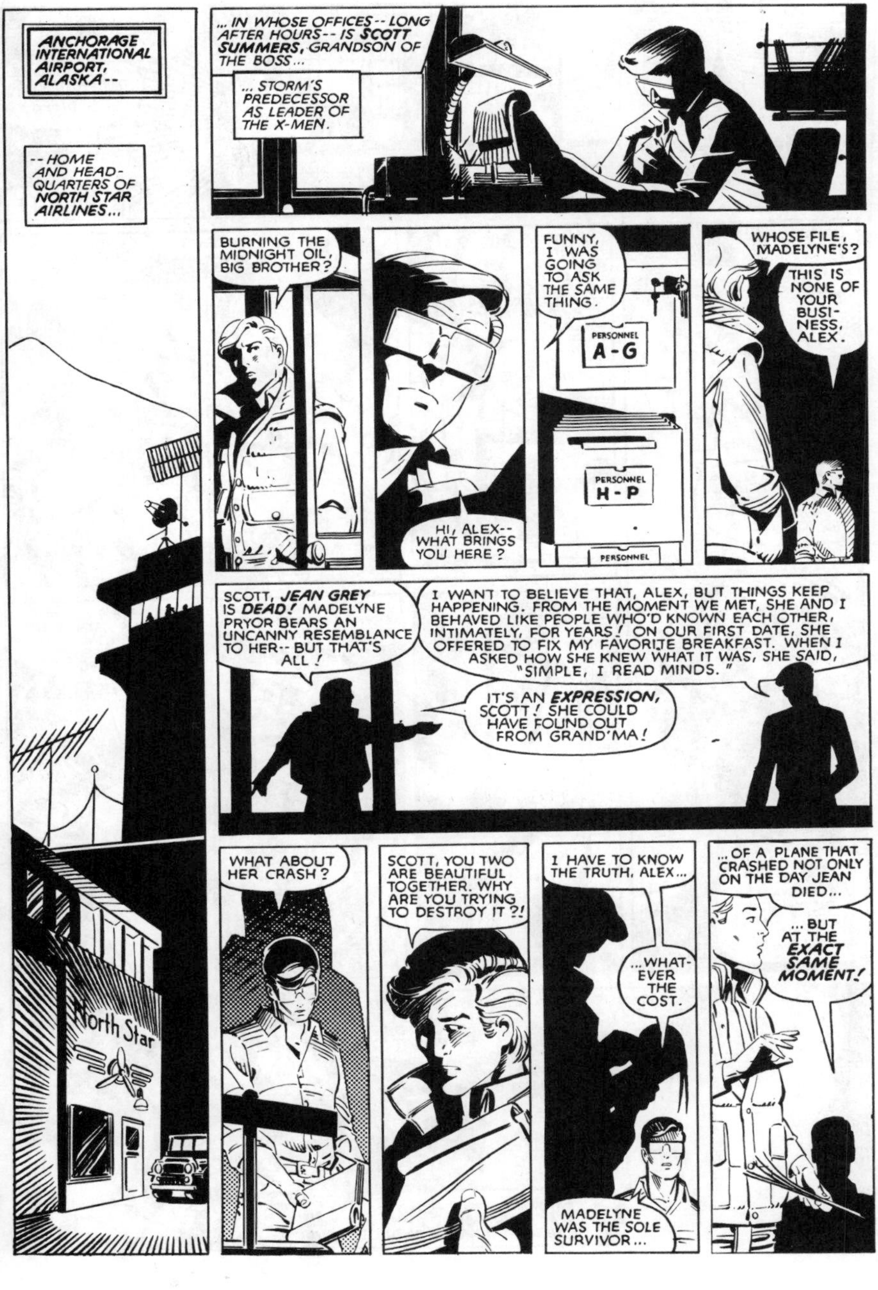
ANCHORAGE INTERNATIONAL AIRPORT, ALASKA--
--HOME AND HEADQUARTERS OF NORTH STAR AIRLINES...
...IN WHOSE OFFICES-- LONG AFTER HOURS-- IS SCOTT SUMMERS, GRANDSON OF THE BOSS...
...STORM'S PREDECESSOR AS LEADER OF THE X-MEN.
BURNING THE MIDNIGHT OIL, BIG BROTHER?
HI, ALEX-- WHAT BRINGS YOU HERE?
FUNNY, I WAS GOING TO ASK THE SAME THING.
PERSONNEL A-G
PERSONNEL H-P
PERSONNEL
WHOSE FILE, MADELYNE'S?
THIS IS NONE OF YOUR BUSINESS, ALEX.
SCOTT, JEAN GREY IS DEAD! MADELYNE PRYOR BEARS AN UNCANNY RESEMBLANCE TO HER-- BUT THAT'S ALL!
I WANT TO BELIEVE THAT, ALEX, BUT THINGS KEEP HAPPENING. FROM THE MOMENT WE MET, SHE AND I BEHAVED LIKE PEOPLE WHO'D KNOWN EACH OTHER, INTIMATELY, FOR YEARS! ON OUR FIRST DATE, SHE OFFERED TO FIX MY FAVORITE BREAKFAST. WHEN I ASKED HOW SHE KNEW WHAT IT WAS, SHE SAID, "SIMPLE, I READ MINDS."
IT'S AN EXPRESSION, SCOTT! SHE COULD HAVE FOUND OUT FROM GRAND'MA!
WHAT ABOUT HER CRASH?
North Star
SCOTT, YOU TWO ARE BEAUTIFUL TOGETHER. WHY ARE YOU TRYING TO DESTROY IT?!
I HAVE TO KNOW THE TRUTH, ALEX...
...WHATEVER THE COST.
MADELYNE WAS THE SOLE SURVIVOR...
...OF A PLANE THAT CRASHED NOT ONLY ON THE DAY JEAN DIED...
...BUT AT THE EXACT SAME MOMENT!

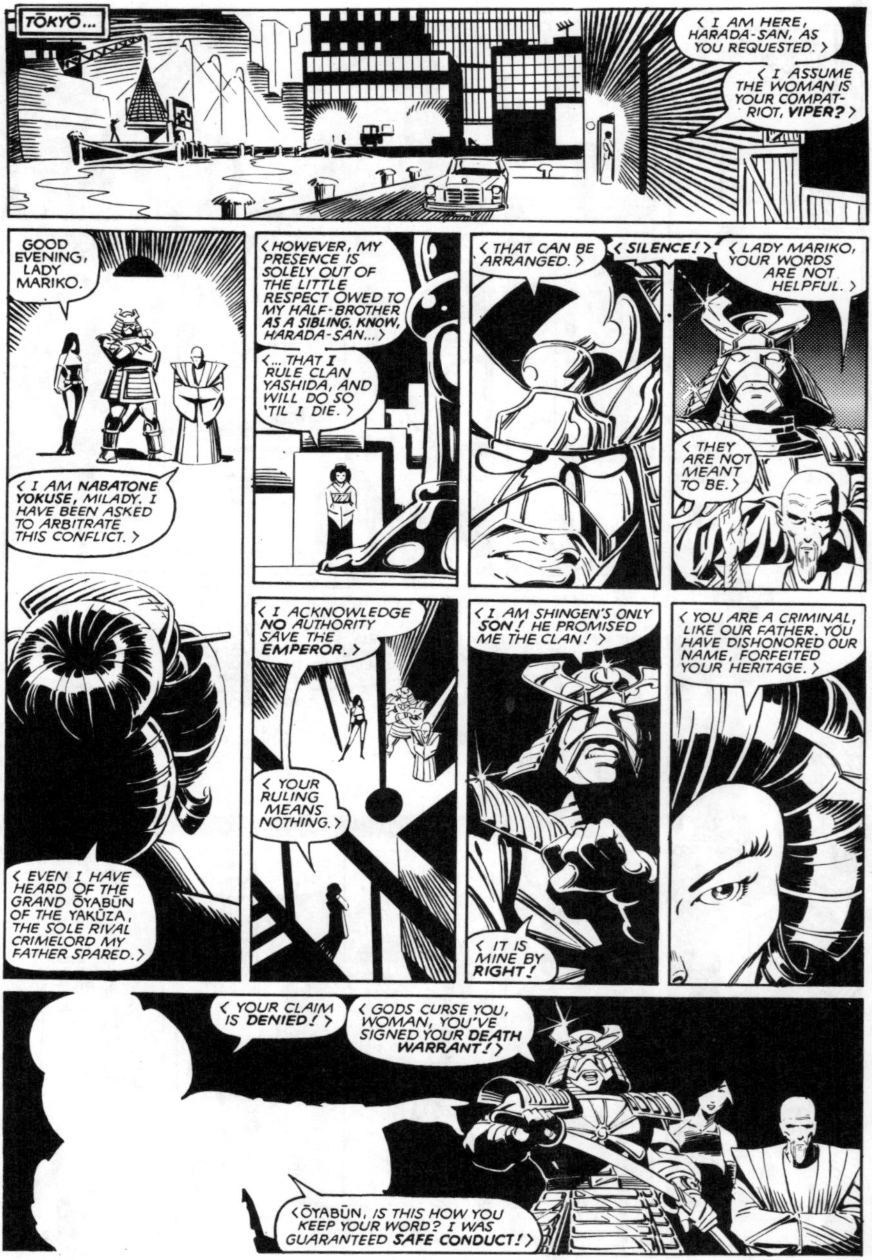
TŌKYŌ...
< I AM HERE, HARADA-SAN, AS YOU REQUESTED. >
< I ASSUME THE WOMAN IS YOUR COMPATRIOT, VIPER? >
GOOD EVENING, LADY MARIKO.
< I AM NABATONE YOKUSE, MILADY. I HAVE BEEN ASKED TO ARBITRATE THIS CONFLICT. >
< HOWEVER, MY PRESENCE IS SOLELY OUT OF THE LITTLE RESPECT OWED TO MY HALF-BROTHER AS A SIBLING. KNOW, HARADA-SAN... >
< ... THAT I RULE CLAN YASHIDA, AND WILL DO SO 'TIL I DIE. >
< THAT CAN BE ARRANGED. >
< SILENCE! >
< LADY MARIKO, YOUR WORDS ARE NOT HELPFUL. >
< THEY ARE NOT MEANT TO BE. >
< EVEN I HAVE HEARD OF THE GRAND ŌYABŪN OF THE YAKŪZA, THE SOLE RIVAL CRIMELORD MY FATHER SPARED. >
< I ACKNOWLEDGE NO AUTHORITY SAVE THE EMPEROR. >
< YOUR RULING MEANS NOTHING. >
< I AM SHINGEN'S ONLY SON! HE PROMISED ME THE CLAN! >
< IT IS MINE BY RIGHT!
< YOU ARE A CRIMINAL, LIKE OUR FATHER. YOU HAVE DISHONORED OUR NAME, FORFEITED YOUR HERITAGE. >
< YOUR CLAIM IS DENIED! >
< GODS CURSE YOU, WOMAN, YOU'VE SIGNED YOUR DEATH WARRANT! >
<ŌYABŪN, IS THIS HOW YOU KEEP YOUR WORD? I WAS GUARANTEED SAFE CONDUCT! >

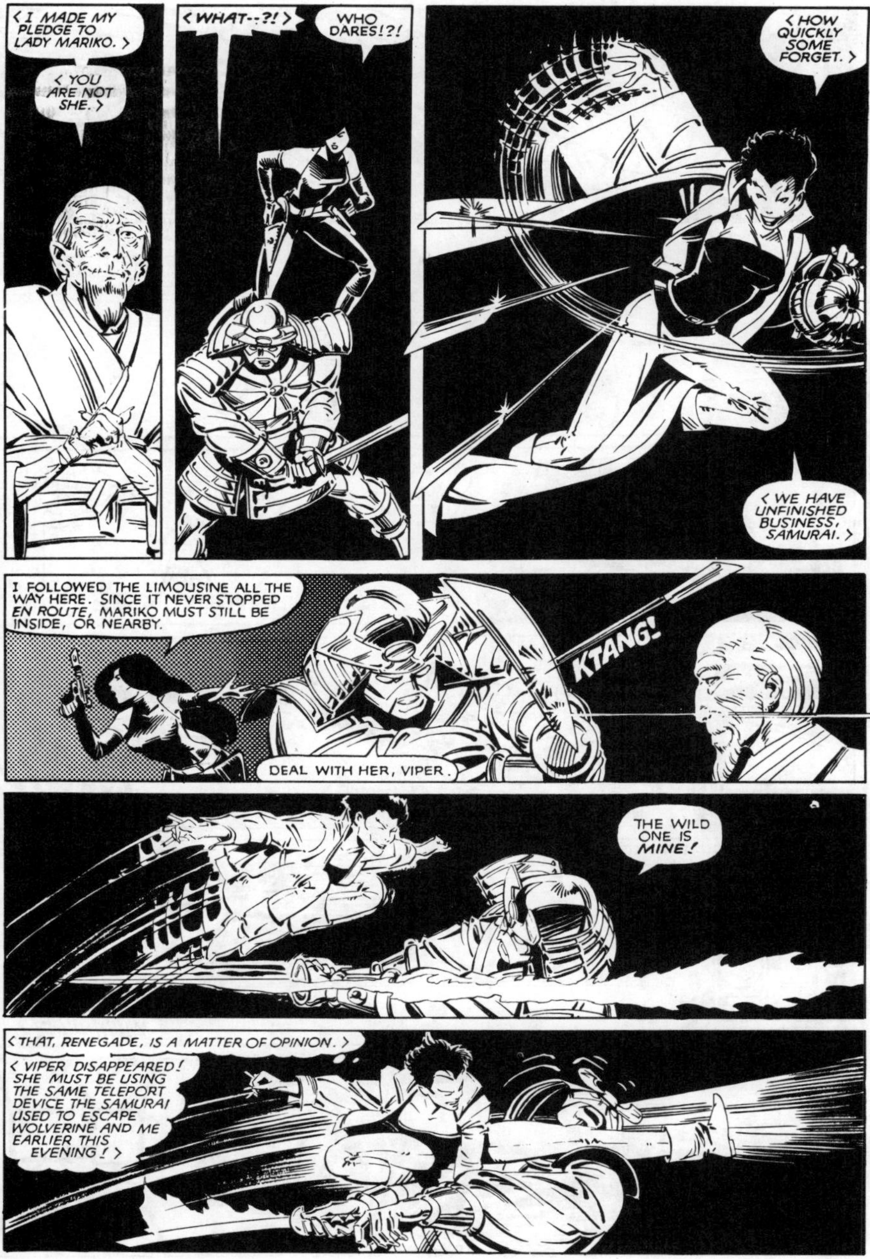

< I MADE MY PLEDGE TO LADY MARIKO. >
< YOU ARE NOT SHE. >
< WHAT--?! >
WHO DARES!?!
< HOW QUICKLY SOME FORGET. >
< WE HAVE UNFINISHED BUSINESS, SAMURAI. >
I FOLLOWED THE LIMOUSINE ALL THE WAY HERE. SINCE IT NEVER STOPPED EN ROUTE, MARIKO MUST STILL BE INSIDE, OR NEARBY.
KTANG!
DEAL WITH HER, VIPER.
THE WILD ONE IS MINE!
< THAT, RENEGADE, IS A MATTER OF OPINION. >
< VIPER DISAPPEARED! SHE MUST BE USING THE SAME TELEPORT DEVICE THE SAMURAI USED TO ESCAPE WOLVERINE AND ME EARLIER THIS EVENING! >

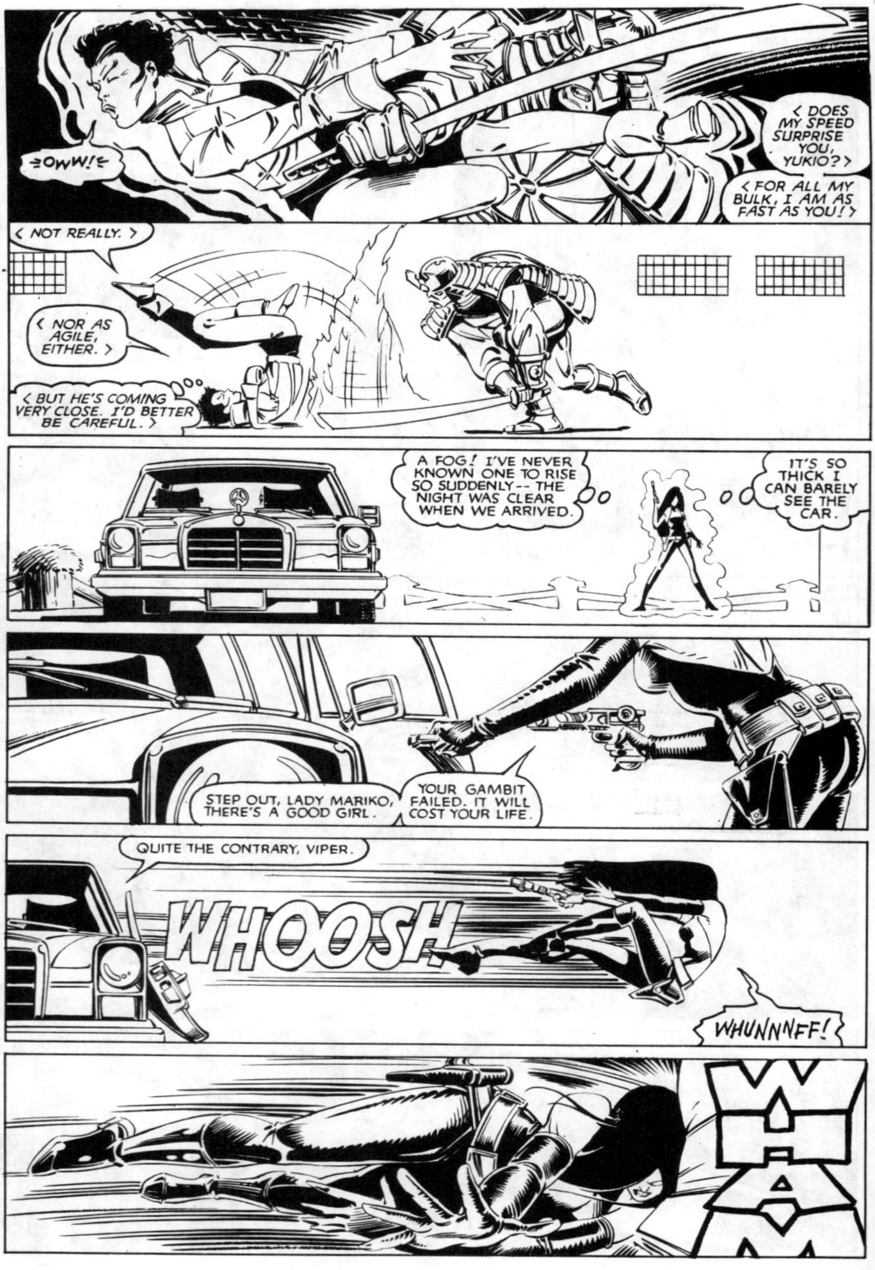

=OWW!=
< DOES MY SPEED SURPRISE YOU, YUKIO? >
< FOR ALL MY BULK, I AM AS FAST AS YOU! >
< NOT REALLY. >
< NOR AS AGILE, EITHER. >
< BUT HE'S COMING VERY CLOSE. I'D BETTER BE CAREFUL. >
A FOG! I'VE NEVER KNOWN ONE TO RISE SO SUDDENLY-- THE NIGHT WAS CLEAR WHEN WE ARRIVED.
IT'S SO THICK I CAN BARELY SEE THE CAR.
STEP OUT, LADY MARIKO, THERE'S A GOOD GIRL.
YOUR GAMBIT FAILED. IT WILL COST YOUR LIFE.
QUITE THE CONTRARY, VIPER.
WHOOSH
WHUNNNFF!
WHAM

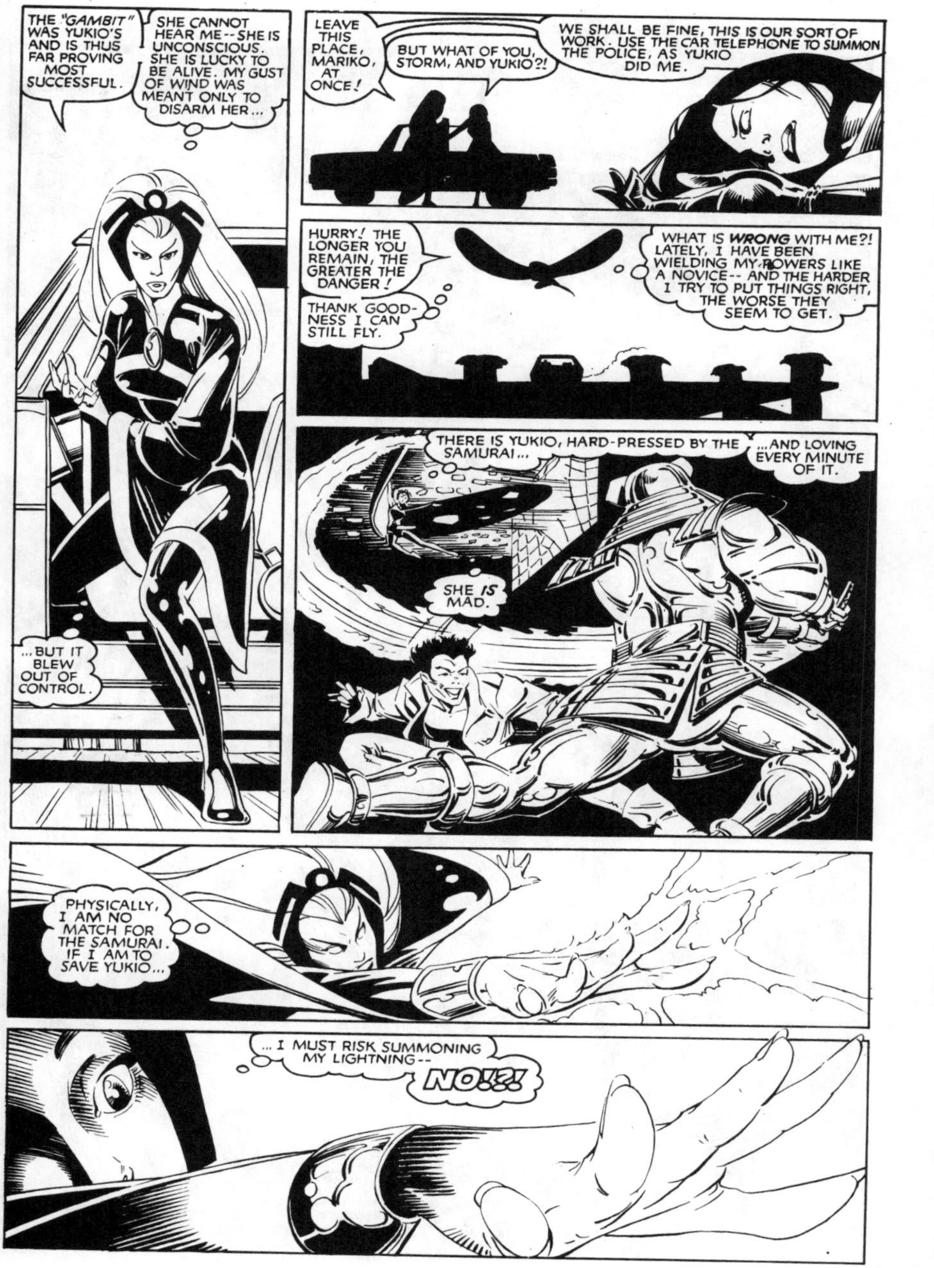
THE "GAMBIT" WAS YUKIO'S AND IS THUS FAR PROVING MOST SUCCESSFUL.
SHE CANNOT HEAR ME--SHE IS UNCONSCIOUS. SHE IS LUCKY TO BE ALIVE. MY GUST OF WIND WAS MEANT ONLY TO DISARM HER...
...BUT IT BLEW OUT OF CONTROL.
LEAVE THIS PLACE, MARIKO, AT ONCE!
BUT WHAT OF YOU, STORM, AND YUKIO?!
WE SHALL BE FINE, THIS IS OUR SORT OF WORK. USE THE CAR TELEPHONE TO SUMMON THE POLICE, AS YUKIO DID ME.
HURRY! THE LONGER YOU REMAIN, THE GREATER THE DANGER!
THANK GOODNESS I CAN STILL FLY.
WHAT IS WRONG WITH ME?! LATELY, I HAVE BEEN WIELDING MY POWERS LIKE A NOVICE-- AND THE HARDER I TRY TO PUT THINGS RIGHT, THE WORSE THEY SEEM TO GET.
THERE IS YUKIO, HARD-PRESSED BY THE SAMURAI...
...AND LOVING EVERY MINUTE OF IT.
SHE IS MAD.
PHYSICALLY, I AM NO MATCH FOR THE SAMURAI. IF I AM TO SAVE YUKIO...
...I MUST RISK SUMMONING MY LIGHTNING--
NO!?!

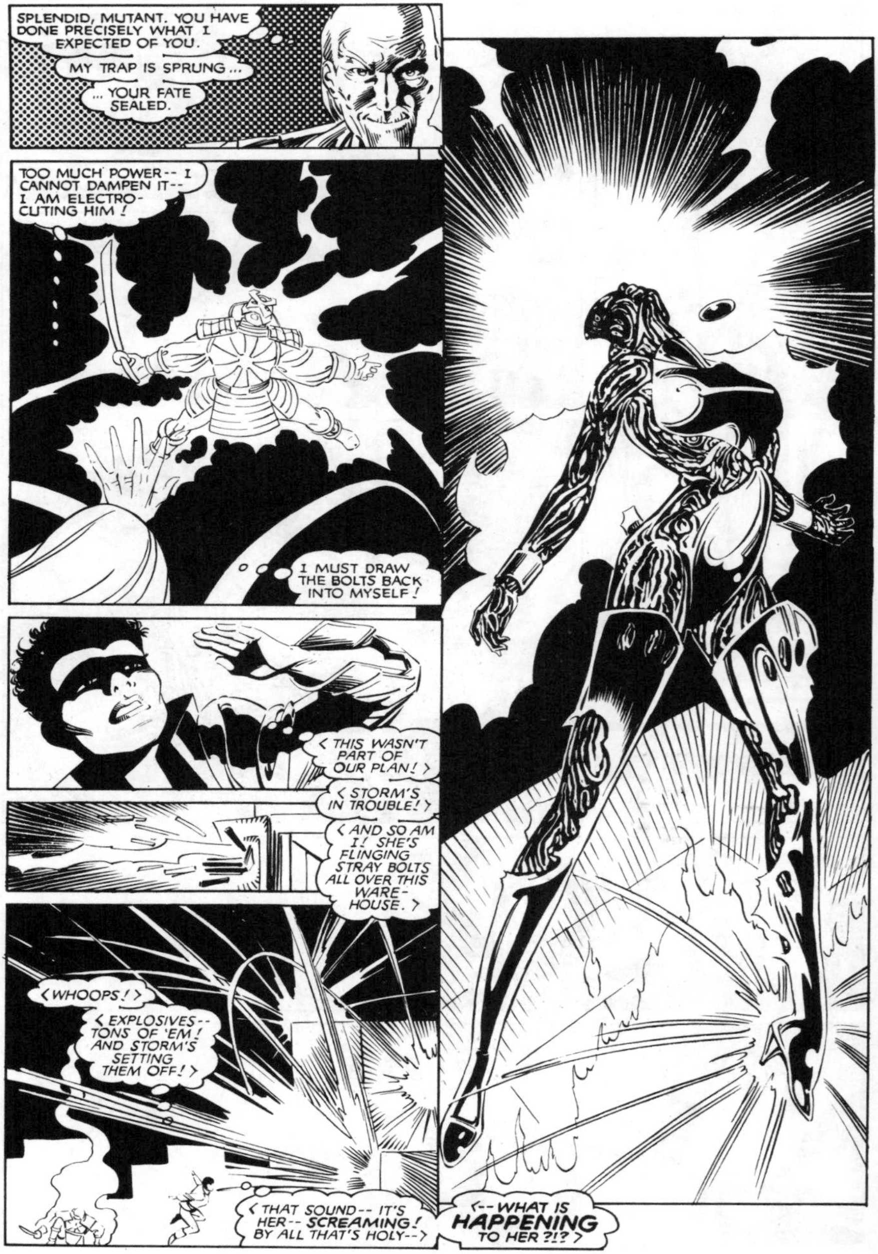
SPLENDID, MUTANT. YOU HAVE DONE PRECISELY WHAT I EXPECTED OF YOU.
MY TRAP IS SPRUNG...
... YOUR FATE SEALED.
TOO MUCH POWER-- I CANNOT DAMPEN IT-- I AM ELECTROCUTING HIM!
I MUST DRAW THE BOLTS BACK INTO MYSELF!
< THIS WASN'T PART OF OUR PLAN! >
< STORM'S IN TROUBLE! >
< AND SO AM I! SHE'S FLINGING STRAY BOLTS ALL OVER THIS WAREHOUSE. >
<WHOOPS!>
< EXPLOSIVES-- TONS OF 'EM! AND STORM'S SETTING THEM OFF! >
< THAT SOUND-- IT'S HER-- SCREAMING! BY ALL THAT'S HOLY-->
<--WHAT IS HAPPENING TO HER ?!? >

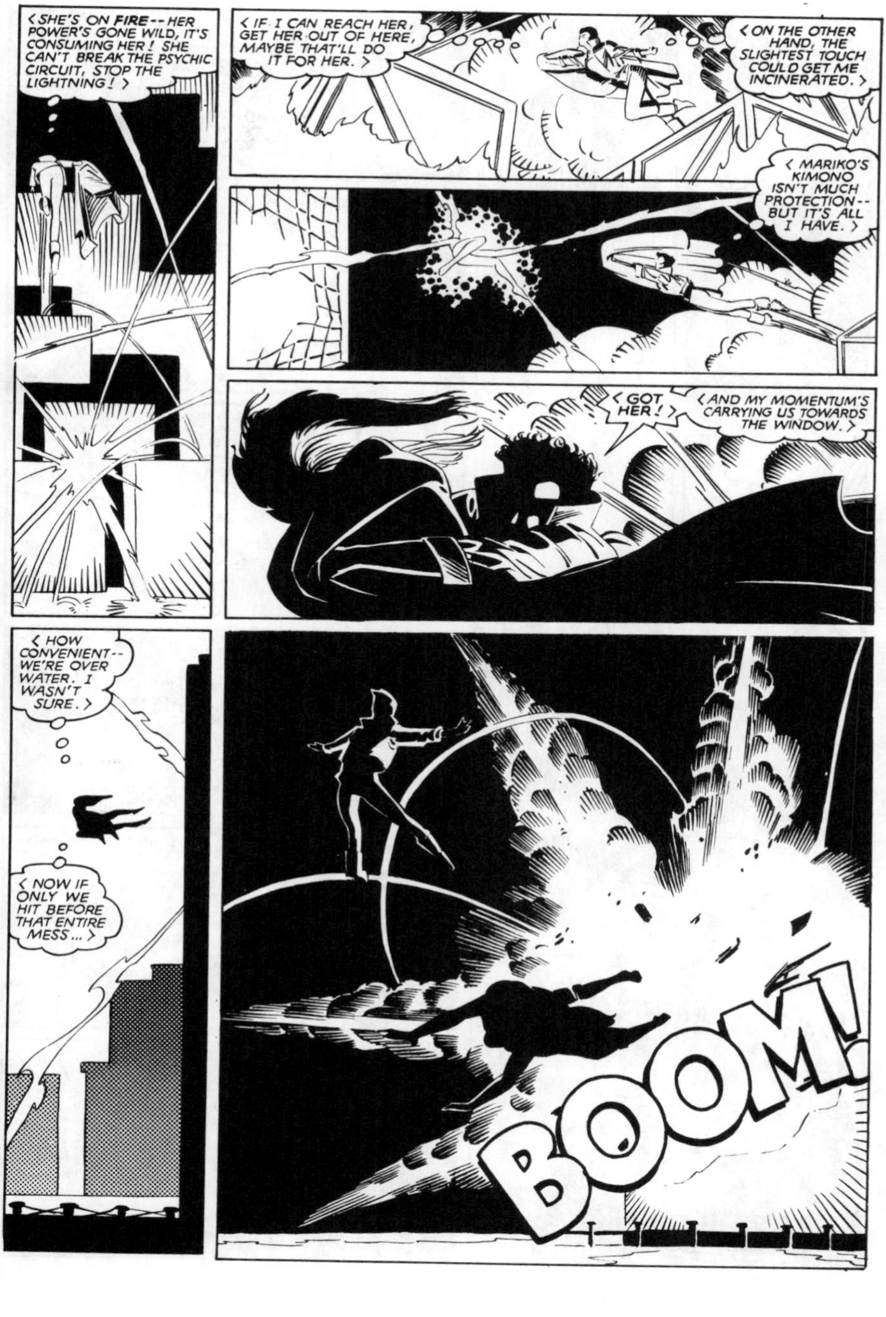

< SHE'S ON FIRE -- HER POWER'S GONE WILD, IT'S CONSUMING HER! SHE CAN'T BREAK THE PSYCHIC CIRCUIT, STOP THE LIGHTNING! >
< IF I CAN REACH HER, GET HER OUT OF HERE, MAYBE THAT'LL DO IT FOR HER. >
< ON THE OTHER HAND, THE SLIGHTEST TOUCH COULD GET ME INCINERATED. >
< MARIKO'S KIMONO ISN'T MUCH PROTECTION -- BUT IT'S ALL I HAVE. >
< GOT HER! >
< AND MY MOMENTUM'S CARRYING US TOWARDS THE WINDOW. >
< HOW CONVENIENT -- WE'RE OVER WATER. I WASN'T SURE. >
< NOW IF ONLY WE HIT BEFORE THAT ENTIRE MESS... >
BOOM!

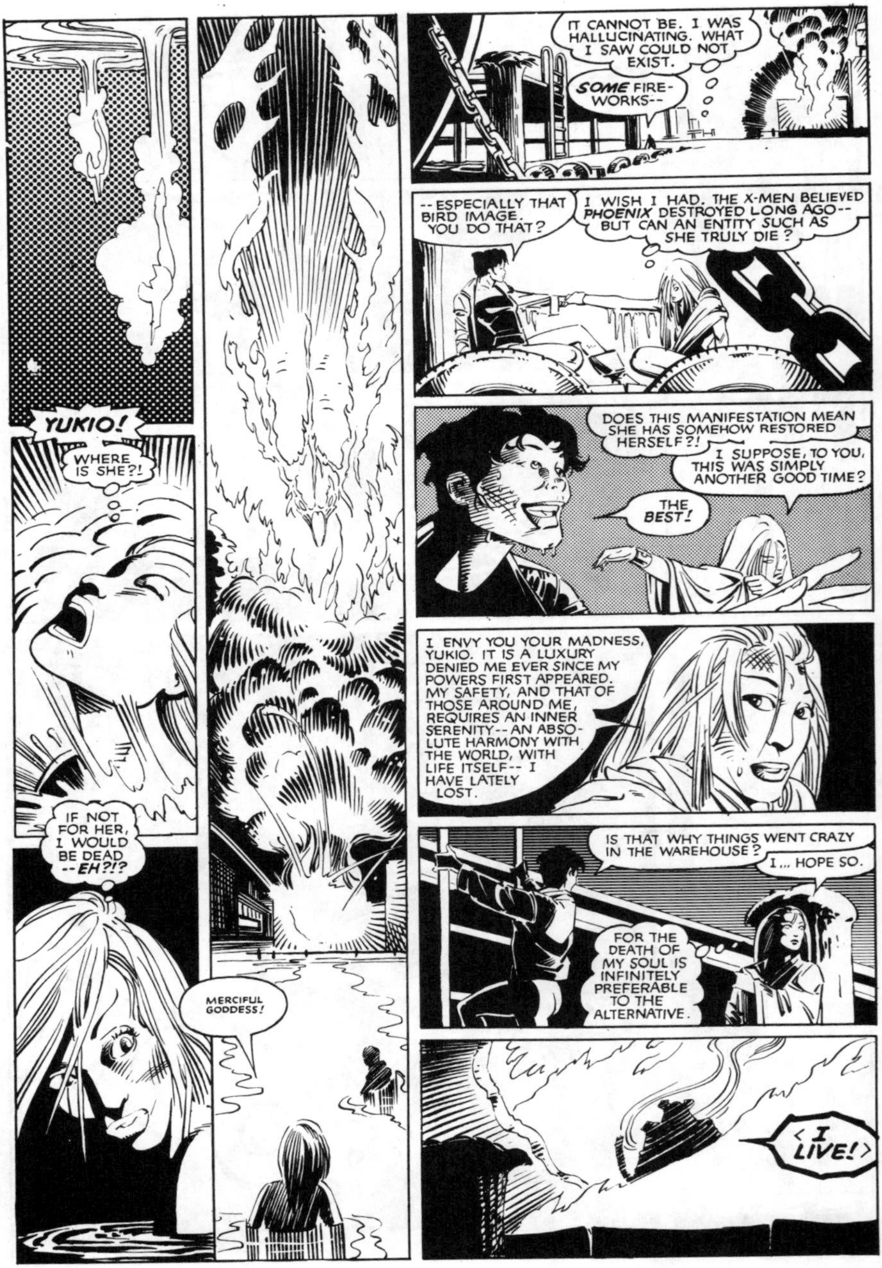
YUKIO!
WHERE IS SHE?!
IF NOT FOR HER, I WOULD BE DEAD --EH?!?
MERCIFUL GODDESS!
IT CANNOT BE. I WAS HALLUCINATING. WHAT I SAW COULD NOT EXIST.
SOME FIRE-WORKS--
-- ESPECIALLY THAT BIRD IMAGE. YOU DO THAT?
I WISH I HAD. THE X-MEN BELIEVED PHOENIX DESTROYED LONG AGO-- BUT CAN AN ENTITY SUCH AS SHE TRULY DIE?
DOES THIS MANIFESTATION MEAN SHE HAS SOMEHOW RESTORED HERSELF?!
I SUPPOSE, TO YOU, THIS WAS SIMPLY ANOTHER GOOD TIME?
THE BEST!
I ENVY YOU YOUR MADNESS, YUKIO. IT IS A LUXURY DENIED ME EVER SINCE MY POWERS FIRST APPEARED. MY SAFETY, AND THAT OF THOSE AROUND ME, REQUIRES AN INNER SERENITY-- AN ABSOLUTE HARMONY WITH THE WORLD, WITH LIFE ITSELF-- I HAVE LATELY LOST.
IS THAT WHY THINGS WENT CRAZY IN THE WAREHOUSE?
I... HOPE SO.
FOR THE DEATH OF MY SOUL IS INFINITELY PREFERABLE TO THE ALTERNATIVE.
<I LIVE!>

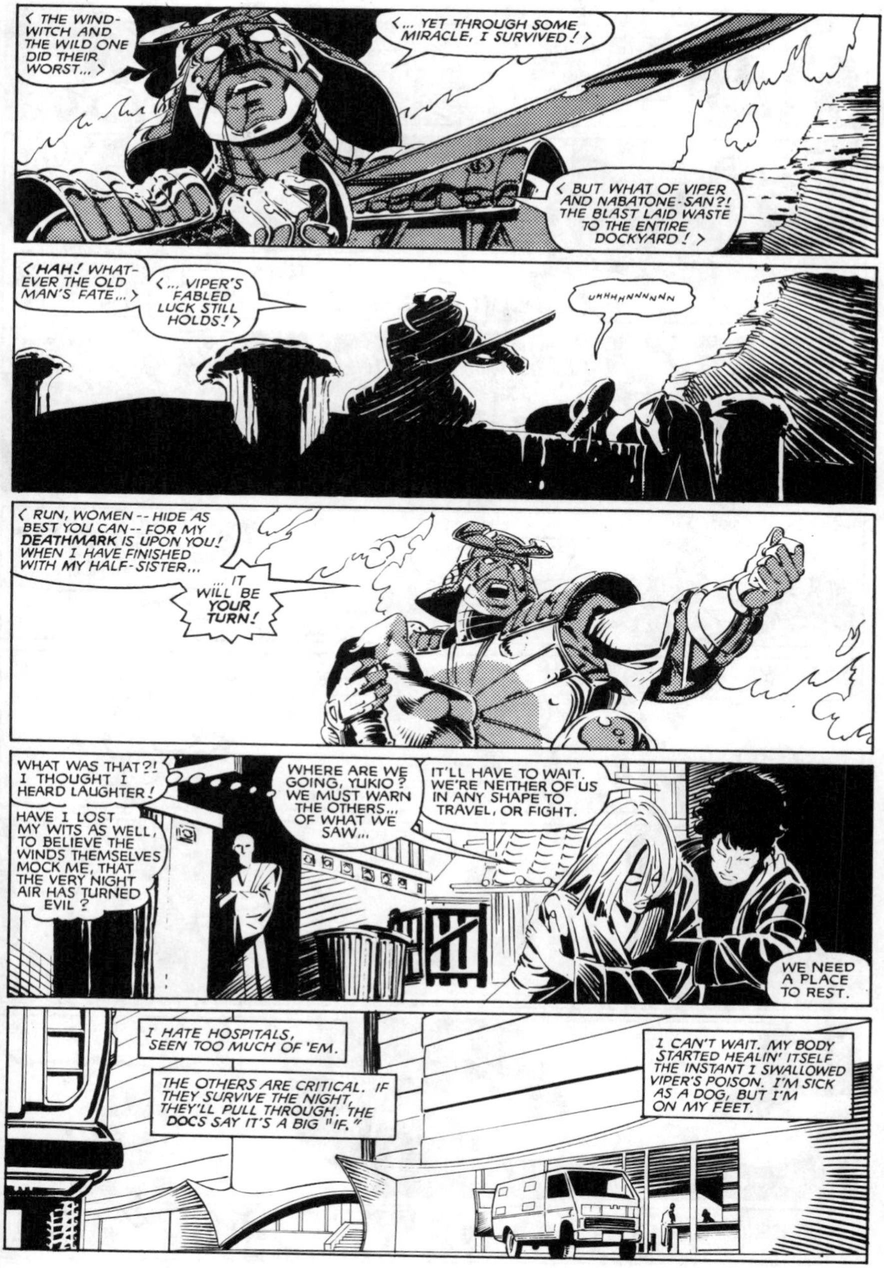
< THE WIND-WITCH AND THE WILD ONE DID THEIR WORST... >
<... YET THROUGH SOME MIRACLE, I SURVIVED! >
< BUT WHAT OF VIPER AND NABATONE-SAN?! THE BLAST LAID WASTE TO THE ENTIRE DOCKYARD! >
< HAH! WHATEVER THE OLD MAN'S FATE... >
<... VIPER'S FABLED LUCK STILL HOLDS! >
UHHHHNNNNNN
< RUN, WOMEN -- HIDE AS BEST YOU CAN -- FOR MY DEATHMARK IS UPON YOU! WHEN I HAVE FINISHED WITH MY HALF-SISTER...
... IT WILL BE YOUR TURN!
WHAT WAS THAT?! I THOUGHT I HEARD LAUGHTER!
HAVE I LOST MY WITS AS WELL, TO BELIEVE THE WINDS THEMSELVES MOCK ME, THAT THE VERY NIGHT AIR HAS TURNED EVIL?
WHERE ARE WE GOING, YUKIO? WE MUST WARN THE OTHERS... OF WHAT WE SAW...
IT'LL HAVE TO WAIT. WE'RE NEITHER OF US IN ANY SHAPE TO TRAVEL, OR FIGHT.
WE NEED A PLACE TO REST.
I HATE HOSPITALS, SEEN TOO MUCH OF 'EM.
THE OTHERS ARE CRITICAL. IF THEY SURVIVE THE NIGHT, THEY'LL PULL THROUGH. THE DOCS SAY IT'S A BIG "IF."
I CAN'T WAIT. MY BODY STARTED HEALIN' ITSELF THE INSTANT I SWALLOWED VIPER'S POISON. I'M SICK AS A DOG, BUT I'M ON MY FEET.

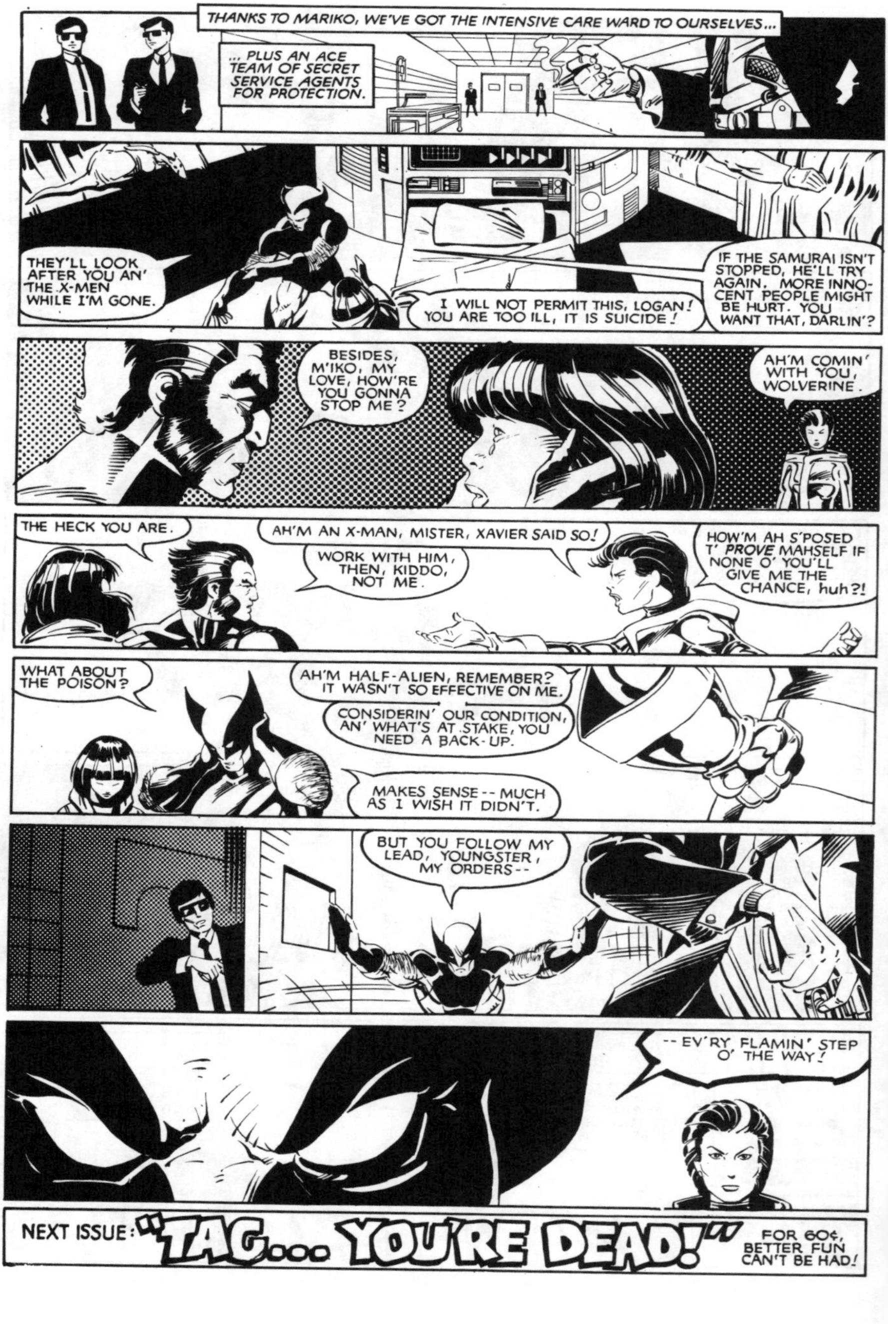
THANKS TO MARIKO, WE'VE GOT THE INTENSIVE CARE WARD TO OURSELVES...
... PLUS AN ACE TEAM OF SECRET SERVICE AGENTS FOR PROTECTION.
THEY'LL LOOK AFTER YOU AN' THE X-MEN WHILE I'M GONE.
I WILL NOT PERMIT THIS, LOGAN! YOU ARE TOO ILL, IT IS SUICIDE!
IF THE SAMURAI ISN'T STOPPED, HE'LL TRY AGAIN. MORE INNOCENT PEOPLE MIGHT BE HURT. YOU WANT THAT, DARLIN'?
BESIDES, M'IKO, MY LOVE, HOW'RE YOU GONNA STOP ME?
AH'M COMIN' WITH YOU, WOLVERINE.
THE HECK YOU ARE.
AH'M AN X-MAN, MISTER, XAVIER SAID SO!
WORK WITH HIM, THEN, KIDDO, NOT ME.
HOW'M AH S'POSED T' PROVE MAHSELF IF NONE O' YOU'LL GIVE ME THE CHANCE, huh?!
WHAT ABOUT THE POISON?
AH'M HALF-ALIEN, REMEMBER? IT WASN'T SO EFFECTIVE ON ME.
CONSIDERIN' OUR CONDITION, AN' WHAT'S AT STAKE, YOU NEED A BACK-UP.
MAKES SENSE -- MUCH AS I WISH IT DIDN'T.
BUT YOU FOLLOW MY LEAD, YOUNGSTER, MY ORDERS--
-- EV'RY FLAMIN' STEP O' THE WAY!
NEXT ISSUE: "TAG... YOU'RE DEAD!"
FOR 60¢, BETTER FUN CAN'T BE HAD!

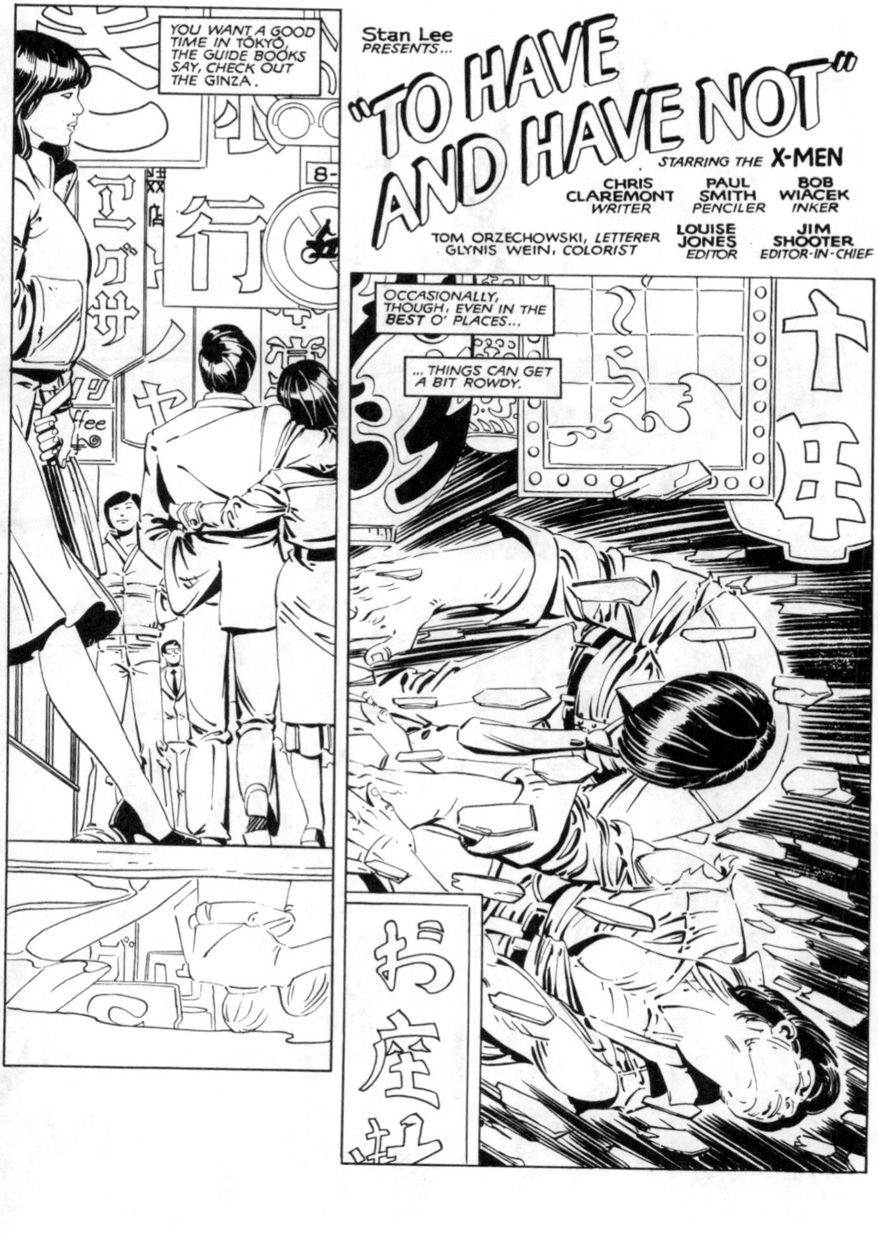
YOU WANT A GOOD TIME IN TOKYO, THE GUIDE BOOKS SAY, CHECK OUT THE GINZA.
Stan Lee PRESENTS...
"TO HAVE AND HAVE NOT"
STARRING THE X-MEN
CHRIS CLAREMONT WRITER
PAUL SMITH PENCILER
BOB WIACEK INKER
TOM ORZECHOWSKI, LETTERER
GLYNIS WEIN, COLORIST
LOUISE JONES EDITOR
JIM SHOOTER EDITOR-IN-CHIEF
OCCASIONALLY, THOUGH, EVEN IN THE BEST O' PLACES...
...THINGS CAN GET A BIT ROWDY.

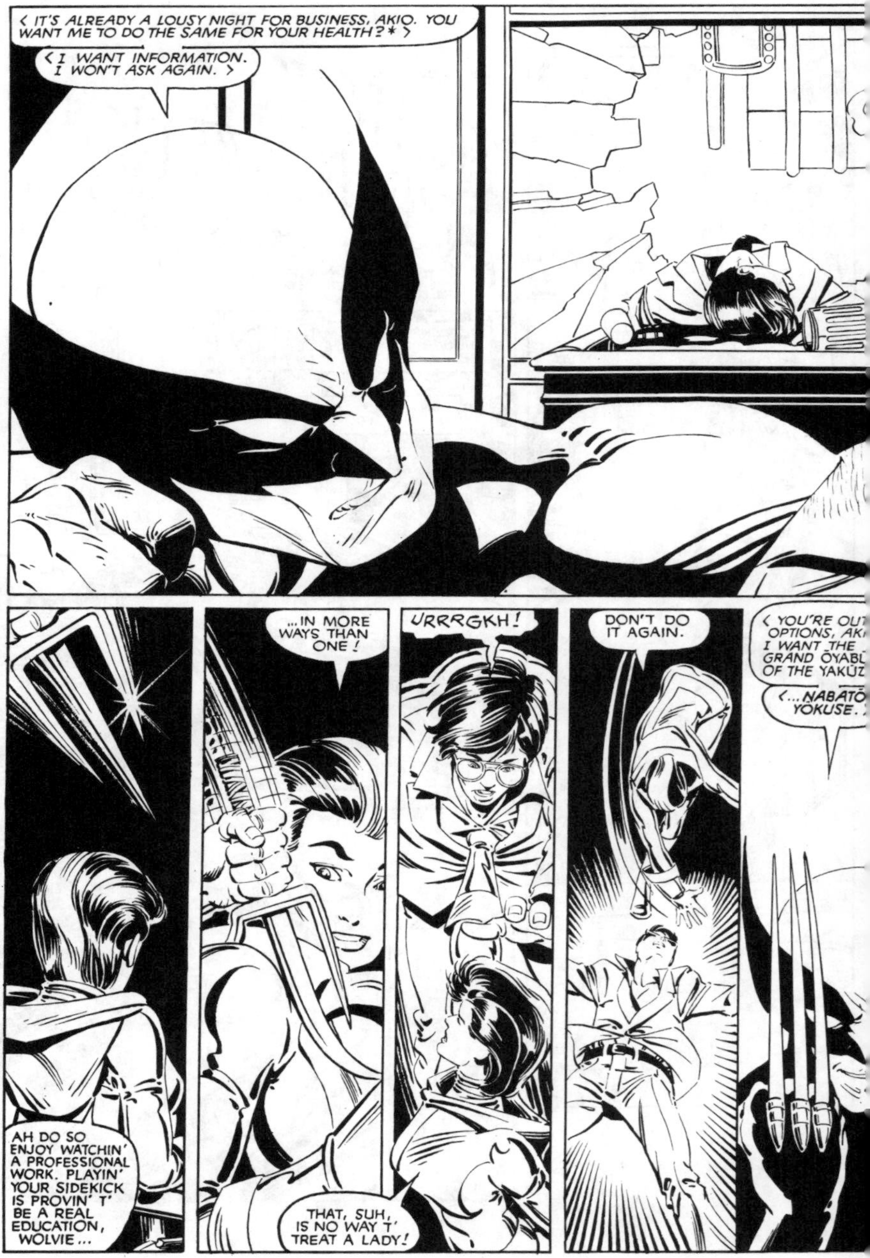
< IT'S ALREADY A LOUSY NIGHT FOR BUSINESS, AKIO. YOU WANT ME TO DO THE SAME FOR YOUR HEALTH?* >
< I WANT INFORMATION. I WON'T ASK AGAIN. >
AH DO SO ENJOY WATCHIN' A PROFESSIONAL WORK. PLAYIN' YOUR SIDEKICK IS PROVIN' T' BE A REAL EDUCATION, WOLVIE...
...IN MORE WAYS THAN ONE!
URRRGKH!
THAT, SUH, IS NO WAY T' TREAT A LADY!
DON'T DO IT AGAIN.

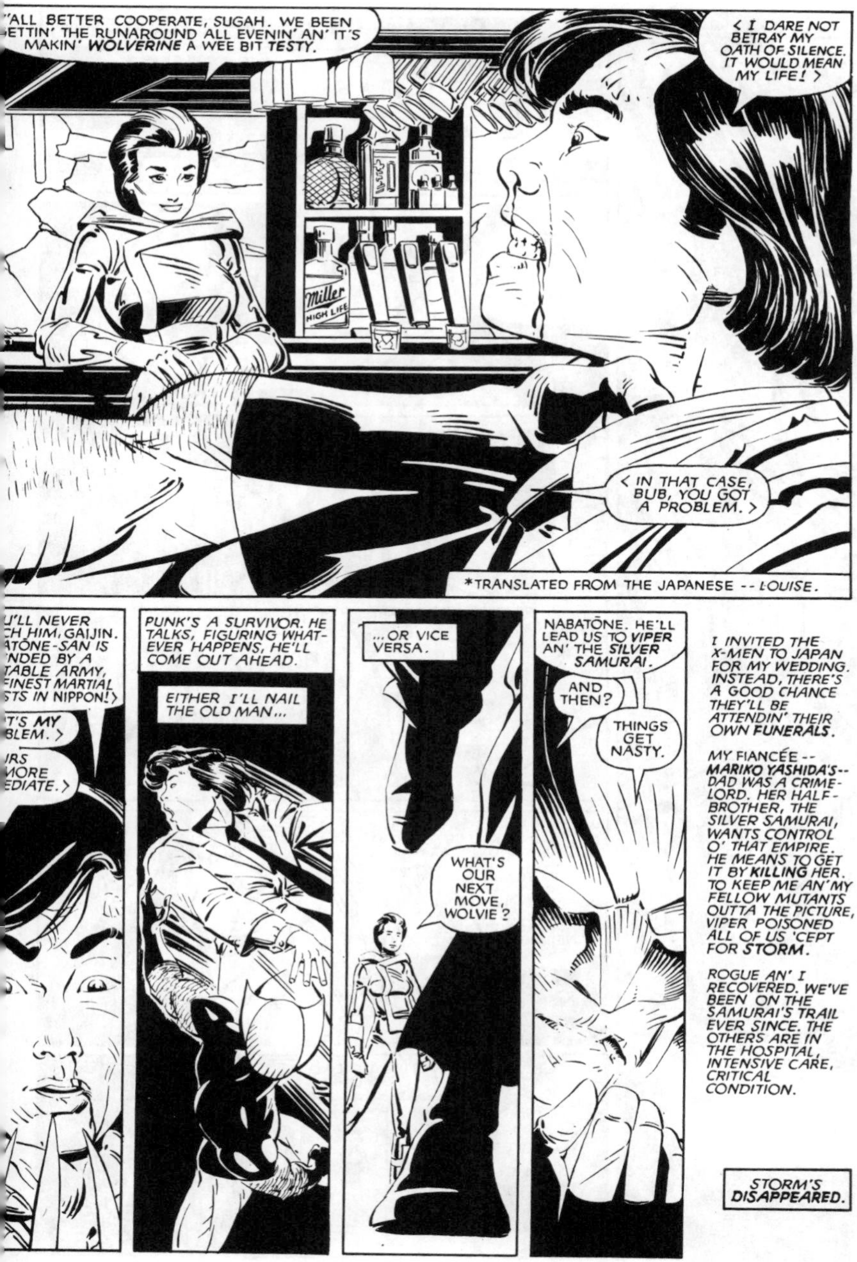

Y'ALL BETTER COOPERATE, SUGAH. WE BEEN GETTIN' THE RUNAROUND ALL EVENIN' AN' IT'S MAKIN' WOLVERINE A WEE BIT TESTY.
< I DARE NOT BETRAY MY OATH OF SILENCE. IT WOULD MEAN MY LIFE! >
< IN THAT CASE, BUB, YOU GOT A PROBLEM. >
*TRANSLATED FROM THE JAPANESE -- LOUISE.
U'LL NEVER CH HIM, GAIJIN. ATŌNE-SAN IS NDED BY A TABLE ARMY, FINEST MARTIAL STS IN NIPPON!>
T'S MY BLEM.>
URS MORE EDIATE.>
PUNK'S A SURVIVOR. HE TALKS, FIGURING WHATEVER HAPPENS, HE'LL COME OUT AHEAD.
EITHER I'LL NAIL THE OLD MAN...
...OR VICE VERSA.
WHAT'S OUR NEXT MOVE, WOLVIE?
NABATŌNE. HE'LL LEAD US TO VIPER AN' THE SILVER SAMURAI.
AND THEN?
THINGS GET NASTY.
I INVITED THE X-MEN TO JAPAN FOR MY WEDDING. INSTEAD, THERE'S A GOOD CHANCE THEY'LL BE ATTENDIN' THEIR OWN FUNERALS.
MY FIANCÉE -- MARIKO YASHIDA'S -- DAD WAS A CRIMELORD. HER HALF-BROTHER, THE SILVER SAMURAI, WANTS CONTROL O' THAT EMPIRE. HE MEANS TO GET IT BY KILLING HER. TO KEEP ME AN' MY FELLOW MUTANTS OUTTA THE PICTURE, VIPER POISONED ALL OF US 'CEPT FOR STORM.
ROGUE AN' I RECOVERED. WE'VE BEEN ON THE SAMURAI'S TRAIL EVER SINCE. THE OTHERS ARE IN THE HOSPITAL, INTENSIVE CARE, CRITICAL CONDITION.
STORM'S DISAPPEARED.

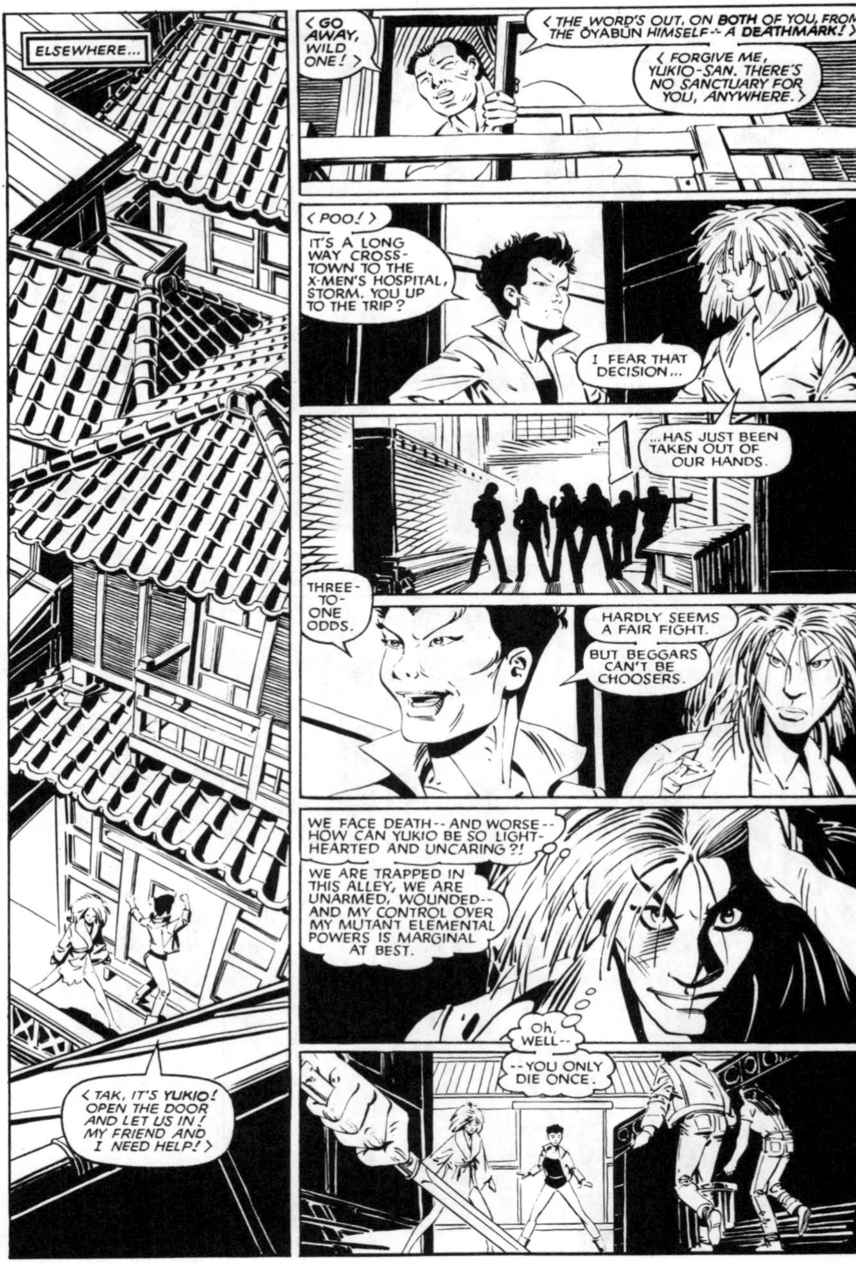
ELSEWHERE...
< TAK, IT'S YUKIO! OPEN THE DOOR AND LET US IN! MY FRIEND AND I NEED HELP! >
< GO AWAY, WILD ONE! >
< THE WORD'S OUT, ON BOTH OF YOU, FROM THE ŌYABŪN HIMSELF -- A DEATHMARK! >
< FORGIVE ME, YUKIO-SAN. THERE'S NO SANCTUARY FOR YOU, ANYWHERE. >
< POO! >
IT'S A LONG WAY CROSS-TOWN TO THE X-MEN'S HOSPITAL, STORM. YOU UP TO THE TRIP?
I FEAR THAT DECISION...
...HAS JUST BEEN TAKEN OUT OF OUR HANDS.
THREE-TO-ONE ODDS.
HARDLY SEEMS A FAIR FIGHT.
BUT BEGGARS CAN'T BE CHOOSERS.
WE FACE DEATH -- AND WORSE -- HOW CAN YUKIO BE SO LIGHT-HEARTED AND UNCARING?!
WE ARE TRAPPED IN THIS ALLEY, WE ARE UNARMED, WOUNDED -- AND MY CONTROL OVER MY MUTANT ELEMENTAL POWERS IS MARGINAL AT BEST.
Oh, WELL --
-- YOU ONLY DIE ONCE.

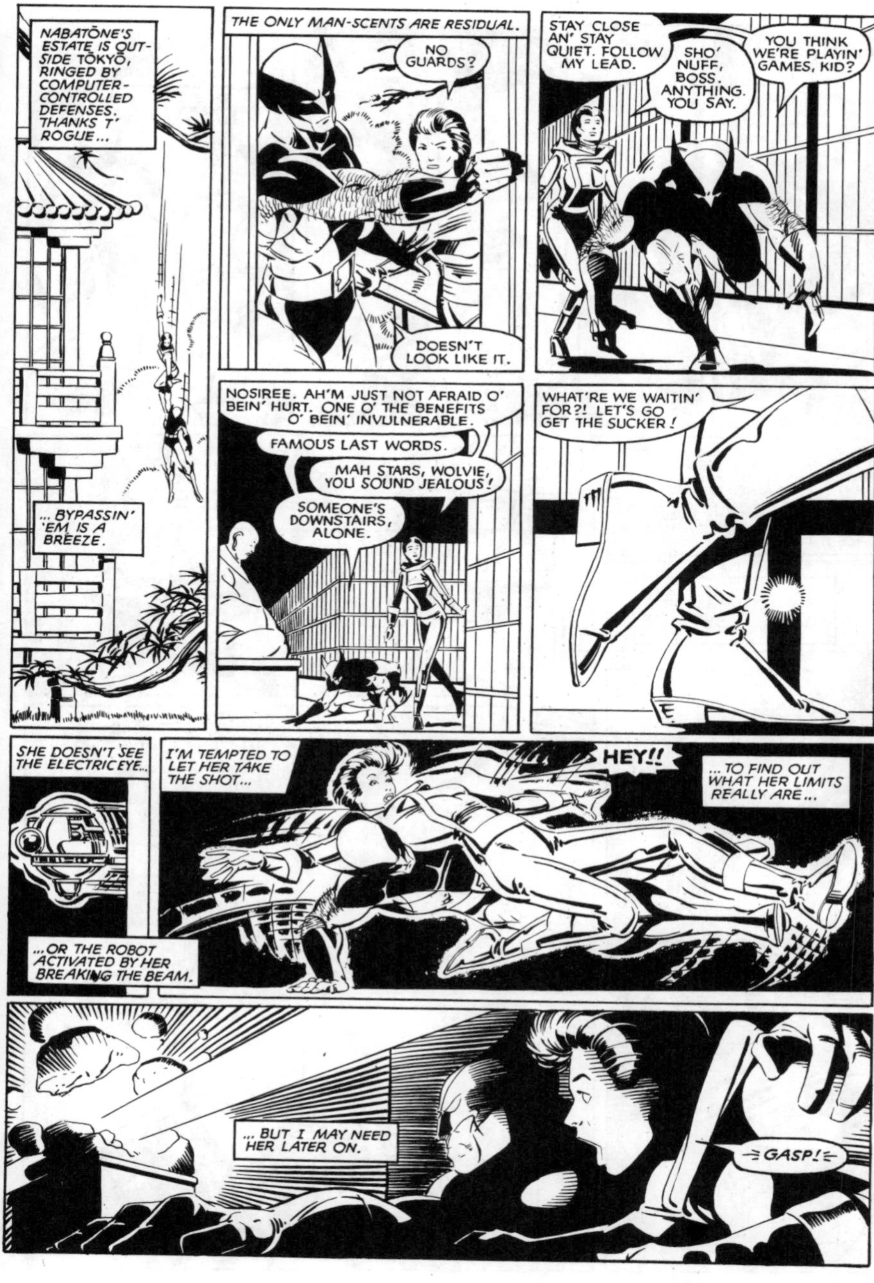
NABATŌNE'S ESTATE IS OUTSIDE TŌKYŌ, RINGED BY COMPUTER-CONTROLLED DEFENSES. THANKS T' ROGUE...
...BYPASSIN' 'EM IS A BREEZE.
THE ONLY MAN-SCENTS ARE RESIDUAL.
NO GUARDS?
DOESN'T LOOK LIKE IT.
STAY CLOSE AN' STAY QUIET. FOLLOW MY LEAD.
SHO' NUFF, BOSS. ANYTHING. YOU SAY.
YOU THINK WE'RE PLAYIN' GAMES, KID?
NOSIREE. AH'M JUST NOT AFRAID O' BEIN' HURT. ONE O' THE BENEFITS O' BEIN' INVULNERABLE.
FAMOUS LAST WORDS.
MAH STARS, WOLVIE, YOU SOUND JEALOUS!
SOMEONE'S DOWNSTAIRS, ALONE.
WHAT'RE WE WAITIN' FOR?! LET'S GO GET THE SUCKER!
SHE DOESN'T SEE THE ELECTRIC EYE...
...OR THE ROBOT ACTIVATED BY HER BREAKING THE BEAM.
I'M TEMPTED TO LET HER TAKE THE SHOT...
HEY!!
...TO FIND OUT WHAT HER LIMITS REALLY ARE...
...BUT I MAY NEED HER LATER ON.
GASP!

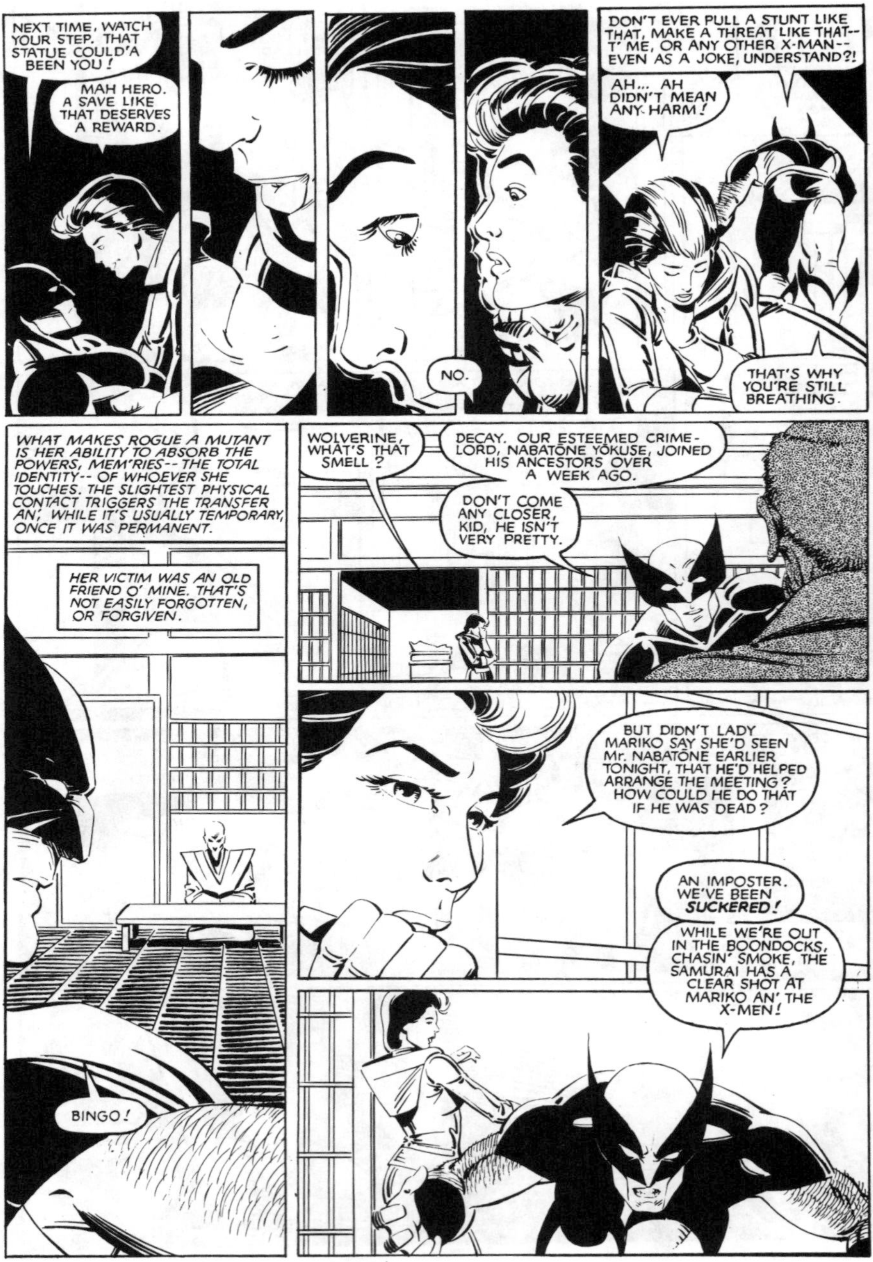
NEXT TIME, WATCH YOUR STEP. THAT STATUE COULD'A BEEN YOU!
MAH HERO. A SAVE LIKE THAT DESERVES A REWARD.
NO.
DON'T EVER PULL A STUNT LIKE THAT, MAKE A THREAT LIKE THAT-- T' ME, OR ANY OTHER X-MAN-- EVEN AS A JOKE, UNDERSTAND?!
AH... AH DIDN'T MEAN ANY HARM!
THAT'S WHY YOU'RE STILL BREATHING.
WHAT MAKES ROGUE A MUTANT IS HER ABILITY TO ABSORB THE POWERS, MEM'RIES-- THE TOTAL IDENTITY-- OF WHOEVER SHE TOUCHES. THE SLIGHTEST PHYSICAL CONTACT TRIGGERS THE TRANSFER AN', WHILE IT'S USUALLY TEMPORARY, ONCE IT WAS PERMANENT.
HER VICTIM WAS AN OLD FRIEND O' MINE. THAT'S NOT EASILY FORGOTTEN, OR FORGIVEN.
BINGO!
WOLVERINE, WHAT'S THAT SMELL?
DECAY. OUR ESTEEMED CRIME-LORD, NABATŌNE YŌKUSE, JOINED HIS ANCESTORS OVER A WEEK AGO.
DON'T COME ANY CLOSER, KID, HE ISN'T VERY PRETTY.
BUT DIDN'T LADY MARIKO SAY SHE'D SEEN Mr. NABATŌNE EARLIER TONIGHT, THAT HE'D HELPED ARRANGE THE MEETING? HOW COULD HE DO THAT IF HE WAS DEAD?
AN IMPOSTER. WE'VE BEEN SUCKERED!
WHILE WE'RE OUT IN THE BOONDOCKS, CHASIN' SMOKE, THE SAMURAI HAS A CLEAR SHOT AT MARIKO AN' THE X-MEN!

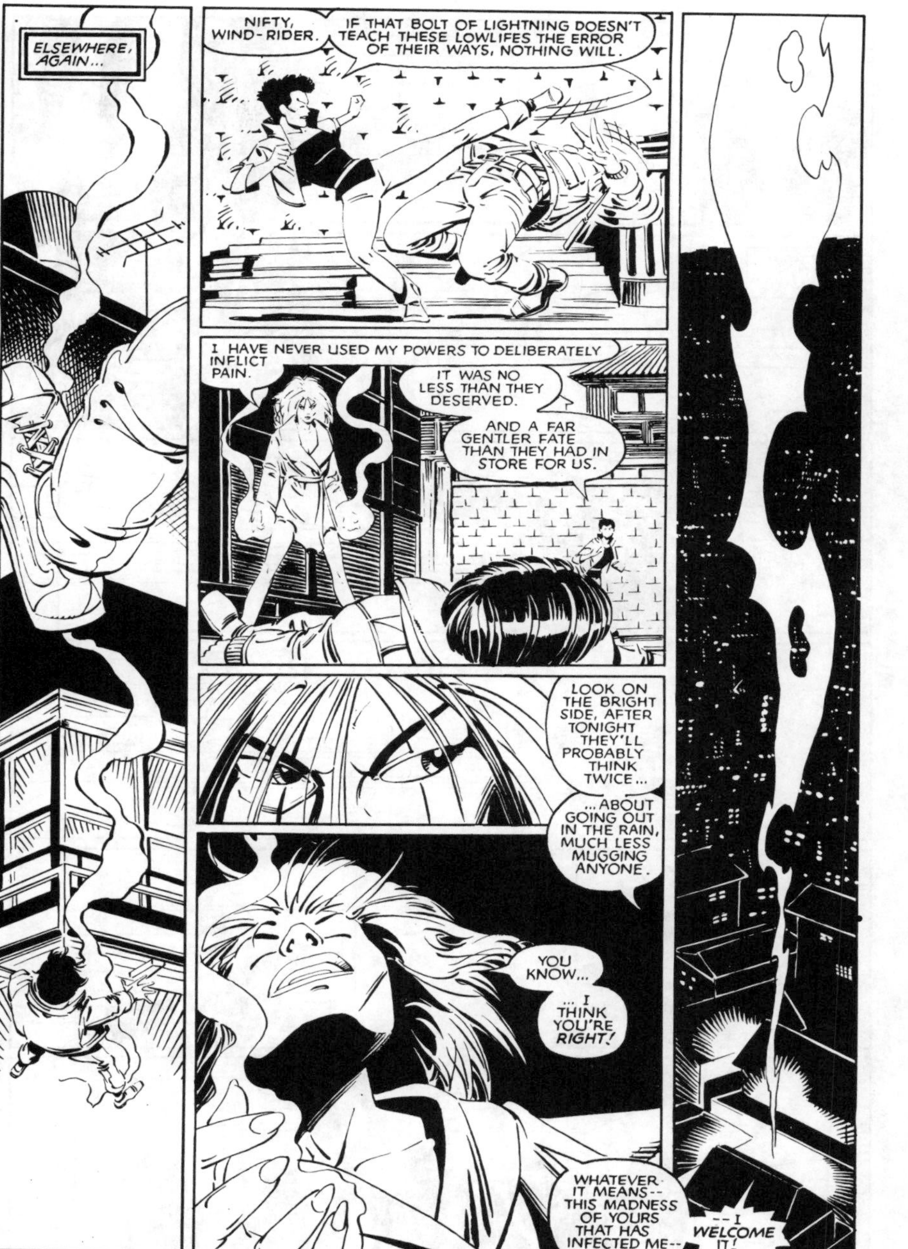
ELSEWHERE, AGAIN...
NIFTY, WIND-RIDER.
IF THAT BOLT OF LIGHTNING DOESN'T TEACH THESE LOWLIFES THE ERROR OF THEIR WAYS, NOTHING WILL.
I HAVE NEVER USED MY POWERS TO DELIBERATELY INFLICT PAIN.
IT WAS NO LESS THAN THEY DESERVED.
AND A FAR GENTLER FATE THAN THEY HAD IN STORE FOR US.
LOOK ON THE BRIGHT SIDE, AFTER TONIGHT THEY'LL PROBABLY THINK TWICE...
...ABOUT GOING OUT IN THE RAIN, MUCH LESS MUGGING ANYONE.
YOU KNOW...
... I THINK YOU'RE *RIGHT!*
WHATEVER IT MEANS-- THIS MADNESS OF YOURS THAT HAS INFECTED ME--
-- I *WELCOME* IT!

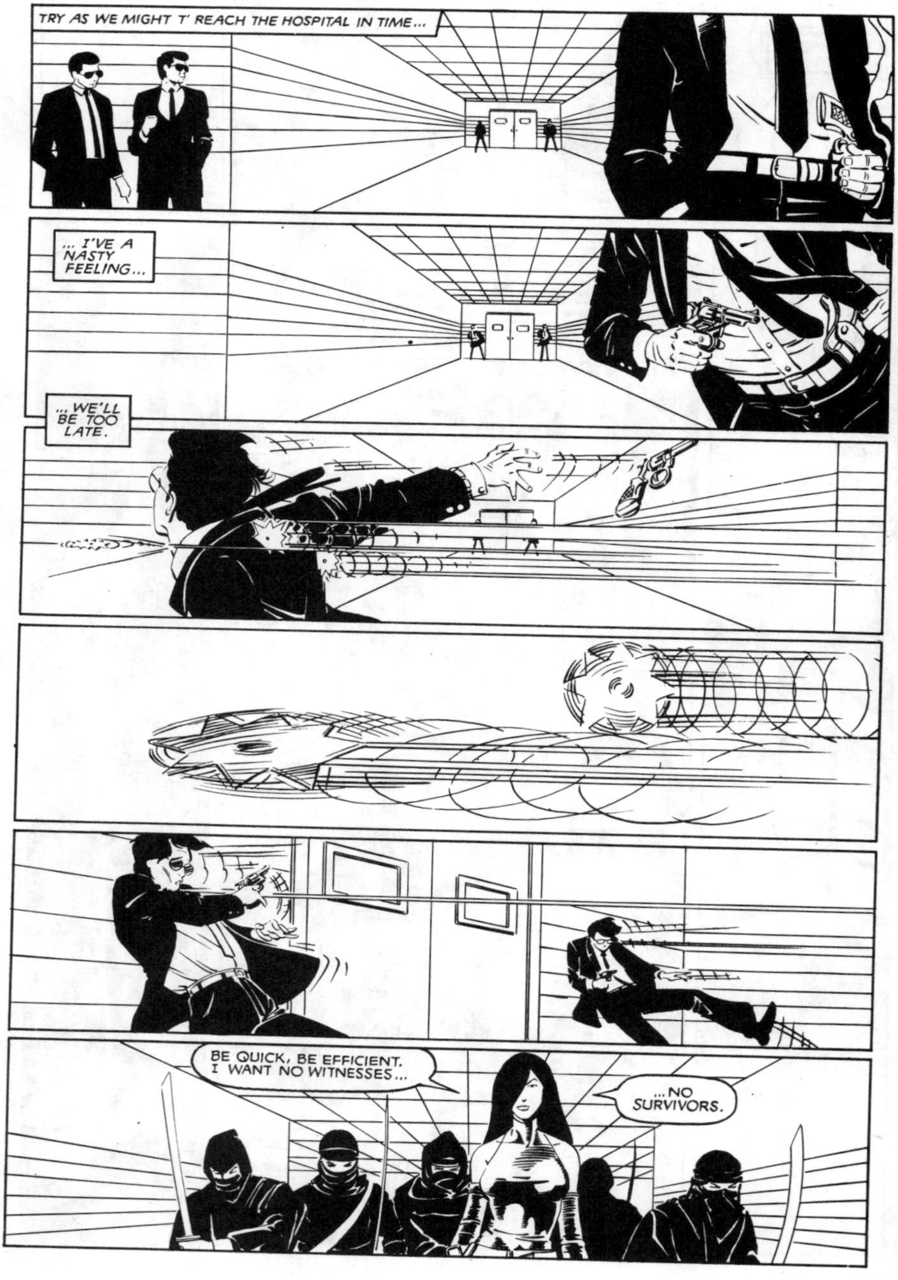
TRY AS WE MIGHT T' REACH THE HOSPITAL IN TIME...
... I'VE A NASTY FEELING...
...WE'LL BE TOO LATE.
BE QUICK, BE EFFICIENT. I WANT NO WITNESSES...
...NO SURVIVORS.

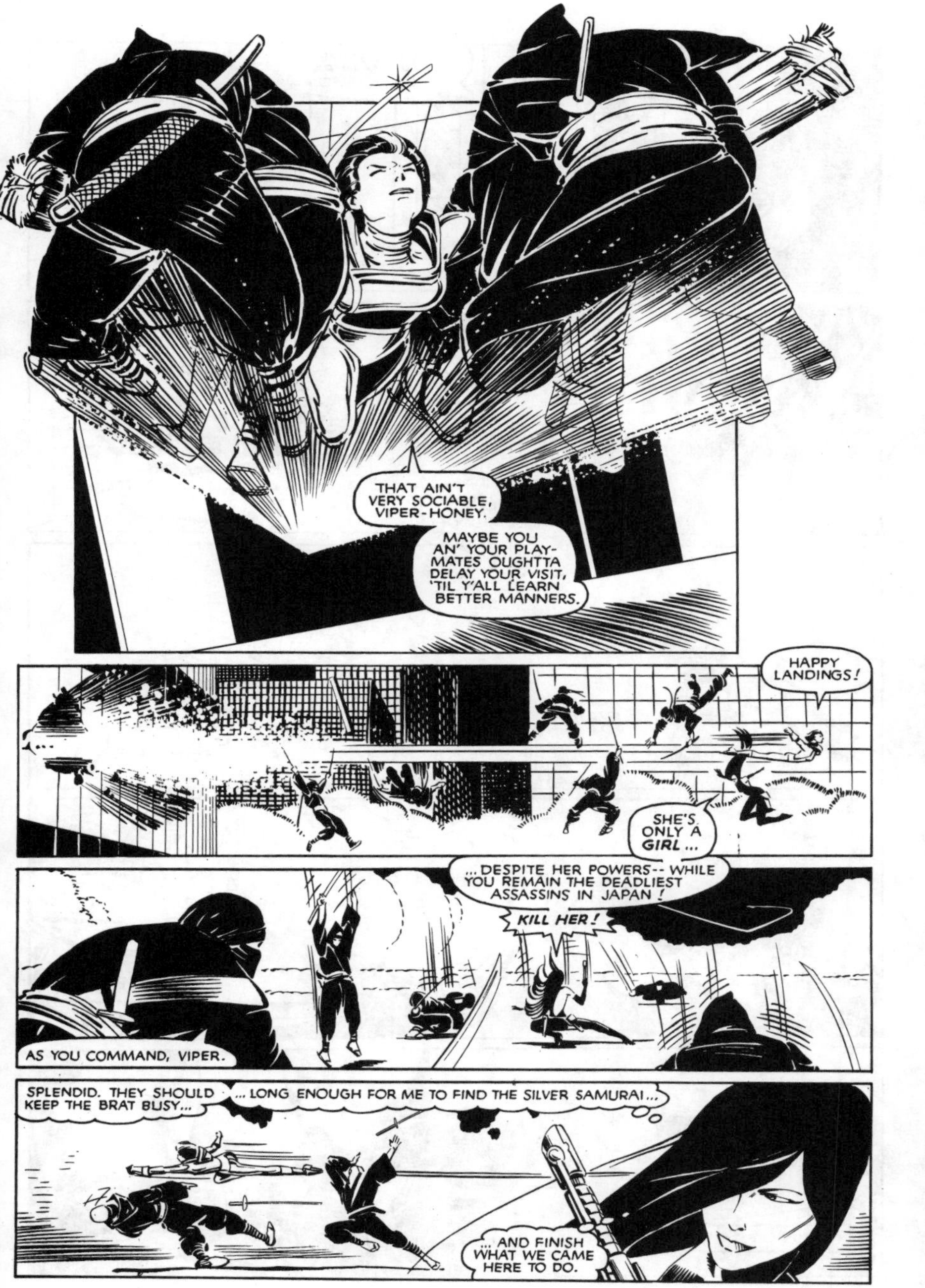
THAT AIN'T VERY SOCIABLE, VIPER-HONEY.
MAYBE YOU AN' YOUR PLAY-MATES OUGHTTA DELAY YOUR VISIT, 'TIL Y'ALL LEARN BETTER MANNERS.
HAPPY LANDINGS!
SHE'S ONLY A GIRL...
...DESPITE HER POWERS-- WHILE YOU REMAIN THE DEADLIEST ASSASSINS IN JAPAN!
KILL HER!
AS YOU COMMAND, VIPER.
SPLENDID. THEY SHOULD KEEP THE BRAT BUSY...
...LONG ENOUGH FOR ME TO FIND THE SILVER SAMURAI...
...AND FINISH WHAT WE CAME HERE TO DO.

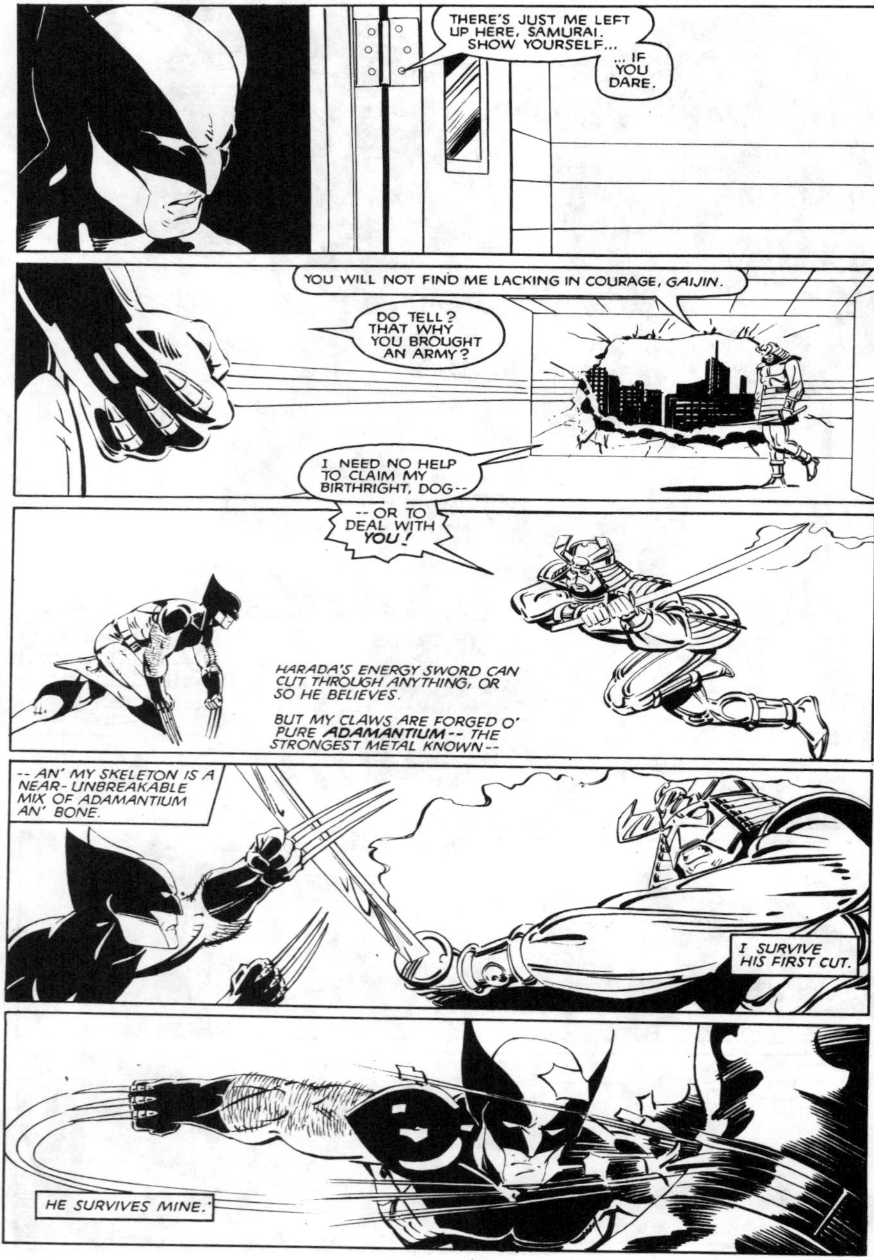
THERE'S JUST ME LEFT UP HERE, SAMURAI. SHOW YOURSELF...
... IF YOU DARE.
YOU WILL NOT FIND ME LACKING IN COURAGE, GAIJIN.
DO TELL? THAT WHY YOU BROUGHT AN ARMY?
I NEED NO HELP TO CLAIM MY BIRTHRIGHT, DOG--
-- OR TO DEAL WITH YOU!
HARADA'S ENERGY SWORD CAN CUT THROUGH ANYTHING, OR SO HE BELIEVES.
BUT MY CLAWS ARE FORGED O' PURE ADAMANTIUM -- THE STRONGEST METAL KNOWN--
-- AN' MY SKELETON IS A NEAR-UNBREAKABLE MIX OF ADAMANTIUM AN' BONE.
I SURVIVE HIS FIRST CUT.
HE SURVIVES MINE.

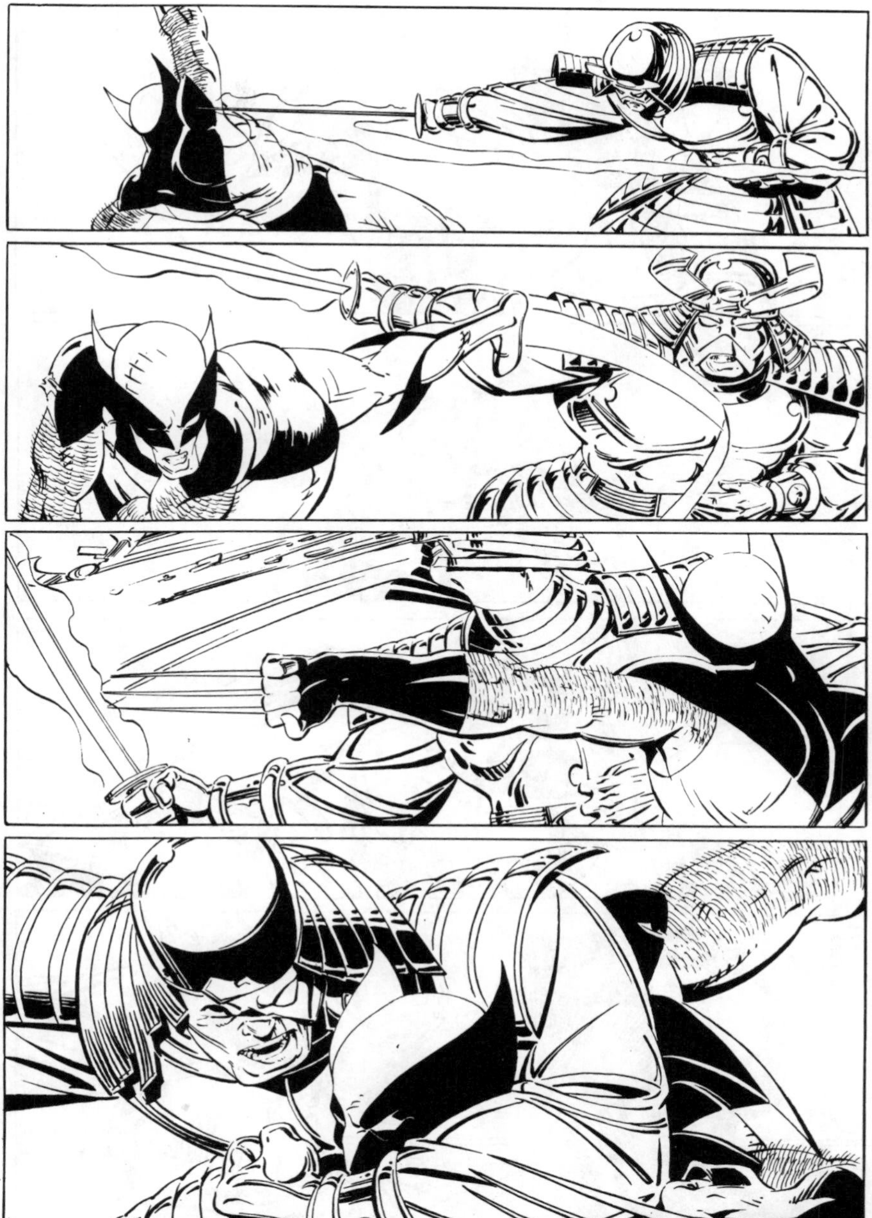

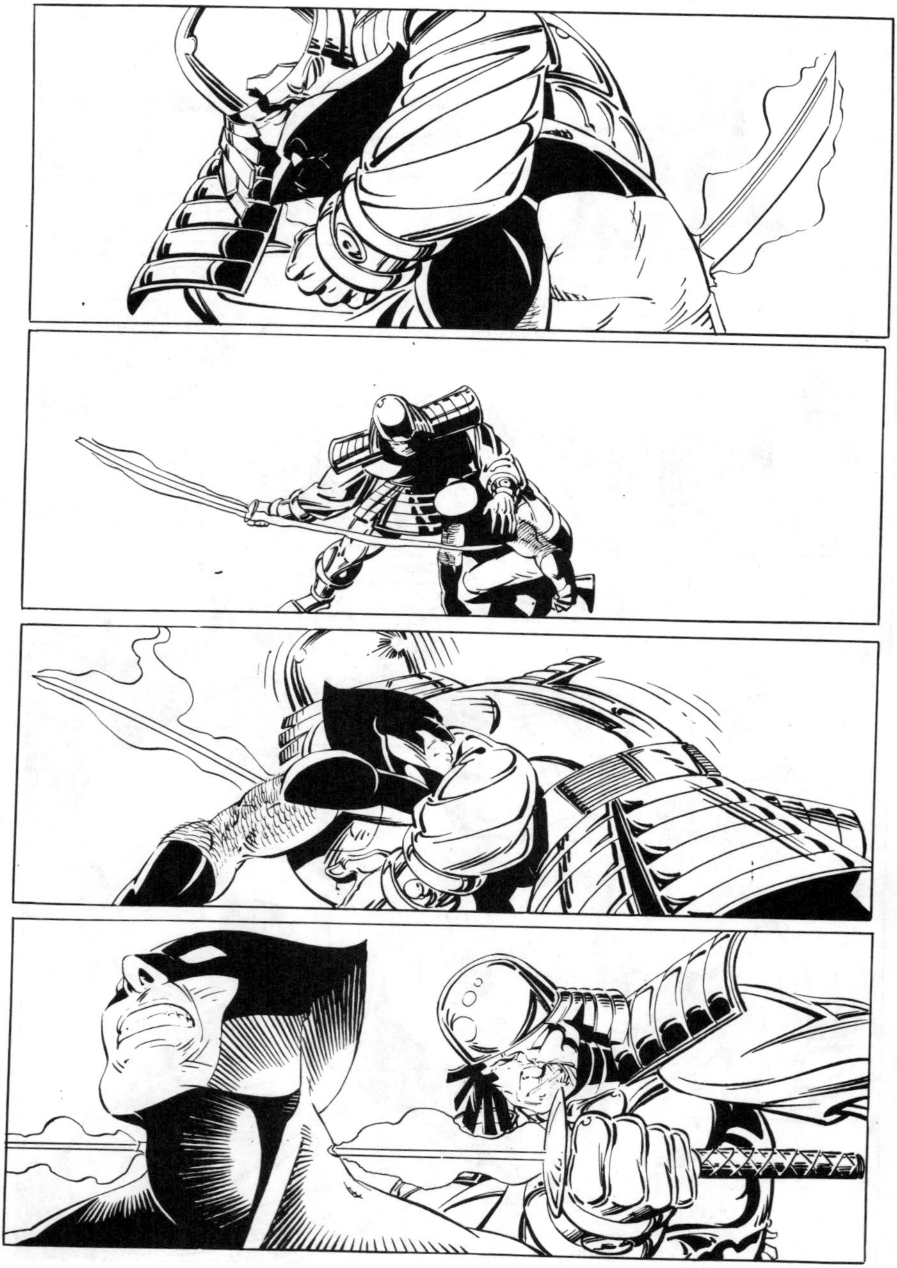

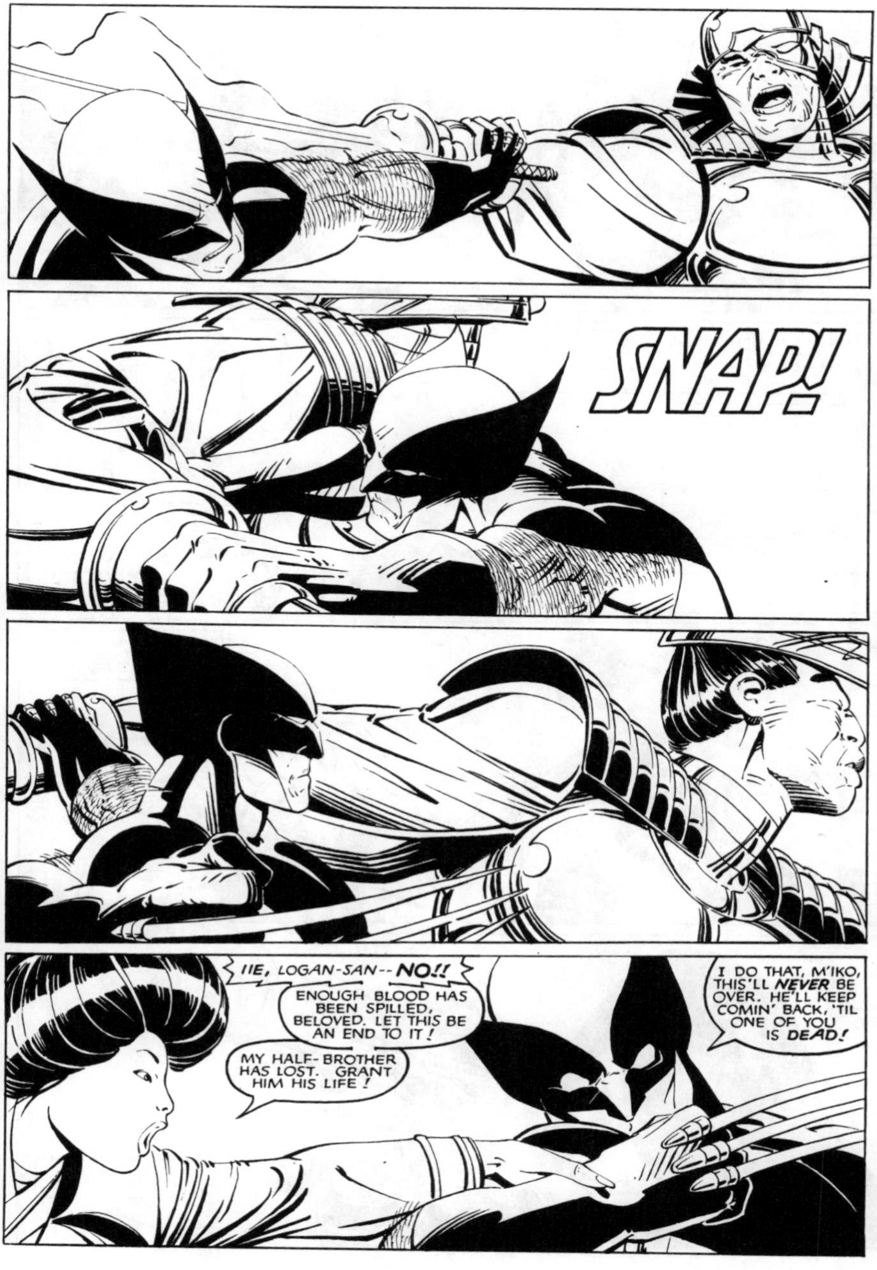
SNAP!
IIE, LOGAN-SAN--NO!!
ENOUGH BLOOD HAS BEEN SPILLED, BELOVED. LET THIS BE AN END TO IT!
MY HALF-BROTHER HAS LOST. GRANT HIM HIS LIFE!
I DO THAT, M'IKO, THIS'LL NEVER BE OVER. HE'LL KEEP COMIN' BACK, 'TIL ONE OF YOU IS DEAD!

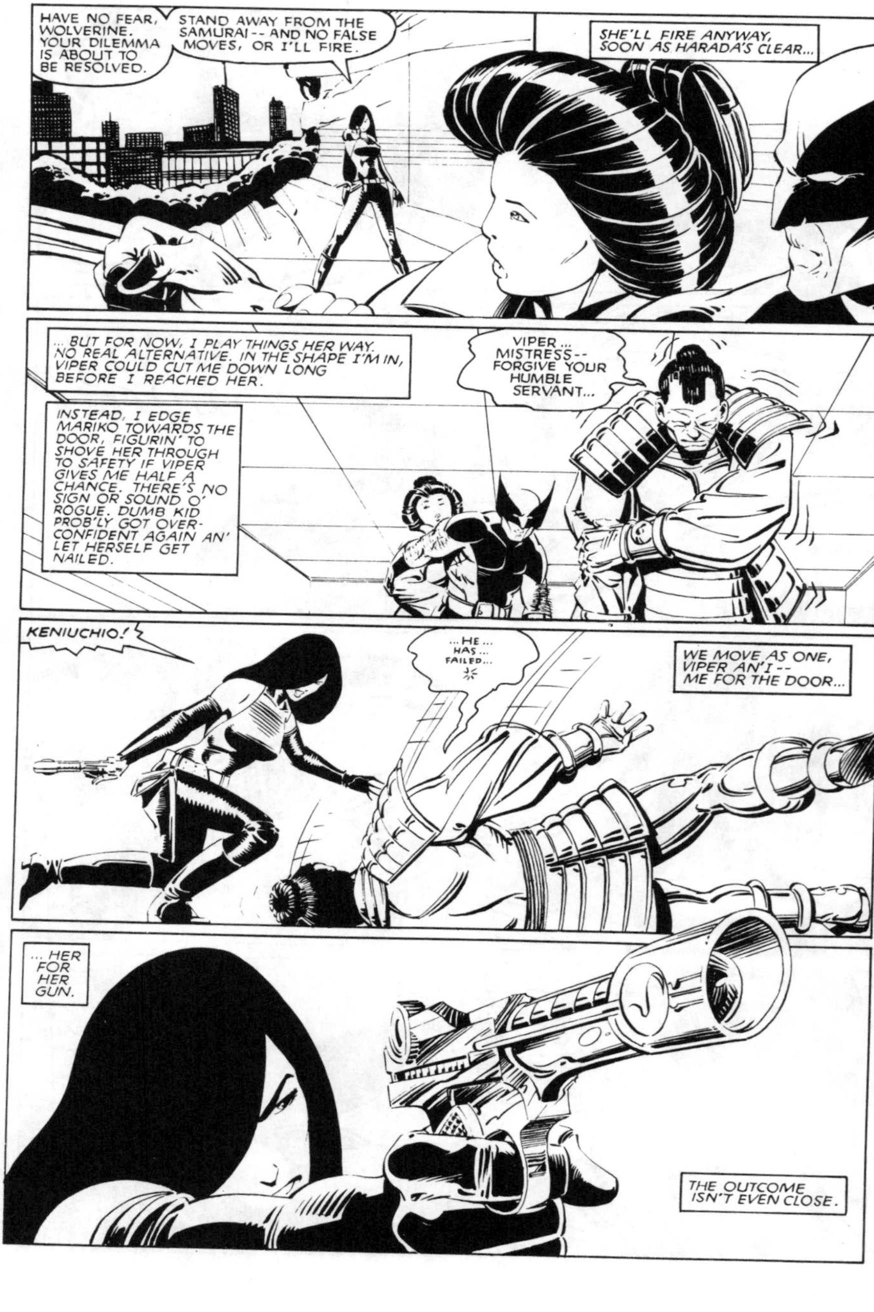
HAVE NO FEAR, WOLVERINE. YOUR DILEMMA IS ABOUT TO BE RESOLVED.
STAND AWAY FROM THE SAMURAI -- AND NO FALSE MOVES, OR I'LL FIRE.
SHE'LL FIRE ANYWAY, SOON AS HARADA'S CLEAR...
... BUT FOR NOW, I PLAY THINGS HER WAY. NO REAL ALTERNATIVE. IN THE SHAPE I'M IN, VIPER COULD CUT ME DOWN LONG BEFORE I REACHED HER.
INSTEAD, I EDGE MARIKO TOWARDS THE DOOR, FIGURIN' TO SHOVE HER THROUGH TO SAFETY IF VIPER GIVES ME HALF A CHANCE. THERE'S NO SIGN OR SOUND O' ROGUE. DUMB KID PROB'LY GOT OVER-CONFIDENT AGAIN AN' LET HERSELF GET NAILED.
VIPER ... MISTRESS-- FORGIVE YOUR HUMBLE SERVANT...
KENIUCHIO!
...HE ... HAS ... FAILED...
WE MOVE AS ONE, VIPER AN' I -- ME FOR THE DOOR...
... HER FOR HER GUN.
THE OUTCOME ISN'T EVEN CLOSE.

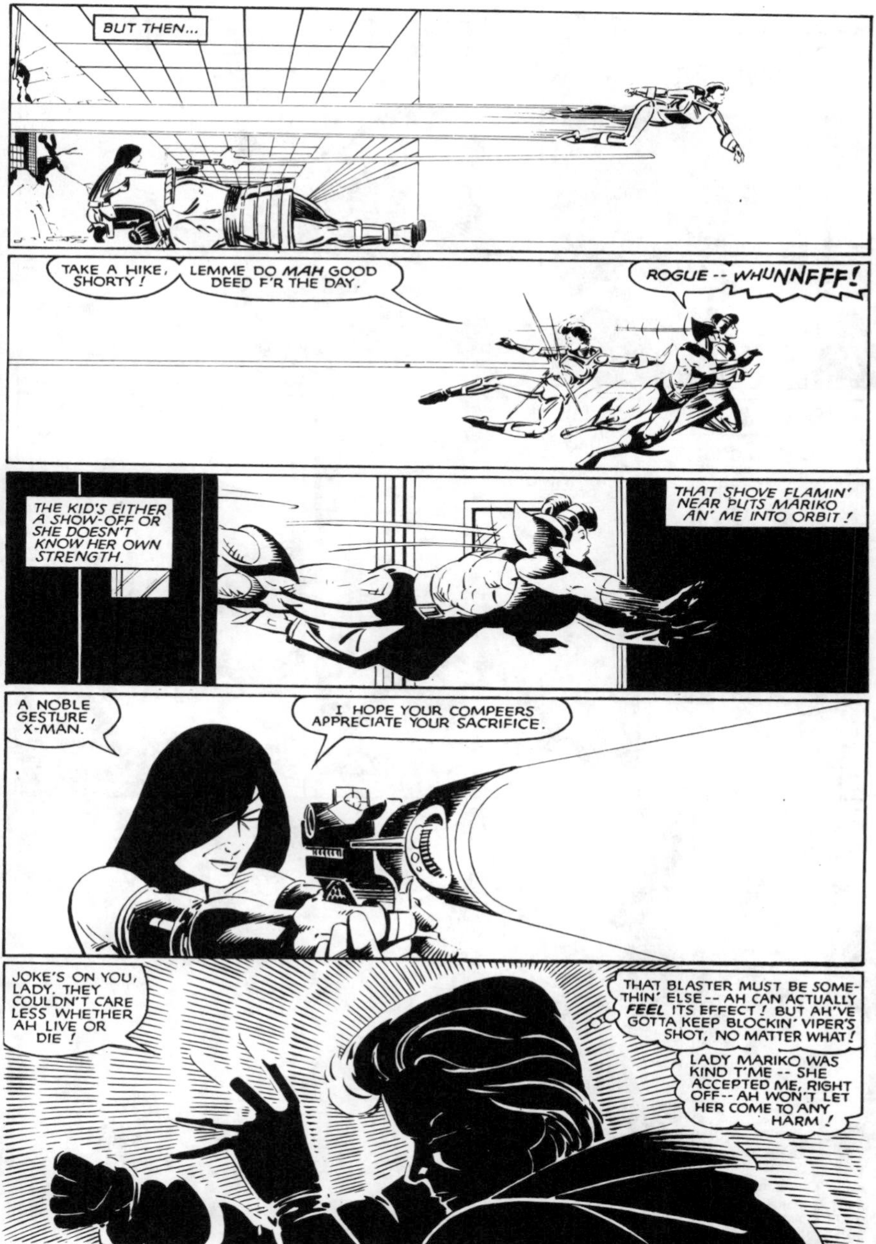
BUT THEN...
TAKE A HIKE, SHORTY!
LEMME DO MAH GOOD DEED F'R THE DAY.
ROGUE -- WHUNNFFF!
THE KID'S EITHER A SHOW-OFF OR SHE DOESN'T KNOW HER OWN STRENGTH.
THAT SHOVE FLAMIN' NEAR PUTS MARIKO AN' ME INTO ORBIT!
A NOBLE GESTURE, X-MAN.
I HOPE YOUR COMPEERS APPRECIATE YOUR SACRIFICE.
JOKE'S ON YOU, LADY. THEY COULDN'T CARE LESS WHETHER AH LIVE OR DIE!
THAT BLASTER MUST BE SOMETHIN' ELSE -- AH CAN ACTUALLY FEEL ITS EFFECT! BUT AH'VE GOTTA KEEP BLOCKIN' VIPER'S SHOT, NO MATTER WHAT!
LADY MARIKO WAS KIND T'ME -- SHE ACCEPTED ME, RIGHT OFF -- AH WON'T LET HER COME TO ANY HARM!

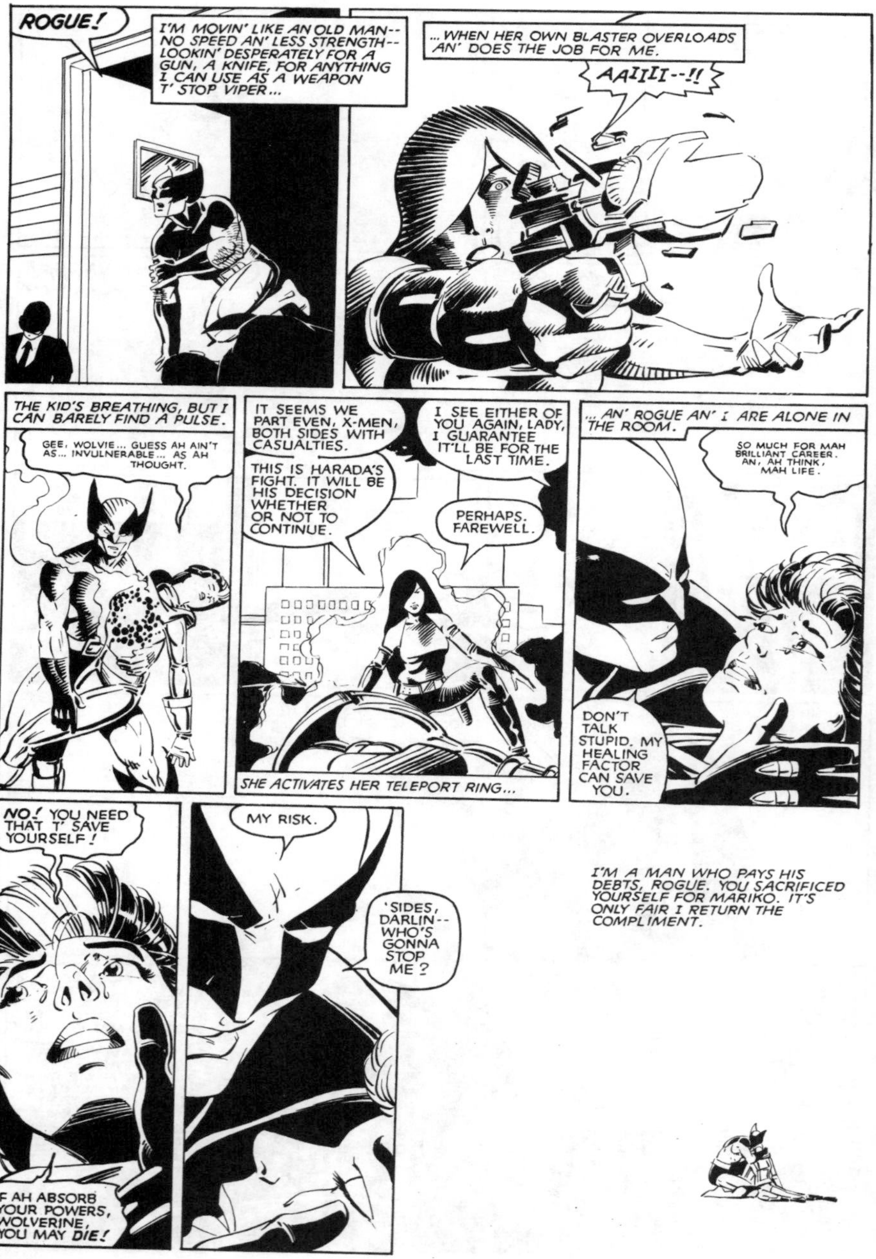
ROGUE!
I'M MOVIN' LIKE AN OLD MAN-- NO SPEED AN' LESS STRENGTH-- LOOKIN' DESPERATELY FOR A GUN, A KNIFE, FOR ANYTHING I CAN USE AS A WEAPON T' STOP VIPER...
...WHEN HER OWN BLASTER OVERLOADS AN' DOES THE JOB FOR ME.
AAIIII--!!
THE KID'S BREATHING, BUT I CAN BARELY FIND A PULSE.
GEE, WOLVIE... GUESS AH AIN'T AS... INVULNERABLE... AS AH THOUGHT.
IT SEEMS WE PART EVEN, X-MEN, BOTH SIDES WITH CASUALTIES.
THIS IS HARADA'S FIGHT. IT WILL BE HIS DECISION WHETHER OR NOT TO CONTINUE.
I SEE EITHER OF YOU AGAIN, LADY, I GUARANTEE IT'LL BE FOR THE LAST TIME.
PERHAPS. FAREWELL.
SHE ACTIVATES HER TELEPORT RING...
...AN' ROGUE AN' I ARE ALONE IN THE ROOM.
SO MUCH FOR MAH BRILLIANT CAREER. AN, AH THINK, MAH LIFE.
DON'T TALK STUPID. MY HEALING FACTOR CAN SAVE YOU.
NO! YOU NEED THAT T' SAVE YOURSELF!
IF AH ABSORB YOUR POWERS, WOLVERINE, YOU MAY DIE!
MY RISK.
'SIDES, DARLIN-- WHO'S GONNA STOP ME?
I'M A MAN WHO PAYS HIS DEBTS, ROGUE. YOU SACRIFICED YOURSELF FOR MARIKO. IT'S ONLY FAIR I RETURN THE COMPLIMENT.

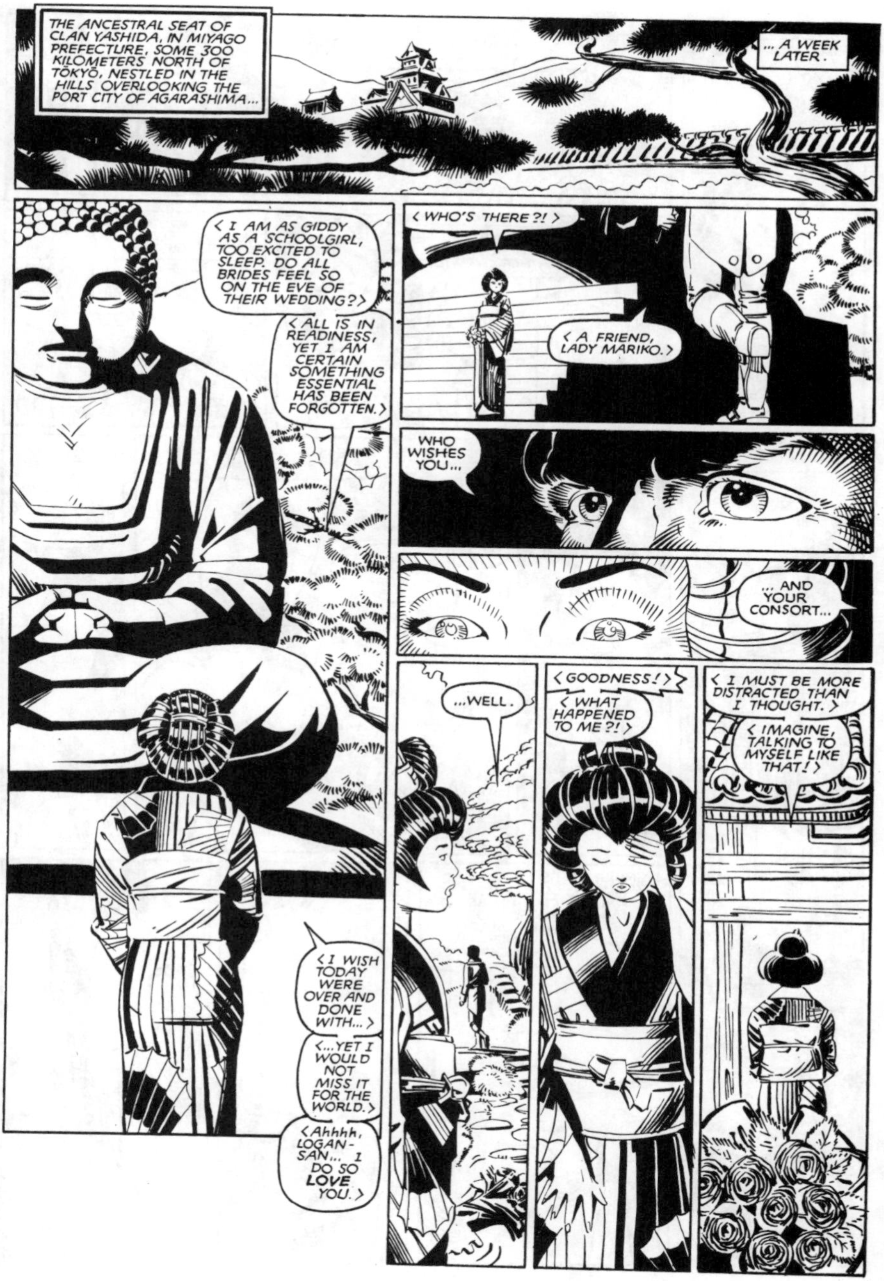
THE ANCESTRAL SEAT OF CLAN YASHIDA, IN MIYAGO PREFECTURE, SOME 300 KILOMETERS NORTH OF TŌKYŌ, NESTLED IN THE HILLS OVERLOOKING THE PORT CITY OF AGARASHIMA...
...A WEEK LATER.
< I AM AS GIDDY AS A SCHOOLGIRL, TOO EXCITED TO SLEEP. DO ALL BRIDES FEEL SO ON THE EVE OF THEIR WEDDING? >
< ALL IS IN READINESS, YET I AM CERTAIN SOMETHING ESSENTIAL HAS BEEN FORGOTTEN. >
< I WISH TODAY WERE OVER AND DONE WITH... >
< ...YET I WOULD NOT MISS IT FOR THE WORLD. >
< Ahhhh, LOGAN-SAN... I DO SO **LOVE** YOU. >
< WHO'S THERE?! >
< A FRIEND, LADY MARIKO. >
WHO WISHES YOU...
...AND YOUR CONSORT...
...WELL.
< GOODNESS! >
< WHAT HAPPENED TO ME?! >
< I MUST BE MORE DISTRACTED THAN I THOUGHT. >
< IMAGINE, TALKING TO MYSELF LIKE THAT! >

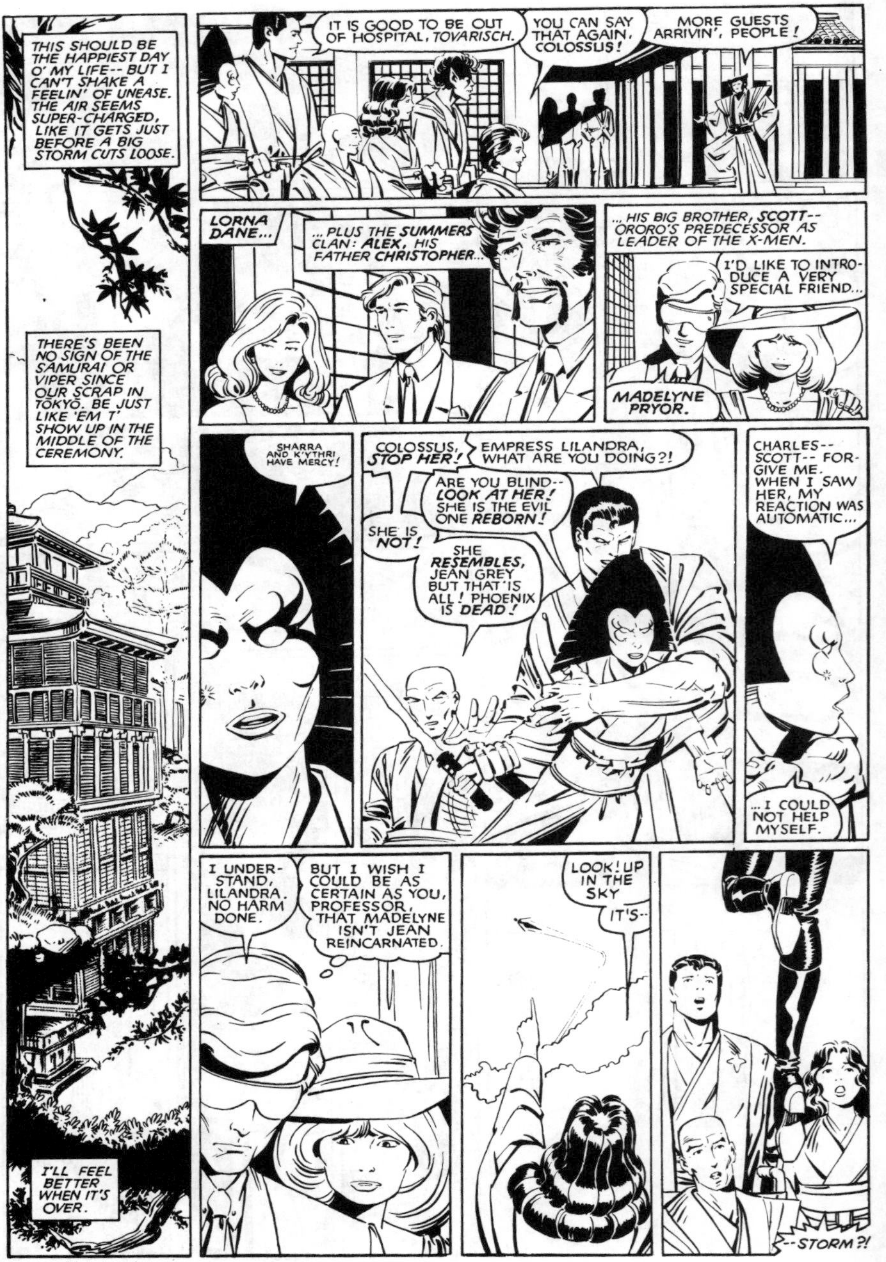
THIS SHOULD BE THE HAPPIEST DAY O' MY LIFE-- BUT I CAN'T SHAKE A FEELIN' OF UNEASE. THE AIR SEEMS SUPER-CHARGED, LIKE IT GETS JUST BEFORE A BIG STORM CUTS LOOSE.
IT IS GOOD TO BE OUT OF HOSPITAL, TOVARISCH.
YOU CAN SAY THAT AGAIN, COLOSSUS!
MORE GUESTS ARRIVIN', PEOPLE!
LORNA DANE...
...PLUS THE SUMMERS CLAN: ALEX, HIS FATHER CHRISTOPHER...
...HIS BIG BROTHER, SCOTT-- ORORO'S PREDECESSOR AS LEADER OF THE X-MEN.
I'D LIKE TO INTRODUCE A VERY SPECIAL FRIEND...
MADELYNE PRYOR.
THERE'S BEEN NO SIGN OF THE SAMURAI OR VIPER SINCE OUR SCRAP IN TŌKYŌ. BE JUST LIKE 'EM T' SHOW UP IN THE MIDDLE OF THE CEREMONY.
SHARRA AND K'YTHRI HAVE MERCY!
COLOSSUS, STOP HER!
EMPRESS LILANDRA, WHAT ARE YOU DOING?!
ARE YOU BLIND-- LOOK AT HER! SHE IS THE EVIL ONE REBORN!
SHE IS NOT!
SHE RESEMBLES, JEAN GREY BUT THAT IS ALL! PHOENIX IS DEAD!
CHARLES-- SCOTT-- FORGIVE ME. WHEN I SAW HER, MY REACTION WAS AUTOMATIC...
...I COULD NOT HELP MYSELF.
I UNDERSTAND, LILANDRA. NO HARM DONE.
BUT I WISH I COULD BE AS CERTAIN AS YOU, PROFESSOR, THAT MADELYNE ISN'T JEAN REINCARNATED.
LOOK! UP IN THE SKY
IT'S--
--STORM?!
I'LL FEEL BETTER WHEN IT'S OVER.

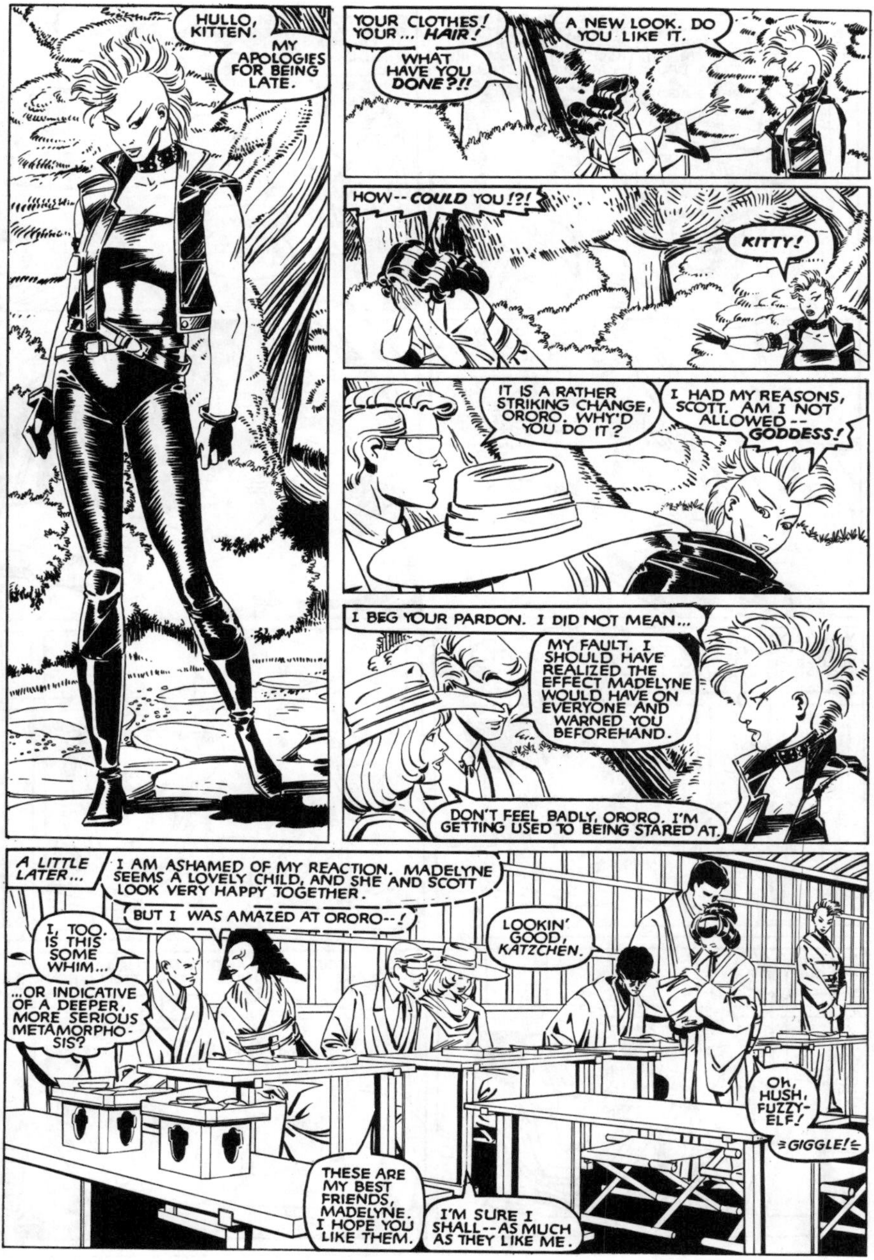
HULLO, KITTEN.
MY APOLOGIES FOR BEING LATE.
YOUR CLOTHES! YOUR... HAIR!
WHAT HAVE YOU DONE?!!
A NEW LOOK. DO YOU LIKE IT.
HOW-- COULD YOU!?!
KITTY!
IT IS A RATHER STRIKING CHANGE, ORORO. WHY'D YOU DO IT?
I HAD MY REASONS, SCOTT. AM I NOT ALLOWED-- GODDESS!
I BEG YOUR PARDON. I DID NOT MEAN...
MY FAULT. I SHOULD HAVE REALIZED THE EFFECT MADELYNE WOULD HAVE ON EVERYONE AND WARNED YOU BEFOREHAND.
DON'T FEEL BADLY, ORORO. I'M GETTING USED TO BEING STARED AT.
A LITTLE LATER...
I AM ASHAMED OF MY REACTION. MADELYNE SEEMS A LOVELY CHILD, AND SHE AND SCOTT LOOK VERY HAPPY TOGETHER.
BUT I WAS AMAZED AT ORORO--!
I, TOO. IS THIS SOME WHIM...
...OR INDICATIVE OF A DEEPER, MORE SERIOUS METAMORPHOSIS?
LOOKIN' GOOD, KATZCHEN.
Oh, HUSH, FUZZY-ELF!
GIGGLE!
THESE ARE MY BEST FRIENDS, MADELYNE. I HOPE YOU LIKE THEM.
I'M SURE I SHALL--AS MUCH AS THEY LIKE ME.

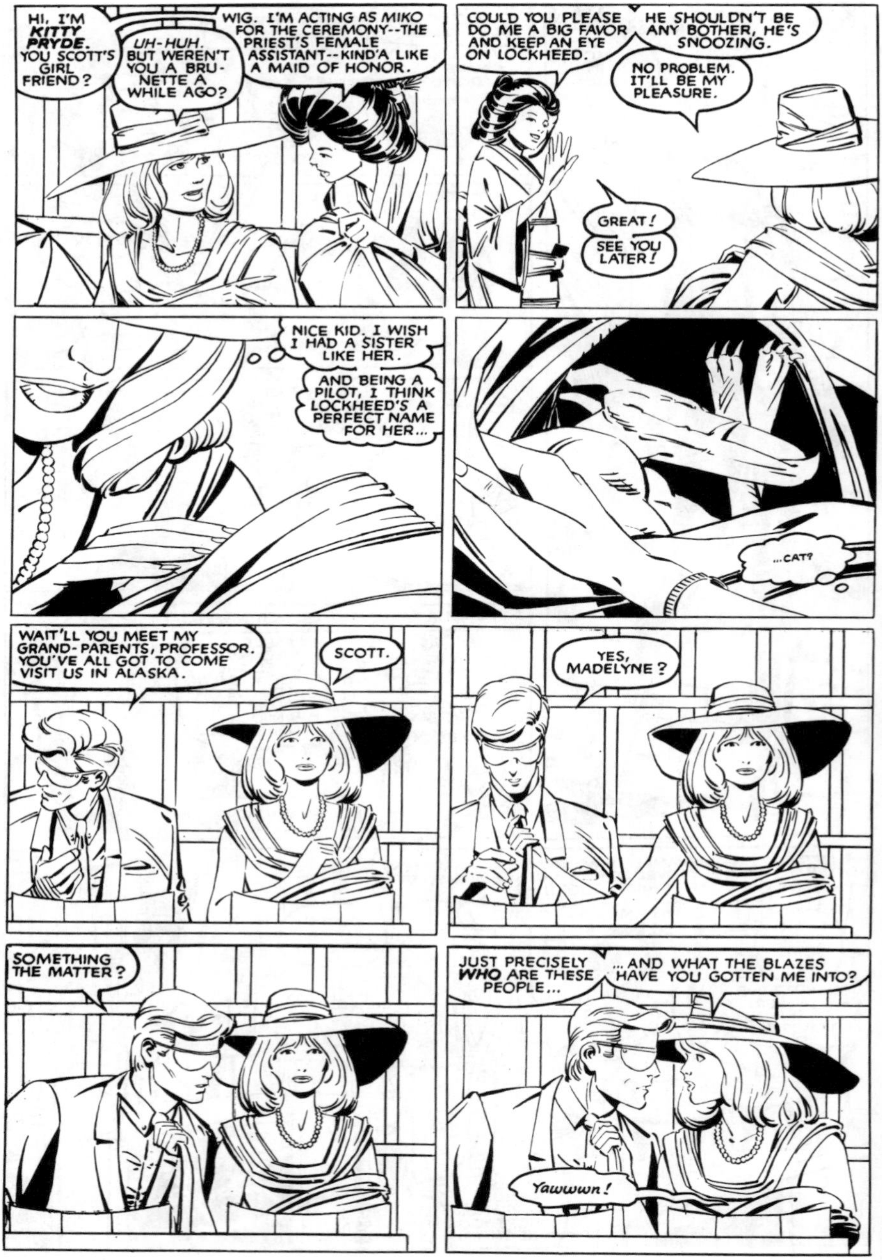

HI, I'M *KITTY PRYDE.* YOU SCOTT'S GIRL FRIEND?
UH-HUH. BUT WEREN'T YOU A BRU-NETTE A WHILE AGO?
WIG. I'M ACTING AS *MIKO* FOR THE CEREMONY--THE PRIEST'S FEMALE ASSISTANT--KIND'A LIKE A MAID OF HONOR.
COULD YOU PLEASE DO ME A BIG FAVOR AND KEEP AN EYE ON LOCKHEED.
HE SHOULDN'T BE ANY BOTHER, HE'S SNOOZING.
NO PROBLEM. IT'LL BE MY PLEASURE.
GREAT!
SEE YOU LATER!
NICE KID. I WISH I HAD A SISTER LIKE HER.
AND BEING A PILOT, I THINK LOCKHEED'S A PERFECT NAME FOR HER...
...CAT?
WAIT'LL YOU MEET MY GRAND-PARENTS, PROFESSOR. YOU'VE ALL GOT TO COME VISIT US IN ALASKA.
SCOTT.
YES, MADELYNE?
SOMETHING THE MATTER?
JUST PRECISELY *WHO* ARE THESE PEOPLE...
...AND WHAT THE BLAZES HAVE YOU GOTTEN ME INTO?
Yawwwn!

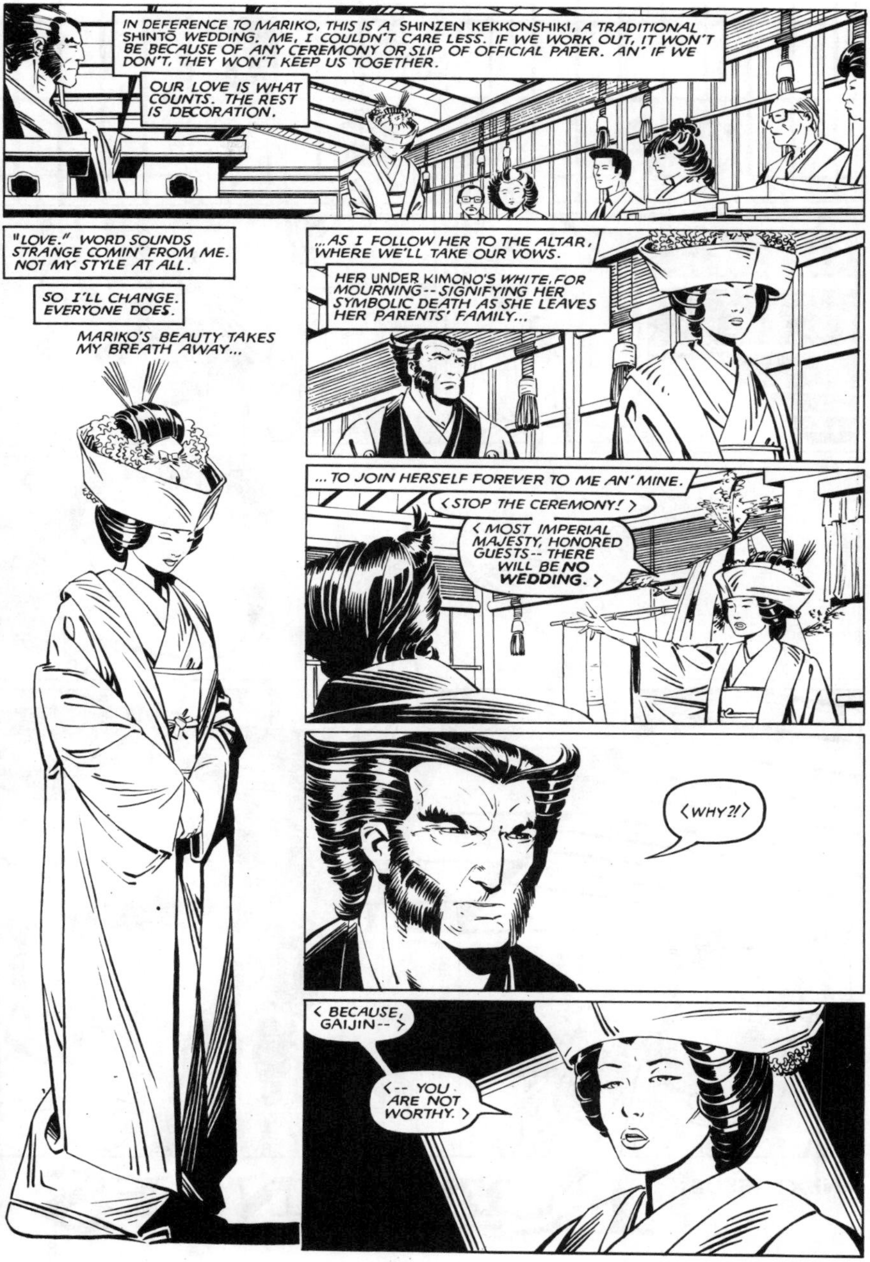
IN DEFERENCE TO MARIKO, THIS IS A SHINZEN KEKKONSHIKI, A TRADITIONAL SHINTŌ WEDDING. ME, I COULDN'T CARE LESS. IF WE WORK OUT, IT WON'T BE BECAUSE OF ANY CEREMONY OR SLIP OF OFFICIAL PAPER. AN' IF WE DON'T, THEY WON'T KEEP US TOGETHER.
OUR LOVE IS WHAT COUNTS. THE REST IS DECORATION.
"LOVE." WORD SOUNDS STRANGE COMIN' FROM ME. NOT MY STYLE AT ALL.
SO I'LL CHANGE. EVERYONE DOES.
MARIKO'S BEAUTY TAKES MY BREATH AWAY...
...AS I FOLLOW HER TO THE ALTAR, WHERE WE'LL TAKE OUR VOWS.
HER UNDER KIMONO'S WHITE, FOR MOURNING--SIGNIFYING HER SYMBOLIC DEATH AS SHE LEAVES HER PARENTS' FAMILY...
...TO JOIN HERSELF FOREVER TO ME AN' MINE.
‹STOP THE CEREMONY!›
‹MOST IMPERIAL MAJESTY, HONORED GUESTS-- THERE WILL BE NO WEDDING.›
‹WHY?!›
‹BECAUSE, GAIJIN--›
‹--YOU ARE NOT WORTHY.›

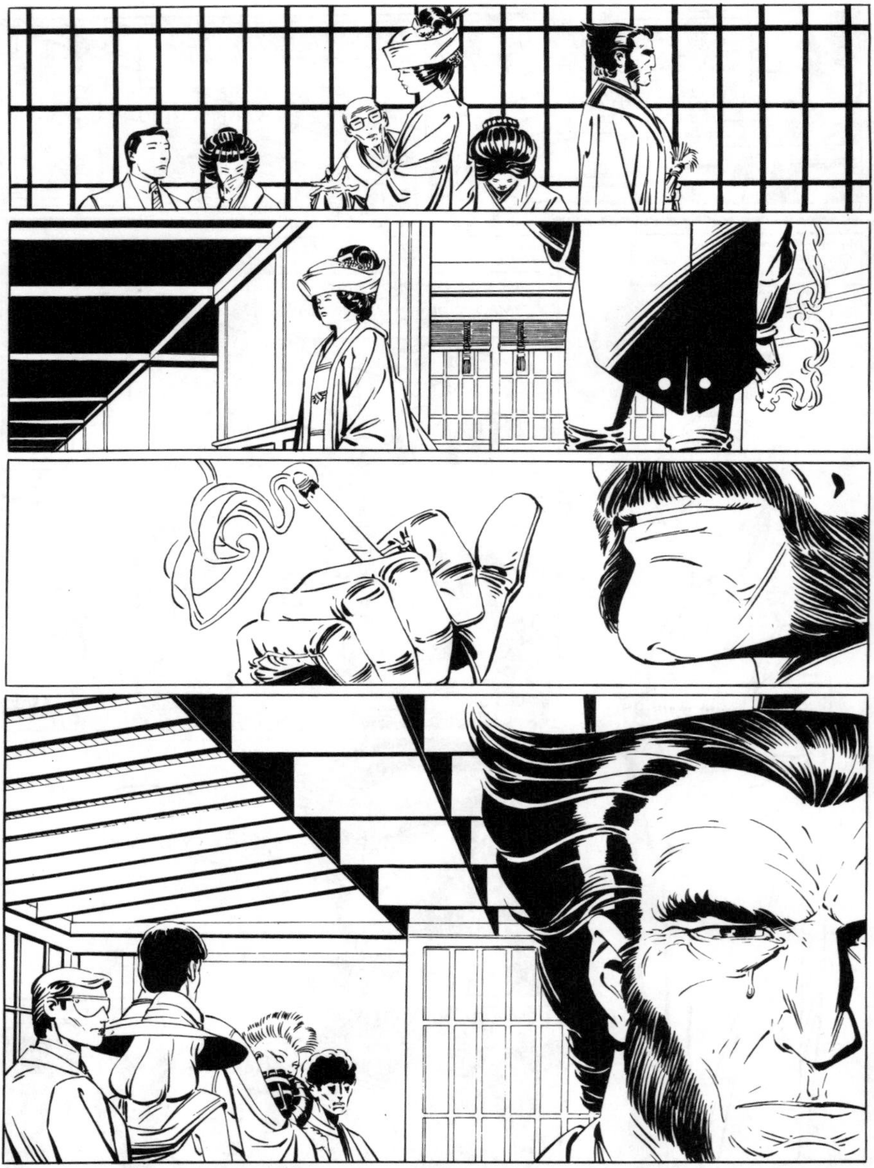

NEXT ISSUE: ROMANCES

BACKPACK PROFILE

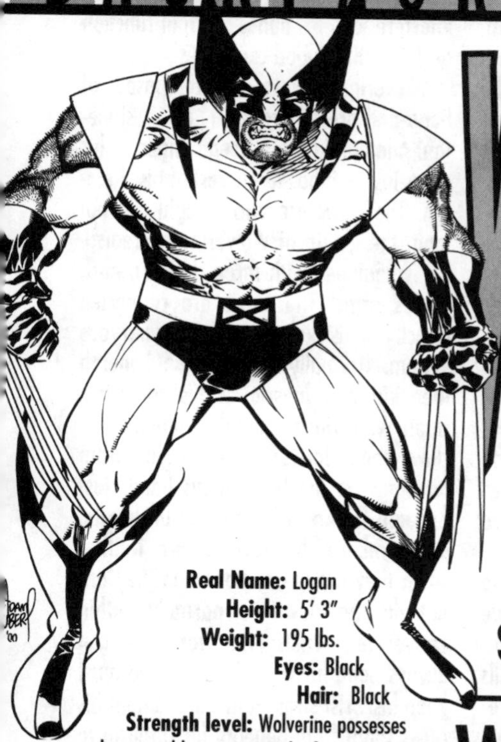

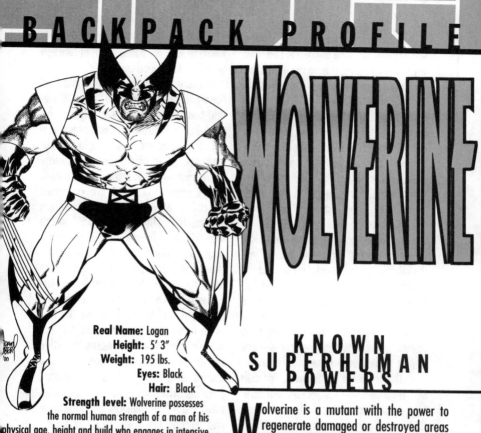

WOLVERINE

Real Name: Logan
Height: 5′ 3″
Weight: 195 lbs.
Eyes: Black
Hair: Black
Strength level: Wolverine possesses the normal human strength of a man of his physical age, height and build who engages in intensive regular exercise.
Occupation: Adventurer; captain in the Canadian armed forces, assigned to intelligence (retired)
Identity: Secret, known to certain members of the Canadian government
Legal Status: Citizen of Canada, now permanent resident in the United States; no criminal record
Former Aliases: Weapon X, Patch
Place of birth: Unknown
Marital Status: Married
Known Relatives: Akiko (adopted daughter), Viper (wife)
Group Affiliation: X-Men
Base of operations: The Xavier Institute, Salem Center, Westchester County, New York; the Princess Bar, Madripoor
First Appearance: INCREDIBLE HULK #180
Origin: (partial) MARVEL COMICS PRESENTS #72-85, ALPHA FLIGHT Vol. 1 #33-34

KNOWN SUPERHUMAN POWERS

Wolverine is a mutant with the power to regenerate damaged or destroyed areas of his cellular structure at a rate far greater than that of an ordinary human. This power is not subject to Wolverine's will; the regeneration occurs automatically. The speed with which the healing occurs varies in direct proportion to the severity of the damage Wolverine has suffered. For example, Wolverine could fully recover from an ordinary gunshot wound in a less than vital area of his body within an hour. However, it took Wolverine almost two months to fully recover from the injuries he sustained in a duel with Shingen Harada, which included one from a sword that went all the way through his trunk. Wolverine can regenerate the cells of his nervous system, although ordinary human adults cannot. It is not yet known whether Wolverine could regenerate an entire organ or body part such as a limb.

Wolverine's "fast healing ability" makes him virtually immune to poisons and most drugs. For example, it is nearly impossible for him to become intoxicated from drinking alcohol. He also has a limited immunity to the fatigue poisons generated by bodily activity, and hence he has greater endurance than an ordinary human being.

Wolverine's senses are superhumanly acute, and are comparable to those of certain animals. For example, he can track someone by smell just as a dog or wolf can. His sense of hearing is only slightly less developed than that of Daredevil. It is unknown whether Wolverine can see into the infrared and ultraviolet portions of the spectrum. It is unknown whether Wolverine's senses of taste and touch are superhumanly acute. In part Wolverine's superhuman senses comprise a separate mutant power of his, but they are also due in part to his power of cellular regeneration. Thanks to the latter power, the cells of Wolverine's sense organs do not atrophy, or at least do not do so at the rate that an ordinary human's might.

The Weapon X Project bonded molecules of adamantium to Wolverine's skeleton. Although Magneto removed the adamantium, Apocalypse later bonded the metal back to Wolverine's skeleton again. Adamantium is an artificial alloy developed by Dr. Myron MacLain and is the hardest metal known to science. It can be cut with a special subatomic particle beam; otherwise, for all intents and purposes, adamantium is virtually indestructible. As a result of being laced with adamantium, Wolverine's bones are virtually unbreakable. The presence of adamantium in his skeleton does not interfere with his bones' normal function of generating blood corpuscles.

Wolverine's claws are composed of bone and are natural parts of his skeleton. Adamantium has been bonded to his claws just as it has to the rest of his skeleton. The claws are each roughly a foot long, the length of Wolverine's forearm. He is equipped with three claws on each of his arms. The claws are connected directly to his skeleton and to his nervous system. Normally they remain beneath the skin and muscle of his forearms. Upon Wolverine's mental command, the claws shoot forward and emerge from openings on the back of his hands just beneath his knuckles. He can unsheathe any number of his claws at once. Neither when they are in use nor when they are not do the claws lie partially within Wolverine's wrists; therefore, he can always bend his wrist. However, he must keep his wrist straight at the moment his claws shoot from beneath his forearm to and through the openings in his hands. The openings through which the claws emerge remain sealed when the claws are not in use, and open upon the same mental command that shoots the claws forward. The claws are slightly curved. Wolverine uses the claws as weapons. The hardness of adamantium and their sharpness allow Wolverine to use them to cut through virtually any substance depending on its thickness and the amount of force he can exert. Wolverine's fast healing ability made it possible for him to survive and quickly recover from the procedure by which adamantium was bonded to his skeleton.